A MUSLIM MISSIONARY IN MEDIAEVAL KASHMIR

A Muslim Missionary in Mediaeval Kashmir

(Being the English translation of *Tohfatu'l-Ahbab*)

Translated from Persian,
with Annotations and Introduction
by
KASHINATH PANDIT

VOICE OF INDIA
New Delhi

This book is the English translation of a Farsi manuscript, *Tohfatu'l-Ahbab*, persumably written in AD 1640. A transcript copy of the manuscript exists in the Research and Publications Department of Jammu and Kashmir State under Accession Number 551.

First published, 2009
First reprint, 2018
Reprint 2022

ISBN 978-81-85990-85-9

www.voiceofin.com

Published by Voice of India, 2/18, Ansari Road, New Delhi – 110 002.
Printed at Replika Press Pvt. Ltd.

For the historians writing
on Mediaeval India

Contents

Acknowledgement

I am thankful to Dr. Tejnath Dhar, a dear friend and colleague at the University of Kashmir, who took pains to go through the draft and suggested many improvements and modifications in the translated text. I am also thankful to a large number of friends and well-wishers who prompted me to undertake this academic project in the hope that it will be an addition to the corpus of historical knowledge about mediaeval Kashmir.

I did most of my work in the rich library of Iran Cultural House in New Delhi. I am thankful to its functionaries and the Cultural Counsellor of the Islamic Republic of Iran in India for the facilities made available to scholars and researchers at this library.

Finally, I wish to to pay homage to my late teacher and guide, Dr. Zabihullah Safa, former Professor at the Faculty of Letters, University of Teheran, Iran, whose profound scholarship, sharp independent critical judgement and a high standard of scholarly research have been a constant source of inspiration for my academic pursuits.

Kashinath Pandit

Introduction

This is the English translation of a Farsi work *Tohfatu'l-Ahbab*, the biography of Shamsu'd-Din Muhammad Araki, an Iranian Shi'a Muslim missionary of Nurbakhshiyyeh order who is reported to have visited Kashmir for the first time in AH 882/AD 1478.[1] He was born in Solghan in Northern Iran in the year AH 828/AD 1424. Some hagiographers have tried to trace his descent from the line of Imam Musa Kazim.

We do not have convincing information about the life and works of the author of Shamsu'd-Din Araki's biography, namely *Tohfatu'l-Ahbab* except that he calls himself Muhammad 'Ali Kashmiri. He often accompanied his father on their visit to Shamsu'd-Din Araki in his hospice at Zadibal, Srinagar. It appears from the biography that he was an eye-witness to many events connected with Araki's mission in Kashmir. Like his father Mulla Khaleelullah, he was a staunch follower of Shi'a Nurbakhshiyyeh faith brought to Kashmir by Araki. The colophon of J&K Researcah Library manuscript of *Tohfatu'l-Ahbab* bears the year of transcription as AH 1052/AD 1642.

Manuscripts of the work are preserved in J&K State Research Library, and in the private collection of Agha Sahib of Budgam, Srinagar. Both are defective because the first and the last chapter, out of a total of four chapters of the work, are completely missing. The MS in the British Museum, too, suffers from the same defect. However, a manuscript copy

[1] *Baharistan-i-Shahi*, ed. Akbar Haideri, p.38.

containing all the four chapters is preserved in the private collection of Barat library in Barqchhan Khaplu, Baltistan, a part of the original Sate of Jammu and Kashmir but at present under the control of Pakistan. Muhammad Reza Akhund Zadeh of Khaplu brought out its Urdu translation (*Tohfeh-e Kashmir*) from Lahore in 1997.

Shamsu'd-Din Araki had traveled from Srinagar to Askardu propagating Nurbakhshiyyeh faith, first in the valley of Kashmir and then in what is now called Gilgit and Baltistan. His mission in the southern foothills of Karakorum Range of the Himalayas was more than successful, and he left behind many people who have, ever since, stuck to his faith and Sufi order. Therefore, preservation of a genuine and unabridged manuscript copy of Araki's biography by a descendent of a family of his faith in distant Askardu seems understandable. In a personal letter that I received from the owner of the manuscript while I was in correspondence with him, he said that a scholar from an American University had visited him sometime back and made a photocopy of the manuscript. I found that this scholar was Shahzad Bashir, Assistant Professor of Religion at Carleton College in Minnesota. I contacted him and came to know that he had produced a work on Nurbakhshiyyeh sect of Sufis, under the title *Messianic Hopes and Mystical Vision*. In the introduction to his work, Shahzad says that he drew most of the material for his monograph from the biography of Shamsu'd-Din Araki titled *Tohfatu'l-Ahbab*. On close examination of his work, I found that he had ignored Chapter IV altogether though he had made for himself a copy of the original unabridged text. I corresponded with him briefly when I took up the translation work in hand. Though he agreed to send me a copy of the two usually missing chapters of the manuscripts, it never materialized. I hope he has used the contents of *Tohfatu'l-Ahbab* very faithfully in view of its importance for a serious student of mediaeval Kashmir history.

In the meanwhile, one Ghulam Rasul Jan, a teacher at the Persian Department of Kashmir University, published in 2008 annotated Urdu translation together with the Persian text of one part of the work. In the introduction of this Urdu translation (Volume I) he says that he visited Khaplu (in Askardu) and stayed as a guest of Muhammad Reza Akhund from whom he obtained a photo copy of the manuscript. He confirms that the manuscript is complete and in a good shape.

Ghulam Rasool Jan has devoted one full chapter of his work to the life, descent and environs of Muhammad Ali Kashmiri, the biographer of Shamsu'd-Din Aaki.

Mulla Akhund himself translated the original Persian text into Urdu, which has been published in Pakistan under the title *Tohfeh-e Kashmir* in 1997. I obtained a copy of this translation also, and on comparing it with the original text, I found that the Urdu translation leaves out almost all ornate portions of the text. As a Persian prose work, its style is boring and redundant, which no genuine scholar of Farsi literature will approve. That could be a reason among many others why Iranian historians and hagiographers (*Tadhkirah navisan*) have overlooked it. Nevertheless, its value as an important history of mediaeval Kashmir dealing with an eventful phase of her social history has not to be underestimated, particularly when we find that the author has tried to be very honest in recording the events connected with the person whose biography he is writing and most of the events to which he was an eye witness. It is this historical value that prompted me to take up its translation into English. The theme of the work is technical in a sense. This necessitated exhaustive footnoting of the text in order to facilitate readers to overcome discrepancy in their historical knowledge of Iranian Sufism. This was a stupendous task and asked for immense labour, research and concentration that took six long years to bring it to completion. I hope researchers in the field of social history of Iran as well as those in the history of Muslim missionaries in Kashmir will find it useful and instructive. Maybe more well-meaning researchers will think of re-interpreting aspects of mediaeval history of Kashmir.

Before introducing some aspects of mediaeval Kashmir, which the book unravels, we need to know Shamsu'd-Din Araki, the Shi'a Muslim missionary from Iran whose life and works have become the theme of this biography. We also need to know some of more important personalities relevant to our study of the book.

Kashmiri historians writing in Farsi have mentioned his name as 'Iraqi (with Arabic alphabet *ain*) and not Araki (with Arabic *alif* and *kaf farsi*). But I take recourse to Iran's geography and topography, and call him Araki and not 'Iraqi. 'Iraq is a country to the west of Iran whose people speak Arabic. The region that straddles Irans western border with Iraq has been traditionally called 'Iraq-e-'Ajam, the latter part being the name given by the Arabs to Iran. The region is called 'Iraq-e-'Ajam because the people in the region are bi-lingual and bi-cultural. Khuzistan, the south-western province of Iran is culturally more Semitic than Irano-Aryan. Since Shamsu'd-Din did not originate from this border region, there appears no reason why he should be called 'Iraqi. On the other hand, we learn from his biography that he originated from Solghan, which lies close to the northern province of Gilan in Iran. We have a sub-region in present-day Iran called Arak and we have evidence to show that he hailed from this region. As such, he has to be called Araki. Furthermore, his life was cast in the social and cultural milieu of this region, which is reflected at several places in the course of this work. This strengthens the inference that it is safer to call him Araki.

My presumption is that Araki was of Kurdish ethnicity. It is based firstly on a references made by the biographer to Araki's connection with the Safavi order of Sufi's with their establishment in Gilan, the northern province of Iran touching on the shores of the Caspian Sea. Regarding the Safavis and Safavi connections, we shall be speaking in detail later in this introduction. But the following excerpt from Nasrullah Falsafis history of the Safavis is an indirect reference to the assembly of Sufis in Gilan.

> "A group of people from the region of Qaracheh Dag was among the old adherents of Safavi order (of *Sufis*); they continue to be so even now. When owing to overwhelming threat from his enemies, Shah Ismail (Safavi), retreated to Gilan, he spent a couple of years in Lahijan where the Sufis of this (Safavi) order used to come frequently to his presence. Groups of Sufis from Qaracheh Dag also paid him occasional visits. These groups (of *Sufis*) are still considered as strong protagonists of the old Lahijani school of *Sufis*,[1] and owing to their title (Safavi–Lahijani), they enjoy precedence over other groups of *Sufis*."[2]

The readers will find more information on Safavis and Lahijanis in the footnotes to the text. Secondly, it has to be noted at this point that Araki had close links with the Lahijani school of Sufis, and in all probability, with other Sufi centers in the province of Gilan, which he often visited. As we shall know later in this introduction, many Sufis from Qaracha Dag, who kept visiting Lahijan in Gilan and took their abode in those regions permanently, were of Azerbaijani Kurdish stock. This leads us to presume that Araki descended from one of these immigrants to Gilan.

To a dispassionate but inquisitive reader, Araki appears a controversial figure on a few counts. It is because of conflicting reports that come to our notice either from his biographer or from historians who have written on mediaeval Kashmir. If we accept what the biography says about what brought Araki to Kashmir, it becomes clear that he was not on a diplomatic but a private mission though funded by the royal exchequer of the Timurid ruler Mirza Bayaqara[3] (AD 1470–

---

[1] See Shamsu'd-Din Muhammad Lahiji, pp.19–20 infra.

[2] *Zindagani-e Shah 'Abbas I*, Nasrullah Falsafi, Teheran 1369 AH(s), p.237. Also see *'Alm Ara-e 'Abbasi*, MS, National Library, Teheran, pp. 622–33

[3] He was the grandson of Bayaqara, son of Omar Shaykh, son of Timur. See *Taraikh-i-Adabiyyat dar Iran*, Zabihullah Safa, Teheran, vol.iv, p.526.

1505) of Herat. But as we proceed with the contents of the biography, we find Araki behaving in a manner as if he was an accredited emissary of the Timurid ruler to the court of the Sultan of Kashmir. The shift in Araki's mission from a procurer of medicinal herbs and elixirs from Kashmir for his ailing ruler-patron of Herat to that of an accredited emissary is significant. This is what makes him controversial.

The biography gives us an insight into how the idea of obtaining medicinal herbs from Kashmir was thrown up at the court of the Timurid ruler of Herat. We are briefly told of the discussion among the courtiers about the assignment for Araki, suggestion of royal physicians, and the rulers consent to providing financial and logistical support to Araki's long travel to a distant place Thus the entire mission was essentially for obtaining desired herbs and medicines from the mountains of Kashmir.

It has to be noted that in ancient Tukhara[1]—geographical region comprising modern NWFP of Pakistan, Northern Afghanistan and Southern parts of Tajikistan—or the Hindu Kush[2]—Badakhshan mountain range, Kashmir was known as the 'land of sorcery (*jadu-e* Kashmir) where apart from other mysteries, effective medicinal herbs were also found in the mountains.[3]

There is no hint in the biography that he planned to visit Kashmir with a definite mission of propagating Islam among local non-Muslims. That he was a zealous follower of Nurbakhshiyyeh order and sect is sufficiently stated in the biography but his extra-territorial religious mission and adventures are not stated explicitly.

---

[1] For Tukhara, see *Rajatarangini*, vol.ii, section on Ancient Geography of Kashmir, A. Stein, 1892.

[2] *Kush* is the corrupted form of *Kuf/Kaf* (in Pahlavi) and *Kuh* in Farsi meaning a mountain. Hindu Kuh (Hindu Kush) means the mountain that marks the watershed between India and the region beyond the mountain. Calling the Hindu Kush as the 'Killer of Hindus" is absolutely wrong.

[3] A fabulous extraction called *Salajeet* in Ayurvedic medical science is said to cure many diseases especially arthritis. Oral tradition says it was obtained from rocks in Tibet.

Two things related to Araki's first visit to Kashmir are noteworthy. One is that after arriving in Kashmir, he lay low for some time and even resorted to the option of *tqiyah* or dissimulation in the sense that he did not disclose to anybody in the initial stage of his visit that he had found conditions conducive to propagating his faith among the people in Kashmir. He gave out that he was an adherent of Kubraviyyeh-Hamadaniyyeh Sufi order, a plea that made him acceptable to local Muslim ecclesiastical fraternity and sections of Muslim community. The fact of the matter is that he was closely studying social contours of Kashmirian society at that time caught as it was in a grim struggle for its identity and social ethos ever since the mission of Mir Sayyid 'Ali Hamadani and his son Mir Muhammad Hamadani to Kashmir, a century and half ago.

The second thing to note is that he made objective assessment of partial success of Mir Sayyid 'Ali Hamadanis mission (AD 1381 or 1371) (sic)[1] inferring that the prospect of reviving it with renewed zeal along new lines would not be a forbidding task.

Araki made correct assessment of hopelessly weak and fragmented central authority in Kashmir kingdom. He found that power and influence in Kashmir at that time (15–16th century) virtually rested with autonomous regional commanders and feudal chiefs (*zamindars*). Mutual rivalry, lust for power, court conspiracies, betrayals and deceit and nominal authority of the Sultan were the characteristics that had rent the Kashmirian society asunder.

Therefore, Araki set for himself the task of creating adequate logistics, the most important factor of which was to rope in some of the powerful Kashmirian commanders and landlords. Convinced of the imbecility of Kashmirian royalty, he rightly, in the interest of his mission, almost ignored the Sultan, who, on his part, considered it a good riddance.

---

[1] *See Baharistan-i-Shahi*, tr. K.N. Pandit, Calcutta 1991, p.34.

One more event that makes Araki a controversial figure is his presenting a letter from the ruler of Herat to Sultan Hasam Shah (AD 1475) of Kashmir. According to the biographer, Mirza Bayaqaras letter was presented under established norms of protocol meaning in a formally summoned royal court where high ranking courtiers, nobles and distinguished personalities were present. Araki even had the audacity of snubbing the ruler of Kashmir for not observing established protocol of receiving the letter sent by a friendly neighouring ruler. He meant that the Sultan should have risen on his feet, taken the letter from the hands of the envoy who placed it on a golden or silver platter, kissed it and touched it with his forehead and eyes. Araki has betrayed contempt for Kashmiris. He charged that the courtiers of Kashmir Sultans were ignorant of norms of etiquette they needed to show to an emissary from a foreign king to their Sultan. This exposed his hypocrisy of posing as a visitor and not an accredited emissary.

Apart from these conflicting reports, some questions arise after going through the contents of the biography. It does not tell us anything about contacts existing between the caretakers of Hamadani mission in Trans-Oxiana/Khurasan and its hangers-on in Kashmir after Mir Sayyids final departure from Kashmir in AD 1384.[1] Why is not there any clear mention of nature and scope of interaction between the followers of Hamadaniyyeh order in Kashmir and those of Nurbakhshiyyeh order in Khurasan/Mavara-an-Nahr (Trans-Oxiana) in the intervening period since we are told that the two orders were ideologically complimentary besides operating almost in the same geographical region? What was the connection between Shamsu'd-Din Araki and Kashmir's earliest converts to Hamadaniyyeh/Nurbakhshiyyeh order like Baba 'Ali and others? How did the Kashmir royalty and

[1] See *Waqa'at-e-Kashmir*, (tr.) Shamsu'd-Din Ahmad, 2001, p.63.

nobility so easily succumb to the intimidation of Araki and his band of followers in the matter of faith, and what were the compulsions for them to give him much more importance than he deserved even as a missionary? To what extent should we accept the impressions of Mirza Haider Dughlat[1] about Araki that he was a pretender and a hypocrite who mislead the people of Kashmir along a wrong path and induced them to move away from the true faith? And finally, why is the last phase including the circumstances that led to the death of Araki left out of the biography? Why did the first and the last chapter of the complete manuscript of the biography disappear from a maximum number of the available copies of the manuscripts? A serious researcher is expected to deal with questions like these. Eventually, a researcher will need to find out the contours of social and political conditions of Kashmir when Araki arrived in the valley for the first time in AD 1486. Actually after the death of Sultan Zainu'l-'Abidin in AD 1473,[2] Kashmir kingdom gradually lost its cohesion and centrality. The post Zainu'l-'Abidin period is a sordid story of court conspiracies, warring and rebellious Damra chiefs, defiant commanders and landlords, hatred and rivalry between the locals and outsiders for political power, and polarization of society along sectarian divide in which task Araki made conspicuous contribution. Araki roped in contemporary Damra commanders—Musa Raina being the foremost among them—as was done by the founder of first Muslim ruling house of Kashmir who had preceded him by nearly two centuries.[3]

---

[1] Author of *Tarikh-i-Rashidi.*

[2] *Baharistan-i-Shahi*, (tr.) K.N. Pandit, Calcutta, 1991, p.74.

[3] Shah Mir, the fugitive from Swat, who later on usurped Kashmir throne (AD 1339) consolidated his position by entering into matrimonial relations with Kashmiri Damra chiefs. He married his daughter Guhava to Kotaraja of Bringa (in district Anantnag) and his grand-daughter to Lusta, the chieftain of Shankarpora (Pattan). See *Rajatarangini of Jonaraja*, tr. J.C. Dutt, p.29. Also see *Sufism in Kashmir*, Rafiqi, p.12fn.10.

Kashmir society at this time, though outwardly converted to Islamic faith, remained dismally bogged with its strong pre-Islamic moorings. Nearly a hundred and fifty years after the mission of Mir Sayyid 'Ali Hamadani, Kashmirian society was still struggling to adapt and reconcile fully to the new social and political structure. To Kashmiris, Islam was a religion and a philosophy not of indigenous growth but of foreign origin. As such, any foreigner coming from the Islamic lands such as Turan, Khurasan, Iran, Iraq or Arabia was naturally shown the highest regard because his interpretations of *Qura'n*, *hadith* and the tenets of faith were taken as the final word. For a long time many distinguished Kashmiri houses and personalities vacillated between the new and the old traditions or for quite sometime they continued to accept one part from each till the time came when they had to make a final choice. Araki came to Kashmir at a time when her society still continued to struggle for identity, an issue that stemmed from the phenomenon of a profound social transformation taking shape in the late 14th and early 15th century AD.

Araki very ably analyzed and understood this phenomenon of social commotion with its political ramifications, and converted it into the harbinger of a change that would break ideological barriers hitherto isolating the landlocked valley from the rest of the Muslim lands in the neighbourhood. It may be said that on finding the ground fertile for unfolding his vast religious mission in Kashmir, Araki played down his role of royal emissary from the ruler of Herat, and concentrated more on his religious mission viz. Nurbakhshiyyeh doctrine, by converting more and more Kashmiris to it. This is the reason why he claims to have carried forward the Hamadaniyyeh mission in Kashmir and seeks the blessings of his forerunner Mir Sayyid 'Ali Hamadani for its success.

A strong reason for the rapid success of Araki's mission was the deep rivalry between Sunni Baihaqi Sayyids and Kashmiri nobles and commanders of indigenous origin. The struggle in essence was for political power and ascendancy and not for faith. But up to a certain limit, the indigenous groups were comparatively more tolerant. The Sayyids did not welcome the presence of Araki much less his propagation of Shi'a Nurbakhshiyyeh order. Therefore, Araki pinned hope in befriending and winning over to his side some of the powerful indigenous commanders and nobles particularly those who contested power with the Sayyids or their partisans. With overt and covert support from influential official circles on the one hand—for, Kashmir bureaucracy of the time was not favourably disposed towards Baihaqi Sayyids—and his munificence in occasionally providing free meals and lavish gifts to ordinary people on the other, Araki confidently resolved to demonstrate the operative part of his great mission. And that part being easily achievable was of destroying all symbols of Hindu civilization and large scale conversion of the community of infidels and polytheists to the new faith. Its details are recorded in the fourth chapter of the biography. He had the compulsion of impressing upon the fresh converts the divine ordination of his mission.

As the story of Araki's activities gradually unfolds in the biography, we get a clear picture of the mission which he was determined to fulfill in Kashmir. Reacting to reports brought to him about how Hindu customs and way of life were still prevalent in Kashmir despite conversions forced on people a century and half ago the biographer writes, "He (Araki) said that the purpose of his visiting Kashmir region was to pull down the idol houses of infidels and polytheists. His first task was to put an end to the customs, traditions and habits of the *kafirs* (infidels), and also stamp out corruption and aberration (that had seeped into their lives)". "Now it is my duty to put and end to these innovations and the customs of the infidels", he exclaimed. We get a vivid description of how he and his followers whom he called *sufis* and dervishes, after the fashion of Safavi Sufi Order of the days of Safavi rulers in Iran, destroyed scores of temples, raised mosques on their ruins and forces conversion on the Hindus of Kashmir. He thanks God Almighty for granting him success in this mission.[1]

We have said that the historical value of the biography cannot be underestimated though we are aware that the work has seldom been given the credit of a reliable source of the history of cotemporary mediaeval Kashmir. Kashmiri historians and hagiographers writing in Farsi have not concealed their sectarian prejudice against Araki and his mission. The same is true of their treatment of other histories written by Shi'a historians, *Baharistan-i-Shahi*.[2] is another example.

Before Araki, four well known Sufi orders that initially originated in Iran or Trans-Oxiana and spread to the Muslim world had also reached Kashmir through their missionaries. However, Nurbakhshiyyeh order is the first Shi'a Sufi order that was introduced in Kashmir by Araki in the mid-16th century and perhaps ended with his departure from the scene. Its followers are found in Gilgit and Baltistan, now called Northern Areas by the Pakistani administration besides some other parts of the sub-continent and Iran.

Another aspect of the historical importance of this work is that while recording events connected with the life and mission of Araki, it illuminates several aspects of the social history of a crucial period of mediaeval Kashmir. This is of particular importance because very scant information has been provided to us by the mediaeval Farsi historians of Kashmir on the transformation of Kashmirian society from an indigenous and antiquated civilizational structure into one of a foreign kind. These historians have mostly rationalized this transformation; most of them have ended up providing insipid ecclesiastical discourse and the unnecessary debate on Sufi-Reshi juxtaposition. The serious debate on the nature, depth,

---

[1] See page 106 infra.

[2] Translation and annotation by K.N. Pandit, Calcutta 1991.

and impact of this significant transformation has been more or less sidetracked, and remains relatively unexplored.

A marked characteristic of Kashmir Sufism is that it did not become institutionalized. The history of Iranian Sufism brings to light two broad and vital categories of Sufis: one is of those whose mystical approach is grounded in Islamic faith, its doctrines, principles and practices, so that the possibility of coming into conflict with the faith does not arise at all. Another class, usually known as transcendentalists, seeks to rise above the compulsions of orthodoxy and tradition.[1] It is no wonder that adherents of this class had to suffer persecution from the orthodoxy. It did not spare even the greatest of Iranian Sufis, Jalalud-Din Rumi, whose celebrated *Masnavi* was called "a word of ill omen":

In kalam-e sufiyan-e shoom nist
Masnavi-e Manavi-e Rum nist

Sufism in its traditional form came to Kashmir from Iranian and Trans-Oxianian regions. In pre-Islamic Kashmir, *Rishism* had become the main vehicle of mystic expression. But when Sufism replaced it, beginning with the second half of the 14th century, its adherents had a much more important task before them than that of direct text book application of its principles and ritualistic discipline. Their real task was to popularize Islamic tenets among freshly converted masses by presenting these through the conduit of mystic lore. Doctrinal terms like Allah, Prophet, *Qur'an*, *hadis*, *Jibril*, *wahi*, *jannat*, *dowzakh*,

[1] The author of *Sufism in Kashmir*, too, has come to the same conclusion while discussing causes of differences between the Rishi and other Kashmiri Sufis. He writes," Sufism from the times of Abu Sa'id bin Abu'l-Khair down to the rise of Shaikh 'Alau'd-Daula Simnani to prominence, exhibits two different attitudes towards life; the Sufi as an ascetic and the Sufi as a missionary". See *Sufism in Kashmir from the fourteenth to the sixteenth century*, Abdul Qaiyum Rafiqi, Bhartiya Publishing House, New Delhi. (date of publication not given), p.207

hur o ghilman, *sunnat*, *amr m'aruf*, *nahi munkir* etc. were more frequently used by them in their diction instead of the standard Sufi terminology of later transcendentalists, such as *nafs*, *wahdat*, *kasrat*, *aina*, *qatareh*, *darya*, *zarreh*, *nur*, *aftab*, *mey*, *mugh*, *pir-e mughan*, etc. This left them with little time for institutionalizing Sufism, so as to give it a recognizable place in the new social structure. Furthermore, at no point of time in the history of mediaeval Kashmir do we see royal patronage extended to Sufism so that its institutionalizing would have been facilitated, as, for example, was the case in Iran during the Safavi rule.

Reverting to *Tohfatu'l-Ahbab*, it is important to note that Araki's life and work were cast in a society that had grown and evolved under the overarching Timurid social and cultural ethos of Central Asia. The period of later Timurids of Herat, known because of kings like Shahrukh and Sultan Husayn Bayaqara (AD 1470–1507) had markedly absorbed the true spirit of the great Timurid empire of the 14th century.

In the period between 15–16th centuries many important things happened in Iran and Central Asia. Firstly, the Timurids, like the great founder of the house, formally subscribed to Sunni-Hanafi faith, and extended royal patronage to Sunni saints, ascetics, Sufis, *ulema*, theologians and doctors of divinity. Secondly, Shi'a resentment to Sunni supremacy led to discontent against the ruling structure and state policy and fueled rebellious sentiments among the followers of 'Alis line. Thirdly, a lurking desire in the Iranian mind for a centralized government representing Iran's social, cultural and spiritual aspirations received impetus during this period, and finally culminated in the emergence of the Safavis.

Shamsu'd-Din's thinking was largely shaped by the social milieu of his time. But the people in Kashmir, particularly the ones who converted to his faith (Nurbakhshiyeh) had only a hazy knowledge of Araki's antecedents, his ideology and the contours of a society and culture from which he came.

A careful study of the socio-cultural movements brewing in the regions of Turkistan and Khurasan during 15–16th century AD, first under the Seljuqs and then Timurids, indicates a commotion of sorts shaking Islamic societies that threw up factional and sectarian fraternities, all aspiring to religious and political space. Rebellions, revolts and underground movements in these two regions were the manifestation of the commotion and discontent that has already been mentioned. Therefore, an overview of social and political history of the period under consideration is quite essential.

Without this information, the biography cannot be studied in its proper perspective. We need to know the mindset of Araki when he planned the operative part of his mission in Kashmir. Therefore, I consider it necessary to deal with some major aspects of Iranian society of his day. This task becomes all the more desirable because the biographer has only hinted at social-cultural spectrum of Iran preceding Araki's times. He does not give elaborate information on how Araki carried forward his mission of popularizing Nurbakhshiyyeh doctrine in Kashmir; how far he succeeded in it, what were the obstacles in his path and what were the effects of his adventure. Stating a couple of confrontational discourses with the Sunni *ulema* or a lavish description of the destruction of temples and conversion of idol-worshippers and polytheists leaves a yawning gap.

Keeping this in mind, it is advisable that the entire spectrum of this biography is assessed by bringing into focus two main things: firstly, some prominent personalities who are in the frontline of activity shaping or influencing events, and secondly, some broad aspects of social and political history of the region wherefrom the missionary came and the impact of the social milieu on his life and thinking. These personalities and the events in which they are involved are very closely intertwined, but to keep things straight, we first deal with the leading personalities and then with the social milieu.

Part I

Sayyid Muhammad Nurbakhsh

Born in AH 795/AD 1392 in Qain of Khurasan province, Sayyid Muhammad Nurbakhsh's ancestors had migrated from Lahsa, for which reason, says the author of *Majalisul-Momineen*, he used Lahsavi[1] as his pen name in some of his poetical compositions. As a young man, his father once paid a visit to the shrine of Imam Reza in Mashhad, took a wife and settled down at Qain. Nurbakhsh was a bright student and learnt *Qura'n* by heart at the early age of seven. As a student he visited the study centre (*mahzar*) of Mir Sayyid Sharief Jurjani, and also attended the lessons of Ibn Fahd Hilli (d. AH 741/AD 1340). They were the two renowned scholars of Iraq at that time.

The studious Sayyid Muhammad pursued various branches of learning of his day: rational and traditional sciences including mathematics in which "he claimed to have superseded Plato, and Avicenna (Ibn Sina) in the rest of sciences."[2] Following the custom of the day, he showed inclination towards Sufism and turned to Khwajeh Ishaq Khatalni,[3] the *khalifa* (spiritual successor) of Mir Sayyid 'Ali Hamadani. The author of *Majalisul-Momineen* tells us that his spiritual master Shaykh Ishaq was impressed by his student's brilliance, and, as a result of a dream, conferred on him the title Nurbaksh (light-giving), and even went to the extent of making allegiance (*bai'at*) to him. In this way Khwajeh Ishaq was admitted to the circle of the disciples of Sayyid Nurbakhsh along with the group of his followers perhaps because

---

[1] In the Gulf region.

[2] *Dunbaleh-e Just o Ju dar Tasavvuf-e Iran*, Adul Husayn Zarrinkub, Teheran AH (s) 1366, p.184.

[3] Sometimes written as Khuttalan. But Khatlan seems to be the correct version.
Sipahi badin san biyamad ze chin
Va Soqlab o Khatlan o Turan zamin (Shahnameh Ferdowsi)

Nurbakhsh claimed to be the seventeenth in the line of Imama Musa al-Kazim.

Khwajeh Ishaq is said to have prompted Nurbaskhsh to stage rebellion against the later Timurid ruler Shahrukh in Herat for reasons stated elsewhere in this introduction, and to declare himself Mehdi. But he turned it down saying that it was not the proper time for staging rebellion against "a king like Shahrukh who was holding sway over Iran, Turan, Hind, 'Arab and 'Ajam".[1] But eventually, hot heads among his followers goaded him to do so.

On the issue of Nurbakhsh claiming himself to be the Mehdi, Qazi Nurullah Shushtari says that Khwajeh Ishaq Samarqandi was unhappy with the domination of Sunni rulers, and incited the Sayyid to follow the example of the venerable personalities of olden days who had revolted against the oppressive Abbasids. The purpose was "to cleanse the world of the contamination of tyrants." In the process, he (Khwajeh Ishaq) consented that Nurbakhsh may assume the title of Mehdi and Imam.[2]

Even if we assume that Khwajeh Ishaq was not instrumental in convincing or could not convince Nurbakhsh to revolt against Shahrukh, it is true that he was not averse to Nurbakhsh ambition of staging an uprising against the Timurid ruler of Khurasan. The anti-state *Sarbadaran* movement that had surfaced then and also quelled had left a deep impact on him. He nursed the idea of establishing a Sufi-Shiite government in Khurasan, which had previously found favour with the adherents of Hurufi sect and Safavi Shaykhs.

What Sayyid Muhammad Nurbakhsh actually contemplated was a religious-political movement in Khurasan. Although Shaykh Ishaq and a good number of his followers

---

[1] *Majalisu'l-Momineen*, p.204

[2] Ibid, p.205.

subscribed to Nurbakhsh's idea of establishing a theocratic state, it did not find favour with all the Sufis of Kubraviyyeh-Hamadiniyyeh order. For example, Sayyid 'Abdullah Barzishabadi, one of the lieutenants of Khwajeh Ishaq, neither accepted making allegiance to Sayyid Nurbakhsh nor supported his defiance to the ruler. He had also declined to call the Sayyid *Mehdi.*

As Nurbakhsh announced himself the Mehdi, a claim supported by Khwajeh Ishaq, the state authorities took note of the development. They both were at Kuh-i Tiri, close to the fort in Khatlan, from where they were arrested, along with some other Shaykhs. Under Shahrukh's orders Khwajeh Ishaq was executed (AH 826/AD 1422), and Sayyid Nurbakhsh was taken prisoner; he was sent to Herat and then to Shiraz where, at the end of the day, Ibrahim Sultan, the son of Shahrukh and the governor of those regions, set him free.

Before long Sayyid Nurbakhsh created his influence among the Feeli and Bakhtyari tribes of Southern Iran, and with their support revived his claim to the caliphate. Some nobles and powerful persons of the region struck coins and read homilies (*khutba*) in his name. From Southern Iran he went to Gilan, but while returning to the Kurdish lands, he was arrested and sent to the royal camp in Azerbaijan. After suffering privations and incarceration he responded to Sultan Shahrukh's order and publicly repudiated—though somewhat ambiguously[1]—from the pulpit in Herat[2] all accusations made against him. He pledged to devote himself only to the task of pursuing knowledge. But this, too, did not secure his freedom until the death of Shahrukh Mirza in AH 850/AD 1446. Finally, he came to Solghan where he acquired some land for cultivation and started a settled life.

---

[1] Dunbaleh-e Just o Ju op. cit.

[2] See Tarikh-e Adabiyyat dar Iran, Zabihullah Safa, Teheran, AH (s) 1366, vol.iv, pp.58–60.

Although in the last phase of his life Sayyid Nurbakhsh had given up the ambition of being called the Caliph, yet he took delight in occasionally calling himself the "promised symbol" (*mazhar-e mowud*) and the "accomplished symbol" (*mazhar-e jame*). He firmly assigned to himself the "realm of the *vali*/saint" (*velayat*) and of a religious guide (*ershad*). In his two letters preserved in the collection of Abu Aala Hayder under the heading *Nushkhah-e Jame-e Murasilat-e Ulul-Albab* in the British Museum,[1] he boasts of his accomplishments in "the Knowledge of the Truth" and "Pursuits in the Unity of Being".

Be khuda gar be zir-e charkh-e kebud
Chun mani hast-o bud-o khwahad bud

Addressing the ruler of his time, he asserts that if there was a learned scholar, a Sayyid who had reached the depths of truth and received light and virtue from the "Being", it was he.

Shaykh Muhammad Lahiji, the author of *Mafatehul-'Ejaz*, a commentary on Mahmud Shabistaris *Gulshan-e Raz* uses almost similar epithets for Sayyid Nurbakhsh and even addresses him as Hazrat Imam.

In any case, his sect being close to Kubravi order of Sufis, came to be known as Nurbakhshiyeh order. His son Shah Qasim Faiz Bakhsh went to Khurasan where Sultan Husayn Bayaqara treated him well. Shaykh Lahiji propagated Nurbakhshiyeh order in Shiraz, where he built the Nuriyeh hospice (*khanqah*) in his name. Qazi Nurullah Shushtari, the author of *Majalisul-Momineen*, too, adopted the Nurbakhshiyeh path.

Sayyid Nurbakhsh's treatise *Ar-Risalatul-'Etiqadiyeh* deals with the theme of Sufism, and the subject of the "realm of a *vali* (*velayat*) has been discussed from the Shi'a point of view. *Fiqhu'l-Ahwat*, another treatise ascribed to him, became

[1] Add 7688.

a contentious document because of opposition from the Sunni Hanafi theologians of Kashmir. His *Risaleh-e Al-Huda* substantiates his claim to be the Mehdi, an obsession in the early days of his active life.[1]

The emergence of Nurbakhshiyeh movement is also interpreted as a revolt of Kubraviyyeh Shi'a order against the Timurid ruler of the time, Mirza Shahrukh Gorkani. The uprising provided an excellent opportunity to a group of Kubravis for aligning themselves with the Shi'a faith or at least an occasion to deviate from the practice of hiding their intentions, known to the *Shi'a* as *taqqiyeh.* Although Nurbakhshi movement had essentially religious and political underpinnings, it brought about a split in Kubaviyyeh order, which ultimately led to the gradual strengthening of the Shi'a faction in the regions of Khurasan, Iraq and Fars. Only one group from among them, the followers of Kemalud-Din Khwarazmi, that stay put in Transoxiana remained outside the pale of Shi'ism, notwithstanding the fact that like all the followers of Khwajeh Ishaq Khatlani they, too, assigned the title of *Dhahabiyyeh* to their group.

In any case, the emergence of Nurbakhshiyyeh religious and political movement denied Khwajeh Ishaq Khatlani any chance of propagating Kubraviyyeh order and Hamadaniyyeh teachings. The irony of fate was that his detractors indicted Khwajeh Ishaq Khatlani as an accomplice in the Nurbakhshiyyeh uprising and obtained royal consent for his execution in AH 826/AD 1422.

Pleased with the title of Shaykh Sufi, Sayyid Muhammad Nurbakhsh deemed himself the successor (*khalifa*) of Khwajah Ishaq and an adherent to Hamadani-Kubravi order. Those in Khurasan who had declined allegiance to Nurbaksh at the time he launched his movement, joined the circle of the pupils of Sayyid Abdullah Barzashabadi. We learn from *Majalisul Mominen* that in all probability the followers of

---

[1]For sources on Nurbakhsh see *Rayhanatu'l-Adab*, vol.iv, p.243, *Riyazu'l-'Arifin*, p.104 and *Taraiqu'l-Haqaiq*, vol.iii, p.30.

Sayyid 'Abdullah were called Sufiyeh and were nothing but Sufis. But the followers of Nurbakhsh, better known as a religious and political group, elevated their master to the status of a spiritual leader, Imam, Mehdi and the successor, and called themselves Nurbakhshiyyeh. However, during the last days of his life, Sayyid Muhammad Nurbakhsh gave up his aspiration to be designated the Imam and Caliph owing to political difficulties and the serious opposition of the rulers and administrators of the time. Yet the adherents of Nurbahshiyyeh order still treated him as a spiritual guide and the Shaykh of *Dhahabi* order and the successor to Khwajeh Ishaq Khatlani and also the spiritual leader of the Hamadani Sufi order.

During the early period of Safavi rule in Iran, Shaykh Muhammad Asiri Lahiji made concerted efforts for the propagation of Nurbakhshiyyeh teachings, projecting them as a complement to the system of Khwajeh Ishaq Khatlani and Mir Sayyid 'Ali Hamadani.[1]

After Sayyid 'Ali's death, Kubraviyyeh order of Sufis gradually came close to Shi'a practices under the guidance of his pupil and successor Khwajeh Ishaq Khatlani. There was a split between the followers of the Sayyid after the death of Khwajeh Ishaq Khatlani and among the Kubravis; some were called Nurbakhshiyeh, while the dissenters assumed the name of Dhahabiyyeh. Strangely, though the Nurbakhshiyeh were called both Nurbakhshiyyeh and Nooriyeh at one and the same time; they too were called Dhahabiyyeh.

After the execution of Khwajeh Ishaq Khatlani, the followers of Kubraviyeh-Hamadaniyeh Shi'a order sought allegiance to Sayyid 'Abdullah Barzeshabadi and came to be known *'dhahabiyyeh*. There is some confusion about the nomenclature of *'dhahabiyyeh* because the group is not specific only to Sayyid Barzeshabadi. In a treatise available to

[1] Most of this material pertaining to Mir Sayyid 'Ali Hamadani has been drawn from *Dunbaleh-e Just o Ju dar Tasawwuf-e Iran* by Abdul Husayn Zarrinkub, Teheran AH (s) 1366.

us in manuscript form,[1] Sayyid Nurbakhsh refers to his own *silsila* or order as Kubravi Nurbakhiyeh and uses the epithet *silsilatul-zahab* characterising them as "free of all impurities like pure gold."

* * *

Amir Sayyid 'Ali Hamadani

Among the accomplished divines of Kubravi order who came after Shaykh 'Alaud-Dawleh Simnani (whose followers were known as Rukniyyeh), the most impressive person is Amir Sayyid 'Ali Hamadani. His followers are generally known as Hamadaniyeh faction of Kubravi order. It is said that in his youth he had the opportunity of seeing the last phase of Shaykh 'Alaud-Dowleh Simnani. Nevertheless, Sayyid 'Ali received Kubravi *khirqa* or initiation into that order from the two disciples of the Shaykh, 'Ali Dosti and Mahmud Muzdaqani.

In any case, whatever has been said about his life and thoughts, particularly by his student and disciple Nurud-Din *J'afar* Badakhshi in *Khulasatul-Manaqib*, one suspects that things have been somewhat exaggerated... Hamadanis meeting with Shaykh 'Alaud-Din Simnani when he was still young or, a mere child, as some say it, seems a remote possibility. Again there is no dependable source to ascertain his descent from the famous house of 'Alavis of Hamadan to which Gonbad-e-Hamadan has been ascribed. His great popularity with the Sunnis of Kashmir and Badakhshan regions could be because of his so-called Alavi line of descent, which stood him in good stead for propagating love for the House of the Prophet (*ahl-e bait*). He had links with *Fotovvat* order as well because of his close friendship with men like 'Ali Dusti and others of the *Fotovvat* School and followers of Alau'd-Dowleh Simnani. The author of *Majalis-l-Momineen* has projected him a Shi'a of Dhahabiyyeh Sufi order of his day. (Safavi period). His pro-Shi'a inclinations reflected in his

[1] Teheran University Central Library, Collection (*Majmu'a*) No.3497.

spiritual training and flight have left their impact on the personalities of Khwajeh Ishaq Khatalani and J'afar Badakhshi. They have considered him a link between Kubraviyyeh and the Shi'a of Dhahabiyyeh School. The title 'Ali *Thani*, meaning the peer of 'Ali, and his interest in the teachings of Ibnl-'Arabi link him with Kubraviyyeh—Dhhabiyyeh School.

It seems that the events of his life have not been described in befitting detail. J'afar-e Badakhshis *Khulasatul-Manaqib* is mostly confined to his thoughts and teachings. Yet another work, actually a tract, *Manqabatul-Jawahir*, compiled by Haider Badakhshi, a student of Abdullah Barzishabadi, on the theme in hand is neither based on direct source of information nor devoid of exaggerated stories of miracles. Some chroniclers say he was born on 12 Rajab 713 or 714 AH/AD 1313 or 1314). If we accept this, then he was just a two or three year old infant at the time of the death of Sultan Uljayatu Khudabandeh in AH 716/AD 1335. Hence, the story of he being introduced by his maternal uncle as a seven year old urchin to a gathering of nearly four hundred distinguished scholars, Shaykhs and Sayyids assembled at the court of Sultan Uljayatu on the occasion of laying the foundation of Gunbad-e Sultaniyeh, and all of them, including Shaykh 'Alau'd-Dawleh Simnani, reciting the scripture and tradition for him and he picking it up (in one audition) hardly sounds credible. This story has been recounted in *Khulasatul Manaqib* though with a slight difference, but without mentioning the name of the Sultan.

The tendency among historians and hagiographers to bring in stories about the miracles of Sufis and spiritualists of high status cannot be verified by available evidence or even by any stretch of imagination.

In any case, he traces his descent from his fathers side (Sayyid Shahabud-Din) as well as his mothers side (Bibi Fatimah), from the line of 'Ali ibn Ibi Talib. Both his father and his maternal uncle, Sayyid 'Alaud-Din, were men of substance, and the latter took special interest in his upbringing.

The writer of *Khulasatu-Manaqib* tells us that "on receiving a hint from the unknown" he found his way to the service of Shaykh Mahmud Muzdaqani, a spiritual successor of 'Alau'd-Dowleh Simnani. Muzdaqani is reported to have built a hospice (*khanqah*) or a study centre for religious practices at Muzdaqan, a place somewhere between Hamadan and Saveh. Later on, Sayyid 'Ali joined the services of Taqiud-Din 'Ali Dusti, another disciple and pupil of 'Alau'd-Dowlah. After the demise of 'Ali Dusti, he came back to Shaykh Mahmud Muzdaqani who recommended to him to proceed on long travels to acquire knowledge from divines and learned scholars. Amir Sayyid 'Ali has stated in *Risaleh-e Fatuhiyeh* that he received the Sufi cloak (*khirqah*) from Shaykh Muhammad who was a pupil of 'Alau'd-Dowleh Simnani. Thus Amir Sayyid has manifold spiritual links with 'Alau'd-Dowleh Simnani.

Following Shaykh Mahmud Muzdakanis instructions, Amir adopted the path (of mysticism) under the guidance of close associates of 'Alau'd-Dowleh, and responded to the decree (*futwa*) of thirty-four leading Shaykhs of the day, to go on long travels to impart knowledge to seekers of spirituality and to propagate Islam. According to the author of *Khulasatul Manaqib*, the Sayyid is said to have "traversed the populated one-fourth (*rub'e maskun*) of the globe and discovered one thousand and four hundred spiritualists (*valis*)". His letters reveal that he went on travels to avoid mischief and denigration by his adversaries. We learn from *Khulasatul-Manaqib and Majalisul-Mominen* that his irascible temper came in the way of his longer stay in distant lands. Some writers have disclosed that in the course of an assembly summoned by Timur in Trans-Oxiana, Mir 'Ali failed to control his wild temper, and because of that, always feared the Emperor's wrath.[1]

[1] This repudiates the story carried by many Farsi histories of Kashmir that the Sayyid had left his native place Hamadan for Kashmir with seventy of his followers because he feared the wrath of Timur.

Although Sayyid ʻAli showed extraordinary veneration for the House of the Prophet (*ahl-e bait*), he, nevertheless, was favourably disposed towards the progress of Shafiʻi School. His allegiance to ʻAli and his progeny did not prevent him from giving full respect to the Prophet's Companions (*sohaba*) and the venerable Caliphs (*khulfa-e rashidin*). Thus in this sense his path is similar to that of ʻAlau'd-Dowleh Simnnai in which distancing oneself from the Prophet's Companions is not necessarily required to winning the love for the House of the Prophet.

It has to be noted that his legendary ʻAlavi lineage helped him to instil love for the House of Prophet in the Sunni Musalmans of Kashmir and Badakhshan regions.

The author of *Majalisul-Momineen* and the Sufi doctors of *Dhahabiyyah* order of Safavi era have insisted on his being a follower of Shiʻa faith. This assertion is partly endorsed by his system of guiding people along the path of mysticism. Not much can be deduced on this count either from his literary output or from his effort of propagating the faith. In any case his Shiʻa proclivity to the extent of training and guiding his disciples along the path of mysticism is reflected in the person of Khwajeh Ishaq Khatlani and Jʻafar Badakhshi who considered him a point of connectivity of Kubravi order inclining towards *Dhahbiyyeh* Shiʻism so much so that they sometimes attributed the title "*Ali Thani*" (The Peer of Ali) to him. Another point of connectivity is the acceptance of the mystical teachings of Shaykh Mohiud-Din Ibnul-ʻArabi by the Kubraviyyeh order of Sufis. Sayyid ʻAlis commentary titled *Hall an-Nusus*, on Ibnul-ʻArabis celebrated work *Fususul-Hikam*—a fundamental thesis of Arab Sufism popular among the doctors of Nurbakhshiyyeh order—is apparently based on his lessons. Though it does not endorse the doctrine of Unity of Being (*wahdatul-wujud*) yet it reflects a considerable compatibility between the doctrine of Ibnul-ʻArabi and the thoughts of the Sufis of Kubraviyyeh order. His commentary on *Masharibil-Azwaq*, a popular treatise of Ibn Fariz, is one more step forward on the path of interaction between the mystic practices of Kubrviyyeh order and those prevalent among the Sufis of Egypt and West Asia.

A few Farsi quatrains and fragments attributed to Sayyid 'Ali are insipid and devoid of merit. But he has more than eighty Farsi and Arabic prose works to his credit. Ethics and statecraft form the theme of his more known work *Zakhiratul-Muluk*. According to Zarrinkub, though Farsi and French translations of this text have been published, a critically annotated edition is yet to be written.[1]

His followers are generally known as Hamadaniyeh faction of Kubravi order. It is said that he as a youth did see Shaykh 'Alau'd-Dowleh who was in the last phase of his life. Nevertheless, Sayyid 'Ali received Kubravi *khirqa* or initiation into that order from two disciples of the Shaykh: 'Ali Dosti and Mahmud Muzdaqan.

In any case, whatever has been said about his life and thoughts, particularly by his student and disciple Nurud-Din J'afar Badakhshi in *Khulasatul-Manaqib*, there is an element of exaggeration and speculation. Hamadani's meeting with Shaykh 'Alau'd-Dowleh Simnani when he was still young or, according to some, a child, too, appears a remote possibility. Again there is no dependable source to ascertain his lineage to the famous house of 'Alawis of Hamadan to which Gonbad-e-Hamadan has been ascribed.

As such, the fact of the matter is that the events of his life have not been described in a way as would remove the cobwebs of confusion. Contents of J'afar-e Badakhshis work *Khulasatu'l-Manaqib* are more or less confined to his thoughts and teachings. Yet another work, actually a tract, titled *Manqibatu'l-Jawahir*, and compiled by Haider Badakhshi, a student of Abdullah Barzishabadi on the theme in hand is

---

[1] *Dunbaleh-e Just o Ju dar Tasawwuf-e Iran*, Teheran, AH (S) 1375/AD, p.182. Annotated text of *Zakhiratu'l-Muluk* along with appendices was published by Sayyid Muhammad Alwari. See *Isharaat*, a publication of Iranian History and Cultural Foundation, Tabriz, AH (S) 1458/AD.

neither based on direct source of information nor is devoid of exaggerated stories of miracle-performing.

* * *

Kubravi Order

Two outstanding scholars of Shaykh Najmu'd-Din Kubra's school, Abul-Mafakhar Bakharzi and Azizud-din Nasafi, were inclined towards the philosophy of Ibul-'Arabi of which the most important aspect is Unity of Being or *wahdatul-wujud*. But another outstanding Shaykh of the same order disagrees with Ibnul-'Arbi and dismisses the concept as nonsense and blasphemy. He is 'Alau'd-Dowleh Ahmad bin Sharf Simnani (b. AH 659/AD 1260), Jami in *Nafahatu'l-Uns* and Nurullah Shushtari in *Majalisul-Momineen* have given us extensive information on Simnani's great debates with his opponents on the subject. But gradually for persons like Mir Sayyid 'Ali Hamadani and Muhamad Nurbakhsh, a reconciliation of sorts of Kubravis with the teachings of Ibnu'l-'Arabi did come about somehow. Although leading intellectuals of Nurbakhshiyyeh and Dhahabiyyeh order may not have openly endorsed Ibnu'l-'Arabi's mystic thoughts, yet they never opposed them directly or indirectly.

'Alau'd-Dowleh Simnani received his Sufi cloak (*khirqa*) from Shaykh Raziu'd-din 'Ali Lala, a leading Kubravi Shaykh of his times and training from 'Abdur-Rahman Isfarayani (d. AH 695/AD 1295). Simnani hailed from a distinguished house of nobles of Simnan. With the passage of time, he felt inclined towards mysticism and abandoned his official post with the Mongol administration "in a bid to seek freedom (from material world) like Ibrahim Adham and Shaykh Shibli, the great Sufis of earlier period" as he says in his own work *al-Urwatu'l-Ahlu'l-khalwat*.

However, he continued to serve Arghun, the Mongol ruler at Tabriz for two more years, and then returned to his native town of Simnan where he developed interest in studying mysticism and serving his people. He freed his domestic slaves and busied himself with humanitarian works. Arghun held him in high esteem for his abilities and expected him to return to state service, which, however, he did not want. He used part of his property to meet the cost of constructing a hospice, and distributed the rest among his dependents. In this way he took to the path of the great Sufis of the past: by renouncing the material world and taking to seclusion and meditation.

His father and uncle both had been in the service of Arghun, the last Mongol ruler of Buddhist faith from the line of Chingiz, who had inherited the empire of his ancestor. But he sought assistance from the Muslims for running the administration of the state, and occasionally showed respect to the Sufi Shaykhs and their burial places. Perhaps for a reticent Sufi like 'Alau'd-Dowleh, it became difficult to re-join the services of Arghun, "an idolatrous infidel," particularly when, after overpowering his uncle Sultan Ahmad, he had behaved in a manner that explicitly betrayed the domination of idolatry over Islam.

But his past services in the administration of Arghun had brought Simnani into close contact with Buddhist *bhikshus*[1] and monks, and their association undoubtedly left a profound impact on the Sufi who had made a hospice as his new abode. He found that the systems of the Buddhists and Sufis had strong parallels. While he lived in seclusion at the hospice in Simnan, the Buddhist monks from Arghun visited him occasionally. Simnani preserved the memory of these meetings and the very pleasing manner in which they met him and exchanged ideas with him. Reflections of these intellectual interfaces are available in his work *al-'Urwat* or in *Malfuzat*, which was compiled under the title *Chehel Majlis* by his disciple and student Amir Iqbal Sistani.

[1] Buddhist monks called *Bhikshu* in Sanskrit/Pali corrupted into *Bakhshi* in Farsi/Arabic (translator).

These writings indicate that 'Alau'd-Dowleh Simnani appreciated the spiritual practices of Buddhist monks, though, as is expected from a Musulman, he rejected ideas like incarnation, rebirth and transmigration. Chapter fourth of *al-'Urwah* deals brilliantly with these subjects. Chapter sixth of *Malfuzat* deals with the principles of Hinduism and is remarkable for its freshness and clarity. Such debates are not to be found in the works of other Sufis. "His rejection of Ibnu'l-'Arabi's philosophy of Unity of Being emanates from his close understanding of the teachings of Buddhist monks. This is what can be understood from *al-'Urwah*. The correspondence between him and 'Abdur-Razzaq Kashani, to which Amir Iqbal Sistani has referred, was intended to help Simnani remove doubts of heresy and aberration against Shaykh Mohiud-Din Ibnu'l-'Arabi. But Simnani sent him a strong letter considering the philosophy of Unity of Being condemnable and "worse than other beliefs of the Hindu infidels".[1]

'Alau'd-Dowleh Simnani occupies an important place among the disseminators of Kubravi Sufi philosophy in Iran and India. He seems to be a traditionalist and distances from innovation (*bid'at*) in Islam. But then, like two of his outstanding predecessors in Kubravi order, Shaykh *Sa'adu'd*-Din Hamavi and Shaykh 'Azizu'd-din Nasafi, he also shows definite inclination towards Shi'ism. In a treatise *Manaziru'l-Mahazir-lil-Nazir* he disapproves speaking ill of the Companions (*sahabah*), but considers 'Ali ibn Ibi Talib as the choicest of all Companions of the Prophet calling him "Our Imam". He endorses 'Ali's refusal to accept the Caliphate of Othman. He is emphatic about the concept of *khalafat*, and *Ghadir Khum* address of the Prophet. This treatise carries many quotes from 'Ali as are set forth in *Nehju'l-Balageh*. However despite the fact that he did not accept the caliphate of

[1] *Dunbaleh-e Just o Ju dar Tasavvuf-e Iran*, loc. cit., p.172.

the four *khalifas*, yet he strongly rejected blasphemy against the Companions of the Prophet. He says that although "Our Imam" first declined to show allegiance to the Caliphs but then he did make it and gave his support to the decisions they made. He argues that 'Ali sacrificed his rights for the sake of faith. Why then should his followers go on saying bad words against the Caliphs, he questions. He quotes 'Ali as an example for avoiding extremes of too much of attachment to 'Ali and too much of resentment against the Caliphs. In the same treatise he argues that true Shi'as are not *rafizis* (deviators) but Sufis. In a letter to Maulana Taju'd-Din Kahri included in *Rowzatu'j-Janan* he proudly qualifies his affection for the House of the Prophet (*ahl-e bait*) as *salabiyeh*, *qalbiyeh* and *haqqiyeh* meaning by descent, by heart and as a matter of fact.[1] He is thankful that he is "from the house and a friend of the house" (of 'Ali). Although he accepts the Twelfth Imam as the 'Pivot" (*qotb*) of the Time, yet he does not endorse the Imamia Shi'a views in this regard. Thus concludes Zarrinkub that although his Shi'ism is not deniable yet his association with the *ithna 'aṣhra* is doubtful.

Like Shaykh Najmu'd-Din Kubra, the founder of Kubravi order, it appears that 'Alau'd-Dowleh also pays attention to what is called the light of revelations and turmoil deep inside the heart of one moving along the path of mysticism (*salik*). The epilogue to the commentary of Najmu'd-Dn Razi (on Ibnu'l-'Arabi's *Fususu'l-Hakam*) shows his appreciation for the concept of light of revelations. The Kubravis talk of 'Seven Graces of Heart (*sab'e qalb*) as legacy from Shaykh Najmu'd-Din Kubra. To 'Alau'd-Dwleh, man is the mini-world and presence of Seven Graces in his heart indicates the presence of seven *anbiya* in the cosmic world. Each Grace tells us of spiritual form and the status and stage of the prophethood, which means exposition of that Grace in the cosmic world. Although he is opposed to the philosophy of Unity of Being

[1] *Dunbaleh* ... etc., p.175.

and some other mystical views of Ibnu'l-'Arabi yet his conceding the view of seven heavenly Graces shows that he is not far removed from Ibnu'l-Arabi who speaks of the status of *anbiya* in *Fususu'l-Hikam.*

* * *

Shamsu'd-Din Muhammad Lahiji

One more person who has been praised by Araki as a staunch Nurbakhshiyyeh Sufi, who contributed much to its expansion, is Shamsu'd-Din Muhammad Lahiji, with Asiri as his pen-name. He is counted among the outstanding Sufi Shaykhs of Nurbakhshiyyeh order. He joined the service of Sayyid Muhammad Nurbakhsh in AH 849/AD 1445. Says he, "When eternal grace and divine guidance blessed this *fakir*, I came to the service of *Imam-e Zaman*, Sayyid Muhammad Nurbakhsh to declare my repentance (from sins) and accept his path and procedure in an urge for spiritual enhancement in a way as is known in the history of the great saints."[1]

He says that he remained in the service of Sayyid Nurbakhsh for sixteen years. However, other sources reveal that he stayed for more than twenty years. During his long service, he thrice obtained the consent of his preceptor to become a guide to those who came to him. He has recorded the last instance of seeking permission in his work *Mafatihu'l-'Ejaz*.

After the death of Sayyid Muhammad Nurbakhsh, Lahiji took up his abode in Shiraz where he began guiding Nurbakhshi followers in the province of Fars. He built a hospice in Shiraz named *Khanqah-i Nooriyeh* to which lands were endowed by the rulers of the time.[2] Lahiji died in AH 912/AD 1506 in Shiraz and was buried in the same hospice.

---

[1] For sources of information on Lahiji, see *Majalisu'l-Momineen*, pp.6, 3–9, *Kashfu'z-Zunun*, column 5, 15, *Riyazu'l-'Arifin*, Teheran AH (s), 1316, pp.63–64, *Taraiqu'l-Haqaiq*, vol.3, p.55.

[2] *Majalisu'l-Momineen*, p.309.

Qazi Nurullah Shushtari has given us a detailed account of Shamsu'd-Din Lahiji in *Majalisu'l-Momineen*, particularly his system of guiding students along the path (Nurbakhshiyyeh order) and his belief in Shi'ism. Qazi tells us," It is said that when Shah Isma'il Safavi conquered the region of Fars and Shiraz, he expressed his desire of visiting Shamsu'd-Din Lahiji. On meeting him, he asked him why he (Lahiji) had adopted black colour for his clothes. Lahiji replied that he was in perpetual mourning for the martyrdom of Husayn ibn 'Ali.

Mafatehul-'Ejaz is his important work on mysticism. It is a brilliant commentary on the *Gulshan-e Raz* of Mahmud Shabistari. It is a comprehensive exposition of Sufi thoughts, principles and practices. Qazi Nurullah remarks, "Though many scholars like Qazi Mir Husayn Yezdi and Shah Taju'd-Din Da'i have written commentaries (on *Gulshan-e Raz*), the Shaykh's commentary supersedes them all. After completing the text, the Shaykh sent a copy to Mulla Jami in Herat. He wrote the following quatrain on the front page of the manuscript and returned it to Shaykh Lahiji:

Aye faqr-e tu nurbakhsh-e arbab-e niyaz
Khurram ze bahar-i khatirat gulshan-e raz
Yak rah nazari bar mis-e qalban andaz
Shayad kih baram rah ze haqiqat ze majaz

In the biography, Araki speaks highly about Lahiji at several places. At the same time, he uses very derogatory language against Jami, who was an outstanding Sunni-Hanafi intellectual and a reputed poet of his times.

* * *

Sultan Husayn Bayaqara of Herat

The idea of Araki's first visit to Kashmir originated in the court of Sultan Husayn Bayaqara, the late Timurid prince of Herat. We are told that he suffered from some malaise for which the physicians had prescribed herbal medicines that were available only in Kashmir. Central Asians believed that there were very effective medicinal herbs in the forests of Kashmir. Since these were not available in Central Asia, the court suggested to the ruler of Herat to send a capable person to Kashmir to procure the medicinal herbs.

There is a strong reason to believe that it was a camouflage. There had been interaction between Kashmir and the Trans-Oxianian region in the past. At one time Gandhara was a part of the Kashmir Hindu kingdom. The Shahis of Waihind had blood relations with Kashmir Hindu royalty. Kashmir was very much on the agenda of Mahmud Ghaznavi's Indian expedition. It is only a freak of chance that he did not enter the valley, but his troops did make a clean sweep of Poonch area up to Loren Valley of Pir Panchal. Therefore, the Islamic missionaries must have been aware of the widespread "infidelity and polytheism" of Kashmir.

There is no dearth of authentic historical information on Sultan Husayn Bayaqara's life and times. Some outstanding Farsi histories were written during his reign. Among these are *Matlau's-Saidayn, Rawzatu's-Safa and Habibu's-Siyar*. Daulatshah Samarqandi dedicated his celebrated biographical history *Tadhkratu'sh-Shu'ara* to him, and Amir Alisher Navai assigned one full chapter (*Majlis* 8) of his work *Majalisu'n-Nafais* to his life.

Sultan Husayn Mirza Bayaqara (AH 875–911/AD 1505) took keen interest in the development of Herat, the seat of his kingdom, by ordering developmental works, raising seminaries, endowments, libraries and laying beautiful gardens. In these enterprises he was assisted and guided by his wise and capable minister, adviser and companion Mir Alisher Navai. More than ten thousand students enlisted in the school and the library in the town of Herat, received stipend from the state exchequer.[1] The buildings raised under his or his nobles' orders are all exquisite specimens of mediaeval Muslim

[1] *Tarikh-e Adabiyyat dar Iran*, Zabihullah Safa, loc. cit., vol.iv, p.567.

architecture with style and grace of the Timurid period. Showering lavish praise on Sultan Husayn, the author of *Rauzatu's-Safa* writes: "He evinced keen interest in raising buildings for public welfare, mosques, seminaries, hospices, and caravanserais. He saw to it that towns became prosperous: he purchased proprietary lands from his private funds and gave them in endowment: he built magnificent palaces and imposing buildings and took extraordinary interest in looking to minute details while laying beautiful gardens and parks."[1]

Interestingly, in his monumental work *Tarikh-e Adabiyyat dar Iran*, the celebrated Iranian scholar, Dr. Zabihullah Safa, has given him some space in the chapter on 'Farsi Language and Literature during the Timurid period in volume IV, thereby recognizing his deep interest in literary activities. He tried his hand at composing verses and used Husayni as his pen-name. Safa has quoted five verses from one of his *ghazals*, of which this is the opening verse:

Dar gham-e ishqat mara ney tan na jani mandeh ast
In khayali gashteh vaz an yak nishani mandeh ast

The most important work attributed to him is *Majalisu'l-Ushshaq*, which has a preface and seventy-five chapters (*majlis*). In the part pertaining to poets and gnostics, the author has brought the record down to the times of Jami. In the concluding chapter, the author gives his own life story. The book written in AH 908/AD 1502, has a pleasing style, but Safa does not find it of much historical value.[2]

Curiously, in *Babaur Nameh*, Zahiru'd-Din Babur has repudiated Sultan Husayns claim to the authorship of *Majalisu'l-Ushshaq* and states the following under the name of Kamalud-Din Husayn Gazargahi: " He has a work to his credit titled *Majalisu'l-Ushshaq*, which he had dedicated to Sultan Husayn. Its text is flimsy and full of falsehoods; it is

---

[1] *Rawzatu's-Safa*, Lucknow Edition, vol.7, p.42. See also *Rawzatu'j-Jannat*, Mo'inu'd-Din Asfazari, vol.4, pp.417–19.

[2] Ibid., p.567.

insipid and often shorn of decency, so much so that some of its writings smack of heresy (*kufr*) because he has tarnished the fair name of many prophets and venerable saints (*anbiya wa awliya*) by attributing sensuous stories to them and projecting a paramour for each of them. It is misleading that in the preface Sultan Husayn Mirza has said and written that he has authored the work."[1]

The prosperity of Herat had begun in the reign of Sharukh, and Sultan Husayn Bayaqara carried the process forward till it reached its climax. Kamalu'd-Din 'Abdur-Razzaq Samarqandi has given us a vivid description of a prosperous Herat. During Baysunqars time, it had become the famous seat of men of learning and letters in Iran and Turan. It is important to note that it was in Herat that a great bulk of Farsi works of prose and poetry of eminent writers and poets was copied and manuscripts carried to India. Herat served a link between Indian plains and Iran and Khurasan during this period as it had during the time of the Buddhist ascendancy in India.

We learn from the biography that Araki wanted Kashmir Sultans to imitate the culture of the royal court of Herat. They say he speaks of Herat court shows that he had greatest regard for it though it is not very clear whether he had succeeded in converting Bayaqara to his faith. He presumes he had, but there is not sufficient circumstantial evidence. The way Jami was respected at the court in Herat shows that Sunni faith was in ascendancy at that time.

* * *

Part II

Society under the Timurids (14–15th century)

This was a period of great bloodshed, turmoil and disruption of civilian life in the vast region of Turkistan and Iran. Sometimes a powerful potentate of the Timurid line rose

---

[1] *Babar Nameh*, tr. Abdu'r-Rahim Khan-e Khanan. See *Az Sa'adi ta Jami* (tr.) *A Literary History of Persia*, E.G. Browne, vol.iii, translated by 'Ali Asghar Hekmat, Second Edition of p.634.

from an obscure corner and established his sway over the vast tracts from Trans-Oxiana in the east to Azerbaijan in the west. At the same time, another Turkmen potentate of great intrepidity trampled under the hoofs of his horse the lands of Fars and Kirman, right up to distant Herat in the east. These happenings created such deep despondency among the people that they considered themselves incapable of ruling their land. It was as if they were willing to abandon the woes of running a state to the care of the Turkic-Mongoloid race or "assigning the world to them and the hereafter to self."

Eventually Shahrukh (d. AD 1446) succeeded in quelling insurgents, subjugating hot-heads, and establishing his authority and sway over the empire. He showed great consideration to scholars, men of learning and the *Shaykhs* and *ulema*, who thronged his court. This semblance of order stood the powerful incumbent ruler Shah Isma'il Safavi in good stead, for it immensely facilitated him to forge a centralized government for the empire. We shall say more on Nurbakhshiyyeh connection with the Safavi ruling house at its proper place in this introduction.

Timur's unique personality was a mixture of opposites. Historians have portrayed him a tyrant and a ruthless homicide of immense ferocity, who was also a patron of men of learning and a connoisseur of art. Whenever he found time from shedding innocent blood or sacking and razing cities and towns to dust, he called in men of learning to read him from the histories of Turkistan, Iran and the Arabs. Physicians and astrologers were always present in his court, and he felt very comfortable in their company.[1]

But the celebrated scholar and astute historian of contemporary Iran, Dr. Zabihullah Safa has raised serious doubts about what many historians, besides Moinud-Din Natanzi say in projecting the positive side of Timurs personality. Here is what he writes: "I wonder how this blood-

---

[1] *Muntakhabu't-Tawarikh*, Mo'inu'd-Din Natanzi, Teheran, 1336 AH (s), pp.279–80.

thirsty fiend could boast of keeping company of men of learning and virtues? Unfortunately, this kind of charade is the manipulation of his friends, which exposes his wiliness. If it were not so, he would not have sent all those men of learning, art and skill into exile or put them in concentration camps in Samarqand."[1]

With the exit of Timur from the scene, internal dissensions among his successors and rampant corruption and highhandedness of the nobility disrupted the fabric of Iranian-Khurasanian society. For more than one century that fills the period from the exit of Timur to the rise of the Safavis in northern Iran, it witnessed rapid cultural and intellectual degeneration. Upper classes, lavishly sharing the spoils of Timur's massive loot in Iran, Syria, Azerbaijan, Khurasan and India got addicted to alcohol and cannabis (*bung*), transmitting the curse to the subjugated people, especially in Iran.

In general, we find that the structure of the state and the system of governance established by the Timurids in their vast empire was a virtual continuation of the system that was introduced by the Mongols in the 13th century. Timur and his commanders came from various Chaghatai clans inhabiting great oases of Central Asia. Later Timurids like Shahrukh, Mirza Bayasunqur and Mirza Bayaqara of Herat continued the old Chaghatai tradition with roots in Mongol culture. Dispensation of justice was on the basis of *Yasa-i-Changizi* or the Code of Chingiz.[2] Thus we find no conspicuous change in the administrative system of the state or in the structure of society in comparison to what obtained during the Mongol period.

However, a big difference in the matter of inclination in approach to religion among the people in two epochs is clearly noticed. Having adopted Islamic faith and then voluntarily adapting to Iranian culture, the later Timurids gave up

[1] *Tarikh-i-Adabiyyat dar Iran*, vol.iv, p.21.

[2] *Zafar Nameh*, Sharfu'd-Din 'Ali Yezdi, vol.ii, p.44.

barbarity and ruthlessness for which the Mongols were notorious. They evinced interest in literature, especially poetry, and some of them patronized men of letters. "If the descendents of Chingiz Khan got Iranised too late and familiarized themselves with the Iranian culture still later, the Timurids achieved it too quick and in some cases almost just on the spur of the moment. They soon identified themselves with Iran and its culture," notes the great Iranian scholar Zabihullah Safa.[1]

Tarikh-i-Timuri, the well-known work whose authorship is disputably ascribed to Timur, takes good notice of subjects like faith, respectful treatment of the Sayyids, *ulema*, ascetics and also the rules for dissemination of religious practices under Timur. It shows concurrence between the religious policy of Timur and his successors as stated in the *Tuzukat*—no matter whosoever from among the line of Timur or his nobles compiled it—on the one hand and the fundamentals of Islamic faith and society on the other. This is of much significance to the scope of our study though in regard to imperial court and army structures under the Timurids, the *Tuzukat* has nothing new to add to what we already know of it in the days of the Mongols.[2] Despite that, some organizational practices of Chingiz's times survived through the era of later Timurids. The *quraltai* or the 'grand assembly' was one such practice.[3] Chingiz's Code (*Yasa-e Chingizi*) remained in force under the Timurids until AH 815/AD 1412. Criminal prosecution was carried along a two-fold practice: either in a religious court according to *sharia* law or in an ordinary court where the *Yasa* code was applicable. In the above mentioned year, this practice was discarded under orders from Shahrukh. Thereafter Islamic theological practice became the source of legal dispensation in the Muslim societies of the region.

---

[1] *Tarikh-i-Adabiyyat*, op. cit., p.41.

[2] See *Tuzukat-i-Timur*, Farsi rendition by Abu Talib Husayni Turbati with English translation, Oxford, 1773, and its Teheran edition.

[3] *Zafar Nameh*, Sharfu'd-Din 'Ali Yezdi, vol.ii, p.44.

The social stratification in Islamic society in the period under consideration did not show any sign of variance from the structure obtaining in the previous millennium. The traditional structure of civil society formed of various classes like courtiers, princes, members of royal seraglio, ministers, judges or *qadis*, revenue officials, army commanders and a host of king's companions continued in its original form under the later Timurids.

Religion

Timurids and their courtiers and nobles did not only profess Islam publicly, true or pretentious, but also carried out most of their military exploits in the name of strengthening and popularizing the principles of that faith. Timur projected himself as one who revived Islamic faith and asserted that he provided strength and stability to his empire by adhering to the principles and fundamentals of Islamic religion. "The first code (*Tuzak*) that "shot forth from the lighthouse of his heart" was about the propagation and strengthening of the path (*shariat*) of Muhammad—and he embellished his empire with that law", writes the author of *Tuzukat-i-Timuri*.[1]

Elucidating the edict, Timur boasts of institutionalizing Muslim endowment system by appointing a highly venerable Sayyid as its chief, designated religious judge (*qadi*), decree announcer (*mufti*) and religious Procter (*mohtasib*) for each town, built innumerable mosques and hospices in the empire, raised rest-houses (*caravansarais*) along highways and built bridges over canals. He appointed religious scholars and teachers in all cities to impart teaching of the principles of faith to ordinary people. They were supposed to impart knowledge about religious science meaning commentary, tradition and theology to the people.

These measures prompted religious scholars of the day to give Timur the title of *Mujaddid-e-Din* meaning one who

[1] Op. cit. pp.174, 176.

revives the faith, who according to a notion prevailing with them appears at the end of each century. The "revivers of faith" who had preceded him were Omar ibn 'Abdul-'Aziz, Mamum ar-Rashid, al-Muqtadar billah, 'Azdu'd-Dowleh Deylami, Sultan Snajar, Ghazan and Uljayatu.[1]

Safa says that pretentious religiosity was not exclusive to Timur and his descendants. Its roots are traceable in earlier periods of Iranian history. The Seljuq Turkmen had adopted and used it fully for furthering their political interests in the first half of the 12th century. To be more precise, the practice of kings, rulers, warlords and satraps using Islam as an excuse for their expansionist and political aggrandizement can be traced to Mahmud of Ghazni, the 10th century warrior Sultan of Turkic ethnic stock.[2]

Timur led many incursions to satisfy his greed for the expansion of his empire and lust for loot and plunder. But he called these incursions *ghazavat* (plural of Arabic *ghazava* meaning crusade) or a holy war so as to carve for himself a place among the Islamic crusaders (*ghazis*). Towards the end of his life, he planned a campaign against China and called it "*jihad* against the infidels of Cathay."[3] Actually, he thought that war against the infidels would mean redemption of the sin of ordering large scale carnage of Muslims in his earlier campaigns. In a *quaraltai* called for the purpose, he declared, "In the course of the conquests of Islamic lands, Muslims faced some harm owing to political exigency. Therefore, I would take a step that would redeem those damages. One virtue that is not the lot of every person is to wage war against the infidels and decimate polytheists and heathens. This requires great power and might. It is in the fitness of things that

---

[1] According to the author of *Tuzukat*, the gap of one hundred years between these personalities is not correct.

[2] See *Tarikh-i-Adabiyyat*, loc. cit., vol. i, under Mahmud of Ghazna.

[3] See *Zafar Nameh*, Sharfu'd-Din 'Ali Yezdi, vol.ii, p.447. Cathay is the distortion of Khitai, the word used by Arab and Iranian historians for China.

the army, at whose hands atrocities were perpetrated against the Muslims, marches in the direction of China and Cathay, the lands of infidelity, and fulfills the obligation of waging *jihad* and leading a crusade (*ghazava*) to destroy their idol-houses and fire-temples and build mosques and prayer houses at those sites."[1]

Perhaps this was the reason why during his Indian campaign, Timur kept in mind the need for foodgrains for his troops and ordered forcible acquisition of all wheat and barely stocks of the farmers of Sindh, all of whom were Muslims, and left them to starve, concludes Dr. Safa.[2]

Nizam-e Shami adds, "During this campaign wherever Timur clashed with the idolaters, he fought them in the name of *ghazava*. He traveled a long distance only to put an end to the tyranny and injustice from a group of tyrants. It was in the suburbs of the same city (Delhi) that in consequence of one of his (Timur's) orders, nearly a hundred thousand Hindu infidels and idolaters , who had been captured by his soldiers, were done to death. Such was the magnitude of this holocaust that Grand Maulana Nasiru'd-Din Omar, an employee at the royal court, slew no fewer than fifteen persons, even though he had not slaughtered a lamb in his life time. When Timur captured Delhi he treated Sultan Mahmud and his Muslim soldiers in a manner that obliterates the memory of the carnages at Isfahan and Sistan. Heaps of dead bodies leveled heights and depths of the ground. The massacre, loot and arson continued in Delhi for four days. A large number of people of the city set their houses on fire and burnt themselves and their families alive in it. The number of people taken prisoner was so large as to allow each Timurid soldier take at least twenty of them as his slaves. The only community that escaped the wrath and decimation were the descendants and deputies of the house

[1] Ibid.

[2] Loc. cit., p.46.2, p.193.

of Prophet, Sayyids, *ulema*, *qadis* and *shaykhs*. They were ordered to assemble in the Jamia Mosque of Jahanpanah, Dehli and no harm was done to them."

This is the story of the "revival of Islam" at the hands of the eighth *mujaddid-e-din* who called himself "the master of supernatural feats (*sahib-e karamat*) and "exclusive recipient of Almighty's grace". These deceptive antics notwithstanding, he created a deep impression of his religious commitment on the mind of contemporary society and left a legacy for his descendants and successors to follow. It generated long time culture of showing respect and veneration to ecclesiastical personalities, ascetics, hermits, and men of learning. After Timur, Shahrukh continued this tradition, which lasted till the Timurids were overthrown by Sheybani Khan, the Uzbek warlord, around the first decade of the 16th century.

The explicit show of concern for propagating and popularizing Islamic faith shown by the later Timurids increased people's interest in subtle religious issues related to their day to day life. Although overdoing it incread the danger of descending into religious extremism and prejudice, yet the truth is that in this period of Islamic history, the *Shaykhs*, *Sufis*, theologians and men of learning managed to wield unprecedented influence in the ruling circles as well as the civil society of the times. Thus, it could be said that several centuries of Islamic orthodoxy's resistance to reason and rational sciences initiated by the great Islamic thinkers of 10–12th century like ar-Razi (Rhazes), al- Farabi, al-Kindi, Ibn Sina, al-Khwarazmi and Abul-Haitham reached its culmination in the period of later Timurids when blind faith swept aside the impact of Greek rationalists,[1] and the conservatism of al-Ghazali and the dogmatism of the followers of his school of thought gained prominence.

---

[1] See *Tarikh-i-'Ulum-i -'Aqli dar Tamaddun-e Islami*, Dr. Zabihullah Safa, Teheran, AH (s) 1334. It is a work of invaluable scholarship on the subject.

Caliphate (*Khalafat*)

With their claims of religiosity and "religious revivalists", the Timurids began to imagine that they were the focal point of Islamic Caliphate. We know that after the fall of Baghdad in AH 616/AD 1238, the centre of Islamic Caliphate shifted to Cairo in Egypt and it remained as such for a long time. The fact is that the Abbasid Caliphate of Cairo was an institution only in name and at best a source of benefaction for the *Memluk* of those regions. In AH 923/AD 1517, Ottoman Sultan Salim I (AH 918–26/AD 1512–19) conquered Egypt followed by the annexation of Mecca and Medina, where the homily (*khutba*) was read in his name. As the Ottomans replaced Abbasid Caliphs who had claimed their descent from the Prophet, the legacy of Caliphate in its entirety passed on to Sultan Salim I and then to his successors who now assumed the title of *Amiru'l-Momineen* or 'Commander of the Faithful.[1]

Safavi kings and the *Shi'as* of Imamiyeh School did not accept the tag for the Ottoman Sultans and this was one of the irritants in the relation between the Ottoman and the Safavi regimes. During the ascendancy of Afghans, the Ottoman Sultan coveted annexation of the regions of western Iran to his empire, and even prepared himself to clash with Ashraf Afghan. In order to legitimize his contemplated incursion against the Sunni Afghans, he obtained a decree (*futwa*) from the jurisconsults (*muftis*) of his state asserting that with Ottoman Sultan as the *Amiru'l-Momineen*, no body else had the right to be the religious leader and ruler of the Musulmans. Getting the decree became necessary because the Ottoman soldiers did not think it proper to fight a Sunni adversary. However, a truce was signed between Ottoman Sultan Ahmad III and Ashraf Afghan in AH 1139/AD 1716 on the condition

---

[1] See *Ahsanu't-Tawarikh*, vol.iii, p.461. Also see *Tabaqat – Salatin-e Islam*, tr. 'Abbas Iqbal, Teheran, AH (s) 1312, p.171.

that the Afghans would recognize the Ottoman Sultans title of *Amiru'l-Momineen.*[1]

As successors to the authority of the Prophet of Islam, the Caliphs were supposed to work for the promulgation of the law of God. But the irony was that this duty was now actually performed not by them but by Turco-Mongols, who were fresh converts to Islamic faith. As such, they considered it their right to lay claim to Islamic Caliphate.

The story of the caliphate of Ottoman Turks lies outside the ambit of our study. Hence we refer again to Timur to whom his special historian Nizam-Shami gives appellations like "Protector of Caliphate" (*Khalafat panah*).[2] The successors of Timur, too, received same title from their historians. For example, in the case of Shahrukh, 'Abdur-Razzaq Samarqandi touches on subjects like the "right to the crown of the Caliphate" and the "heights of the sky of Caliphate" etc.[3] Sultan Abu Saeed Mirza is introduced to the readers with the title *Hazrat Kahlafat Panahi.*[4]

When the descendents of Gorkani Timurids in India, meaning the Indian Mughals, came to power, the title of *khalafat* survived with the successors of Zahiru'd-Din Babur. They were given titles like *khalifeh-e bar huqq*[5] (Caliph of the Path of Truth) and *Hazrat khalaft martabat*[6] (Royalty holding the status of Caliph). Other appendages meant for His Majesty were *gavhar-e sahab-e khalafat-e kubra*[7] (The Pearl from the Cloud of the Grand Caliphate) and *doodman-i khalaft* (The Family Unit of Caliphate). The imperial court of the Mughal Emperors received titles like *mauqif-e khalafat-e kubra* (The

[1] Ibid., p.98.

[2] *Zafar Nameh*, loc. cit., pp.171, 269.

[3] See *Matla'u's-Saidayn*, vol.ii, p.6.

[4] Ibid. pp.5, 1019 et al.

[5] See *Sakinatu'l-Auliya*, Dara Shikoh.

[6] See *Shah Jahan Nameh*, Indian edition, vol.ii, p.4.

[7] *Shah Jahan Nameh*, vol.ii, p.80.

Holder of the Status of Grand Caliph), and their capital got the adjunct of *darul-khalafah* (The House/Place/Abode of Caliphate).[1] In an encomium composed in connection with the birth day celebrations of Prince Dara Shukoh, the court poet Kalim of Kashan said:

Yaki akhtar az burj-e shahi dameedeh
Kih nurash girifteh ze mah ta be mahi
Garami khalaf inchunin bayad al huqq
Ze sahib qaran-e khalafat panahi
Ba farr-e Fariduniyash har kih deedeh
Be Dara Shukuhiyash dadeh gawahi

Though the title *Khalafat Panah* has been occasionally used by historians[2] while writing the story of Safavi rulers, in their case, in particular, caliphate meant *khalafat-e murtazavi*[3] meaning the Caliphate of Murtaza ('Ali) and not what it meant for the Sunnis. Dr. Safa is of the opinion that the titles prefixed to the name of Shah Isma'il Safavi were only a matter of convention and adoration and nothing more. On this basis the house of Safavis was called *doodman-i Imamat maqam* meaning the House with the status of Imams.[4] It was believed that Imamate was given to the Safavi rulers only for keeping it in their custody.[5]

Before moving on to the next sub-topic, it has to be noted that Farsi historians have invariably given the title of *Khaqan* to the rulers of the House of Timur. The practice is in evidence in almost all the contemporary histories of the period. Shahrukh Mirza is mentioned with the title of

---

[1] See *Shah Jahan Nameh*, op. cit., Also see *Jahangir Nameh*, Muhammad Saleh Kunboh, events of the year AH 1022 and 1027. See also *Padshah Nameh* of Abdu'l-Hamid Lahori, events of the years AH 1065 and 1037.

[2] See*Ahsanu't-Tawarikh*, by Romlu, p.65.

[3] See *Habibu's-Siyar*, Khayyam Publications, Teheran, vol.iv, p.467.

[4] Ibid, p.234 et al.

[5] *Tarikh-i-Adabiyyat dar Iran*, loc. cit., vol.v, p.200.

Khaqan-i-Saeed[1] and Sultan Husayn Bayaqara with that of *Khaqan-i-Mansur*.[2]

Mehdi (*Mehdaviyyat*)

At many places in the biography it is suggested that Sayyid Muhammd Nurbakhsh, the founder of that order, was called the Mehdi, though there are also hints contrary to it. Nevertheless, historians and hagiographers (*tadhkiranavisan*) have stated that once Nurbakhsh saw that his followers had increased to big numbers he thought that he was the Mehdi. It is, therefore, pertinent to have some idea of what *Mehdaviyyat* is about.

According to the numerous traditions recorded in their works, the Twelver Shi'a (*ithna 'ashrah*) and the Sunnis too believe that Mehdi from the house of the Prophet will appear at the 'end of the time (*akhir-e zaman*). A tradition (*hadith*) attributed to the Prophet says: "If there is only one day left from the full cycle of time of the world, God Almighty will stretch it long so that a person from my line or from my house is born to fill the world with justice as hitherto it was full of injustice."[3]

According to both Shi'a and Sunni traditions, this person (Mehdi) will be from the house of 'Ali ibn Ibi Talib and shall appear at the 'end of time. On this basis, many people from time to time claimed to be the Mehdi and called themselves 'the Expected Imam (*Imam-e Muntazar*). Muhammad Hanafiyeh, the son of Hazrat 'Ali, was the first to do so. Mukhtar bin Ibi 'Ubaydeh Thaqafi led a rebellion in his name and sought revenge from the slayers of Husayn. When Mukhtar was killed and Hanafiyeh died, the followers of Muhammad did not believe that he was dead and expected his

---

[1] 'Abdu'r-Razzaq Samarqandi records this in the introduction to *Matl'au's-Saidayn*. Subsequently, in the rest of the text, he has used only the title and not the name of Mirza Shahrukh. See Safa, loc. cit., vol.iv, p.52fn.2.

[2] *Rawzatu's-Safa*, Indian edition, vol.7, pp.3–5 et al.

[3] See *Loghat Nameh Dehkhuda*, Mehdviyyat, p.176.

return. They say that Muhammad is hiding in Rizvi Mountain where he has access to water and honey. Sometimes later, 'Ali ibn Husayn rose in rebellion against the Ummayids. His followers called him Mehdi. Again, during the Caliphate of 'Abbasids, some other persons claimed to be Mehdi. The Mehdi imposters of Africa in particular became well known. Two among them are quite famous. Ubaydullah founded the Ubaydullahi or Fatimi order, and the second Mehdi incepted al-Muwahhedin, which established sway over Spain. Ubaydulllah, said to be a descendent of the house of 'Abdullah bin Maymun al-Qaddah, was a staunch Shi'a da'i[1] (suicider) who, using the power of remarkable eloquence and sword, had established sway over Tunisia and North Africa. He spread the rumour that the time for the re-appearance of Mehdi had arrived. He would conquer the whole world, resurrect the dead to life, and make the sun rise in the west. However when the "Mehdi" was on his way to meet with his propagator, he was arrested and imprisoned in Tripoli. Some time later, Abu 'Abdullah secured his release. He mounted a horse and the chiefs of the tribes escorted his procession. With tears rolling down his cheeks, he told his fraternity, "Here is your Lord (*mawla*). Friday next, his name will be read out in the homily as "*Mehdi Amiru'l-Momineen*" (Mehdi, the Commander of the Faithful).

However, the full name of Mehdi the founder of the order of al-Muvahiddin was Muhammad bin Tumarth from Masamadeh tribe that lived in the Atlas Mountain of Morocco. In the beginning, he conveyed the tidings of Mehdi's imminent appearance, but soon announced that he himself was the Mehdi. Large groups of Berbers became his followers. After his demise in AH 524/AD 1129 his disciple 'Abdu'l-Momin took time by forelock and induced his followers to capture Morocco. His next target was Spain and the order of *al-Muwahhidin*.

---

[1] The role of *da'i* of Isma'ilis is well known . For more information, see the history of Rashidu'd-Din Fazlullah chapter on Nzam'ul-Mulk Tusi.

Although the number of protagonists of 'Ali in the Ottoman territories was very small, and Ottoman rulers had been fighting against the Mehdavis,[1] yet a few people in those lands, too, claimed to be the Mehdi. The well-known among the impostors was a person of clerical lineage in Kurdistan who announced himself the Mehdi in AH 1066/AD 1655. But when he was arrested and brought before the Sultan, he denied having made any such claim. Nevertheless, his way of conducting himself created a good impression on the Sultan, who admitted him to the circle of royal companions.

Among the impostors of more recent times, the Mehdi of Sudan merits a mention. Muhammad Ahmad was a student of the two famous religious scholars of Khartum. After completing his studies, he went to the Island of Aba, where he spent fifteen years in seclusion, spending his days in an underground cave and often crying on hearing about corruption among people. Fasting and rigid penance weakened him physically. The Bagara tribe in the vicinity of his cave showed him much respect. He announced himself the Mehdi when he was forty years of age, and that tribe quickly accepted him as one and even began worshipping him. In 1300 AH/AD 1882 he dispatched volunteers to the chiefs of the tribes all around who conveyed to them that the expected Mehdi, about whom the Prophet had hinted, had arrived. People thronged to him and he took up his residence on Mount Jadir. His followers defeated the Egyptian government several times and captured many towns. Harassed by threats from the followers of the impostor, the Egyptian government sought help from the British. This brought General Gordon to the scene of operation in Khartum. But he was unable to make any headway against the militia of the impostor and met with his death at their hands. Khartum fell to the Mehdavis, and people

[1] Article 24 of Turkish Religious Law stipulates that the Imam has to be visible and should not conceal himself from the sight of the people who are not supposed to be in waiting. See *Mehdi* by Dormesteter, Farsi translation pp.51–52. Also see *Loghat Nameh*, p.176 under Mehdaviyat.

began to believe that "the Mehdi" regularly received guidance from God and acted according to these supernatural messages. They waited for the day when he would take control of the entire Sudan and then the whole world. But before that could happen, the impostor was taken ill with fever and died on 21 January 1885. With his exit from the scene, the African issue, which had become a mix of Mehdavi anti-British movement, came to an end.

These instances and their end-result apart, the Shi'a firmly believe that the true Mehdi will appear one day and establish a just government over the world. The Shi'a world is still waiting for his appearance.

In Iran, one amongst those who claimed to be the Mehdi was Sayyid 'Ali Muhammad Shirazi who called himself *Bab* meaning 'The Gate,' and his followers were called Babis. He appeared around the middle of the 19th century and his story is well-recorded in the books of history.[1]

Sectarian contours

The type of ultra-Islamism fostered by Timur's descendants on the society of the period under consideration gave rise to a game of sectarian cut-throat competition, from which Shi'ism emerged stronger and more domineering. Though Timurid rulers and princes professed Sunni Hanafi faith, there is no evidence to suggest that any sect of the Sunni or Shi'a faith was pressurized to tow the religious line of the imperial court. In fact, some incidents show the religious liberalism of the ruler. For example, once Mirza Abu'l-Qasim Babur (AH 852–861/AD 1448–56) and his nobles and courtiers were in the royal court. He took a jug in his hand, and looking at some inscription on its outer side said that it was the name of the 12th Imam. A courtier asked when the Imam would appear. "In my time", said Babur Mirza. The courtier said, "Everywhere people trust Your Majesty". The king of good

[1] See *A Literary History of Persia*, E.G. Brown, Cambridge, 1902, vol.iv.

faith said, "Let people hold on to whatever belief they like. I am steadfast on the path of tradition and community (*sunnat wa jamaat*) and subscribe to the line of Imam Abu Hanifa."[1]

Taking advantage of the soft religious policy of the Timurids, the Twelver Shi'a freely propagated the tenets of their faith. They launched recurrent attacks on the Sunni faith to expose what they considered its "corrupt beliefs". One of their acts in this direction was to revive blasphemy against the Companions of the Prophet (*sabb-e Sahaba*) and drop their names from the homily (*khutba*). They raised hue and cry over even the smallest provocation—real or feigned. For example, when Sultan Husayn Bayaqara (AH 875/AD 1470, with whose period we are directly concerned in this biography, adopted "Husayni" as his poetic-name (*takhallus*), the Shi'a in Herat hailed him a member-follower of their sect and said that "soon the Sunni religion would be abandoned and despised". They went to the extent of saying that "the homily (*khutba*) read from the pulpits should be in the name of Twelve Imams, and the name of four venerable Caliphs should be altogether omitted."[2]

An overall assessment of the situation reveals that during the 9th century of Hijra, corresponding to the 15th of Christian era, the Shi'a increased their strength and expanded their sphere of influence in Iran and Khurasan. However, they did not rest content with what they had achieved till then, and nursed the ambition of staging a revolt to overpower the Sunnis and then either grab the Sultanate or, at least, establish Shi'ism as formal religion of the state.

No wonder, therefore, that some social movements with obvious political undercurrents spanned this period of Iranian and Trans-Oxianian history. Three of these are noteworthy. The first is of Biktashiyyeh order of Sufis led by Hajji Biktash (d. AH 738/AD 1337 who ordered that white dress be the

[1] *Matl'au's-Saidays*, loc. cit., vol.i, p.1118.

[2] *Rawzatu'j-Janat*, vol.ii, p.32.

formal dress of the followers of his order to contrast with the green of the "much hated Ummayads."[1] The second movement is called Nurbakhshiyyeh. The third with a much stronger ideology than the rest, was founded by Fazlullah Nasihi Astarabadi (AH 740–796/AD 1339–95) who is known for attaching great significance to the words (of the *Qur'an*), and hence also called the founder of Hurufi movement. Astarabadi pronounced his faith during the reign of Timur and soon found a large following in Iran, especially in the northern region (Azerbaijan, Tabriz, Shirwan, Baku), Khurasan and as far away as Asia Minor. Presuming that the movement was a threat to the security of the state, Timur's son Miranshah—nicknamed by the Hurufis as 'Maranshah (the king of snakes)—ordered the beheading of Astarabadi around AH 796/AD 1393); this was avenged later by Ahmad Lur, a staunch Hurufi activist, who stabbed Shahrukh to death in AH 830/AD 1426 in the Jami'a Mosque of Herat. Investigations into the murder revealed deep and wide network of the Hurufis and their unflinching loyalty to Astarabadi whose work on Hurufi thought called *Javidan-e Kabir* is still a favourite among his followers.[2] The Hurufiyeh sect may not have achieved much success, yet its impact, like that of the Isma'ilis in 11–12th century AD, with which it was very close ideologically, cannot be brushed aside cursorily.

From the Hurufis branched another group under the leadership of Mahmud Pasikhani Gilani, better known as Naimi. Its subscribers were called Nuqtavis. Mahmud was among Fazulullah Astarabadi's adherents but separated from him after he proclaimed the Nuqtavis around AH 800/AD 1397. Though he proclaimed his faith in the beginning of the 9th century AH/14–15th century AD, his teachings were fairly popular during the two following centuries, so much so that Safavi rulers, apprehensive of a threat from them to Shi'a

---

[1] See *Taraiqu'l-Haqaiq*, vol.ii, p.155.

[2] Ibid. For details on Hurufi sect see Clement Huart, *Textes Pensans Relatif a la Secte des Houroufis*, Leyden, 1909. *Tarih-i Adabiyyat dar Iran*, vol.iv, p.63.

Orthodox Church, found it necessary to compass a large scale massacre and destruction of the followers of Mahmud Pasikhani.[1]

Nonetheless, this extreme attitude of the Shi'a community of 15th century Iran met with equally strong resistance from the Hanafi Sunnis of Turkic-Mongoloid stock, making it impossible for them to realize their dream. It will not be far from truth if we consider this sectarian strife as a prelude to some major social-political change that shaped the future of Iran. In the following century, Iran became a Shi'a state, under the ruling house of the Shi'a Safavis. The on-going sectarian divide opened up an important field of Islamic religious studies for both sides: theology (*fiqh*) and jurisprudence. That is why we find many serious, albeit rabid, theologians contribute copiously to this branch of science during the period of our study. It also reminds us of deep sectarian prejudice vitiating the mind of even genuine scholars of literature, religion and theosophy. I cannot resist the temptation of recounting an anecdote about Abdur-Rahman Jami, the reputed intellectual and poet at the court of later Timurid at Herat, whom Edward Browne has praised as "the last of great classical poets of Iran".[2] He was a staunch Hanafi Sunni by faith, but in this biography, Shamsu'd-Din Araki uses exceptionally derogatory words against him.

During the reign of Mirza Babur (AH 852–861/AD 1448–56) Maulana Mazid, a wise and learned theologian from Samarqand, was on a visit to Herat. Once he came to Mirza Babur's court where Abdur-Rahman Jami was already seated. The text of the conversation among them recorded in *Matl'au's-Saidayn*[3] runs like this:

---

[1] For detailed information on Nuqtavis see Dr. Sadiq Kiya's article of remarkable scholarship, titled 'Nuqtaviyan', in volume no.13, of *Iran Kudeh Collection*. Nuqtavis are said to have attracted the attention of Emperor Akbar of India too.

[2] *A Literary History of Persia*, loc. cit., vol.iv.

[3] Loc. cit., vol.ii, p.716.

Mirza Babur: "What have you (Maulana Mazid) to say about cursing Yazid?"

Maulana: It is not right. After all Yazid was from the people of qibla (towards which we the Muslim bow).

Mirza to Jami: This is what Maulana Mazid says, but what is your opinion?

Jami: I send a hundred curses on Yazid, and another hundred in addition (*mazid*).

Apart from Jami's subtle use of pun in the word *mazid*, we find that even among the Hanafi Sunnis of Trans-Oxiana and Khurasan of the period under discussion, there were extremists as well as moderates. While moderates like Maulana Mazid, though conscious of the oppression perpetrated by the Ummayids, would still desist from cursing them, there were others like Jami who would go to extremes. Amusingly, even Jami, whom the incident portrays a rabid Hanafi Sunni, has several panegyrics in praise of 'Ali and his progeny, besides many eulogies.[1]

Sufism (*Tasavvuf*)

Timurid kings, princes and nobles of the 9–10th *hijra*/AD 15–16, patronized Sufi saints and had faith in them. This resulted in the thriving of Sufism and expansion of the influence of Sufi saints within the civil society of the day. It has to be noted that prior to the Timurids, a big difference in ways and means kept the Sufi saints and elders of the faith distanced from each other for many centuries. But the period under consideration partially narrowed the gap, and now differences between the two became less divisive except in some rare case like that of the 'way (*tariqat*) of Sufi poet Shah Qasimul-Anwar[2]. Within this social matrix we see that the leading Sufi saints, too, were recognized as dispensers of Islamic jurisprudence. In other words, leading Sufi luminaries conducted themselves in the manner of religious authorities.

---

[1] See *Kulliyat-e Jami*, Teheran Edition.

[2] See *Nafahatu'l-Uns*, 'Abdu'r-Rahman Jami, Teheran edition, pp.592–93.

As principles of Sufism and mysticism entered the ambit of the 13–14th century institution of pedagogy and many branches of science prescribed for curriculum in seminaries, Sufism was no more a monopoly of the inmates of hospices (*khanqah*). This is why mystic themes and mystic terminology had a profound impact on the various genres of Persian literary output. Dr. Safa is of the opinion that the terms *dervish* and *dervishi* (dervish-hood), as socio-cultural manifestations of post-Timurid period, had surfaced in this background, and then spread fast even among ordinary people.[1] This makes it easy to understand why the biographer of Shamsu'd-Din Araki has used this word very frequently and with its varied dimensions.

Hardships of life and uncertainty of human affairs made ordinary people more responsive to Sufi mystical teachings that emphasized transcendentalism and renouncing of worldly desires. This forms the primary contour of Iranian and Trnas-Oxianian society during the period of her history marked by the onslaught of the tribes and clans of Turkic Slaves, and military campaigns of the Tartar, Mongol, Chaghatai Turk and Uzbek warriors. For the destitute there was no place of safety and refuge except in Divine Providence.

Sufism and *dervish*-ism are two prominent features of the 13–14th century Islamic society of Iran and Trans-Oxiana. But, at the same time, contemporary Sufi personalities were actually of a mediocre level, not only in the field of mystic thought and practice but in other aspects of intellectual excellence as well. There is hardly anything refreshing or new in the mystic domain of this period. Sometimes, the mediocrity of the times was reflected in the unbecoming behaviour or mutual rivalries among these groups. Thus we see that Khwajeh Hafiz of Shiraz, the great Sufi poet of Iran and a contemporary of Timur, is highly critical of hypocritical Sufis of his time. Jami has categorized Sufis into several classes, on the basis of their distinctive characteristics.[2]

[1] Loc. cit., vol.iv, p.67.

[2] *Nafahatu'l-Uns*, Teheran edition, pp.8–17.

We have said that during the time of later Timurids, the gap between Sufism and orthodoxy had been narrowed down to some extent. It is also true that despite wielding considerable influence in contemporary society, the Sufis of the period did not escape censure and disparagement by the stalwarts of the faith. The reason was firstly the feigned devoutness of Timur and his son Shahrukh to Hanafi faith, and secondly, the institutionalizing of resistance to the "heresy (*ilhad*) and the designs of innovation (*bid'at*) in matters of faith, the latter charge being usually ascribed to the Shi'a. Thus at the royal court, a variety of religious issues were raised and discussed at length, which normally should have been the realm of juris-consults of the day.

Under these circumstances, the most effective weapon with the orthodoxy was to issue a decree of heresy against their adversaries. Entrenched orthodoxy has played this old trick with progressive philosophers, enlightened thinkers and outstanding spiritualists during all the periods of Islamic civilization.

On the positive side, exercise in scientific Sufism continued as in previous centuries. The most popular school of Sufi thought focused attention on Ibnul-'Arabi and his senior followers. The last notable protagonist of his school was Maulana 'Abdu-Rahman Jami who wrote *Naqdu'l-Fusus fi sharh-e Naqshu'l-Fususu'l-Hekam Ibnu'l-'Aabi*, a commentary on Ibnul-Arabis celebrated work *Fususu'l-Hekam*. Another important and highly dependable work in the branch of *tasavvuf* produced at this time is the commentary of Shamsu'd-Din Muhammad Lahiji Nurbakhshi (d. AH 913/AD 1507) on the famous Sufi poetical composition (*masnavi*), *Gulshan-e Raz* of Mahmud Shabistari. The biography of Araki has references to both Ibnu'l-'Arabi and Shaykh Lahiji at several places, which shows the popularity of the work during his days and the thoughts contained in it.

It has to be noted that Ibnu'l-'Arabis philosophy has immensely influenced the Kubravi Sufi thought; it has a profound impact on the thought of Mir Sayyid 'Ali Hamadani and the Hamadiniyyeh school of Sufis from whom Sayyid Muhammad Nurbakhsh, too, derived inspiration. At the same time, Ibnu'l-'Arabis's Unity of Being (*wahdatu'l-wujud*), a concept of remarkable importance in the history of Sufi thought has also been severely criticized by both traditionalist Sufis and *muttakalimun* or Doctors of Divinity. Since any comprehensive debate on Sufi philosophy of any of the well-known orders is beyond the scope of this prefatory note, I quote the following passage from the valuable work of Nicholson because Ibnu'l-'Arabi was a major influence on Hamadaniyyeh and later on Nurbakshiyyeh school:

> "He (Ibnu'l-'Arabi) emphasized that Reality is one and indivisible. The creative power of God acts through His servant who is a locus (*mahal*) on which this power is focused. He says: The believer praises the God who is in his form of belief and with whom he has connected himself, and to praise the work is to praise the maker of it; its excellence or imperfection belongs to its maker. For this reason he blames the belief of others, which he would not do, if he were just. Beyond doubt, the worshipper of this particular God shows ignorance when he criticized others, on account of their belief. If he understood the saying of Junayd, 'The colour of the water is the colour of the vessel containing it, he would not interfere with the beliefs of others, but would perceive God in every form and in every belief. He has opinion, not knowledge; therefore God said, "I am in My servants opinion of Me, i.e. 'I do not manifest Myself to him save in the form of his belief. God is absolute or restricted, as He pleases and the God of religious beliefs is subject to limitation, for He is the God is not contained in the heart of His servant; But the absolute God who is contained by anything for He is the being of all things and the Being of Himself, and a thing is not said either to contain itself or not to contain itself"[1]

This short notice of Sufism in Central Asia and Iran at a specific point of time in history will remain incomplete without reference to some of their well-known orders. The most popular Sufi order that influenced people even outside the

[1] *Studies in Islamic Mysticism*, Nicholson, p.159.

region of its birth is that of Naqshbandis. Its followers publicized their principles and practices among people in Central Asia, Iran, Asia Minor and the Indian sub-continent. They were definitely inclined towards the thoughts of Ibnu'l-'Arabi.

Naqshabdiyyeh order, also called *Silsileh-e Khwajahgan*, is attributed to Khwajeh Bahau'd-Din Naqshband (d. AH 791/ AD 1388), a pupil of Khwajeh 'Abdu'l-Khaliq Gejdawani, who, in turn, was the pupil of Shaykh Abu'l- Hasan Kharaqani. As all these eminent personalities bore the title of *Khwajeh*, the order came to be known as *Khwajehgan*.[1] Naqshabandis professed Sunni faith and were distributed in several branches. The author of *Taraiqu'l-Haqaiq*, who had met with many of the members of this order during his sojourns, tells us that a group among them is called *Malamatiyeh*, and yet one more group from among them strictly observes all Sunni religious practices. He says there is a very small group of Naqshbandis that professes the faith of *ithna 'ashra*[2]—the Sect of Twelve.

Cheshtiyeh and Suharwardiyeh Sufi orders originated elsewhere, but flourished in the 14–15th century AD in Delhi and Multan respectively and gradually extended their influence in other parts of India.

As Shi'a faith progressed during the period of our study, Shi'a Sufi orders also grew in number. The earliest order among them is of Safavis, the followers of Shaykh Safiu'd-Din Ardabili about whom we shall know more in the discussion on Safavis in this introduction. The Safavi order of Sufis was incepted first in Azerbaijan and gradually strengthened its position in its adjoining areas. Shaykh Safi claimed his descent

---

[1] Later on word *Khwajeh* was used as a mark of respect and did not remain confined to the Sufis of that order only. Hafiz of Shiraz says:

Wufa az Khwajehgan-e shahr ba man
Kamal-e millat o din bul-Wufa kard

[2] *Taraiqu'l-Haqaiq*, vol.ii, p.158. See also *Nafahatu'l-Uns*, Teheran edition, pp.384–86, and *Zubdatu't-Maqamat*, Indian edition.

from the line of Imam Musa Kazim, and for his school of thought to Shaykh Abu'l-Najib Ziau'd-Din. Sayyid Moinu'd-Din 'Ali better known as Shah Qasimu'l-Anwar is an outstanding Shi'a saint and poet of the 9th century *Hijra* (14–15th century AD) who received his grooming in the Safavi order of Sufis.

The well-known Shi'a Sufi order of this period is of Nematullahis founded by Amir Sayyid Nuru'd-Din Nematullah. Born around AH 730/AD 1329, Nematullah soon found many followers, some of them very brilliant, like Shah Da'i, with followers in different parts of Iran and several other countries.

All the four orders had their followers in Kashmir. 'Abdu'l Qaiyum Rafiqi has made an excellent study on them.[1] Sae'ed Nafici, the well-known Iranian scholar has mentioned these orders under the sub-heading of Sufi orders in Iran and India.[2]

But let us revert to the question of how orthodoxy looked at Sufism in the 7–8th centuries of *hijra*/14–15th century AD. We find that ecclesiasts were not seriously interested in arriving at the core of Sufi philosophy made more complicated by the diabolical style of some of the followers of Shaykh Naju'd-Din Kubra like Ab'u Sae'ed Baghdadid (d. AH 616/ AD 1219) and Ibn Moed Hamavi (AH 650/AD 1252). Whatever they could understand of Sufi doctrines was only superficial knowledge or the top layer culled out from stray writings available to them at random. That is why the 14–15th century orthodoxy openly denigrated Sufis. In particular, Sayyid Murtaza bin Da'i, the author of *Tabsiratu'l-'Awamm* did not spare even the tallest among the early Sufis like Hasan bin Mansur Hallaj, and called him "a sorcerer who claimed to be the God."[3] Nor do Shibli and Bayazid Bastami[4] escape his

---

[1] *Sufism in Kashmir from the Fourteenth to the Sixteenth century*, Bhartiya Publishing House, Delhi.

[2] *Sar Chashmeh-e Tasavvuf dar Iran*, Teheran, 1343 AH (s), pp.197–99.

[3] *Tabsiratu'l-Awamm*, p.122.

[4] Bastami is said to have been greatly influenced by Vedantic scholars from India who often visited the eastern part of Khurasan of those days.

severe censure, as they are charged with heresy. They considered their views on themes like 'Unity of Being or 'Omnipresence of Supreme Being" nothing short of blasphemy.[1]

One more important source that deals with the denigration of Sufis by the orthodoxy is Ibnu'l-Jawzi's well-known work *Talbis-i Iblis*.[2] He has described at length the deviation of Sufis from the right path, meaning the path of faith, and provided copious proof of their heresy, sacrilege and *zandaqa*[3] (meaning reversion to pre-Islamic faith of the Iranians).

This apart, the work is a valuable mine of information. It gives us details about the practical side of Sufi life and their institutions. For example, Ibnu'l- Jawzi says that some Sufis observed *arba'ina*, meaning that for forty days the meditating Sufi subsisted only on dry fruits. Some ate very little and developed the habit of fasting continuously for several days. Sometimes Sufis would desist from drinking water for days on end. Sufis also showed great interest in music; they argued that it is a means of coming closer to God. It helps to get into a trance. They loudly cry *Ya Hoo* (God is Great). They clap their hands with the rhythm of the music and tear apart their clothes in a state of ecstasy, remove their headgear and dance in that state. Sometimes, they tear their clothes into small pieces and distribute them among the people present. Sufis adhered to their faith and did not care either to acquire some skill or to plan for life's requirements. They avoided congregations and Friday prayers, saying that they did not like interference in their life of seclusion and meditation. Sufis always showed humility. Most of them lived a life of celibacy. They liked to go alone into forests and wastelands without any means of subsistence. After arriving at a hospice or an inn, they would wash their hands and face and offer prayer, and then come to the presence of the Shaykh and wish him *salam*. The Sufis

---

[1] *Tabsiratu'l-Awam*, p.129.

[2] Talbis-i Iblis, by Ibn'l-Jauzi, Egypt, 1928, see p.160 et al.

[3] Those having faith in Zend-Avesta. This has been dealt with at its proper place in the text.

would not shed tears or lament on the death of a colleague; in fact, crying over the dead is punishable by expulsion from the Sufi fold.

Acquiring formal education was not the wont of Sufis because they said seeking knowledge obstructed a Sufi in his pursuit of Gnosis. To a Sufi religious knowledge was "manifest knowledge" (*ilm-e zahir*) and the knowledge within ones self was the "knowledge of the spirit" (*ilm-e batin*).

Safavi Sufi Order

In terms of its philosophical formulation, Nurbakhshiyyeh Order of Sufis has to be studied with reference to the Safavi Order that immediately preceded it in Iran. Safavi Sufi order had made a deep impact on the thinking of Sayyid Muhammad Nurbakhsh because he was close to it in time and space. The founder of this order, Shaykh Safiu'd-Din Ardabili has been mentioned at several places in this biography. Therefore, a brief introduction to this order is presented here to give a clear picture of the Iranian society of the day and the intellectual background of Nurbakhshiyyeh order; it will also discuss the factors that contributed to the emergence and growth of Nurbakhshiyyeh order.

It is ironic that although in Iran Safavi era was ushered in as a result of some preceding Sufi movements, yet the history of Sufism in this period was hardly smooth and hopeful. This spell of doom extended even beyond the times of the Safavis till the reign of Muhammad Shah Qajar (AH 1250–62/AD 1834–45). However, it does not mean that because overall conditions were not conducive, Sufism in Iran lost its continuity and fell from public favour. Nor did Iranian interest in universalism subside in any degree. There were two reasons that did not help create conducive atmosphere for Sufism, which have been hinted earlier; we mean "militarization" of Safavi Sufis and domination of religious divines of mediocre scholarship. This reminds us of the conflict between *ahl-e shariat* and *ahl-e tariqat* in the history of Sufism. Under the sub-heading 'Sufis versus the Juris-consults, Dr. Safa has opened an illuminating debate on the subject, which no student of Sufism can afford to overlook.[1] The group of Sufis that rose to ascendancy under Safavi rulers, Shah Isma'il and his son Shah Tahmasp, was bereft of standard training in the branch of mysticism. Its members were more or less ignorant of its high objectives and treated it cursorily. If they betrayed signs of adherence to it, that was out of ignorance and not conviction. At the same time, they bore stupid allegiance to their system of *Shaykhs*. Therefore, any faith in any other manifestation was reprehensible and deserved to be liquidated. "When Qizlbash Sufis of Turkic stock replaced the gown (*khirqa*) of a dervish with the outfit of a trooper, and the rosary with the rapier, and dragged them out of hospices to the battlefields, they, indeed, were not the Sufis though they insisted to be called so and boastfully talked of their chief as Perfect Preceptor (*Murshid-e Kamil*)", writes Dr. Safa.[2]

In the 15th century AD some new Sufi orders arose in Iran. Ghazan was the first among Chingiz's descendents who formally embraced Islam. Thereafter, the *Il-Khans* extended their patronage to Sufi orders at different centres in Iran. A fairly important social group during their reign was of the *Safaviyyeh* order of Sufis founded by Shaykh Safiu'd-Din of Aardabil (d. AH 735/AD 1335). Shaykh Safi was a disciple of Shaykh Zahid (d. AH 700/AD 1401). The people of Ardabil, prior to the rise of Shaykh Safi, were said to be the Sunnis of Shafi'i School.[3] But since the town became the resting place of the founder of the Safavi House, the ruling house and the people who had shown great veneration for the Sufi-saint, considered Ardabil a holy place, next only to the famous Shi'a shrines of Najaf, Meshhad and Kerbala, so much so that during the Safavis, Ardabil was declared a sanctuary for

[1] *Tarikh-i-Adabiyyat dar Iran*, Teheran, AH (s) 1386, vol.iv, pp.71–74.

[2] Loc. cit., vol.v, p.201. Shamsu'd-Din Araki put his Kashmiris Sufis precisely to this type of mission.

[3] See *Shaykh Safi wa Tabarash*, by Sayyid Ahmad Kasravi, Teheran, pp.39–48.

the criminals. Two chains were suspended horizontally and vertically on the main gate of the shrine of Shaykh Safi Ardabili, and any criminal or offender who succeeded in reaching the complex and pulling the chain, was granted security in all circumstances of life.

During their lifetime Shaykh Safiu'd-Din and his progeny acted as preceptors, or *Sufi Pirs* and religious guides whose followers increased quite fast. They and their adherents publicized their faith vigorously not only in Iran but also in Asia Minor, Syria and its adjoining regions. Shaykh Junayd, the grandfather of Shah Ismail Safavi, a contemporary of Qara-Qoyunlo (Black Sheep) ruler Amir Jahanshah, inspired a strong group of his Sufi followers and disciples to conquer lands and seize the reins of their government or in Sufi jargon "to combine visible kingdom with the spiritual kingdom". The Sufis were instigated to fight religious wars and *jihad* against the *kafirs*. He gave unto himself the title of Sultan Junayd. From this time onwards, the woolen gown wearing Sufis (*suf posh*) re-appeared in battle dress.[1] Apprehending retaliation by Amir Jahanshah, Shaykh Junayd took with him a strong group of Sufis and went to Amir Hasan Beg Aq-Qoyunlo (White Sheep) in Dayar Bakr, and married his daughter. When his followers increased in strength, he marched at the head of ten thousand Sufis for *jihad* against the Christians across River Aras.

Sultan Haider, the son of Sultan Junayd, strongly desired to distinguish Safavi Sufis and disciples from the rest, obviously for political reasons. He wanted to remove all

[1]Aruj Beg, Bayat, a Qizilbash chief accompanied Shah 'Abbas' ambassador Husaynali Beg Bayat to Europe where he embraced Christianity and came to be known as Don Juan of Iran. In his travelogue he write that the word Sufi, according to some, has nothing to do with the Greek word Sophis meaning knowledge and wisdom etc. They have erroneously stated that the word has been derived from Sophis. Actually it is derived from word sauf of Arabic which means woolen. As Sufis wear woolens they came to be known as Sufis. See *Don Juan of Iran*, tr. Le Strane, London, p.111. Also see *Zindagani-e Shah Abbas I* by Nasrullah Falsafi, Teheran, 1369 AH (s), p.234fn.1.

visible symbols that distinguished his various Sufi groups from one another since they were drawn from different clans and tribes. He replaced their Turkmen cap with a red 12–cornered head-gear,[1] and with that they came to be called Qizilbash (or Qizlbash).

For some time in the early period of his reign, Shah Isma'il Safavi let his followers and disciples be called Sufis.[2] That is why the Europeans called him the Great Sufi. The title remained with the Safavi house of rulers till it lasted in Iran.

Two titles, viz Qizlbash and Sufi, became synonymous, but gradually, towards the last phase of Shah Isma'il Safavis reign, when almost all Turkic ethnic groups had joined him as his followers and legions, emphasis shifted to Qizlbash while the meaning and implication of the term Sufi became restricted as well as special. It was restricted to such Qizlbash families as had previously shown allegiance to and association with the House of Safavis, and hence commanded more respect than the others. This explains why more known Sufis came mostly from the clans like Romlo, Shamlo and Qajar. The Shah (Safavi ruler) was their chief and preceptor for whom they coined the title of *Murshid-e Kamil* or Perfect Preceptor.

During the reign of Shah Tahmasp, another group of Shi'as, the descendents of the old disciples of the Safavis, arrived from Dayar Bakr and other parts of Asia Minor to Iran, and joined the local Sufi groups. At the time of Shah Tahmasps death, their number in Qazvin alone was around ten thousand.

Among all the clans and groups, Sufis were closest to the Safavi rulers. Their loyalty and faithfulness to the Shah were fully proven. Their chief was called *Khalifa* and the grand

---

[1] Twelve corners of the head dress symbolized twelve Imams though traditionally Sufis used to wer a three-cornered cap representing three renunciations recommended under Sufi teachings, viz. "*tark-i donya, tark-i uqba, tark-I tark.* "meaning renouncing the world, renouncing the hereafter and renouncing renunciation. See Dr. Safa, loc. cit., vol.v., p.144fn.4.

[2] See *Jahan Ara-e 'Abbasi*, MS, *Kitab Khaneh-e Milli*, Teheran. See also *Zindagani-e Shah 'Abbas*, op. cit., p.235.

chief of all the *khalifas* received the title of *Khalitatu'l-Khulafa*. Obviously, he was a personality of high status for the reason that Sufis considered him the deputy of *Murshid-e Kamil*—the Perfect Preceptor. Obedience to him was as important and binding as to the Shah. Under the Safavis, the *Khalifatu'l-Khulafa* was one who had attained something of a formal spiritual status. On the occasion of *Eid* festival, he, along with other Sufis, would come to see the Shah and offer him greetings and a bowl of sugar cubes. The Shah picked a cube or two and put it in his mouth. Courtiers and nobles did the same. Sometimes elders and distinguished persons from all walks of life came to *Khalifatu'l-Khulafa*, to seek his blessings and forgiveness for their past lapses and faults, and bowed before him on their knees. The elated *Khalifatu'l-Khulafa* touched their shoulders with his stick, which meant that their faults were forgiven. This was called *'eteraf* or confession.

The foremost condition for being a true Sufi was to show unflinching obedience to the orders and instructions of the *Murshid-e Kamil*.[1] The meanest sacrifice for the Perfect Preceptor was to give one's life for him. If a Sufi told a lie to the *Murshid-e Kamil*, he was liable to be punished with death, which would be undertaken without delay.[2] During the second year of Shah 'Abbas Is reign, Shah Vardi Khan, the son of *Khalifa* Ansar Qaradaglo, and the Governor of Qaracheh Dag, rose in revolt against the Safavi rule and joined hands with J'afar Pasha, the Turkic Governor of Tabriz. At that time, the western part of Azerbaijan and the city of Tabriz were under the Ottoman rule. Turkish warlords, too, had made incursions

---

[1] The Shi'a concept of *hulul-e sirr-e uluhiyyat* reincarnation of the Supreme Being lies behind it.

[2] *'Alam Ara-e 'Abbasi* records that Bolgar Khalifa, the *Khalifatu'l-Khulafa* in the days of Shah Isma'il II had told a lie and the Shah said to his Sufis," A *khalifa* who tells a lie to the *Murshid-e Kamil* deserves reprisal." Thereupon the crowd of Sufis pounced on the *Khalifatu'l-Khulafa* and delivered him some hard kicks till he succumbed to death.

into Qaracheh Dag. As Shah 'Abbas Safavi was in Khurasan at that time, no support from him was possible. Three years later in AH 1001/AD 1592 Shah 'Abbas captured the defiant Sufi commander and ordered his execution. Twenty-five years later in AH 1023/AD 1614 associates of the executed Sufi were rounded up and executed for the crime of violating Sufi discipline.

A group of people of Qaracheh Dag had, from olden days, remained devoted to the Safavi order of Sufis. During the reign of Shah Isma'il, when he had moved to Gilan owing to threats from his enemies, the Sufis of this order visited him often. The local Sufis, too, would visit him occasionally. The Sufis of Safavi order who had been visiting Shah Isma'il in Lahijan are still called Safavis-Lahijanis. In the biography of Shamsu'd-din Araki, we come across references to Safavis-Lahijanis, and the inference one can draw from this is that Araki had been in contact with this group.

Royal Guard

Safavi kings chose their bodyguards from the group of devoted Sufis[1] called *Qurchiyan* and *Qaravulan*. A special contingent of Sufis (*Qaravulan*) functioned as the royal bodyguard. They were supposed to be always ready to carry out the orders of the king.[2] The personnel of royal bodyguard always sported large moustaches, and like all Qizlbash wore red headgear. Their arms comprised a sword, a dagger and a pick-axe, which was slung by shoulder. Each group consisted of about three hundred Sufis. Whenever the Shah signaled that

---

[1] *Zindagani-e Shah 'Abbas* I, op. cit., p.238.

[2] The Sufis are reported to have eaten the flesh of a person if he said or did anything against the wishes of the *Murshid-e Kamiil* meaning the Shah. *Rawzatu's-Safa* records that when the dead body of Sheybak Khan Uzbek was brought to Shah Isma'il after former's defeat in the battle of Merv, the Shah, out of acute anger and vengeance, struck several blows at the dead body with his sword and ordered the Sufis to eat his flesh, which they did instantaneously.

a person to be killed, the Sufis tore him to pieces in his presence or trampled him under their feet, or kicked him to death. At times, they ate him up alive.[1]

This group of Sufis, the bodyguard of the Shah, was always with him wherever he went, except when he was relaxing in the company of the royal seraglio (*harem*). At that time, they were replaced by eunuchs. The royal palace was a sanctuary, and anybody managing to enter it could not be thrown out even by the Shah. All that the Shah could do was to order that no food be given to him, which eventually forced him to leave the palace voluntarily. Often the Sufis deployed for the security of the Shah used asylum-seekers for their self-aggrandizement. On Friday nights and also on festival nights, the Sufi guards assembled at a specific place in the royal complex and indulged in *zikr* (continual recitation of prayer). During the reign of Shah 'Abbas II and Shah Suleyman, this specific place was called *Tawoos Khaneh*.[2]

When Shah 'Abbas learnt that Sufis were conspiring against him to reinstate his deposed father Khudabandeh on the throne second time, he became cold towards them. Jalalud-Din Muhammad Yazdi[3] has recounted this episode in detail in his manuscript history.

'In the year AH 998/AD 1589 Shah Muhamamd Khudabandeh, partly because of his lust for power and partly because he was misled by misguided associates, came to the group of Sufis who had gathered for *zikr*. He asked them to rise in unison and put a question to Shah 'Abbas as to who was their *Pir-e Kamil*? They should ask that since the existence of father obstructs the son to become *Pir-e Kamil*, he should recognize Khudabandeh as the Shah, and not spoil the world and not destroy habitations or convert them into deserts.

The assembled Sufis got busy in chanting (*zikr*). Shah 'Abbas had received intelligence about their intentions. He

[1] *Zindagani-e Shah 'Abbas*, Nasrullah Falsafi, op. cit., p.238.

[2] *Travelogue* by Chardon, Paris, 1811, vol.vi, p.375.

[3] *Tarikh-i Shah'Abbas*, Jalau'd-Din Muhammad Yezdi Munajjim, MS Kitabkhaneh-e Milli and Kitabkhaneh-e Malik, Teheran.

took Muhammad Quli Beg Chaghatai with him and headed towards the assembly. After taking his seat in the balcony, he asked them, "It is not a Friday night. Are you assembled for a session of *zikr* to celebrate the birthday of one of the Imams? The Sufis said they had a problem, in response to which the Shah said," But this is not how you can solve your problem. Choose an eloquent person from amongst you and send him to me with two more companions for talks, and I shall solve your problem." The Sufis assigned the task to one who was the source of conspiracy, with two other Sufis. When they came to the presence of the Shah, he spoke just two words with them, and ordered his attendants to put them to death. The Shah himself killed the main conspirator with his sword and retired to his place. The Sufis in that assembly took to their heels without even the footwear.[1]

This marked the decline of Sufi power in the reign of Safavis. As the Shah lost his confidence in the Sufis and thus gave them cold shoulder, the Sufis lost their influence, power and status so much so that having been sidelined from the status of royal guards they now worked as sweepers, menials and gatekeepers. Rumour spread that the Sufis met in secret assemblies at night under the pretext of *zikr* sessions, but indulged in unbecoming acts.

However, despite the fact that Sufis had lost their old and formal status and influence at the royal court, many of them still respected them and trusted their spiritual status. After all, people had got used to believing in their mystical powers. For example, snatching a morsel from them was considered to have a curative effect. Even people of high status from among the elite and powerful government functionaries sought morsels from the platter of Sufis.

To sum up, we find that the social fame of the Safavi ruling house began from the hospice and got mixed up with the Imami faith of *ithna 'ashra*. For its military and political achievements, this house depended on the fighting personnel

[1] *Tarikh-i-Shah 'Abbas*, Jalalu'd-Din Muhammad Yezdi Munajjim, MS copies, *Kitab Khaneh-e Milli* Teheran and *Kitab Khaneh-e Malik*, Teheran.

who had chosen to be the disciples of Safavis. They were the Turkmen from the regions of Anatolia, Syria, Dayar Bakr and the western Caspian Sea areas. These people, spread out among a number of clans, had migrated to these areas during the heyday of Seljuq Turks and influenced the history and politics of Asia Minor and parts of Iran. These groups had shown their inclination towards Shi'a faith as early as the 13th century.[1] It was even rumoured that when the Mehdi would appear, the Turks would accompany him and fight on his side.[2]

These groups gradually joined the Safviyeh Sufi order during the rule of the descendents of Shaykh Safiu'd-Din Ardabili (d. AH 735/AD 1334). Some historians think that the presence of these groups within the Safavi Order became a catalyst for the House of Shaykh Safi to shift from *Shafi'i* to *ithna 'ashra* faith. Hamdullah Mustawfi (d. cir. AH 730/ AD 1329) tells us in *Nuzhatu'l-Qulub* that the people of Ardabil were of Shafii faith and disciples of Shaykh Safiud-din. Ibn Bazzaz, who gives extracts from the life of Shaykh Safiud-Din in *Safavatu's-Safa*, does not give any hint that the Shaykh was an adherent of Shi'a faith. Even some of his descendents, too, stuck to his faith until the time they found it expedient to make a shift. This shift happened around AH 830/ AD 1426 when Shaykh Junaiyd came to loggerheads with Jahanshah of Qara-Qoyunlo on the issue of religious leadership (of Musualmans). He had to take refuge with Amir Hasan Beg Bayandar, the chief of Aq-Qoyonlu a Twelver Shi'a, and married his sister Khadija Begum. Sultan Haider was born of this Shi'a woman.[3]

Perhaps it was not too difficult to change over from Shafi'i to Imami (Twelver) faith because from among the sects of Sunnis, the sect of Shafi'i is closest to the fundamentals of Imamis. Muhammad bin Idris, the founder of Shafi'i sect bore personal allegiance to 'Ali ibn Ibi Talib and his House. Apart

---

[1] Safa, loc. cit., vol.v, p.189.

[2] Ibid., vol.ii, pp.190–91.

[3] Also see *Tarikh-i-Siyasi wa Ijtema'i-e Iran: Az marg-i Timur ta marg-i Shah 'Abbas, Abul Qasim Tahiri*, Teheran, p.133 et al.

from many encomia for Husayn and the Martyrs of Kerbala, he has composed many elegies as well.[1] We are aware of the presence of Shafi'i scholars in the assemblies organized to commemorate the martyrs of Kerbala during the ascendancy of Sunni-Hanafi Seljuqs.[2] The Shafi'i like the Twelver Shi'a believe in the (Occultation?) of Mehdi (*ghaibat-e Sahib-e Zaman*) and his return (*raj'at*).

After the House of Shaykh Safi embraced the Imami faith and made a departure from the faith of their ancestors, they tried to raise its status to its previous heights. Shaykh Safi, the founder of the Safavi Order of Sufis, was projected as the purest Shi'a, though of course, historians and informed persons, who were opposed to that house knew their background. This is reflected in the letters sent by Ubaydullah Khan Uzbek to Shah Abbas Safavi.[3] One of the letters is very amusing and merits a mention. 'A Referring to the claim of the Safavis to be the descendents of Hazrat Ali, Ubaydullah writes to Shah Abbas, "You claim to be the progeny of Hazrat Murtaza Ali. The question is whether you are or not? Now since you claim you are his offspring, let it be said that the Prophet (pbuh) has said that a person telling the father of another person that he is his father, whereas actually he is not, (such a person) cannot find entry into the paradise. And if you are the offspring of Hazrat Ali Murtaza, who the devil did he exhume from the grave and set on flames..?"[4]

---

[1] *Kitabu'n-Naqsh*, Teheran, AH (s) 1331, p.402.

[2] Safa, loc. cit., vol.ii (fifth ed.) p.195.

[3] See *Ahsanu't-Tawarikh*, p.230.

[4] The allusion is to the attack of Shah Isma'il Safavi on Shirwan in AH 907/AD 1501 in which the dead body of Sultan Khalil Pasha of Shirwan was exhumed and set on fire by way of avenging the killing of his grandfather Sultan Haider. See *Ahsanu't-Tawarikh*, p.47. It could also allude to the destroying of the grave of Abu Hanifatu'l-N'aman, the religious preceptor of the Hanafi Sunni School by the order of Shah Isma'il Safavi after his conquest of Baghdad in AH 914/AD 1508. Hayrati the poet, too, alludes to it in this verse:

Shi'a bar goor-e Hanifeh momina didi chih kard
Hast ridangah-e Shi'a sajdeh gah-e Sunniyan

See *Fihrist-e Kitabkhaneh-e Danishgah-i Teheran*, Muhammad Taqi Danishpijoh, vol.iii, fn. p.2157.

Reflecting on this scenario, Dr. Safa concludes, "These negative reflections emanated from those who knew whether the Safavis were in truth descendents of the illustrious House of Ali or not. Nevertheless, in the days of Shah Ismails ascendancy, the claim had come to stay with his followers so much so that his successors had no need to contradict this fiction and fallacy. The red-barrette Qizlbash even began to believe that the Safavi kings (*murshid-e kamil*), whether awake or in sleep, were in direct communion with the venerable Imams. But what is more significant than all this is that the Shaykhs of the Safavi Sufi order and their disciples believed in the concept of 'Re-incarnation of the Essence of Divine Primacy in the body of their preceptor,[1] an entity that subsequently emerged with the title of *murshid-e kamil*.[2]

A close study of the biography in hand shows that the status which Shamsu'd-Din Araki has tried to confer upon Sayyid Muhammad Nurbakhsh in the realm of spirituality (*velayat*) has actually been borrowed from the tradition laid down by the Sufis of Safavi order, to which the biographer has referred at several places. "Safavi Sufis were not the only ones to believe in this concept; there were their contemporaries like Nurbakhshiyyeh, Pasikhaniyan, Hurufiyyeh and Mushashayyeh who also subscribed to it", concludes the celebrated scholar of Iran.[3]

Kashinath Pandit

[1] See *Dairatu'l-M'aarif-e Islami* (new edition), vol.4, p.51.
[2] Safa, op. cit., vol.v, p.143.
[3] Ibid., p.143fn.4.

Chapter I
Araki and Nurbakhshi Preceptors

This chapter contains the following themes: Hazrat Mir Shamsu'd-Din Araki comes to the presence of Sayyid Muhammad Nurbakhsh; prediction made by Sayyid Muhammad Nurbakhsh; poignant elegies on the death of the Sayyid, Araki's training (in religious attainments) by Shaykh Mahmud Bahri, Maulana Husayn Kokai, Shaykh Mahmud Sufli, Burhanu'd-Din Baghdadi, Shaykh Asiri Lahiji and Shah Qasim Faiz Bakhsh; Asiri coming to the presence of Sayyid Muhammad Nurbakhsh, Shaykh Muhammad Ghaibi falling into trance, Faiz Bakhsh as the successor to Sayyid Muhammad Nurbakhsh, activities of Faiz Bakhsh in Khurasan and Arak, and the reasons for dispatching Mir Araki to Kashmir.

People endowed with the attributes of love and sincerity are enlightened souls: they know that Araki[1] belonged to the Safaviyyeh,[2] in the town of Khurasan[3] in Arak. This tribe is

---

[1] Arak is the name of a province in Iran with Farahan to north, Qom to east, Mahallat to south and Shazand Mountain to west. Sultanabad is its present capital. *Loghat Nameh* Dehkhuda, vol.vi, p.1610.

[2] This refers to the tribes that formed the Safavi ruling house of Iran in 16th century. Shaykh Safi Ardabili was the patron-saint of the Safavi ruling house founded by Shah Isma'il in AH 907–930/AD 1501–23, a follower of Shaykh Safi Ardabili. Historians have tried to trace the geneology of Shaykh Safi to Imam Musa Kazim. Araki has been linked to this line. See *Tohfatu'l-Ahbab*, edited by Ghulam Rasool Jan, Srinagar, 2006, vol.1, p.440.

[3] *khwar* (Pahlavi meaning the Sun, Avestic *hur*) +*shed* (Sanskrit *shweta*, Pahlavi *sheid* and Farsi *sefid* meaning white or bright). *aas* is from defunct verbal noun *aasdan* in Pahlavi meaning to come. *an* is suffix. Hence Khur+as+an (*Khurasan*) means from where the Sun comes or the East (of Iran).

well known in those countries (lands).[1] His birthplace was called Kandaleh, (which is) in the vicinity of Solghan,[2] and his ancestors were in possession of its territory from the ancient times. His father Dervish Ibrahim was one among the dedicated disciples of the *Qutb*[3] of the Time, Imam Muhammad Nurbakhsh. His mother came from a Sayyid house of Qazvin.

In the service of Nurbakhsh

As a child, Araki occasionally accompanied his father on visiting the Imam (Sayyid Nurbakhsh). These visits earned him Imam's, affection and care. He listened to his exhortation and sermons, and finally joined the circle of his disciples. His father, Dervish Ibrahim, was then of advanced age. For a long time, he had done penance, and remained in seclusion at the shrine of the Imam. For this reason, he (Dervish Ibrahim) had forbidden his son to leave his family and become a recluse. He told the Imam that owing to his physical infirmity and old age, he was unable to look after his family. Therefore he had entrusted it to the care of his worthy son (Araki). But if he decided to forsake his family and home, and become a recluse and live the life of celibacy, what would happen to the members of the family and its affairs? It was a matter of concern. He requested the Imam to counsel Araki and induce him to return to his home and look after the family so that he (Dervish Ibrahim) could devote himself to meditation and penance without any distraction.

---

[1] This sentence confirms that Araki belonged to the clan subscribing to the order of Shaykh Safi Ardabili.

[2] A village on the outskirts of Teheran (Rey in medieval times). *Loghat Nameh*, p.344. This is the reason why I have used Araki and not Iraqi as is generally done by scholars.

[3] Literally meaning Pole. Title of a *wali* (spiritual leader) who has the authority of governing a city or a land in the realm of spirit, *ibid*, p.344.

Sayyid's prediction

The Imam called Mir Araki to his presence and said, "Muhammad, you should think of serving your father because service to parents means earning happiness in the hereafter. As long as your father is alive, look after his family. Penance and acquisition of religious knowledge come after that. Should I continue to live, I shall impart training to you. But if I be no more, my disciples and followers will impart knowledge and training to you." Araki acquiesced to the command of the Imam and returned to his home, to the satisfaction of his father.

He earnestly began discharging responsibilities of the household. However, he occasionally came to the Imam and got benefit from his sermons and assemblies. A few years later, his father breathed his last. He got more occupied with family matters. Once he had to travel to Syria and Egypt to meet material requirements (of the family). He was forced to halt in Egypt for several months because of the construction of a wall for the security (of the town). He lived those days in the hospice of Shaykh Muhammad Samarqandi,[1] who was a faithful disciple of the Imam.

The debate

Araki said that Shaykh Muhammad Samarqandi was the *Shaykhu'l-Islam*[2] of Samarqand, and Maulana Ahmad

---

[1] Nurullah Shustari has mentioned his name adding that Samarqandi had written a memoire on the life and spiritual attainments of his mentor (*Pir*). See *Majalisu'l-Momineen*, MS, fol.374b, J&K Research Library.

[2] Title given to Sufi Shaykhs and men of learning around the middle of the 4th century *hijra* (10–11th century AD) In early Memluk era in Egypt and Syria, the title was more a mark of respect than anything formal. But when the title was given to the Grand Mufti of Turkey it gained some status and became a formal title. In 17th century this title was given to influential Muftis. During the Saffavi period in Iran, the title was given to a person who headed the judiciary. The Prime Minister appointed him. *Encyclopedia of Islam.* See also *Loghat Nameh*, p.152.

happened to be the *Qadi* of the time (of that town). Once, these two persons said that one Sayyid Muhammad Qaini had declared himself the promised Mehdi[1] and assumed the name Sayyid Muhammad Nurbakhsh. Their intention was to engage the Imam (Nurbakhsh) in a theological debate in order to falsifying his claim that he was the promised Mehdi. They would challenge his claim of providing leadership to the people of the world (meaning Muslim world) and carrying them to a state of ecstasy. He had wanted to declare himself "Imam" Nurbakhsh, and raising his pontifical banner in the world desired to establish his Shaykhdom in the hospices of Khurasan and Arak. These two persons were among the stupid *ulema* and brainless scholars of their day in Samarqand and Trans-Oxiana.[2] They proceeded towards Arak. Covering the long distance by stages, they arrived in Gilan[3] where they enquired of local people the group that Imam Nurbakhsh owned, and made friends with. They said that the Sayyid was affectionate towards the dervishes.[4]

---

[1] Also Mehdi-e Zaman. Muhammad bin Hasan 'Askari, titled *Imam-e-Zaman/ Sahibu'z-Zaman/Imam-e-Muntazar/Hujjatu'l-Qaem* was born in Samra in AH 255/AD 870. From the time of his disappearance up to the death of his fourth lieutenant in AH 326/AD 937, the period is called *ghaibat-e sughra* (Lesser Occultation). *Ghaibat-e kubra* (Greater Occultation begins from the time of the death of Abu'l Hasan 'Ali bin Muhammad Samra. Shias are waiting for the reappearance of Mehdi. In the middle of the month of *Sh'aban*, Shia hold a feast (*jashn*) to remember the return of Mehdi. See *Aynu'l-Shia*, vol.iii, part iv, p.326. See also *Loghat Nameh*, p.178. The issue of Nurbakhsh declaring himself Mehdi has been discussed in the Introduction.

[2] *Mawara an-Nahr* of Arab and *Wara Rud* of Farsi/Dari/Tajik/Russian historians. The Greeks called it Oxus while Arab historians and geographers called it Jayhun.

[3] Northern province of Iran, bordering on the Caspian Sea. Among its major towns are Rasht, Bandar Anzali, Mowqanat, Tawas and Lahijan. See *Loghat Nameh.*

[4] Its meaning has many dimensions like followers of the sect of Nurbakhsh or Nurbakhshiyyeh, volunteers and crusaders in the path of Islam of Nurbakhshiyyeh order, people of singular devotion, faith and trust in Imam Nurbakhsh etc. *Dervish* is used in a specific sense throughout the text. In the context of Kashmir, Nurbakhshiyyeh *dervish* invariably means a mercenary and a crusader who works for the spread and propagation of Islam.

In those days the Imam lived in Nurabad, known as (Kurah) Shaft (?) in earlier days. The name Nurabad was given to it after he had laid the foundation of a hospice there.

The above-named two persons came to the presence of the Imam in the guise of *qalandars*.[1] Those present in the assembly had (not?) expected them to come in that guise and initiate a debate with the Imam. Gifted with the knowledge of the invisible as the Imam was, he summoned them to his presence and enquired of them about the hardships of a long journey. They were in the middle of a casual talk when the *mu'ezzin* (one who calls for prayer) of the Imam gave a call for prayers.

Maulana Burhanu'd-Din Baghdadi used to perform the duties of *Imama:* that is, leading the mass in the assemblies of the Imam. If he was not available, the Imam himself performed this function. After performing the daily ritual (*sunnat*) and *nafl*,[2] the Imam invited Mulla Muhammad Samarqandi to perform the duties of leading the mass despite the fact that Mulla Burhanu'd-Din was very much present in the gathering. He considered it mandatory to abide by his instructions and began to lead the prayers.

During his conversation with the two persons, the Imam tried to win their heart. After making the prayers, their eyes

---

[1] de Sacy attributes the tribe to Shaykh Karandal. Ivanov says that his forty years of research has not yielded the root of the word. *Kalantar* in Farsi meaning the elderly person does not sound logical as the root because of Arabic q and not Farsi letter *k* with which it begins. He could not find it in Arabic, Turkish, Hebrew, Sanskrit and other languages. In Russian *kalika* was used during the Middle Ages almost with the same meaning. *Loghat Nameh*, p.451. The definition of *qalandar* given by the author of *Taraiqu'l Haqaiq* (Tehran, vol.iv, p.354) is the opposite of what Iqbal conveys in this Urdu verse:

Qalandar juz do harf-e la illah kuchh bhi nahin rakhta
faqih-e shahr Qarunhai loghat ha-e Hejazi ka

[2] voluntary religious act and a prayer rendered in addition to the needed or desired one (*wajib*).

met with some spiritual light. The celestial bliss engulfed them and the Imam captivated their hearts with love and affection. Thus immediately after performing *namaz* (Islamic prayer), they declared their allegiance to the Imam and decided not to go away from his doorstep. They were admitted to the circle of disciples and hence undertook to do various types of penance, submission, acquisition of spiritual knowledge and training. Thus, they thanked God Almighty for having blessed them with right direction (through the Imam).

Shaykh Samarqandi

Once, the ruler of Samarqand wrote a letter of chastisement to Shaykh Muhammad Samarqandi. He replied that rulers were deprived of patronage because of their timidity. Once, friends and acquaintances in Samarqand wrote to him (the Shaykh) to abjure outwardly asceticism and mendicancy. His reply was that as long as his hand was in the hands of Nurbakhsh, he would receive heavenly bliss. Shaykh Samarqandi usually wrote in verse using *Feraqi* as his pen name (*takhallus).* We shall hear more of him in the pages that follow.

After acquiring prescribed training in the branches of spiritual science, and after crossing the stages set forth for perfection, both of them (scholars) gained prominence in their respective fields of knowledge. They were authorised to administer repentance (*tauba*). 'The Cream of the Time' meaning the Imam permitted them to train and discipline seekers of spiritual knowledge. He directed Shaykh Muhammad Feraqi to proceed on a pilgrimage to Iraq, Arabia, Syria and the twin holy shrines (meaning Mecca and Medina). The Imam appreciatingly called him 'Chosen among the Gnostics (Verses).

After performing the stipulated obligations of pilgrimage to the House of God (Mecca), he proceeded on a pilgrimage to the shrine of the Holy Prophet. On his return, he settled in Egypt.

Sayyid's death

In Egypt, Mir Shamsu'd-Din Araki camped in the hospice of Shaykh Muhammad Feraqi. Some disciples of the Shaykh from Khurasan and Arak used to visit this place. A group that had arrived from Arak brought the sad and tragic news of the Imam's demise. This snatched Araki's peace of mind and left him woe-begotten and lamenting. Leaving some of his tasks unfinished, he collected his nick-knacks, took packhorses and proceeded towards Arak. After covering a long distance, he arrived at his native place where he off-loaded his baggage. Leaving all responsibilities of his household to the care of his brother, he proceeded on a visit to the shrine of the Imam in Solghan (Soljan) in Iran. At that point of time, the Nuriyyeh hospice of the Imam had been just completed. The Imam's holy body remains buried in it. After coming to the shrine, he performed all rites connected with the mourning (of the dead).

Enquiries about Nurbakhsh

A few days later, he got interested in knowing about the life and ideas of the Imam. He collected detailed information on the subject from dervishes and vicegerents (of the Imam), He learnt of his high spiritual status from their oral account. Thereafter, he looked for the successors of the Imam and his disciples from whom he would gather information on the Imam's school/sufi order. The first resource person he met was Shaykh Mahmud Bahri, the brother of Pir Hajji Bahrabadi. He ranked among the middle-level disciples of the Imam but was quite knowledgeable. Among his close associates he was a man of status and merit. He was perfect in imparting training and discipline to students and seekers of spiritual knowledge and capable of winning the hearts of his students.

Shaykh Bahri trains students

Once, in the assembly of Pir Hajji, a serious discussion followed among men of excellence and conviction about training disciples and mystics. Some dervishes[1] said that if merit and capability were inherent, then training and discipline imparted by the spiritual guide would become effective forthwith. But many a time a disciple diligently strives to acquire these qualities. Even though the spiritual guide also does his best to help him, yet he remains deprived. "A blacksmith invests whatever labour and skill is at his command to bring lustre to the glass. Likewise, the spiritual guide takes pains to embellish the mirror of a disciple's heart. If the iron and the glass did not have intrinsic merit in them, the blacksmith's labour would be futile."

Pir Hajji Bahrabadi repudiated the analogy. He argued that if the blacksmith was gifted with perfection and mastery in his skills, he would still turn iron into glass, though, of course, its lustre would not be of permanent nature and would wear out because of the inferior quality of the substance (iron). This line of argument prejudiced the audience against him. They said that if this were the case then everybody would rush to the patriarchs to become saints and savants. Pir Hajji challenged them by telling them to bring idiots and ignorant to him and he would guide them on the path of righteousness. The audience dispersed, and then brought together a band of gamblers, vagabonds, foolhardy people who did not believe in God, knew nothing about the Prophet, and were ignorant about Islam and Islamic faith. With hearts hard as stones they had refused to accept any guidance. Forty of them were brought to Pir Hajji.

A single look of the Pir (Master) captivated them: they forthwith embraced Islamic faith, made recantation[2] and

---

[1] The word *Dervish* is variously used in Farsi. The author uses it for disciples and adherents of Nurbakhshiyyeh order.

[2] Meaning they recited *kelima.*

expressed repentance.[1] After the first stage was crossed, Pir Hajji started delivering sermons on the ways of the mystics, doing penance and methods of acquiring spiritual knowledge. He had such a success in imparting training to them that in one sitting in seclusion, he issued certificates declaring that forty men had earned the stage of full attainment (of spiritual eminence). Now they were authorized to obtain allegiance from mendicants, and guide devotees along the path of spiritual knowledge.

Ordinary people would not trust the veracity of this story. Even some people with a modicum of spiritual insight, too, were loath to accept it. They subtly complained to the Imam (Sayyid Nurbakhsh), who rebuked them in these words, "You too appear to be blind and heartless like other ordinary people. You should open your inner eye and examine for yourselves whether the certificate was given to them rightly or wrongly". As a result, they began to dig deeper into this matter. After conducting necessary tests, they reported to the Imam that thirty-nine out of forty persons had perfected their training. They could not ascertain the position of the odd one. The Imam said that one who had rightly issued certificates in favour of 39 could not be faulted in the case of the remaining one. He told them that in his opinion, the status of the fortieth person was higher than the rest of them in the realm of spiritual knowledge. This could have been the reason why they failed to assess him properly. The Imam said, "This is the period of appearance of guardianship (*velayat*)[2] and no wonder these perfectionists and researchers were brought up under the prospective *velayat*. Maybe they had been trained under the observant eye of the *Qutbu'z-Zaman*[3] (the Pivot of the Time). Maybe the *Qutbu'z-Zaman* has appeared on the earth. How am

---

[1] Repentance (*tauba*) over sinful deeds is accptable to allow entry into the Islamic fold.

[2] Spiritual domain in Shia theology.

[3] See fn. p.2, supra, fn.6.

I to explain (these concepts) through this broken tongue and broken pen."

In the presence of Shaykh Mahmud

The reason why Araki decided to stay in the company of Shaykh Mahmud Bahri was to conduct research on the life and spiritual attainment of Imam Nurbakhsh. He wanted to adopt his line of spiritual perfection. Of all the disciples, Shaykh Mahmud Bahri had the distinction of being better informed about the details of the life, spiritual attainment, mysteries, penance, mystic practices, etc. of the Imam. He was well-informed on known and unknown movements, practices of fasting and observance of the rules and practices of prayers of the blessed soul (Imam Nurbakhsh). He did not absent himself from the service of the Imam even for a fraction of a minute and was always present in his assemblies and gatherings to the extent of providing water to him for ablution. And when the Imam confined himself to the cell (*chilleh*),[1] the Shaykh waited outside the door. When he stepped out of his cell for ablution, the Shaykh carried the jug of water and accompanied him. Thus Araki spent two years in the company of Shaykh Mahmud Bahri. During that period he sought his views on many theological matters. The fund of information about the Imam and his life and achievements, which Araki could collect during those two years, was so comprehensive as if he had spent his entire life in the service of the Imam.

Maulana Husayn Kokabi (Kokai ?)

Araki joined the services of Maulana Kokai. He was among the disciples of the Imam. He was well versed in rational and transmitted sciences besides being a leading scholar of Arabic. He had accomplishments to his credit in the branches of apocalyptic and contemplative sciences. In the field of

---

[1] Forty days during which ascetics go into seclusion for prayer and fasting. For more details see *Loghat Nameh*, p.345.

induction and deduction, he was like a vast ocean. In temporal and spiritual sciences, his forehead reflected the rays of Imam Nurbakhsh's radiance. In his work, *Sahifa-e-Aulia*,[1] the Imam included him among perfect Shaykhs. Araki asserted that the Imam had said a number of times that after him, Mulla Hussain Kokabi had all pre-requisites to hold the *velayat*.[2]

During the lifetime of the Imam, Mulla Hussain Kokai served as the tutor of Shah Qasim Faiz Bakhsh and the progeny of the Imam. He designed a course (of study) for the womenfolk and daughters of the Imams house who had the gift of high level of intelligence. He translated the chapters pertaining to ablution, prayers, tradition, obligations and imperatives of *Ahwat*[3] theology into Farsi. All the female pupils preferred to read the Persian version of *Ahwat* and learn it by heart.[4]

---

[1] Also mentioned as *Sahifatu'l-Aulia*, the work is reported to contain biographical sketches of some contemporary personalites like Shaykh Bahau'd-Din Kashmiri, Shah Qasim Faiz Bakhsh, Shaykh Muhammad Alwandi and Pir-e Hamadan. This poetical composition has not been published so far though its MSS are easily available in oriental research libaries. The author of *Tohfat'l-Ahbab* has copiously drawn from it.

[2] According to Shi'a theology the institution of spiritual guardianship/domain of the community is called *velayat*. The guardian is *vali*.

[3] *Ahwat* is the title of a work by Sayyid Muhammad Nur Bakhsh on Nurbakhshiyyeh theology. Some historians including the author of *Waaq'at-e-Kashmir* have erroneously ascribed its authorship to Araki. It is believed that the original MS of this treatise is no more extant now though its recensions are available. Ghazi Muahammad Naeem believes that at least 14 MSS of the work exist in Baltistan alone. See *Mir Sayyid Muhammad Nurbakhsh aur Maslak-e Nurbakhshiyyeh*, by Ghazi Muhammad Naeem, Islamabad, pp.244–45. Nadvah-e-Islamiyyeh Nurbakhshiyyeh in Karachi has published the Arabic text of *Ahwat* with its Urdu translation under the title *Al Fiqh al-Ahwat*. Nurbakhshiyyeh tenets are still observed by the Nur Bakhshiyyeh sect in the Karakorum foothill regions. See *Baharistan-i-Shahi*, tr. K.N. Pandit, Calcutta, 1991, p.159, fn.87 and *Tarikh-i-Kashmir* by Malik Haider MS. Research and Publications Department, Government of Jammu & Kashmir, Acc. No.934, f.52b.

[4] It means that the original *Ahwat* was written in Arabic language.

Fiqh-e Ahwat

During his second visit to Kashmir, Amir Shamsu'd-Din Araki brought with him a copy of *Fiqh-e-Ahwat* so that his family members and children were imparted lessons from it. He used to resolve issues in accordance with this text and observe prayers and fasting set forth in that book. Elderly people of this land, children, young and old, and disciples and sympathisers read the same text and observed the rites, obligations and commandments laid down in the book. In regard to the question of wiping over (*mas+ha*)[1] the longboot (*mowzeh*)[2]—a practice followed by the leading religious divines of Nurbakhshiyyeh order—Maulana Husayn Kokabi has clarified the matter in his translation. Had he not lived in the company of the Imam and observed the practices, he would have declared the wiping of the legging permissible.

Mir Shamsu'd-Din Araki spent three years in the service of Maulana Husayn Kokai, strictly following the religious practices authorised by him. For the most of time he lived in seclusion, meticulously observing the prayer schedule, recitation and the telling of beads. The Maulana blessed Araki, which enriched him with spiritual knowledge.

Infatuation for a wali

Mir Shamsu'd-Din has disclosed that during the days of his training by Maulana Husayn, he came to know a young person who infatuated him. Deep intimacy with him made him restless. The Maulana came to know about it and admonished Araki for indulging in what was forbidden.[3] But Araki's heart was inflamed by love, which could not be extinguished

---

[1] *Mash u'r-raqaba* means wiping the neck, a practice of the Muslims before engaging themselves in prayer.

[2] Leather legging still in use in Central Asia.

[3] Sodomy among the inmates of a hospice was not uncommon in the history of the Sufis.

by sermons and warnings. The Maulana deliberately sent him away on some errand to a distant place, which would ordinarily take a day's travel on foot. But Maulanas instructions were that he should halt there for the night and return the next day. Araki could not bear even one day's separation from that youth. After carrying out the errand, he returned post haste the same day. However, since he had to cross the river, and the boatman supposed to ferry him had left the place, he was obliged to spend the night on the bank of the river. He longed for his friend and passed the night restlessly. On reaching the hospice, he came to know that the Maulana had breathed his last the same night. He was stunned and shocked and enquired of attendants and disciples how the departing hour had come for the Maulana. They told him that he did not die of any disease. After performing mid-day prayers, he took a stroll with his disciples in the garden where he had grown melons. He took a spade in his hand and struck it into the soil with full strength. This caused rupture in the vein of his heart and he fell on the ground. His disciples assembled around him. He lifted his hands and uttered the prayer, "Oh God! As you have delivered me from the prison house of the world and liberated me from this abode of destruction, please liberate him (Shamsu'd-Din) also from his distraction." Thus Mir Shams came to know (through the disciples of the Maulana) that the Maulana had prayed for him in his dying minutes. It cooled down his infatuation for the youth. When burial rites were over, Mir Shams visited the grave of the departed soul for three consecutive days to offer prayers and chant hymns. Then he sought permission from the attendants and disciples to leave the hospice. They told him that they had agreed among themselves that for one year nobody would leave the group, and they would be the keepers of the grave (shrine). If he decided to join them, he was welcome. But Araki excused himself saying that he was in search of a spiritual guide to help him find the path leading to the Supreme Being (God). On the third day, he took leave of them and proceeded in search of his spiritual guide.

Mahmud Sufli

Araki came to Mahmud Sufli, a disciple of Pir Hajji Bahrabadi. He was one of the forty persons trained by Bahrabadi in spiritual skills and to whom he had issued certificates of competence (*khat-e-irshad*). He was authorised to obtain allegiance from students and accept recantation from the seekers of truth. He had attained perfection in these practices. He had built a house and a hospice on the outskirts of the city. People seeking the right path used to receive instructions and lessons in training in that hospice. Mir Shamsu'd-Din came to him, offered allegiance (*bai'at*)[1] to him and undertook spiritual training in the path of the Prophet. He demonstrated his ability to pick up skills of physical prowess and control over the self so as to perform even the hardest of penance. He spent two years in the hospice of Mahmud Sufli. He found that under his training the rays of spiritual guidance had begun illuminating his inner self. Shaykh Mahmud had made special arrangements for his training. He had attained a distinguished place in the science of revelations and miracle-performing, and in supernatural feats. Thus he had reached highest place among the ascetics of his days.

---

[1] *Bai'at kardan* figuratively means binding oneself in obedience. In Islam the tradition of giving hand in the hand of one to whom allegiance is made has a history. When Ka'aba was retaken, the Prophet obtained allegiance from his male followers by asking them to put their hands on his hand. He then asked the womenfolk for their allegiance. He put his hand into a pitcher full of water and the women folk in their turn put their hands into it one by one. Thus the men and women of Mecca announced their allegiance to the Prophet. *Persian Encyclopedia* and *Loghat Nameh*, p.554. Nasir Khusrav says:

goftam kih kanoon an shajar-o dast chigune hast
an dast kuja juyam-o an bai'at-o mahzar

Burhanu'd-Din Baghdadi

Another teacher from whom Amir Shamsu'd-Din received further training in the branches of spirituality was Maulana Burhanu'd-Din Baghdadi. In the realm of mysticism very often an aspirant trainee has to surmount several difficult and hard stages in the course of training at higher level. In order to arrive at these stages, he invariably stands in need of a guide with outstanding accomplishments to his credit. Many Shaykhs and spiritualists depute their disciples to accomplished guides for streamlining their skills in mysticism. For example, we know that Shaykh 'Ammar Yasser[1] (d. AH 582/AD 1186) had sent Shaykh Najmu'd-Din Kubra[2] in

---

[1] He was among the Companions of the Prophet. His father 'Asha was from Yemen. Sameyeh, also known as Umm 'Ammar, was his mother. *Taju'l-'Urus* and *Loghat Nameh*, p.87. He died in AH 582/AD 1186). 'Ammar was known for his asceticism as Nasir Khusrav says:

pasand ast ba zohd-e' Ammar o Bu Zar
kunad madh-e Mahmud mar Unsuri ra?

[2] The founder of Kubravi order of Sufis of 6–7th century *Hijra*. Listed among his pupil are eminent men such as Najmu'd-Din Razi and Bahau'd-Din Walad. He had renounced worldly life, and was given the title Abu'l-Janab (meaning one who had gone away to a side). He was also called *wali tarash* (carver of *walis*) for accepting as many as 12 disciples—all Shaykhs and learned men. He lived in Khwarazm and when Chingiz Khan sent him a word that since orders of a massacre of Khwarazmians had been issued, he (Najmu'd-Din) should come out and join his services because otherwise he could get killed. Najmu'd-Din replied that he had spent eighty years of his life with the Khwarazmians and it would be faithlessness to betray them in their hour of distress. He met with his martyrdom in Khwarazm in AH 618/AD 1221. *Tarikh-i-Guzideh*, p.789. Rashidu'd-Din Fazlullah writing his history in AH 710/AD 1310 is the first historian to say that he was martyred in Khwarazm. But Ata Malik Juwayni makes no mention of the event although the fist section of his work *Tarikh-i-Jahangushay* deals entirely with Khwarazm. Ibn Batuteh writes categorically that Kubravi's grave existed in Khwarazm. *Loghat Nameh*, p.366. For more details see *A Literary of Persia*, E.G. Browne, vol.ii, p.491 et seq. The following couplet is attributed to him:

divist durun-i man kih pinhani nist/ bardashtan-i sarash asani nist
imanash hazar bar talaqin kardam/ an kafir ra sar-i musalmani nist

the presence of Shaykh Rozbehan[1] in Egypt for upgrading his spiritual knowledge. Thus, Shaykh Rozbehan liberated Shaykh Najmu'd-Kubra from demerits like ego, repudiation of saints and objections to the institution of Shaykhdom and its upholders. He wrote a letter to Shaykh 'Ammar saying that those (seekers of spirituality) whose inner-self collected the rust of ignorance should be sent to him for an exercise in purification. Shaykh 'Alau'd-Din Simnani's[2] work *Iqbaliyyeh* gives fuller details on this subject.

Following the aforementioned principle, Shaykh Mahmud Sufli sent Amir Shamsu'd-Din to the assembly (class) of Maulana Burhanu'd-Din Baghdadi who was one of the accomplished and leading disciples of the Imam[3]. He was gifted with innovative faculty of resolving theological riddles. The depth and expanse of his knowledge can be judged from his writings, which included *Bahr'ul-Manaqib fi Fazail-e 'Ali bin Ibi Talib*. This treatise contains careful research on the qualities and merits of the *Choicest of the Jurisconsults* (meaning Hazrat 'Ali). In his pursuit for truth, he was among the highly accomplished masters of his time. His status and position in the realm of spiritual attainments can be understood from the fact that besides conducting Friday congregational prayers, he used to lead the daily prayers, too, at the hospice of the Imam. In his work *Fiqhu'l-Ahwat*, the Imam (Nurbakhsh) has spelled the criterian for the Imam (conductor of Islamic prayers) fit to lead the Friday prayers. A person who had the honour of conducting public prayers in the presence of the Imam (Nurbakhsh) is too exalted a personality for my estimation. There is no scope of doubting the merits of such a

[1] Renowned spiritualist of 7th century *hijra* had met with Abu'-Najib Suharwardy in Alexandria and accepted the Sufi gown (*khirqa*) at the hands of Shaykh Sirraj Mahmud. He died in AH 606/AD 1209. See *Nafahatu'l-Uns* of Jami, Teheran edition, p.235.

[2] He died in AH 736/AD 1335 in Sufiabad at the age of 77. *Makashifat* is his well-known work. See *Loghat Nameh*, pp.2–3.

[3] Nurbakhsh.

person; doing so is tantamount to misleading people. (God protect us from such an aberration.)

In short, Araki spent nearly six years in the company of illustrious saints and with their blessings rubbed off rust from his heart's mirror. He converted base metal into gold and thus prepared himself for accepting leadership in the realms of spirituality.

Shaykh Muhammad Lahiji Asiri[1]

Shaykh Lahiji was peerless among the thousands of disciples and followers of the Imam. He could influence even casual visitors so much so that they ultimately ended up becoming his disciples. His sermons touched the heart of the audience: he administered recantation to them and accepted their allegiance. He bestowed black gown (*khirqeh*)[2] and headdress to many people who recognised him as the lieutenant of the great spiritual leader. These ordinations did not fall to the share of other disciples of the Imam. This was why some of his successors and Shaykhs began criticising him. Their main objection to bestowing black gowns was that there was a recognised procedure through which a learner had to go through before he was bestowed with spiritual authority. In the first stage, a devotee had to serve the guide and learn to obey

[1] Qazi Nurullah Shustari considers Lahiji a spiritual descendant of Sayyid Muhammad Nurbakhsh to the extent that in a couplet the latter called him his spiritual son. (*Majalisu'l-Momineen*, MS, p.307). He bult a hospice in Shiraz called Nuriyyeh. Asiri was his pen-name. Lahiji died in AH 912/AD 1506.

[2] When the perfect Sufi (Shaykh) through intuition and intelligence looks into the inner self of a disciple and discerns in him signs of spiritual advancement and a sincere desire to arrive at the truth, he clads him in a special robe called *khirqeh*. A *hadith* has been cited. Once, some linen was brought to the Prophet. Among it was a blackish small blanket. The Prophet took it in his hands and said," I give it to Umm Khalid." It bore yellow and red patches on it. The Prophet told Umm Khalid that that was good for him. *Loghat Nameh*, p.451. When a Sufi meets another Sufi of higher spiritual attainment, he takes off his *khirqeh* and places it before the other as a Sufi traditional mark of respect for a Sufi of superior status.

his orders and instructions. The second stage was to elicit their allegiance, administer recantation, and call them to true faith. The third stage was to put them through severe penance and spiritual practices to strengthen their determination. Unless a seeker resolves to render service, accepts the ways of obeisance and regulates his life by conforming to what the guide permitted or not permitted, he could not be admitted to the fold (of the Sufis/disciples).

Views on Nurbakhshiyyeh

His answer was that "people generally lagged behind in their pursuit of spiritual knowledge, truth and the means of seeking the truth. I wish they could come out of ignorance and complacency and strive to liberate their lives. In order to achieve this objective, it is necessary for them to hold on to the 'strongest handle' (*urwatu'l-wusqa*)[1] meaning the true faith and hold fast to the line of proper direction (*silsilatu'l-huda*). This was not possible without accepting the practices and precepts of the Imam. I believe that people should join Imams circle and associate themselves with him and his *silsila* or order. In my opinion the example of *ahl-e bait* (Members of the family of the Holy Prophet) is that of the Ark of Noah. Whosoever jumped on to that ark, found himself a liberated person; and the one, who refused to jump, was drowned. In short, Shaykh Lahiji worked hard and made elaborate arrangements for a large number of people to embrace the dignified order of Nurbakhshiyyeh. In most of his writings Lahiji has used the attributes of *Imam-e-Zaman* and *Mehdi-e-Zaman* for Imam Sayyid Muhammad Nurbakhsh. Of his verses and *mathnavis* (long poems) that reached this land (Kashmir) one is *Asrar-e-Shahud*. It underlines love as the condition for seeking the truth and nearness to God etc.

---

[1] *Qur'an*, *Sura al-Baqr* verse 257. Strong grip. *Loghat Nameh*, p.209. Maulana says in the *Mathnavi*:

urwatu'l-wusqast in tark-i hava/
bar kashid in shakh-i jan ra bar sama.

He has also given an account of his coming to the presence of the Imam.

(verses)

The Imam had considerable regard for Asiri because he was the most outstanding of his disciples. Many a time, he had spoken very high of him. Learned scholars have given him a respectable place in their works. The Imam had almost declared him his spiritual successor. Once he dispatched him to Shiraz[1] for briefing Yusuf Mirza who, in turn, would transmit spiritual guidance to the people of that town. The letter meant for Yusuf Mirza contained pieces of advice, besides high appreciation of Shaykh Muhammad Lahiji. The substance of his words of approbation was that meeting with him (Lahiji) was as good as going on a pilgrimage to Mecca.

In Asiri's service

Shamsu'd-Din Araki benefited from his contemporary Shaykhs, erudite scholars and religious divines. He entered the services of Shaykh Asiri Lahiji at a time when the latter was in Shiraz, the prime city of spiritualists.[2]

In Shiraz, Lahiji built a hospice and guided people along the path of true faith. Before Araki actually came to his presence, the Shaykh had learnt through intuition and insight (into the secrets of the world) that a person—recipient of God's blessings, and popular among the people (of the world)—would be coming to meet with him. When, after covering a long distance, Araki arrived at the hospice,

---

[1] Shiraz is the famous capital city of the southern province of Fars and the birhplace of many Iranian celebrities, such as Sa'adi, Hafiz and Mulla Sadra. Originally, *shathra+racha* in Pahlavi and *shahr-e raz* (= Shiraz) in later Farsi. Since it was ussed as a headquarter of many ruling houses in the course of history, Shiraz preserved official records of great historical value, and hence *Shahr-e- raz* (the city of secrets) or Shiraz. See my Urdu work *Hafiz ki Shairi*, Anjuman-e-Taraqqi-e Urdu, Delhi, 1977.

[2] *be Shiraz aay o faiz-e ruh-i qudsi begir az mardum-e sahib kamalash* (Hafiz of Shiraz).

Shaykh Lahiji received him with a warm embrace. Then Araki declared his allegiance (*bai'at*)[1] to The Shaykh and submitted to the procedures and practices introduced by him (in his hospice). He rendered service to the devotees who had gone into retreat (*chilleh*)[2] and undertook to run errands for them. Thus, he subjected himself to rigorous training and service (of the mendicants and devotees) at this hospice. Eventually, this hard labour raised him to higher level of knowledge and practice in the realm of mystic science and spiritual merits. He was gradually heading to become a man of learning who would possess mystic powers too. For six long years, he rendered service at that hospice and acquired knowledge from saints who had perfected the skills in mysticism and did not waste a single minute of his life. Out of this period, he spent four years exclusively serving the disciples of Lahiji. And this labour did not go unrewarded.

Araki has said that at the hospice of Asiri Lahiji, where he spent many years, he became intimate with a kitchen attendant. His three year long infatuation for this young person was so profound as to make him completely forget himself; for a time he was indifferent towards part, the world and religion.

Love is an attribute of every mystic vicegerent (*wali).* When love fills his heart then all that remains with him are emotions not intellect . All renowned Shaykhs and mystics have worked hard during the course of their training to bring themselves to the playing field of love. They remain intoxicated with divine love. Shaykh Mohiu'd-Din 'Arabi (Ibnu'l-'Arabi)[3] has recordd that in Mecca, Shaykh

---

[1] P.14fn.1, supra.

[2] Forty days retreat.

[3] Born in AH 560/AD 1165 in North Africa, Abu Bakr Mohiu'd-Din commonly known as Ibnu'l-Arabi is foremost among the founders of systematized Sufism. Among his celebrated works are *Futuhat-e Makiyyeh* and *Fususu'l-Hikam.* The latter work is a compendium of the principles and practices of Sufism. He is considered the originator of the philosophy of "*hama ust*" meaning Omnipresence of God.

Rozbehan[1] developed infatuation for a young man. He abandoned the robes which the puritanic and abstinent usually wear. When the spell of infatuation was over, he resumed his normal robes. Shaykh Najmu'd-Din Kubra[2] (martyred AH 618/AD 1221) says that once on the banks of the Nile in Egypt, he caught sight of a damsel, and was infatuated by her. The spell was so devastating that for several days he did not eat anything. The flame of love engulfed his entire self and he felt that if there existed anything between the earth and the sky, it was only the flame of love. The truth is that temporal love is precursor to eternal love and the spiritualists have practiced it. Attractive body is the manifestation of heavenly light, which emanates from the Creator. A human being is entitled to seek that light and use it for the embellishment of his soul, his inner self. Thus, we have the physical beauty (*husn-e-surat*) and spiritual beauty (*husn-e-sirat*). Love, whether worldly or cosmic, is sheer benefaction conferred by God Almighty. However, the doctors of Qishriyyeh[3] and Mu'atazilah[4] schools keep themselves away from these experiences.

---

[1] Najmu'd-Din Kubra perfected his knowledge of mysticism from lessons from Shaykh Rozbehan of Egypt. He had made him his virtual son and given him his daughter in marriage.

[2] See p.16 supra, fn.1.

[3] One who pays attention to the literal meaning of the *Qur'an, hadith*, permitted and forbidden etc. not accepting allegorical meaning (*ta'vil*) and inference (*tanzil*) is called Qishriyyeh. Abu'l-Qasim bin Abdu'l-Karim, a renowned sufi of 4 /11th century.

[4] An important Islamic sect, which appeared towards the end of the Umayyids in 2nd century A.H. Its founder Wasil b. 'Atta, a student of Hasan-i Basri (nicknamed *'adli naubat*), differed with and marched away from his teacher, who said, "*a'etezil mana*" (he has gone away from me). Thus, Wasil's followers came to be known as *mu'atazila*. See Zabihullah Safa, *Tarikh-i Adabiyyat dar Iran*, vol.i, pp.52–57. Also see *al-farq baynu'l-firaq* (tr.) pp.17, 111. For further information on the principles and beliefs of Mu'atazila, see *'Ilmu'l-Kalam*, by Allama Shibli Nu'mani, Azam Garh, 1993 ed., p.17 et seqq.

Menial jobs

Mir Shamsu'd-Din Araki said, "Once during the retreat, the devotees (in Lent) gave me some linen (turbans and trousers) of different colours for washing. The festival (*Eid*) of Lent (*chilleh*) was round the corner. After making usual morning prayers and recitation (*awrad*), I began to work at the laundry. I spread out washables on stones and beat them under foot until mid-day prayer without a minute's break. The devotees brought more linen for washing. This kept me busy until afternoon prayers. By the evening prayer, I felt the rumbling in my stomach. My intestines had hardened and I could not move. For a couple of days, I could not even ease myself. It was after some medication and treatment that I regained normal health and got rid of constipation. However, the symptoms of this ailment remained with me for the rest of my life, and increased with the passage of time. I had to go for medication to relieve myself of constipation; I invariably took grape juice, and vegetables like spinach and soup. Despite all these (dietary) precautions, my normal digestive system was not fully restored."

Habits

In short, Mir Shamu'd-Din Araki had to undergo rigorous training and do hard labour to reach the stage of perfection. He often kept vigil at night, fasted during the day, adhered strictly to the time schedule for prayers and recitations, and performed all religious obligations with meticulous regularity. He acquainted himself with the knowledge of seven dimensions (levels) of the inner self[1] and different occult inspirations.

---

[1] The illusion may be to seven long chapters of the *Qur'an* from *sura baqra* to *sura tauba*, or to seven stages (*maqam*) through which a Sufi must pass to attain spiritual excellence. For more details see *Tarikh-i Tasawwuf dar Iran*, by Qasim Ghani, 2 vols. Teheran, 1342 AH (S). For the significance of numerical 7 in Avestic tradition, see Muhammad Moin's *Shumarah-e- Haft*, published in Teheran. Maulana says:

haft shahr-e ishq ra 'Attar gasht
ma hanuz andar kham-e yak kucheh em.

He traversed the realms of spirituality and found the secrets of the expanses of *jabrut*[1] and *lahut*,[2] the highest stages in journey in mysticism. From journey to God, he entered the expanses of journey with God.[3] He understood the concept of One-ness of God, the concepts of absorption in God (*fana fi'llah*) and preservation in God (*baqa bi'llah*). He had all these attainments during his six years service to Shaykh Lahiji in his hospice.

Shah Qasim Faiz Bakhsh

Shaykh Muhammad Lahiji used to visit Shah Qasim Faiz Bakhsh once or twice in a year. He would make a pilgrimage to the shrine of Imam Nurbakhsh too. During these visits, he would leave behind Amir Shamsu'd-Din to take care of recitation, performance of other duties and reception and guidance of the devotees (dervishes). He took with him a group of his devotees to provide them with an opportunity of being in the presence of Shah Qasim Faiz Bakhsh, and serve him for a while.

Amir Shamsu'd-Din desired to visit the shrine of the Imam. He got an opportunity during Lahijis seventh visit to Shah Qasim. Lahiji and Amir Shamsu'd-Din stayed in the service of Shah Qasim for about a month.

Shah Qasim closely watched Araki's noticeable behaviour, aptitude for service, purity of spirit and other qualities. He tested his steadfastness (in pursuit of truth), lofty courage and the level of his seriousness. He found him possessed of all these qualities. He appeared to him the pure and luminous mirror of his own heart. This was why he

---

[1] The world of God's power as against *nasut*. For fuller information on four categories into which the Sufi philosophy distributes the universes, see *Hikmatu'l-Ashraq* edited by Henry Corbin, p.246.

[2] Invisible world or the world of spirit as against *nasut*. Khaqani says:

az 'la' rasi be sadr-i shahadat kih aql ra
az 'la' wa 'hu'st markab-e lahut zir-e ran

[3] *sayr il'allah, sayru'n fi'l allah, sayr ma'allah*

prompted him to become his associate and stay in his service and company. Amir Shamsu'd-Din also discerned in him the light of spirituality and eminence and showed his willingness to be at his service. Shah Qasim desired Shaykh Lahiji to let Araki stay with him which was readily accepted. Having finished with his duties and obligations, and having left Amir Shamsu'd-Din in the service of Shah Qasim, Shaykh Lahiji left for his native place Shiraz. Shamsu'd-Din bowed his head in thanks to God Almighty who had bestowed upon him the opportunity of getting admitted into the service of Shah Qasim. His coming to this saint was like a drop of water getting absorbed in the ocean.[1]

Amir Shamsud-Din Araki said," Bayazid Bistami,[2] the foremost among the mystics, said that after receiving training in spiritual excellence from learned and exalted Shaykhs (of his time), he was admitted to the service of 'Abdallah bin Ja'afer bin Muhammad as-Sadiq.[3] He acquired from him knowledge about the secrets of the Caliphate (*khalafat*)[4], and the significance of the truth of being the preceptor (*Imamat*).[5] He attained precise understanding (of ins and outs of the domain of the Imam) and its rationale as stands endorsed by him (Ja'afer as-Sadiq). He also realised his faults

[1] This is a very popular allegory in Sufi thought. Individual soul is like a drop of water (*qatreh*), which when submerged into the ocean (universal soul) (*fana fi Allah*), finds immortality in the ocean (*baqa bi Allah*).

[2] Tayfur ibn I*sa*, (AH 181–261/AD 797–874), the celebrated mystic—also called *Sultanu'l-'Arifin*—was of fire-worshippers' ancestry (Attar in *Tadhkiratu'l-Awlia*). His followers were called Tayfuria, See *Nafahatu'l-Uns* of Jami, p.38 and *Majalisu'l-Momineen* of Qazi Nurullah Shustari to whom orthodox theologians were hostile. In AH 713/AD 1313, Uljayatu built a dome over his grave in Bistam, Khurasan. Commentators say that he was greatly influenced by the Vedantic thought and the teachings of the *Upanishads*. See *Loghat Nameh*.

[3] Sixth Imam in the Shi'a sect of Twelve (*ithna ashra*). Further notice on him is available in *Habibu's-Siyyar* of Khwanda Mir, vol.ii.

[4] The Caliphate of the Sufi pontiff or the spiritual domain of the Imam.

[5] The institution of the Imam in Shi'a sect.

and shortcomings and declared that if he had not joined the service of Imam Sadiq, he would have died an infidel.

As a pupil of Shah Qasim, Amir Shamsu'd-Din Araki attained a high degree of spiritual perfection and erudition. Repeating the words of Bayezid Bistami (or Bastami), he remarked that if he had not got the opportunity of coming to the presence of the great spiritualist (meaning Shah Qasim), it would not have been possible for him to reach the heights of perfection. Among the disciples, devotees and learned associates of Imam Nurbakhsh, Shah Qasim had the distinction of becoming his lieutenant and deputy. This proves that he was endowed with intrinsic worth.

Estimation of Faiz Bakhsh

The Imam (Nurbakhsh) himself had mentioned on several occasions his high estimation of Faiz Bakhsh. Many a time he had lucidly explained his attainments. In the *Sahifatu'l-Awlia*, he paid glowing tribute to Faiz Baksh. Once, Imam Nurbakhsh said to Amir Shamsu'd-Din, "If I survive, I shall provide you spiritual guidance. In case I die, my disciples and devotees will do that job." Imam's three-dimensional intuition (*'elmu'l-yaqin, 'ainu'l-yaqin* and *haqqu'l-yaqin*)[1] convinced him that Shah Qasim would reach the stage of mastering the science of revelation (*Sahib-e-Kashf*).[2]

---

[1] These are ascertaining through deduction, witnessing the truth and arriving at the truth. Three stages in Sufi thought are (i) dispensing worldly affairs (b) coming out of the world, and (c) finding the image in the Paradise. See *Farhang-i Mustalahat-e 'Urafa*, p.497. Also see Shabistari's *Gulshan-i Raz* (*muqaddimeh*), p.106.

[2] While a prophet performs a miracle (*m'ujaza*), a Sufi of high attainments is capable of revelation (*kashf*) and foretelling (*karamat*). One who makes revelations is *sahib-e kashf* meaning the master of revelation. The authorized Sufi spiritual guide would give two types of written certificates or letters of authority to a disciple after the latter is admitted into the fold. One was *khatt-e-irshad* meaning the certificate authorising the disciple to guide fresh entrants into the fold. The other was *khatt-e-rahi,* which was something like a passport or a document of identification (perhaps) enabling the Sufi to enter a hospice for board and lodging purpose.

In the circle of the disciples of Shah Qasim Faiz Bakhsh, nobody enjoyed as high a status as Araki did. He became the deputy to the Shah. In one of his poems, the Imam entreated his pupils and devotees to be in the service and company of Shah Qasim Faiz Bakhsh.

(verses)

Shah Qasim made gradual progress in the field of mysticism. This is why the Imam stated in *Fiqh-e-Ahwat*, "O son! You the learned and erudite seeker of a true guide, may God bestow upon you the divine light to comprehend the truth of *haqiqat*, *tariqat* and *shariat*.[1]

The Exalted Imam granted him the Certificate of Passage/ Passport—(*khatt-e-rahi*) to undertake long journeys. It contained full description of his attainments and merits (in the field of mysticism). It authorized him to accept allegiance and recantation from the mendicants who had chosen path of mysticism. (Here follow two folios giving the text of the certificate. It enjoins upon fresh recruits to feel elevated when admitted to the service of Shah Qasim).

Araki has said that Shah Qasim Faiz Bakhsh had acquired profound knowledge of the various branches of sciences. At the age of seven, he observed the movement of seven stars and its effect etc. He could make astrological tables, and had gained mastery in that branch of science. Learned men of his times were astonished at the erudition of the Shah when he was still so young; they thought of it a miracle. When he stepped into adolescence, he diverted his energies towards theological sciences. No learned scholar could surpass him in his high level of scholarship in that branch.

Shah Qasim's scholarship

Araki said that Shah Qasim was in Khurasan. Many learned men of those parts visited him frequently and benefitted from

---

[1] Three passages to spiritual attainment. For more information see Qasim Ghani's *Tarikh-e Tasawwuf dar Iran*, 2 vols., loc. cit.

his discourses. Prominent among them were Maulana Husayn Waizi[1] and Maulana Qusji,[2] both were renowned scholars in rational and deductive branches of learning. Their writings had made a profound impact on the scholars of those days. Once, in the course of a discussion about the movement of heavenly bodies and their impact, he told Maulana ‘Ali Qusji that he had some difficulty in resolving some problems of astronomical science. He asked him to stay back and resolve them for him. Maulana Qusji felt embarrassed and said that although he had reached advanced age, his intelligence was still much lower than that of Shah Qasim, and could not muster courage to speak in his (Shah Qasim's) presence. If the Shah could not resolve them, it was not possible for an old man like him to tackle the problem. Amir Shamsu'd-Din says that he was personal witness to this exchange of civilities. Amir Sayyid J‘afar Nurbakhshi said that Shah Qasim lived in his house in Khurasan. A group of people adhering to the Qishriyya School (of theology?) showed more prejudice towards the house of Mustafa than that of Marwan.[3] Out of malevolence, they spoke ill of Shah Qasim to his servants. They said that they had not heard a single word of mysticism from the mouth of Sayyid Nurbakhshi; he did not say anything about godly persons nor did he make enquiries into the comments of his father about our (Qishriyyeh) group. The Qishriyyeh scholars would sometimes meet with Sultan

[1] The author of *Anwar-e Suhayli.*

[2] A 15th century intellectual had attainments in mathematics and astronomy. Mirza Ulugh Beg put him in charge of his observatory in Samarqand. He was sent on an official assignment to the Court of Sultan Muhammad of Turkey for whom he wrote a treatise in the science of Astronomy. For further notice see *Tarikh-e Nazm-o-Nasr dar Iran*, Z.U. Safa, Teheran 1363 AH (S), pp.269–70.

[3] He was born in Mecca in 2nd century *hijra.* 'Ali granted him pardon and he, in turn, showed allegiance towards 'Ali. Mu'awiyeh made him the Governor of Medina, but al-Zubayr turned him out and he went to Syria and then laid his claim to Caliphate when Jordanians made allegiance to him. He was the first to strike Syrian dinar. *Muntahau'l-‘Arab.*

Husayn Mirza[1] and propose that if permitted, they would seek from Shah Qasim Nurbakhshi his explanation of some mystical themes set forth in the *Fususul-Hikam*[2] of Ibnu'l-'Arabi. Sultan Mirza agreed to call Shah Qasim to his presence and himself initiate a debate so that nobody had the audacity of misbehaving with him. When the meeting commenced and the volume of *Fususu'l-Hikam* was placed before the audience, Shah Qasim began his lecture on its contents without opening the book. On hearing the style of presenting his views, the audience was cut to its size. Nobody had the courage to ask any question, and his discourse continued for several days. After some days, he realised that the intention of those people (Qishriyyeh) was only to test his scholarship. Therefore he brought with him a book and showed it to the audience saying, "All of you consider *Fususu'l-Hikam* a comprehensive work on mysticism. My father, Sayyid Muhammad Nurbakhsh used to start the class of the beginners in the science of mysticism with lessons from this book. However, this work was not much useful for his pupil. Instead of this book, the one which I have placed before you remained with him a desk-book on the subject. You may go through the book and understand its contents so that after a couple of days a discussion could be held on how much you have understood it. In response to an enquiry from Sultan Husayn Mirza, Shah Qasim said that the author of the book entitled *Tajlilu'l-Zat* was Shaykh Najmu'd-Din Kubra.[3]

---

[1] The ruler from the later Timurids of Herat. d. AH 911/AD 1505.

[2] A fundamental treatise on the principles and philosophy of Sufism.

[3] Also called *Wali Tarash,* he was the founder of Kubravi order of Sufis in 6–7th/12–13th century. He was in Khwarazm when Chingiz Khan attacked and captured it. Chingiz sent a message to Najmu'd-Din advising him to come out of the city as he was going to order a massacre of the Khwarazmians. The Shaykh said that he had spent eighty years of his life in peace and comfort with the Khwarazmians and it would be faithlessness to betray them in their hour of trial. He was martyred in Khwarazm in AH 618/AD 1221. In this context I am tempted to quote this meaningful verse of Hafiz of Shiraz:

be khuban dil madeh Hafiz bebin an bewafayi ha
kih ba Khwarazmiyan kardand Turkan-e Samarqandi

For more information on the alluded event, see my *Hafiz ki Shairi*, Anjuman-e Taraqqi-e Urdu, New Delhi, 1977. Sources: Hamdullah Mustawfi *Tarikh-i-Guzideh*, p.789 and *Jam'eu't-Tawarikh.* For more information on the alluded event, see my *Hafiz ki Shairi*, Anjuman-e Taraqqi-e Urdu, New Delhi, 1977.........

He said that he had no hesitation in becoming the pupil of one who would read just one page of that book and then deliver a lecture on it. He asserted that *Fususu'l-Hikam* and *Fatuhat-e-Makki* of Ibnu'l-'Arabi,[1] the works of Shaykh Shihabu'd-Din Suhrwardy,[2] and the panegyrics of Abu Hanifa Omar Ibnu'l-'Aridh, the standard works of renowned mystics were no more than a prologue to the work he had spoken about.

The Qishriyya critics carried that book to Mulla Jami,[3]

... ... Sources: Hamdullah Mustawfi *Tarikh-i-Guzideh*, p.789 and *Jam'eu't-Tawarikh*. However, 'Ata Malik Juwayni makes no mention of the event in his *Tarikh-i-Jahangushay*. Ibn Batuteh says that he had visited his grave in Khwarazm. Hamdullah Mustawfi quotes the following quatrain of Najmu'd-Din: *divist durun-e man kih pinhani nist/ bardashtan-e sarash be asani nistimanash hazar bar talaqin kardam/ an kafir ra sar-e musalmani nist.*

[1] Born in AH 560/AD 1164, Mohiu'd-Din Ibnu'l-'Arabi was an outstanding Sufi precptor from Andalusia. He travelled extensively in Asia Minor, where contemporary rulers and leading personalities showed him great respect. He died in Damascus in AH 638/AD 1240. He wrote no fewer than 200 books and tracts, some of which like *Fusus'l-Hikam* and *Fatuhat*-e *Makki* are still among the source of information on the doctrines of Sufism. Some of his contemporaries accused him of harbouring the concpt of re-incarnation (*hulul*). His originality in interpreting philosophical concept of the Unity of Being (*wahdatu'l-wujud) and Discovery* of the Manifest (*Kashf-e-shahud*) infuriated religious extremists. However, some of his contemporary or later contemporary theologians like 'Abdu'r-Razzaq Kashi, Siyuti and Firuzabadi tried to simplify his thoughts. See *Loghat Nameh* of Dehkhuda, (under Ibnu'l-'Arabi), p.320.

[2] Renowned mystic and founder of Suharwardiyeh order of Sufis, Abu Hifs Umar Shihabu'd-Din was born in Suharward, a town in Zanjan province of Iran, and lived during 6–7th/12–13 century. He was a student of Shaykh Sa'adi and Awhadu'd-Din Kirmani. *Awarifu'l-Mu'arif* is his well-known work on mysticism.

[3] Born in AH 817/AD 1414 in Kharjard, Jam, Nuru'd-Din Abdu'r-Rahman Jami studied almost all branches of science prevalent in his days. He was an outstanding poet and prose writer. A contemporary of Mirza Shahrukh, Jami was a staunch follower of Naqshbandiyyeh order of Sufis and held Khwajeh Ahrar in high esteem. Jami is known to be critical of the Shi'a but at the same time historians and commentators have called him a controversial figure. See *Epilogue* written by 'Ali Asghar Hikmat and incorporated in Allama Qazvini's work titled *Jami*. He has many works to his credit including two most famous of them, namely *Baharistan* and *Tohfatu'l-Ahrar*. Nurbakhshis are highly critical of Jami; they even did not hesitate to call him "faithless". Amusingly, Nurbakhshi thinkers and writers of contemporaneous times produced two books almost borrowing the title from Jami's works. These are (i) *Baharistan-i-Shahi*, a history of Kashmir written in AD 1622 (translated into English with annotations and published by this writer in 1991), and (ii) *Tohfatu'l-Ahbab* (the work in hand)

a fervent advocate of Naqshbandiyyeh order.[1] Though they joined heads they could not comprehend even a single proposition in it, not even the simple meaning. In utter helplessness, they returned the book to Sultan Husayn Mirza. In reply to a question of Sultan Husayn Mirza if Muhammad Nurbakhsh used to deliver lessons to his pupil from *Fususu'l-Hikam*, he repeated that the beginners received lessons from that work. Even four or five year old children too listen to the Imam delivering lessons from this work and they understood something of its meaning.

Mir S'adu'l-Huqq Akbar

Once the Imam was delivering a lesson from *Fususul'-Hikam* to Pir-e Hamadan Mir Sa'du'l-Huqq Akbar. The son of the Imam, who was one or two years younger to Shah Qasim Nurbakhsh, was present in the class of Pir-e Hamadan. A delicate and profound theme from the work came up for discussion and explanation. Pir-e-Hamadan could not comprehend it. He could not comprehend even the substantiation made by the Imam during that discourse. Mir Sa'du'l-Huqq was hardly four or five years old at that time. He looked at Pir-e-Hamadan, smiled and said that, he (the Imam) had explained it but still he did not understand. Pir-e-Hamadan looked at him sternly and asked what he had understood from those discourses. Then the Imam turned to Pir-e-Hamadan and told him reproachingly that even a child of five years had understood what he said. It showed that he was too naive a learner.

The company of the Imam from early days of his life had helped him develop the faculty of discovering the truth and cleansing inner self of impurities. Mystics attain these qualities

[1]One of the four main Sufi orders founded by Khwajeh Bahau'd-Din Naqshbandi (6/13 century) in Bukhara. *Dalilu'l-'Ashiqin* is his work on Sufism. He died in AH 791/AD 1388 and remains buried at Qasr-e 'Arifan in Bukhara. His followers are also called *Khwajehgan*. See *Ibn Khallikan* vol.i, p.213 and *Rayhanatu'l-Adab*, vol.i, p.183.

only after doing rigorous penance. When the Imam passed away, all the leading spiritual personalities, his lieutenants and the Shaykhs of the day unanimously agreed to make Shah Qasim his successor.

Shaykh Muhammad Ghaibi

In the towns and villages of Arak and Khurasan people widely mourned the death of the Sayyid. His devotees shed tears on this sad event. Many of them composed elegies to commemorate the poignant occasion. Included among them was Shaykh Muhammad Ghaibi, who happened to be away from Solghan (Iran) at that point of time.

(verses)

Araki said that Shaykh Muhammad Ghaibi hailed from Solghan (Iran) where his ancestors owned landed, moveable and immovable properties besides a hospice, which was under their control. He was among the followers of the last category (of the Imams). When the fame of the venerable Imam reached the people of Arak and Khurasan, Shahrukh Mirza[1] ordered his expulsion to lands beyond the Oxus. He took up residence at a village called Shifat (?), a well-known town of Gilan. People from adjoining places who thirsted for divine knowledge came to him. Stimulated by the urge to seek truth, Maulana Ghaibi gave up his home and his properties, and proceeded on self-imposed exile to Gilan. As he came to the presence of the Imam, he found that thousands of people from Iran and the Arab world had gathered there. People were ready to sacrifice their lives and other material possessions for his sake. All yearned for access to him. Owing to a large crowd of people assembled there, many could not get a chance to come closer to him. Shaykh Ghaibi found that he was far less resourceful than others. Therefore, he sat silently in a corner and hung his head ruminating over his position. After some

[1] Youngest son of Timur who ruled at Herat from 1409–47 AD.

time, a person, who happened to know Shaykh Ghaibi, recognised him and called him. The Shaykh sought from him information about the ways of the life of devotees, their religious and spiritual practices and the system of Lent and seclusion. The acquaintance informed him about the severe penance and spiritual training, that the followers were to undergo. Shaykh Ghaibi found that he did not posses enough strength to undergo the prescribed penance and spiritual training. Therefore, he lost the hope of benefiting from these exercises. He enquired of his friend if there was any other kind of service, which he could render to please the Imam. His friend said that he could not make out what service the Shaykh could render when there were many servants and attendants running a host of errands. However, if he stayed there at least for one year, he might be able to find some odd job for himself. The acquaintance added that he had heard from the Imam that he was disposed to admit a person, who would bring him the news about the death of Shahrukh, to the hospice and help him achieve spiritual eminence without undergoing severe penance and training prescribed for the purpose. Shaykh Ghaibi thought that bringing the news of Shahrukh's death to the Imam was much easier a task than to undertake harsh penance for gaining access to the Imam. He decided to go to Balkh[1] and stay there. At that time, Balkh was the capitol of the kingdom of a despicable person (Mirza Shahrukh). Now he waited for the death of Shahrukh.

[1] Ancient Bactria. In the inscriptions of Darius the place name is Bakhtri, in *Vedas* as Bhakri, *Avesta* as Bahli and original Bayodro. After Alexander's conquest, Balkh was the centre of Graeco-Bactrians, then of Kushans and Hephthalites. In pre-Islamic times it was a Buddhist centre and famous for the cloister of Navabahar, the head of which were the Barmaks (Barmecides) who seem to have established political control over the city. It was also famous for Zoroastrian tradition with fire temples. See *Barmakyan* translated by Meykadeb, Teheran.

Letter to Shahrukh

One day he learnt that a messenger of Imam Muhammad Nurbakhsh had arrived in Balkh to deliver his letter to the *dajjal*[1] of the times (meaning Mirza Shahrukh). Maulana Muhammad Ghaibi asked some of his known persons to procure him a copy of that letter. After reading its contents, he inferred that the days of waiting were over and that the king was very near the end of his life. (Text of the letter is omitted).

Shaykh Ghaibi in Geelan

The detestable Shahrukh did not survive long. Within a year of receiving the letter in question, he descended into the depths of hell. Leaving Balkh, Maulana Ghaibi proceeded post-haste to Gilan; he shortened the time of by reducing three stages to one. He arrived in Shifat hospice, which stood on the heights (of a hillock). Some Sufis (mendicants) had occupied a portion of those heights. They served water to the pilgrims and looked after their comfort. The pilgrims who come from

---

[1] Antichrist, the false claimant, called Abu Yusuf, who will appear at the "end of the time" (*akhiruz-zaman*). According to Islamic tradition he will immediately precede Mehdi and will perpetrate atrocities and oppression for forty days or forty years. Mehdi will put an end to him and restore justice in the world. Blind of one eye and born of a Jewish mother, he remains tied to a rock on an island. He rides a donkey and has a good quantity of food and water with him. Probably he will appear in Khurasan or Kufa or from the Jewish locality in Isfahan. He claims to be God and performs miracles to mislead people. *Mehdi's* struggle against him is the struggle of virtue against vice or that of light against darkness as in Zoroastrian mythology (*Ahuramazda* vs Angaramenu/*Ahriman*), which has gone into the Jewish tradition. See *Lughat Nameh*, p.271.

Iskandar amad o dar-e yajooj dar girift
Isa rasid o naubat-e dajjal dar guzasht (Khaqani)
kujast sufi-e dajjal chashm mulhid shakl
bigu bisuz kih Mehdi-e dinpanah rasid (Khwajeh Hafiz)

Iran[1] with the intention of meeting with or serving or paying obeisance to the Imam would first come to the post of Sufis. After partaking of food and drinks, they proceeded to the hospice of the Imam. Sufis briefed them about the hospice. The mendicants stationed at or coming down from those heights could be seen from a distance.

Maulana Ghaibi came down from the post of the Sufis on the heights. At that time, the Imam was sitting outside the hospice, and there was a crowd of dervishes, mendicants and seekers of spiritual excellence around him. Some of them said that they had seen an armed horse-rider coming down the heights toward the Sufis.

Foretelling

The Imam said, "This rider has to bring an exciting piece of news for the gentry and the ascetics. Wait till we hear it from him." As the crowd waited rather impatiently, the armed rider entered the courtyard of the hospice and dismounted. Without waiting even for a moment, without detaching arrows and the quiver from his accoutrement, and without laying down his sword and shield, he came to the presence of the Imam and conveyed: "O Venerable Imam! The despicable Shahrukh has gone to hell." The Imam cast a glance, full of affection and benevolence at him and saw the light of *velayat*[2] in his eyes. He smiled gently, which was as good as alchemy for Maulana Ghaibi. Thereafter Shaykh Ghaibi fell in a trance and began to dance with arrow and quiver still slinging from his shoulder. He uttered the loud cry of dervishes (*hoo/yahoo*).[3] He brandished the sword, shield and arrow in the air. Many gnostics and seekers of truth stood up to join him in his ecstatic

---

[1] At this point of history, it appears that Khurasan meant the kingdom of later Timurids, which included some eastern parts of present Iranian territory.

[2] p.9fn.2 supra.

[3] The Sufis' utterance made intermittently during ecstasy and trance. *Allah hoo* or ya hoo is the most frequent expression Sufis use when an ecstatic mood overtakes them. Hoo means great, majestic, limitless and endless etc. It also means void, desolate and intangible.

dancing. Everybody present shared in the trance and the grace bestowed upon the audience by the Imam. In his presence they danced and raised *hoo* as if angels in heavens too got rapturous after beholding that spell of mysterious ecstasy of the dervishes. Those in the stage of *malakut*[1] (the world of angels) and attired in green, and the inmates of the hospice of *jabrut*[2] (one of the four mental or spiritual stages for a Sufi) and clad in black gowns,[3] all fell into a trance. In an emotionally charged state, tears rolled down their cheeks.

One Shaykh Muhammad Samarqandi had adopted *Firaqi* as his pen name. He was present in the assembly of the Imam and composed the following panegyric (*ghazal*) on this occasion:

anam kih zahr dar kaf-e man angabin shavad
div az latafatam bemisal hoor-e-'ain shavad

On the same day, the Imam conferred upon Shaykh Muhammad Ghaibi the authority for accepting allegiance (*bai'at*)[4] as well as repentance (*tauba*) from prospective mendicants.[5]

---

[1] Loc. cit. The Subtle World.

[2] The World that demonstrates God's power. loc.cit.

[3] This indicates that the two categories of Sufis wore gowns of two different colours; the green was for those who had reached the angelic stage and the black for those who were at a lower stage. 'Abbasid Caliphs are reported to have introduced black gowns for the royalty and the state flag was also of black colour (See Ibnu'l-Athir, *al-Fihrist*). The Sufis appear to have carried forward the tradition.

[4] Binding oneself in obedience to a mentor or spiritual/religious guide. In Islam the tradition of giving hand in the hand of one to whom allegiance is made, goes to the Prophet himself. After seizing Ka'aba, the Prophet obtained allegiance from his male followers. He asked them to give their hand into his hand. Having done that, the Prophet asked the female followers to declare their allegiance to him. They did so but instead of giving his hand into their hands; the Prophet asked for a pitcher of water, put his hand into it, took it out and then asked the womenfolk to put their hands into the pitcher one by one. They did as directed and the ritual of *bai'at* was thus completed. *Persian Encyclopedia* cited in *Loghat Nameh*, p.554. Nasir Khusrav Qubadiani says:

goftam kih kanun an shajar o dast chihguneh ast
an dast kuja juyam o an bai'at o mahzar

[5] Repentance as well as acceptance.

The chronogram for the date of Imam's death has been recorded in the fragment *'sirraj-e-khuda'*, which corresponds with AH 869/AD 1464. Many poets composed elegies on his death.

Shah Qasim as successor

After performing the death rites (of the Imam), and acknowledging condolences for the departed soul, all followers, Shaykhs, devotees and students of the Imam presented themselves at his hospice. They came to Shah Qasim collectively and said, "We fervently desire to remain in the service of the *Shah-e Velayat*, the Protector of the Land (meaning Shah Qasim Faiz Bakhsh). You may kindly take care of Imams mission as his successor and lieutenant. You will kindly lead the devotees and followers of the Imam and improve their spiritual levels. We do not recognize anybody else as the successor and lieutenant of the Imam." But Shah Qasim turned down their offer and said, "I do not bother myself about leadership. I would advise you to dispatch two dervishes (inmates) to Hamadan[1] to call Pir-e Hamadan so that we install him as the successor of the Imam. This is because the Imam preferred him over the rest of his followers."

Shaykh Alwandi

Pir-e Hamadan's real name was Shaykh Alwandi. He was among the first rank followers of the Imam. All of Imam's subordinates have praised him saying that he held a higher position and status in spiritual eminence in comparison to others. He has composed a *mathnavi* (long poem) titled

---

[1] Hagmatana of Pahlavi texts and Ecbatana of Greek historians. The town, situated to the west of Teheran, is famous for the tomb of great philosopher Abu 'Ali Ibn Sina (Avicenna d. AD 1002)

gushayam raz-i lahut az tafarrud
namayam saz-i nasut az hayula (Khaqani)

Wardat-e-Ghaibi. In *Sahifatu'l-Aulia*, Shaykh Alwandi has been profusely praised for his big achievements. An encomium ascribed to him in that work begins with this verse:

ay naqd-e- nowe insan vey rahnuma-e eyan
mushkil kusha-e asan har dard ra tu darman...

Nurbakhsh in trance

Amir Shamsu'd-Din Araki said: Once I enquired about the account of the Imam from Shaykh Mahmud Bahrai. He gave me full detail and recounted this story that he had heard from the Imam himself. The Imam had said, "Once I rambled in the high spheres and made thousands of rounds and went beyond the cosmos until I reached the endless sphere of *lahut*[1] which is the eternal world. There again I made thousands of rounds and found myself liberated from all encumbrances of person, action and perception. I found that for me all the worlds—*jabroot, malakoot* and *nasoot*[2]—had disappeared and that I had got submerged in God. In each of the thousands of rounds, I found total effacement, and, after effacement, I found revival and immortality. During the period of revival, I murmured these verses. During the gaps of effacement, I ascended to a state of dance and music (*wajd wa samaa*):[3] The poem begins with this verse:

[1] Alwand is the mountain to the north of Hamadan. Its older form is Arvand as used by Maliku'sh-Sh'uara Bahar in one of his compositions.

[2] From t-he Arabic root *lah* meaning the World of God. According to Sufi thought, the place of perennial life in things is *nasut*. It is in this world that a traveller along the path of spirituality (*saluk*) attains *fana fi Allah*—immersion in Allahnd then he attains the stage of immortality or eternity in the world of *lahut*.

mahram-e nasut-e ma lahut bad
afarin bar dast o bar bazoot bad (Maulana)
gushayam raz-i lahut az tafarrud
namayam saz-i nasut az hayula (Khaqani)

[3] Trance is allowed in Sufism. In fact it became inseparable from the life style of the Sufis, especially those of the Dancing Dervishes. For details, see relevant portions in Qasim Ghani's *Tarikh-e-Tasawwuf dar Iran* in 2 vols. under *sama'a*

aye ahl-e- dard jooshi wey ashiqan khurooshi
kaz dast-e- mey furooshi noshide aim nooshi.

Dervish Mahmud Bahri says: Once towards the closing part of the night, Pir-e Hamadan emerged from the door repeatedly uttering a thousand times words in praise of angels. He also recited couplets from the above-cited *ghazal*. In the night of *m'eraj* the Holy Prophet had returned from the sphere of *lahut* back to the sphere of *nasut* (ascension). He had brought thirty thousand secrets of the eternal world for Hazrat 'Ali in particular. The Holy Prophet had heard these secrets from God Almighty and ordered that these were not for disclosure.[1] Sufis discourage revealing of heavenly secrets.

In the morning Hazrat 'Ali brought in ten thousand secrets before the Holy Prophet and gave their full commentary.

The Imam heard the messages of the eternal from Pir-e Hamadan. He was surprised and asked where he had been in those wee hours. Pir-e Hamadan answered, "I was sitting in a corner and you were in a state of trance. I beheld with my own eyes the hilarity of trance, and I heard your *ghazal* as well, which I have learnt by heart". Many such events happened between the two. The Imam has recorded the spiritual excellence of Pir-e Hamadan in his work *Sahifatu'l-Aulia*.

The Imam has recorded some events pertaining to Pir-e Hamadan also in his *Kitab-e Nuriyyeh* too, which had been compiled for Shaykh Shihabu'd-Din Umar. It contains thoughts on rays of spirituality, transience and permanence, explained with examples. *M'erajiyyeh* treatise also contained two events pertaining to Pir-e Hamadan. People of extraordinary eminence like him are very rarely born.

Alwandi's succession

Shaykh Alwandi arrived at the shrine of the Imam in Solghan (Iran). After fulfilling all customary obligations pertaining to

[1] Sufis discourage revealing of heavenly secrets. Hafiz of Shiraz says:
goftam an yar kez u gasht sar-i dar buland
jurmash in bud kih asrar hoveyda mi kard

the rituals of condolence, Shah Qasim called all senior Shaykhs, devotees, dervishes and followers and told them that he wanted Pir-e Hamadan to be the vicegerant of the Imam. Therefore, all devotees should formally express their allegiance to him, obey his orders and follow his instructions and observe his verdict about the prohibited and the permitted. On hearing these words of Shah Qasim, Pir-e Hamadan demonstrated utmost humility, and tears rolled down his cheeks. In choked voice he said to Shah Qasim," I try to assess my own condition with searching eyes to know my status. Through the knowledge of the physical eye and the eye of belief,[1] I have learnt of your superior and lofty achievements in the realm of spirituality. I shall be too brazen faced a fellow to put your hand on my own. Kindly be affectionate and munificent to me and do not push me in the death trap of aspirations. In truth, I have not yet entered the life (of spirituality/Sufism) and you want me to put my hand on your hand. I am disappointed and hopeless of my life."

Having said this, he turned to the dervishes, followers and Shaykhs of the Imam and said, "My dear friends! It speaks of your lack of intelligence and of your ignorance that we have more than a hundred times read in the work of Amir Sayyid 'Ali Hamadani, (the Second 'Ali),[2] titled *Masharibu'l-Azwaq*[3] that with the Imam—the guide—among us; it is only blindness to submit to somebody else".

---

[1] *aynu'l-yaqin wa ilmu'l-yaqin.*

[2] (*'Ali Thani*) Ibn Muhammad bin 'Ali bin Yusuf Hamadani d. AH 786/ AD 1384. Another title given to him is *Amir-i Kabir* meaning "Grand Lord". In the beginning of the Memluk kingdom, this title was given to all those who had seniority in service and in years. Consequently, there was a whole group of Amirs of whom every individual was called *al-Amir al-Kabir*. In the days of Shaykh-al-Umari (AH 752/AD 1352) the title was reserved for the Commander-in-Chief (*Atabek al 'Askar*) of the kingdom. Thereafter it became the most common title of the Commanders-in-Chief, besides that of his rank. See M von Berchem, CIA, 1: Egypt, pp.276, 292 et al. Also see *Encyclopaedia of Islam*, vol.i, p.444.

[3] The *Loghat Nameh* mentions his only two books, namely *Ikhtiyarat as-Sultan fi at-tasawwuf* and *Awrad-e-Fathiyyeh* The author of *'Ayanu'l Shi'a-e Amoli* includes him among the Shi'a divines of his day (p.34). *Loghat Nameh*, pp.282–83.

When dervishes and mendicants heard these words of Pir-e Hamadan, they decided to show their allegiance to Shah Qasim and follow his instructions. He taught them the ways of a Sufi s life such as seclusion, penance, virtue and methods of spiritual achievement (*tariqat*).

Mir Araki and Shah

Mir Shamsu'd-Din Araki had the honour and privilege of entering the service of Shah Qasim who, in turn, bestowed benedictions upon him. Before entering the service of Shah Qasim, Mir Araki had a dream, which he related to Shah Qasim. "In the dream, I found myself going along a path by the side of which many streams, rivulets and rivers were flowing. There was plenty of water. I made ablution and took a dip in the waters of each stream. But I did not feel satisfied and no ablution provided me consolation. At last, I came to a place where a big river was flowing on its bank, I took off my clothes and plunged into its waters. I had a bath and I began swimming in the water. This bath and this ablution gave me complete satisfaction." Shah Qasim interpreted the dream in these words: "In the path of mystic attainments and penance, you have acquired knowledge and training from many spiritual guides and Shaykhs. However, that did not bring you satisfaction. Now God willing you will find satisfaction and consolation in my service. Here, after doing penance and spiritual exercise, you will attain your goal. You should (a) have lofty courage, (b) make no room for doubt and skepticism, (c) always be devoted to me, (d) always follow what I permit and what I forbid, (e) never falter in rendering service, and (f) observe strictly all duties and obligations with determination." Thus, Amir Shamsu'd-Din Araki heard the exhortations and sermons of Shah Qasim from his own tongue. He resolved to abide by his instructions in order to achieve his real objective. He was always ready to perform the duties assigned to him. If Shah Qasim summoned any one of his servants at the hospice to run some errand, Araki would feel unhappy why he was not be doing it. For days and nights, he would wait for someone to run an odd errand. All that he did was more than what any other devotee could do. Shah Qasim felt very happy with his etiquette and cultured habits. He prayed for Shamsu'd-Din Araki.

Travels

Once, Shah Qasim proceeded on a journey to Khurasan. He rode a swift horse. "As we proceeded, he handed a bottle of acid to me. During the travel, he spoke of high position of the Imam in the science of mysticism. He got so much absorbed in recounting details that he forgot he was riding a fast running horse. We had covered nearly twenty forsakhs (thirty miles) and arrived in a village. In response to his question, I told him the name of the habitat. In surprise, he loudly said that we had gone ten stages farther. He asked for the bottle of acid, which I handed back to him. He was very happy and prayed for me thrice saying, "May you be honoured in this world and hereafter".

Once, Mir Araki came out of his house with the intention of bringing himself to the service of Shah Qasim. On arriving at the hospice, he found that Dervish Shahi, whose anthology of verses is well known, was sitting on the threshold. He was waiting to send his obeisance and thanks to Shah Qasim through somebody going that way. When he saw me, he handed over a melon to me requesting that I present "his humble gift" to Shah Qasim. He took it in his hand and cast a look at me and then smiled and recited this verse:

man na shahi khawahm o ney khusravi
anchih mi khwaham man az tu an tui
(I do not want either kingship or monarchy/ All that I want is you and you alone)

Master and disciple

A disciple of Shamsu'd-Din Araki said that he thought the relation between a preceptor and his disciple was like that of lovers. In the beginning, the lover seeks the beloved.

Ultimately, the beloved seeks the lover. However, in the beginning, one is desirous of becoming the pupil, but in tuth the preceptor seeks the pupil. He used to say that the heart of the preceptor is thousand times more lovingly and affectionately inclined towards the pupil. Once we used to say that the love of a master for his disciple was hundred times more than the love of a mother for her child.

Amir Shamsu'd-Din Araki showed great steadfastness and perseverance in learning the skills of mysticism through practical observance of penance and training in the presence of Shah Qasim. His rank and status among the disciples was elevated, with the affection, guidance and supervision of the Shah, he began to soar higher in the skies of spiritual sciences. He equipped himself with all outwardly and inwardly secrets of transcendence to mystic world and understood the truth of its various stages viz. *jabroot, nasoot*, *malkoot* and *lahoot*.[1] He mastered all the three stages of knowledge viz. *'ilmu'l-yaqin, 'ainu'l-yaqin* and *haqqu'l-yaqin*.[2] The veil of illusion was removed from his eyes and now he could see the truth. These lofty qualities of spirit endeared him to Shah Qasim, who believed that religious tenets of the Islamic religion were fully reflected in his appearance (in the world).

The Title

Shah Qasim conferred the title of Shamsu'd-Din upon him. He told his disciples that thereafter, they should call him by the name Shamsu'd-Din Muhammad Araki. (Here the author has one paragraph which describes the technical attainments of Araki in the field of mystical and religious training).

In short, Araki acquired perfection in all the branches of training and self-discipline only through the guidance of

---

[1] loc.cit., pp.35, 43.

[2] The definition of the three terms is: 'ascertaining through reason, ascertaining through vision and arriving at the truth'. According to Sufi thought, the first is dispensing worldly affairs; the second is exit from the world and the third and last is finding the image in paradise. See *Muqaddimeh Gulshan-e Raz*, p.106 and *Farhang-i Mustalahat-e 'Urafa*, p.497.

Shah Qasim. He gave him permission to accept allegiance from his followers,, approve forgiveness, issue decrees, guide disciples, lead prayers and accept leading the seekers of knowledge in their pursuit of mystic sciences.[1]

Shah Shams and Araki

Shah Qasim entrusted his eldest son Shah Shamsu'd-Din to the care of Araki so that he would learn the skills of doing penance and sitting in *chilleh.* He learnt the principles and etiquette of the 'path of mysticism.[2] From this teacher, he came to know many things even about worldly wisdom. He prepared to give up mundane ways of life and seek higher values. Araki said that at one time Shamsu'd-Din sat among his friends showing affection to his relatives and dear ones. The assembled people there talked about current affairs. After having their supper they continued their leisurely talk. Then Shamsu'd-Din addressed the assembly requesting them to tell him about the deficiencies they had found in his character. He said he would endeavour to overcome bad habits if these were brought to his notice. People in the audience spoke of various things, such as clothing, gait, mannerism etc. But, all these did not fall in the category of vices. Araki, in his turn, said that his friends were only taking recourse to expediency and not identifying the real vices. On Shamsu'd-Din's insistence, Araki said that the major vice was miserliness, which, he said, could overshadow all his good qualities. Surprised, Shah Shams asked when he had acted miserly. Even after serving meals to all friends present, he was still called a miser. Araki told him that he had been the disciple of Shah Qasim. If he had forty gold coins in his hand, he would give these away to the disciples together with the meals served to them and would never speak a word about it. But, it was strange that being the son of Shah Qasim, he had spoken about forty gold coins and still did not consider it bad manners. Thereafter Shah Shams increased it to sixty gold

[1] These are the supreme powers vested in a Sufi saint of the highest level.

[2] In the technical language of Iranian Sufism it is called the Path (*suluk*) and one choosing to go along the Path is called *salik.*

coins (*shahi*) and enhanced the daily allowance (of his devotees) as well.

In short, Shamsu'd-Din Araki brought up Shah Shamsu'd-Din as his pupil. When he completed his training and studies under Arakis personal supervision, Araki conferred upon him (Shah Shamsu'd-Din) the authority to accept allegiance (*baiat*) from his followers. Thus, as a mark of regard and respect for the spiritual leadership of Shah Qasim, Araki was the first to offer his allegiance to Shah Shamsu'd-Din. After him, the members of the house of Shah Qasim and all the people connected with it offered their allegiance to Shah Shamsu'd-Din as a mark of continuity of spiritual leadership.

The divines

Many people in the path of asceticism have offered allegiance to the divines. This was by way of setting an example for others. The system never gave rise to corrupt practices nor did it bring any blemish to the fair name of the preceptor. It is also observed that many divines offered their allegiance to the lieutenants of their fathers or grandfathers. They received training from them until they reached a higher status in the hierarchy. Shaykh Muhammad Azkani[1] became the *pir* or the preceptor of Amir Sayyid 'Ali Hamadani. However, divines did quarrel with the preceptors of their fathers or forefathers. Amir Sayyid Muhammad Hamadani, the son of Amir-i Kabir (Sayyid 'Ali Hamadani), had to go into exile from the place and house of his father and was forced to go on a long journey in alien lands.[2] Misled by the devil and the Satan, he could

[1] See *Loghat Nameh.*

[2] See *Baharistan-i-Shahi,* (tr.) K.N. Pandit, Calcutia, 1991, pp.37–38. This is a curious revelation and is not found in many important histories of Kashmir, and as such, merits further investigation. On the face of it, one may say that Muhammad Hamadani had given up the sect professed by his father. Dedmari, the author of *Waqa'at-e-Kashmir* says that Mir Muhammad married Bibi Bara'a, the daughter of Seh Bhatt who had converted to Islam and assumed the name of Malik Saifu'd-Din. After his conversion he became Prime Minister during the reign of Sultan Sikandar, the Iconoclas. See *Waqa'at-e-Kashmir* (tr.) Shamsu'd-Din Ahmad, Delhi 2001, p.72 et seq.

not protect himself from the enmity and opposition of the followers of his father. Many among the progeny of the *pirs* and preceptors overpowered the followers of their fathers while dealing with worldly matters. Without obtaining permission from their fathers, they occupied the seat of their fathers or grandfathers and posed as their successors.[1]

In his work *Kashfu'l-Haqaiq*, Imam Sayyid Muhammad Nurbakhsh has expressed his disappointment with such type of *pirzadgan* (meaning the sons of religious divines).

In short, despite enjoying the authority to accept allegiance or repentance from others, and despite ascending the special seat of spiritual guidance (*masnad-e irshad*), Amir Shamsu'd-Din Araki remained in the service of Shah Shamsu'd-Din and continued to impart training and refinement to him meticulously.

Faiz Bakhsh and Shams'u-Din

As long as Shah Qasim remained at his station and in his country, he would dispatch Amir Shamsu'd-Din to the followers and admirers of the Imam in different countries and regions. *Zakat*[2]—money and other offerings would also be sent along with him. Besides, Shah Qasim would also send through him letters to the elders and notables of those lands. These letters generally carried the theme that Shamsu'd-Din Araki was the choicest among the disciples and foremost among the crusaders and that they should make allegiance at his hand because that was tantamount to making allegiance to him (Shah Qasim).

[1] This is an indirect insinuation aimed at Muhammad Hamadani. Is it that Muhammad Hamadani openly deviated from his father's path of Shi'a propensity and went along the Suuni path? (tr.)

[2] Giving up a portion of wealth one may possess in excess to what is needed for sustenance. *Zakat* is one of the five pillars of faith. *Zakat* money can be given in support to those fighting for God (*al muqatelun fi sabil Allah*). Other taxes/ voluntary subscriptions are *kharaj, sadaqa, 'ushr* etc.

Sultan Husayn Mirza[1]

Shamsu'd-Din Araki said: When Sultan Husayn Mirza became the ruler of Khurasan, the reins of (spiritual) power and authority over Iran and Turan[2] also passed into his hands. A group of Khwaje Abdulla Naqshbandis[3] disciples and humble followers came to the ruler, and exhorted him to invite their mentor ('Abdullah Naqshbandi) to his court. They impressed upon him that it would be a mark of good omen for the monarchy. They also insisted that the ruler should make allegiance at his hand and obtain guidance from him. Since 'Abdullah Naqshband happened to be the patron-saint of the

---

[1] Also called Sultan Husayn Bayaqara, he was the ruler of the house of later Timurids at Herat (Hari of *Chehar Maqala* of Nidhami Uruzi of Samarqand). A man of letters, he used Husayni Gorkani as his pen-name. He has a *Diwan* to his credit and wrote a treatise titled *tanzil* on the theme of Sufism. Kamal'd-Din Husayn Fanai dedicated his work *Majalisu'l-Ushshaq* to him, which was later on published in India in his name. See *Hayatu'l-'Arifin*, vol.i, p.317, and *Sabk Shinasi* of Taqiu'd-Din Bahaar, vol. iii. The Indian edition of *Majalisu'l-Ushshaq* carried colourful stories of sexuality and sodomy of some of the ancient prophets, religious and Sufi personalities. It also carries pencil sketches of these stories.. See *Loghat Nameh* Dehkhuda, Husayni Bayaqara, p.646.

[2] According to *Shahnameh*, the geographical region that formed the kingdom of Tur—the son of Feridun—came to be known Turan. But we also come across the twin names of *Tur o Tajik* indicating the two distinct ethnic groups of Central Asian regions. It appears that Khurasan and its adjoining eastern regions up to the Amu River formed the traditional region of Turan. It has to be noted that Amu has changed its coure with the passage of time. Previously it woauld disgorge in the Aral Sea but after it changed its course it took the direction of the Caspian Sea. Now it dries up before reachig its destination. For detailed information on ethnic groups see Babajan Ghafurov's monumental work on Tajikan.

[3] Nasir'u'd-Din Abdullah, genrally known as Khwajeh Ahrar, was a distinguished scholar-saint descending from the line of Naqshbandi Sufis. He is reported to have been a pupil of Shaykh Ya'qub Charkhi and Nizamu'd-Din Khamosh. He was the guide and mentor of Maulana Abdu'r-Rahman Jami. The rulers of Turkistan, and in particular Abu Saeed, showed him great consideration. He died in AH 896/AD 1490 in Samarqand. *Hazrat Khwajeh Naqshband aur Tariqat-e Naqshbandiyeh* by Shamsu'd-Din Ahmad, Srinagar, 2001, p.572. For more details see *Tarihi Adabiyyat dar Iran*, Safa, *op. cit.*

progeny of Amir Timur, the goodwill and obeisance of the house of Timur was associated with that order (*silsilah*). Shahrukh Mirza and his offspring were acquainted with and devoted to that order.

But Sultan Husayn Mirza did not pay attention to their words; he did not accept their advice. Shahrukh Mirza and his progeny were also devoted to Khwaja 'Abdallah. They had no idea that the descendants of Mirza Sharukh would once again ascend the throne of the kingdom. The offspring of the Mirza received no special attention during their childhood. The reason for this animosity and revengefulness was that during the heyday of his power, Sultan Husayn did not maintain relations with Khwaja 'Abdallah. He had no liaison or connection with any of his (Naqshbandi's) disciples or camp followers. Even during the dominance of Mir 'Ali Sher[1]

---

[1] Alisher ibn Ulus or Kichkaneh was the celebrated minister of Sultan Husayn Bayaqara. A learned scholar, poet, administrator and public official, he wielded a facile pen both in Turkish and in Farsi. In his Turkish poems he used *Navai* as his penname (*takhallus*) and *Fani* in Farsi. Born in AH 844/AD 1440, he was a classmate of Sultan Husayn Mirza. As students, the two had made a pledge to help each other if they rose to great heights in life. Sultan Husayn Mirza, a descendant from Chaghatai of Chingiz's line, came to rule over Transoxiana, Kashghar, Balkh and Badakhshan regions. Alisher Navai dedicated himself to academic pursuits. On receiving an invitation from Sultan Husayn, Alisher left his native place Samarqand and came to the court of the Sultan in Herat where he was given the high post of the Lord of the Royal Seal (Mohrdar). Shortly after, Sultan Husayn made him his Prime Minister and with that he rose to great eminence. Scholars visited his rich library. One of them was Khwandamir, the author of the famous *tadhkira* titled *Habibu's-Siyar*. Finally, he relinquished his official position, became a recluse (*dervish*) and interacted for most of his time with the famous contemporary poet Abdu'r-Rahman Jami. However, Sultan Husayn continued to hold him in high esteem. He built many tombs and shrines including those of Imam Reza, Shaykh Faridu'd-Din 'Attar in Nishapur and of the mystic poet Qasimu'l-Anwar in Langar. In all, the number of these structures is computed at 370. He died in AH 906–07/ AD 1500–01. See: *Majm'au'l-Fusaha*, vol.i, p.3195; *Tadhkira Nasirabadi*, p.470; *Fihrist-e Kitabkhaneh-e Majlis*, Teheran, vol.iii, p.367; *Fihrist-e Kitabkhaneh-e Sipahsalar*, Teheran, *Habibu's- Siyar* (Khayyam Publications), vol.iv, pp.137, 159 et al.; *Dasturu'l-Wuzara* of Khwandamir, pp.397, 404 et al.; *Tohfa-e Sami*, p.179 and *Miratu'l-Khayal*, p.172.

too, Sultan Husayn Mirza did not accept any word of the *Khwajehgan*.[1] His heart was with the Nurbakhshiyyeh order.

Invitation

Sultan Husayn Mirza invited to his presence the prominent disciples of the Imam in Khurasan and felt comfortable in their company. Through them he came to know about the lofty qualities of Shah Qasim. This prompted him to seek his company, and he yearned for a meeting with him (Shah Qasim). He sent many letters and missives to the saint along with many exquisite gifts and invited him to a visit. The Sultan responded to these letters vigorously. Owing to the entreaties of the ruler and his eagerness to visit the holy city of Meshad, and above all to enjoy the change in climate, Shah Qasim decided to proceed to Iran and Khurasan.

Shrine of Imam Reza

Covering stage after stage, he arrived at the holy shrine of Shah-e-Khurasan (Imam Reza), where he rested for a few days. Sultan Husayn Mirza received the news of his arrival in Meshad. He dispatched a delegation of his courtiers and confidants to the holy town to accord him formal reception. After meeting with him in that town, the team escorted him to Herat with due protocol. Sultan Husayn Mirza stood up from his throne, mounted a horse, and rode about two miles for Shah Qasim's reception. After the meeting, he escorted Shah Qasim to the palace in Bagh-e-Zagan.[2]

---

[1] The followers of Khwajeh Bahau'd-Din Naqshbandi and adherents of his Sufi order are called *Khwajehgan*. The inference from this sentence is that contrary to the disposition of the later Timurids of Herat, Sultan Husayn Mirza adhered to Nurbakhshiyyeh rather than Naqshbandiyyeh order of Sufis. Thus, contrary to what his father Shahrukh Mirza professed, he was not of Sunni but of Shi'a faith.

[2] A famous park and the seat of mediaeval royalty in Herat. It was destroyed in AH 875/AD 1470. During its heyday, the place was decorated profusely for an occasional jamboree. Owing to its colourfulness, it had received the epithet *par-e tawus*, meaning the wing of the peacock (*Waqa'atu'j-Jannat fi Awsaf-i Madinatu Herat*, vol.ii, p.48). "The Uzbeks took 'Ali Quli Khan Shamloo and his companions to Bagh-e Zagan, the largest park in the town, and tore them up into pieces in AH 997/AD 1588," *Zindagani-e Shah 'Abbas Awwal*, vol.I, p.126. "This garden was also the scene of reception given to the Indian fugitive prince Muhammad Humayun Gorkani" (*'Alam Ara-e 'Abbasi*, p.98).

zauq-e gulgasht-i Khurasan rafteh ast az yad-i ma/ dar sawad-e Hind sayr-e Bagh-i Zaghan mi kunam ('Ali Quli Salim) *pas angah garden sar afraz sarvsu-e Bagh-i Zaghan kharaman tadharv (Hatifi)*

The Sultan showed him extraordinary hospitality and ordered a great feast in his honour. A few days later, the Sultan and his queen Khadija declared their formal allegiance to Shah Qasim, and the saint, in return, accepted their vow of abstinence (from prohibited). Courtiers and senior government functionaries hosted feasts in his honour by turns.

Nurbakhshiyyah in Herat

A number of government functionaries, eager to reform and purify their lives came to Shah Qasim. They were admitted to the fold with due honour. A number of leading personalities of the town, men of higher and of lower ranks, one and all, came to pay him obeisance. Their number increased day by day. The minister of the royal court, Mirza Cheetah, became the most sincere and dedicated devotee of the saint and accepted allegiance to him. He was admitted to the fold of his disciples. In this way, the Nurbakhshiyyeh order (of Sufis) grew day after day and the genuine[1] Hamadaniyyeh pathway (*tariqah*) was adorned with ever-increasing lustre. The Naqshbandis could not keep going. Many scholars and men of erudition in Khurasan, who had kept their heart's mirror clean from the rust of enmity against the Sayyids, and who did not entertain inimical disposition towards the members of the family of the Holy Prophet (*ahlu'l-bait*), came to his august presence. They entered his services and soon benefited from him by acquiring religious knowledge.

Chilleh

Shamsu'd-Din Araki said: "(When) the winter set in (in the lands of Khurasan), Sultan Husayn Mirza made a fervent request to Shah Qasim that he greatly desired the saint to enter into Lent (*chilleh*) in Herat enabling him (the Sultan) to see in person the ways of Hamadaniyyeh order and the line (*silsilah*) of Nurbakhshiyyeh system and tradition. He believed it would

[1] The word "genuine" indicates that there existed controversy over the sect to whom the followers of Hamadaniyyeh order belonged, viz. Shia or Sunni.

enable him to understand the ways and methods of the faith. After some persuasion, Shah Qasim reluctantly acceded to the request.

There was a building of large dimensions in Bagh-e-Zaghan. Shah Qasim selected it for lent. Separate cells were made in the walls of the building and each window made up a separate room. The corners of the compound were reserved for offering congregational prayers and recitations. The lent house (*chilleh khaneh*) and the confines for secluded meditation were repaired. The news of Shah Qasim performing *chilleh* spread all around the province of Khurasan. The reputed Shaykhs and divines housed in various hospices in towns all flocked to Herat. A large number of uninvited people also headed towards Herat. They, too, wished to enter lent in the presence of Shah Qasim. The season was also conducive for the lent and the event received wide publicity in the length and breadth of Khurasan.

As the time of going in for lent drew near, people in large groups squatted in the compound. Shah Qasim came out in the large compound and found a host of Shaykhs and dervishes sitting in clusters. Some of them wore colourful robes with black turbans on their heads; others were clad in black from head to foot with turban—ends fallen on their shoulders. He did not like the groups of people in these costumes. They came to him saying that they desired to enter lent in his presence. Though he was not happy with them, still he treated them with due regard, neither accepting nor rejecting their request.

After performing the dusk-time prayers, Shah Qasim spoke to the groups of dervishes as these words: "I beg all dervishes and Shaykhs to excuse me. Please oblige me by returning to your places because it is not possible for me to concede your request of going into lent along with me. The ruler has insisted on me to perform the *chilleh* so that he acquaints himself with the procedures of lent. If the king wanted only to have a look at those going into lent, I would have shown you to him. But the fact of the matter is that he wants to know the procedure for the observance of lent and not just to see the faces of lent-goers."

Having heard the objection, the dervishes were impressed and prepared to return to their native places.

Then Shah Qasim ordered all his servants and attendants, who were always at his command, to make arrangement for furnishing water sacks, chefs, firewood collectors, fodder suppliers and many others with specific skills for routine services during the lent. Having made these arrangements, the *chilleh* commenced.

Amir Shamsu'd-Din reported that Shah Faiz Bakhsh invariably made secret prayers during each night when on a move.

Sultan in the presence of Faiz Baksh

Except the people closest to him, nobody knew anything about his personal life. He always kept himself away from public gaze. Sultan Husayn, along with a group of his courtiers, was present when the dervishes went into lent. He saw with his own eyes the procedure and associated practices and protocol of this exercise. He told Shah Faiz Baksh to leave behind one of his disciples so that (through his instrumentality) he would also become part of the dervishes and obtain more information about the rules and regulations of the practice of going into lent. Shah Faiz Baksh replied, "Your Majesty should exert control on your mind. Pay me regular visits and light a lamp or two in the lent house." Thereafter, Sultan Husayn Mirza regularly went to the lent house twice or thrice a week where he closely observed the behaviour of the dervishes in lent. Sometimes he learnt the rules from them. He would meet with Shah Faiz Baksh a couple of times during a year, sit with him for some time and benefit from his company. He invariably came to see Shah Faiz after the latter completed the *chilleh.*

Shamsu'd-Din had not intended to seek seclusion on the instructions of Shah Faiz Baksh when he went into lent in

Herat. He spent the night in the lent house reciting (prayers) and chanting hymns. During the day, he looked after the affairs of the household besides spending some time in training the new comers. He had to look after the training and schooling of the servants and attendants engaged in performing household chores. He would distribute eatables among the dervishes. At the time of breaking the fast, he literally became their humblest servant.

Ulema show allegiance

At the end of the forty-day long lent a large group of people comprising nobles and distinguished personalities of Herat, besides a number of learned men and theologians of Khurasan became his sincere and respectful devotees. Prominent among them like Mulla 'Ali Qusji, Maulana Husayn Waiz,[1] Maulana 'Abdullah Hatifi[2] and many others reputed for their scholarship, declared their allegiance to Shah Faiz Bakhsh. They have written about their allegiance to and respect for him in their works.

Enmity of Mullas[3]

There was a group of ignorant *mullas* and stupid sinners whose hearts were besmeared with prejudice and animus against the House of the Holy Prophet (*Ahlu'l-bait*). They nursed malice and enmity towards the progeny of 'Ali waliu'llah ('Ali the Apostle of God). They found that in the

---

[1] A literary figure of considerable eminence, Husayn Waiz Kashifi (d. AH 910/ AD 1502) is the author of a fine specimen of Persian prose work, namely *Anwar-e Suhayli*, which is an abridged recension of *Kalileh wa Dimneh*. *Raudatu's-Shuhada* is his important and valuable biographical work. See *Majalis'n-Nafais* of 'Alisher Navai, *Tehran*, pp.93–94.

[2] Hatifi was a contemporary but a junior of Jami. He was a poet who is said to have written three *mathnavis* in reply to Nizami's *khamsa*.

[3] Mulla invariably means the clergy of Sunni sect whereas for the clergy of Nur Bakhshyeh sect he uses the term dervish/sufi/*ulema* etc. It is almost contemptuous use of the term *mulla*. Most of the members of Hindu priestly class in Kashmir who were converted to Sunni Muslim faith were invariably given the epithet *mulla*.

company of Shah Qasim Nurbakhsh, Sultan Husayn Mirza was gradually ascending to spiritual and temporal heights and status and that the *ulema* and the distinguished scholars were turning to Shah Qasim in larger numbers day after day. Out of envy and malice, vices ingrained in the blood of these wretches, they resorted to creating disturbances. They started teasing the attendants of Shah Qasim and leveling false allegations against his servants. As long as Sultan Husayn Mirza was not afflicted with disease and illness, and Mir 'Ali Sher,[1] his prime minister, was not that powerful, the employees of the hospice of Shah Qasim were not faced with any danger or harm.

The credibility and influence of Shah Qasim increased day after day. Sultan Husayn Mirza continued to show him more respect and regard. After having performed the lent, Shah Qasim often used to say that he never did an act of dissimulation. He said that in the present lent, he had been hypocritical and he did not know what would be the fruit (treatment) that God Almighty might give him in return of it.

Abu'l Ma'ali's demise

Amir Shamsu'd-Din Muhammad said: "Shah Abu'l-Ma'ali was the youngest son of Shah Qasim. He was the apple of his father's eye. Shah Abu'l-Ma'ali was with him during his travels in Khurasan. His other sons stayed back in Arak. Abu'l-Maali suddenly took ill and was confined to bed for a few days. Shah Qasim sent for the physicians of Khurasan to examine him. He took upon himself the duty of giving the patient regular medical treatment but all efforts for his recovery failed. After a few days, destiny played its role, and he had to proceed from this world of labour and suffering to the other world of peace and tranquility. Shah Qasim immensely grieved the demise of this dear child. In a state of utter despondency, he said that the death of his dear son was

[1] loc. cit. p.

the result of that lent, which he had not undertaken for the sake of God Almighty.

Buried in Herat

Sultan Husayn Mirza and the elders and nobles (of Herat) and friends and associates from far and near joined the condolence meeting held in connection with the demise of Shah Abu'l-Ma'ali. Sultan Husayn had earmarked a nearby place for his grave. The walls of this graveyard were adorned with gold, silver and rubies carrying various designs of tile and marble work. The Sultan suggested to Shah Qasim to bury the dead body (of Abu'l-Ma'ali) in that graveyard. He thought that after his death, his dead body would find a place adjacent to the grave of a descendent of the Prophet. This should be the source of God Almighty's grace upon him (Sultan Husayn). However, Shah Qasim declined the offer and begged to be excused on the ground that his house was of dervishes, and did not have any connection with royalty so that their dead are buried in their graveyard. Shah Qasim desired his son's body to be buried in the graveyard of the dervishes and the king should be satisfied with it. Thereafter, Shah Qasim instructed me as this, "Shamsud-Din Muhammad, go to the site of the grave of Amir Husayn Sadat, and dig a grave towards its foot for my son where he will be laid to rest." This Amir Husayn Sadat is the author of the work *Nuzhatu'l-Arwah* and among the prominent vicegerants (*khalifa*) of Shaykh Bahau'd-Din Zakariya.[1]

---

[1] Also called Bahau'l-Haqq, Shaykh Zakariya (AH 578–661/AD 1182–1262) was the foremost spiritual successor to Shaykh Shihabu'd-Din Suharwardi, and the founder of Suharwardiyyeh order of Sufis in India. Born at a place near Multan, he travelled to Khurasan, Bukhara and Medina to acquire knowledge. After returning from the pilgrimage of Mecca, he joined the services of Shaykh Suharwardi in Baghdad and became his disciple. On the behest of his spiritual guide, he built an impressive hospice in Multan. A Sufi of strong personality, he did not permit anybody to show him traditional obeisance. In due course of time, a large number of people in Sindh, Punjab, Herat, Bukhara and Hamadan became his disciples. Among his more prominent followers were Fakhru'd-Din Iraqi (the author of a mathnavi *Ushshaq Nameh*) and Amir Hasan Harawi. See Browne's *A Literary History of Persia*, vol.iii, pp.46–47, 99, 194; *Riyadhu'l-'Arifin'*, p.174, and *Nafahatu'l-Uns* of Jami, p.329.

Among his works are *Zadu'l-Musafirin*[1] *Kinzu'l-Ramuz* and *Bai'at Nama Husayni*. He remains buried in the protected area of Herat.

The burial

After performing the funeral rites over a dead body, the coffin was brought to the graveyard where Sayyid Amir Husayn had been laid to rest. Among the people who joined Shah Qasim in the funeral procession were Sultan Husayn Mirza, his ministers, nobles, courtiers and court officials, Sayyids, *ulema*, scholars, friends, well-wishers and men from different occupations. When the burial was over and the rites were performed, Shah Qasim declared mourning for three days. Thereafter he instructed Shamsu'd-Din Araki that for the ensuing forty days he should get together the recitors at the shrine of Abu'l-Ma'ali for recitations from the holy book, especially the *sura furqan*. He was told to perform this duty without any fault and with meticulous regularity. Shamsu'd-Din said that the recitors and those who had learnt the *Qura'n* by heart, as well as the poor and the mendicant who assembled at the grave, were served bread and soup every day. After forty days of recitation, a big meal was served to all recitors and mendicants, after which they dispersed to their respective destinations.

Shaykh Muhammad Lahiji

At a time when Shah Qasim had made Khurasan and Herat his stations, Shaykh Muhammad Lahijhi came to Khurasan from Shiraz on some mission.[2] He also wanted to meet with Sultan Husayn Mirza. On his arrival in Herat, Shah Qasim told Araki that Shaykh Lahiji was in town and he would be their guest for a few days. He was to be looked after well and all assistance

---

[1] This should not be confused with the famous work of the same title (or Zadu'l-Musafir) of Nasir Khusrav Qubadiyani, the reputed poet of Ismai'ili faith.

[2] The nature of the mission has not been made clear to us. But in any case it appears to be an important one.

had to be extended to him for completing his mission. Shah Qasim arranged a special tent, which Shaykh Lahiji occupied and continued with his mission. He would call upon Shah Qasim once or twice a day to discuss some difficult matters pertaining to the mysteries of the path of spirituality. Sometimes Shah Qasim would also visit him in his private residence and spend some time in his company. Once when Shah Qasim was with the Shaykh, in the course of their conversation, Shah Qasim asked some questions about material sciences.

Shaykh Lahiji's son happened to be with his father and he began addressing the enquiry of Shah Qasim. He became very aggressive in his presentation, which weighed heavily on Shah Qasim. But he lowered his head and kept quiet. In fact, Shah Qasim virtually ignored what he said. Araki says that he was too greatly disgusted with the way in which Shaykh's son addressed Shah Qasim. He knew by experience that whenever his heartbeat intensified it indicated for sure that some serious damage or tragedy was about to happen. "I told the people present in that gathering that the youth was likely to meet with some physical or mental danger. A few days later, that young person was taken ill. Medicines were administered but to no avail, and finally he expired. He, too, was buried in the graveyard of Mir Husayn Sadat.

Ascetic in Herat

Amir Shamsu'd-Din Muhammad Araki said: There lived an ascetic in Khurasan. He was counted among the ones who were absorbed in the thought of Creator. He had abandoned all worldly connections and had severed relations with his kinsfolk. He had chosen a sequestered place to live in; cast only a perfunctory glance on his visitors and attributed acquiring his faculty of absorbing the rays of spirituality to Amir Sayyid Zainu'l-'Abidin. Staying in an old mosque in Herat, his fame had spread in Khurasan and Arak. Kings,

Sultans and great persons all desired to meet with him. However, he never stepped out of the mosque and maintained no connection with anybody.

If at any time he emerged from the mosque, he behaved very rudely with the people out there. He humiliated them and kept them away by denouncing and repudiating them. He had to be entreated a thousand times before he listened to any one. Despite all that he would avoid meeting the supplicants. Several leading personalities spoke very high of him to Sultan Husayn Mirza with the purpose that the Sultan might be motivated to seek him.

At last, one day Sultan Husayn Mirza decided to proceed to the place of the ascetic for a meeting. A group of *mullas* accompanied him on the mission. On his arrival at the mosque, the ascetic declined to come out. People entreated him and tried to prompt him for a meeting with the Sultan. But, he would not budge. Thereupon Sultan Husayn Mirza suggested that Shah Qasim be requested to come over to the place so that the ascetic might come out to see him. The *mullas* did not want the ascetic to come out while the Sultan was there. If he did come out, he would, as usual, insult the Sultan and cause him embarrassment. However, Sultan Husayn did not understand the hidden purpose of the *mullas*. He then dispatched one of his confident employees to Shah Qasim with the request to come to the place urgently.

Shah Qasim mounted a camel and proceeded towards the mosque where the Sultan had arrived. As Shah Qasim came close to the mosque, the ascetic drew a heavy sigh and demonstrated his eagerness. People standing outside tried to listen intently to what he said. Suddenly he burst into reciting this *ghazal* in a melodious voice:

mujdeh aye dil kih masiha nafasi mi ayad
kih ze anfas-e khushash buy-e kasi mi ayad[1]

---

[1] This is a celebrated *ghazal* of Khwajeh Hafiz of Shiraz.

Reciting the concluding verses of the *ghazal* in question, the ascetic came out of the mosque, moved briskly towards the camel, which Shah Qasim rode, held the camels nails and kissed them, and in ecstatic mood recited in loud voice the concluding verse of the *ghazal*. Sultan Husayn Mirza observed how in all humility the ascetic bowed before Shah Qasim. Addressing Shah Qasim, the Sultan said that he was eager to meet with the ascetic. He had come several times but each time he was disappointed. This time again the ascetic cared least for him and did not come out of the mosque. That was the reason why he had requested Shah Qasim's presence at the spot, and this stepping out of limits might be excused because, after all, he (Sultan) was a devotee.

Rumours in Khurasan

During the three days of Shah Qasim s rest in Khurasan, people in Arak suddenly floated a rumour that Yaqub Shirazi had arisen at the head of a strong force and captured the capital of Arak and was now heading towards Khurasan for capturing some of its parts. Owing to the serious illness of Sultan Husayn Mirza, the rulers and lords of the region were viewing with each other in their adventurous designs. This rumour spread like wild fire and reached the ears of Sultan Husayn Mirza. His generals and functionaries expressed serious concern. Sultan Husayn Mirza called his advisers, secretaries, counselors and government functionaries to discuss the matter. After serious deliberations, they decided to dispatch someone to Arak to gather intelligence so that preparations for a battle were taken in hand. They also decided unanimously that they needed to take Shah Qasim into confidence. One of his disciples proceeded to Arak to take stock of things in person and ascertain the veracity of the rumours. Moreover, many of Shah Qasim's devotees were fully acquainted with the topography of those regions. The advisers and senior government functionaries of Sultan Husayn made humble submission to Shah Qasim that they were impatient to receive his munificence. They hoped that Shah Qasim would dispatch one of his attendants to Arak for ascertaining the truth in the rumour. On their part, they would start preparations for a war. They entreated the Shah that only one of his servants should undertake this mission. Shamsu'd-Din Muhammad was to run the errand. He had instructions to go post haste and return quickly. Sultan Husayn Mirza ordered that necessary arrangements for Araki's mission be made, and he (Araki) proceeded towards Arak.

Departure

Sultan Husayn Mirza ordered that horses be kept ready at each stage of Arakis arrival for ensuring his quick movement. Mir Shams made good use of this facility and combined three to four stages into one.. If one horse looked fatigued, he rode another. In this way, three days journey was reduced to one day. Thus the distance from Herat to Daresht,[1] which usually took one month to cover, was done in twelve days, and he arrived in the house of Shah Qasim. He conveyed to his people about his (Shah Qasim's) welfare. In Daresht Amir Shams was taken ill with diarrhea. A physician who lived in the house of Shah Qasim was sent for. He prescribed wild animal's roasted meat and Amir Shamsu'd-Din recovered within a couple of days.

On making an enquiry about the rumoured attack of Yaqub Shirazi, he learnt that it was baseless. Only false rumours were spreading in Khurasan. Amir Shams halted at Daresht for one more day so that the "princes of high order" (meaning the sons of Shah Qasim) could write letters for Shah Qasim, giving information about various events. All relatives, acquaintances, near and dear ones took time to write their tales about the pangs of separation and their eagerness to see him back. On the third day, Amir Shamsu'd-Din started on his

[1] Now called Taresht. It is situated to the west of Teheran. See *Tarikh-e nazm-o-nasr dar Iran*, Saeed Nafici, p.274.

return journey to Khurasan carrying with him the bunch of letters for Shah Qasim. On the twelfth day, he presented himself before Shah Qasim in Herat. The entire journey took him twenty-five days in all. Soon after the afternoon prayers, he met with Shah Qasim and presented him the bunch of letters. He read them and was delighted to know about the welfare of his sons and relatives. Then Shah Qasim instructed Amir Shamsu'd-Din to proceed to the court of Sultan Husayn Mirza and report to him what he had come to know about Yaqub Mirza's adventure because he (Sultan Husayn) was impatiently waiting for news and had been regularly enquiring about Araki. His impression was that he (Araki) would have arrived in Arak that day while in reality he was back from this long journey. Thereupon Shah Qasim prayed for Araki's health and sought God's blessing for him.

Mir Araki awarded

Though it was an odd time of the day (evening), Shah Qasim sent an informer to the court of Sultan Husayn to convey him the news of Araki's arrival. The Sultan had thought that the rumour of Yaqub's attack might be true since Shaykh Shams had returned post-haste. Immediately he sent his messenger to Araki to confirm the truth about the rumour. Amir Shams passed on the letters to the messenger—the letters he had brought from Arak. Then he asked the messenger to convey to Sultan verbally that the rumour was entirely false and baseless. Sultan Husayn was very happy to know the truth. He sent the messenger back to Amir Shams saying that he (Araki) should go and see Shah Qasim that very moment. Both of them were expected to be with him the next day to take stock of the latest situation in the light of the information collected by Amir Shams. After receiving the message, Amir Shams went to the lodging of Shah Qasim, and spent the night with him. Next day in the morning both of them came to the palace of Sultan Husayn Mirza.

The Sultan mounted the throne and held the court (*durbar*), in which all nobles, ministers, and leading personalities were present. Amir Shamsu'd-Din recounted the entire story and the situation of the regions he had recently visited. His reports gladdened everybody. The nobles, chiefs, satraps and leading personalities of the town who had gathered there were relieved of the anxiety created by the rumour of the uprising led by Yaqub Mirza. Everybody appreciated the speed with which Shamsu'd-Din Araki had completed the difficult mission. The Sultan conferred many presents on Shamsu'd-Din Araki, which included many precious things.

Kashmir mission

Amir Shamsu'd-Din Araki said: Shah Qasim took care of Sultan Husayn Mirza's treatment of some ailment. He had found some relief in his chronic illness (under the treatment of Shah Qasim). He felt slightly better and stronger. This was the reason why Sultan Husayn Mirza had rejected other physicians and continued with the treatment by Shah Qasim. In his turn, Shah Qasim also took great pains to provide him the best possible cure. However, the appropriate medicine, which Shah Qasim administered to his royal patient, was not available (in the region of Herat). The Sultan ordered for procurement from places mentioned to him. His employees had to search and procure it and then only could Shah Qasim prescribe the medicine. Once Shah Qasim said that there were some medicines which were necessary for the treatment of Sultan Mirza. But procuring these herbs and elixirs was a very difficult task. These were found in the mountains of Kashmir and the rocks of Tibet.[1] Kashmir was a place far away and the

[1] Reference could be to the famed medicinal compound called *shilajeet* by the Indian physicians. People in olden times believed that *shilajeet*, sort of black coloured hardened jelly was obtained from special rocks in the mountain heights of Tibet and Ladakh in Kashmir region. *Shila* in Sanskrit means a rock stone. Classical Persian poets have often used the term *mushk-eTabbati* meaning the Tibetan musk.

long-distance travel was fraught with many hardships. It would take a long time to go and come back.

The Cause of Causes (God Almighty) had ordained that in the 'proposed world' (*'alam-e-ijab*) the auspicious steps of Amir Shamsu'd-Din Muhammad would bring cure to the sick, and true guidance to the people steeped in ignorance and those who had gone astray from the right path.[1] The dazzling rays of this Sun (Shams)[2] of true guidance would kindle the candles of truthful direction to remove the darkness of *kufr* (infidelity) and aberration. The visit became a source of spiritual guidance and discipline for the sinful and the heretical (people of Kashmir).[3]

Sultan Husayn Mirza pondered over the matter. His enlightened mind could not think of any person other than Shamsu'd-Din Muhammad who was capable of undertaking the mission. Thus under the supreme ordination of the Divine Will of the Lord, and also as a result of deep introspection and wisdom of Sultan Husayn Mirza, it was resolved to approach Shah Qasim with the request that Amir Shamsu'd-Din Muhammad be deployed to proceed to those regions (Kashmir and Tibet). Since he had completed the mission to Arak at a record time, it was, therefore, expected that he would show the same urgency in going to Kashmir, procuring the herbs and returning to Herat. After a couple of days, Sultan Husayn Mirza requested Shah Qasim who, in turn, kept it pending for a

---

[1] This sentence clearly shows that the primary purpose of Araki's visit to Kashmir was to procure herbs and medicines. His effort of propagating Islam of Nurbakhshiyyeh sect in Kashmir was only a by-product of the actual mission. The illusion is obviously to the valley of Kashmir as a stronghold of Hinduism.

[2] Pun on the word 'Shams'. The allegoric use of *Shams*, darkness, *kufr*, aberration, guidance are self explanatory, keeping in mind the achievements of Araki in Kashmir as we shall see in the pages to follow.

[3] The sentence reveals that even at this point of time, Islamic faith had not taken firm roots in Kashmir and those who had been converted to it earlier were given to proselytizing.

few days. However, because of Sultan Husayn insistence Shah Qasim could not avoid according his permission. He told Amir Shamsu'd-Din in soft tones that he did not want to keep him distanced from his company even for a moment for Shah Qasim did not feel relaxed and comfortable without his company. But the request from the ruler could not be ignored. He could hardly reject it? Amir Shamsu'd-Din said, "Your auspicious tongue has uttered the words. I bow in obedience. I promise to lay low my head in deference to your instructions. Should your holiness choose to cast me into leaping flames or order me to jump into the fatal whirlpools, I shall not hesitate even for a single minute to obey your command. I can never think of not proceeding to Kashmir when Shah Qasim desires me to undertake the visit."

On the following day, Shah Qasim went to see Sultan Husayn Mirza and announced that he had acceded to the Sultan's desire and that Shamsu'd-Din Muhammad would proceed to Kashmir to procure the medicines. He told Sultan Husayn Mirza to appoint him (Shamsu'd-Din Araki) as his emissary so that befitting presents were sent to the rulers and kings of those lands. The secretaries and scribes were directed to write letters to the rulers and other leading personalities of those lands (Kashmir) commensurate with their status.[1] Orders were also issued for providing Shaykh Shamsu'd-Din with equipment and expenses of the two-way journey.

It took Araki a few days to arrange equippage for this journey. Travel expenses, equipment, horses, arms and many other requirements were taken care of. Letters from the Sultan

[1] It is not clear whether the courtiers and officials at the court of the ruler of Herat had full knowledge of the rulers, nobles and courtiers of Kashmir and Tibetan regions. However, it is certain that concerned circles at the court of the rulers of Herat were aware of the mission of Mir Sayyid 'Ali Hamadani, his son Mir Muhammad Hamadani and their Sayyid companions to Kashmir.

were made ready for local rulers in Kashmir and Tibet. Shah Qasim chose a very auspicious day and time for the departure of Araki. The full details of this long travel and happenings related to it will be recorded in the second chapter of this work.

Chapter II
Araki's First Visit to Kashmir: His Miracles, Kashmiris, and Araki's Return

Two systems are provided for a beginner on the path of spirituality. These are: serving the guide and following his precepts.

First system

Enlightened minds are eager to move towards God Almighty. In doing so, they eschew attachment to their place of origin and habitat. People dear to God go out in search of a spiritual guide and preceptor. This entails travels to foreign lands and forsaking their families, children and wife. Only after severing these connections can they hope to find a spiritual guide. The company of the preceptor lends purpose to their lives. We know of several preceptors who did that. After undertaking long journeys, Shaykh Najmu'd-Din Kubra[1] (d. AH 618/AD 1221) came to the presence of 'Ammar Yaser[2] (d. AH 582/AD 1186). 'Alau'd-Din Simnani, the great spiritualist (d. AH 736/AD 1335) had to traverse the expanses from his native place Simnan to Baghdad to meet with

---

[1] pp.16fn.1, 21, 28 supra.

[2] p.16fn.2 supra.

Shaykh 'Abdu'r-Rahman Isfaraini[1] (d. AH 766/AD 1364), Shaykh Ali Dosti[2] (d. AH 734/AD 1333) and Shaykh Mahmud Muzdaqani,[3] all had to undergo rigours of travel and suffer privation in order to find their spiritual guide Shaykh 'Alau'd-Dawleh. The honourable Imam and the cream of the progeny of the Sayyid of Sayyids (the Holy Prophet)—meaning Sayyid Muhammad Nur Bakhsh[4]—had to cover several stages (of physical journey) to come to the presence of Khwajeh Ishaq (martyred AH 826/AD 1442) and to attain a high status in the spiritual world. Thus the Cause of Causes has helped many sincere scholars and travellers along the path of divinity, to help them to come into contact with spiritualists of various

[1] *In Nafahat'l-Uns*, Jami says 'Alau'd-Dowleh Simnani descended from a princely house of Simnan. At the time of his departure for Hejaz in AH 687/AD 1288, he met with Shaykh Nuru'd-Din Abdu'r-Rahman. Two years later, he received permission to guide his pupils. During a period of 16 years when he took up his abode at the hospice of Sakakiyeh, Simnani went into retreat no fewer than one hundred-fortytimes. He died in AH 736/AD 1335 at the age of 77 and was buried in the graveyard of 'Imadu'd-Din'Abdu'l-Wahhab. *Kitab-e Makashifat* is his well-known work in mysticism. Iranian scholar Muzaffaru'd-Din Qazi published a tract with the title *Asar wa ahwal-e 'Alau'd-Dowleh* in which he listed 28 works of Simnani. See *Habibu's-Siyar*, (Khayyam Publication), Teheran, vol.iii, p.220, *Tadhkira* of Daulatshah Samrqandi, pt.iv, *Atashkadeh Azer* (Shu'ara-e Simnan), and *Hidayatu'l-'Arifin*, vol.i, p.108.

[2] See *Loghat Nameh*

[3] See p.69 infra

[4] Muhammd bin 'Abdallah (Sayyid) Musavi Khurasani, generally known by his title Nurbakhsh was a 9th century (AD 14–15th century) leading personality who founded the Nurbakhshiyyeh order of Sufis. Born in Qain (Khurasan) in AH 795/AD 1392, he first received lesson from Ibn Fahd Hilli and later on became a disciple in the system (*tariqat*) of 'Alau'd-Dowleh Simnani and Khwajeh Ishaq Khatlani. The latter conferred the title of Nur Bakhsh upon him, and finally elevated him to the position of a spiritual guide (*masnad-i irshad*). However, owing to a mischief of wile people, he became the target of the anger of Sultan Sharukh Mirza, which forced him to go into hiding. After the death of Shahrukh in AH 850/AD 1446, he reappeared in Rey and began his spiritual and religious mission. He died in Solqan in AH 869/AD 1464 and remains buried there. See *Rayhanatu'l-Adab* vol.i, p.243, *Majalisu'l-Momaneen*, p.119, *Riyadhu'l-'Arifin*, p.154 and *Taraiqu'l-Haqaiq*, vol.3, p.30.

categories like *aqtab, afrad, akhyar* and *awtad*).[1] Through their intercession, the seekers have been able to reach the heights of perfection.

Second system

At times God Almighty desires that the seekers of spiritual guides and preceptors need not step out of their homes and lands. God Almighty does not disperse their food in far off lands and climes. From their birth up to the end of their lives, they continue in their places of origin. God Almighty sends the spiritual guide to them in the light of the Qura'nic verse *inallaha ta'ala muttaka li yesauqu'l ahl ilalah*, so that the seekers have the fortune of receiving the excellent quality of guidance. Thus if they are true and sincere in their quest, a perfect guide is sent to them. Therefore, many perfect teachers have forsaken their homes and material comforts and volunteered to undergo travails of long and arduous journeys to provide the nectar of guidance to the thirsty. In order to fulfil their mission, they have travelled from clime to clime and region to region. God Almighty ordains that those who attain high position in the realm of spirituality take abode among the fortunate people in countries and towns who are to receive training and guidance from them. Such exalted persons as guide the people along this path are in truth the inheritors of the Holy Prophet as the holy book says *inalazina ya bay aunak inam ye bayaun allah*. They are the recipients of the power of accepting allegiance from people. They deserve to be called lieutenants of the Imam. There are a large number of

---

[1] *Qutb* literally means the pole/pivot. *Aqtab* is its plural. According to Sufi tradition, there is one supreme spiritual leader, the *qutb* at one given cycle of time. *Awtad* is the plural of *watad* meaning the centre—peg of a millstone. The *Qur'an* says: *awa j'alna al-jabal awtaden*. According to Sufi concept four persons out of a total number of 350 (*afrad*) are called *awtad* who hold firm four corners of the world Their status is one step below the *qutb*. *Akhyar* is plural of *Khayyar* meaning benevolent people, which again is a category of the Sufi group. See *Tarikh-e Tasavvuf dar Iran*, Qasim Ghani loc cit.

such venerable personalities who have guided the people. The great mystic Shaykh Mahmud Muzdaqani (d. AH 826/ AD 1422) gave up his home and native land and took abode in Hamadan *velayat*. Under his guidance and supervision grew the pivot of the mystics (*qutbu'l-aqtab*) and the compendium of virtues like Amir Kabir Sayyid io'Ali Hamadani.[1] This master of the science of names and definitions, the knower of the degrees of *velayat* (spiritual realm), the object of obeisance of people of excellence and the person embellished by the divine rays (meaning Amir Kabir Sayyid 'Ali Hamadani), had travelled thrice round the inhabited part of the globe.[2] He traversed the Tukharistan[3] lands from the west to the east not staying at any one town or country. The region of Khatlan[4] was the birthplace of the renowned mystic Khwajeh Ishaq. Amir Kabir once spent eight months of winter at that place in the house of Avlad 'Ali Shah. After some time, Mubarak Shah bin 'Ali Shah, the grandfather of Khwajeh Ishaq, came to know of the spiritual excellence of Amir Kabir. He watched

---

[1] For the title Amir Kabir, see fn. pp.63–73 supra.

[2] *rub'a-maskun* or *haft iqlim* meaning one fourth of the globe, which, according to the Arab geographers, is inhabited by human beings. They computed this area at 12 thousand *kroh* long and 6 thousand *kroh* wide. They distributed the earth into 360 parts, each part called degree (*darajeh*), and each *darajeh* measuring 67 *kroh*. See *Kashshaf-e Estelahatu'l-Funun*. Nizami says:

Iraq az rub'a maskun ast bahri
waz an bahreh Madayen ast shahri

[3] Tukharistan of early and middle ages is the name of the region south of Amu Darya extending to eastern basin of river Kabul. Turkhara is repeatedly mentioned by Kalhana in *Rajatarangini*. Tukhara and Sogdiana are often mentioned in the annals of mediaeval Central Asia. Sogdiana is the region of Zarafshan valley in which Samarqand is situated.

[4] Arab geographers have assigned Khatlan to *Ma'wara'an-Nehr* region. "*wa chun kardeh amad navahi-e Balkh wa Tukharistan wa Termiz wa Qubadiyan wa Khatlan be mardum akandeh bayad kard kih har kuja khali yaft wa fursat deed gharat kunad wa furu kubad.*" *Tarikh-e Baihaqi*, edited by Qasim Ghani and Fayyaz, Teheran, p.92 Ferdowsi says in *Shahnameh*:

sipahi beyamad badinsan ze Chin
ze Suqlab o Khatlan o Turan zamin

his merits and his ways from close distance. He studied him fully and found that all the superior qualities and virtues of a true Sayyid were in his personality. The authority of accepting allegiance from many Shaykhs and elderly persons was bestowed on him. He also enjoyed the power and authority of accepting repentance from those who wanted it.

Khwajeh Ishaq

One morning, Mubarak 'Ali Shah took Khwajeh (Ishaq) along with him to the presence of Amir Kabir. He also carried an unfettered arrow in his hand and placed it in front of him. Amir Kabir asked him the reason for bringing his son to his presence. He also wanted to know the meaning of bringing the arrow. Mubarak Shah said that it was his grandson and he desired Amir Kabir to bestow upon him the privilege of lifting it and accepting him as his disciple. Amir Kabir wanted to distance himself from these matters. He turned down the request and asked what quality in Ishaq prompted him to make him accepted as his (Amir's) disciple. By trying to distance from what Mubarak 'Ali wanted him to do, Amir Kabir only intensified his (Ishaq's) eagerness to become his disciple: *al insan haris ila ma man'a*, (a man is greedy about what is forbidden to him). Mubarak Shah was unhappy with Amir Kabir's refusal. He asked which religion recommended creating obstructions in a person's path. Amir Kabir discerned his eagerness and told him in soft words, "I shall accept your word among my disciples but I entreat you not to disclose my secrets to anybody".[1] Thereafter Amir Kabir placed his hand on the head of adolescent Khwajeh between his forehead and

---

[1] An important principle of Sufism is not to disclose the spiritual powers of the Shaykh. Hafiz of Shiraz says:

goftam an yar kazu shud sar-e dar bulan
jurmash in bud kih asrar hoveda mi kard.

or

Sirr-e khuda kih salik o arif be kas na goft
dar hayratam kih badeh farosh az kuja shanid.

eyes. This is the practice observed by the (Sufi) preceptors and teachers. He (Khwajeh Ishaq) had the privilege of becoming his disciple. However, owing to his adolescent age, he could not undergo the (prescribed) rigours of penance and meditation.

After some time, Amir Kabir proceeded on a long journey. Twelve years later, he learnt that the rare mystic Khwajeh Ishaq had attained the strength of rendering service to the seekers of Allah. After travelling to the regions far and wide, he returned to the region of Kaplan (Khatlan?).

The Discourse

The river Aqsu[1] flows close to Khatlan. Amir Kabir halted on its bank when by chance Khwajeh Ishaq, accompanied by a group of his relatives, brethren, and friends suddenly appeared from somewhere. They were on a hunting expedition. Amir Kabir told him that he wanted to cross the river, and if somebody from his (Khwajeh Ishaq's) party was crossing. Thereupon Khwajeh Ishaq said that he (Amir Kabir) could mount one of his horses or even his own as it was a strong beast. Amir Kabir mounted Khwajeh Ishaq's horse and sat behind him on the saddle. Khwajeh Ishaq addressed him "Dervish, you should hold me fast." (*dervish, mi bayad kih mara mazboot girifteh bashi*). Amir Kabir answered. "I shall hold you tightly and not let you go till eternity (*chunan mazbut giriftamat kih ta qayamat tura az dast ne guzaram*). Amir Kabir's pleasing words and his attention greatly impressed Khwajeh Ishaq. Indeed, he found that he had surrendered to Amir Kabir. This was the result of immense love and affection that Amir Kabir poured out to him. After dismounting the horse on the other bank of the river, Khwajeh Ishaq said, "Do you have an appointed place and a house to go to? (*Dervish ja*

---

[1] *Aq* in Turkish/Uzbeki means white against *qara* meaning black. Hindi *kala*.

mau'dudi wa manzili dashteh bashi?) Amir Kabir smiled and said, "You are my destination and your heart is my home. Otherwise, wherever the nightfall overtakes a dervish, it is his lodging" (*mau'id-e man tust wa manzile man dile tust wa illa dervish har kuja kih shab amad sara-e ust*). Then Khwajeh Ishaque invited him to stay with him for some time. Amir Kabir readily accepted the offer.

Association

Khwajeh Ishaq had given himself up to worldly and physical attachments and had forgotten that in the days of his boyhood, he had made allegiance to Amir Kabir. He had forgotten all those pledges and had also forgotten the understanding that existed between the two. The words of love and affection, uttered by Amir Kabir were, meant to arouse him from deep slumber. These made him shun ignorance and lassitude. We can imagine the happiness that this event must have brought to Khwajeh Ishaq. True love defies explanation.

In short, Khwajeh Ishaq took Amir Kabir to his house and for many years he stayed in the house of 'Ali Shah to impart spiritual teaching to Khwajeh Ishaq. The latter now revived his oath of allegiance and started doing penance and undergoing rigorous training. He devoted himself to learning the ways, traditions, formalities and specificities of spiritual training under the guidance of Amir Kabir. Under the close guidance of the saint, Khwajeh Ishaq attained the degree of *velayat* (meaning he became a *vali* or the holder of spiritual realm) and finally rose to be the *Qutb* (the Pivot).

Through the instrumentality of Khwajeh Ishaq, a large number of Shaykhs and scholars, and also his friends, relatives and members of fraternity, and lots of people from far and near received spiritual training from that great master and guide, Amir Kabir. His company and the training of the seekers of truth and travellers along the divine path brought immense benefits to them. Among the recipients of his guidance and blessings are Maulana Nuru'd-Din J'afar Badakhshi[1] whose status and position (in spiritual domain) are described by Amir Kabir in these words: "If Bayezid Bistami[2] (d. AH 426/ AD 1034) were alive today, I would have still looked up to Maulana Nuru'd-Din." Likewise, Khwajeh Shamsu'd-Din Khatlani, the elder brother of Khwajeh Ishaq Khatlani, also happened to be among his disciples. Once Amir Kabir said to Maulana Nuru'd-Din J'afar, "You do not pay as much regard to my instructions as Khwajeh Ishaq and Khwajeh Shamsu'd-Din pay. You should observe for yourself how these two persons steal a march over others in obeying my orders. They have gone much ahead of you in their spiritual journey and it will take you fifty years to catch up with them."

Amir Kabir brought up these species of spiritualists of high rank under his guidance and training. Perhaps it was because of Khwajeh Ishaq that they could come to the presence of an eminent person like Amir Kabir. A large number of his followers and disciples emerged in those lands (Khatlan and Tajikistan) because his auspicious steps touched that soil. The existence of a large number of shrines of the Shaykhs and *valis* (spiritualists) in those lands is a proof of Amir Kabir raising a large number of Sufis in those parts. People pay visit to their shrines. In truth, these shrines are the places that angels should visit.

First visit to Kashmir

There were two reasons for Araki's visit to Kashmir. At the face of it Shah Qasim directed him to proceed to Kashmir to procure herbs and elixirs to cure the ailing Sultan Husayn Mirza. We have already dealt with this earlier in this work. However, there was also a deeper and more cogent reason. The Creator of the Universe and the one who has assigned name and character to the manifest world (God Almighty)

---

[1] Author of *Khulasatu'l-Manaqib.*

[2] p.24fn.2.

ordained that he (Araki) bestow his grace on the people of Kashmir.[1] Baba 'Ali,[2] the chief of the seekers of God and the chief of all the spiritualists (of Kashmir), was to be adorned with the robes of allegiance to Shamsu'd-Din Araki. He was to take the seat of grace. The very sight of Araki was enough to transport Baba 'Ali and his followers to a state of trance. Overwhelmed by the feeling of spiritualism, he left his family and children and took to seclusion. He went in search of a preceptor and guide, and had to undergo many privations in that path. God Almighty did not arrange his food and water in any foreign country. Therefore, he had not the chance to travel to distant lands. He returned to his home hoping that the Will of God Almighty would grant him his wishes. The *Qura'n* says: The one who sought me, found me; the one who knocked at the door, entered the house.[3]

In Kashmir, the seekers of God made him their guide. He proved a spring of sweet water for the thirsty (of divine munificence). He became the healer of the painfulness (scar) of ignorance.

Let it be known that Amir Sayyid 'Ali Hamadani stayed on in the *velayat* of Khatlan in the lands of Badakhshan. Through Khwajeh Ishaq, many sincere and devoted people of those regions became the recipients of his favours and guidance. Like this, through Hazrat Baba (Baba 'Ali), Shamsu'd-Din

---

[1] I do not rule out the possibility of He with capital H meaning God Almighty in this sentence.

[2] Baba 'Ali Najjar is said to be the first Kashmiri divine who embraced Nurbakhshiyyeh order at the hands of Araki. Dedmari calls him "stupid" and "hypocrite". He was a disciple of Baba Ismael and developed close association with Araki. When Baba Ismail grew old and retired, Baba 'Ali became active and popular. Before arriving in Kashmir, Araki is said to have sent a letter to Baba 'Ali expressing that he had forsaken worldly desires and intended to proceed to Kashmir as the lieutenant of Sayyid Muhammad Nurbakhsh. See *Waqa'at-e-Kashmir*, tr. Shamsu'd-Din Ahmad, Srinagar, 2001, p.122.

[3] Maulana says:

goft Payghambar kih chun kubi dari
akharash zan dar birun ayad sari (Mathnavi)

Araki became the preceptor and guide to many people in Kashmir. All this munificence flowed owing to the auspicious footsteps of Shamsu'd-Din Araki on this (Kashmir) land. We shall speak more about these spiritual personalities in the chapters that follow.

Departure from Khurasan

At the time when Shamsu'd-Din Araki took leave of Shah Qasim for his travel to Kashmir, Sultan Hasan Shah,[1] son of Haider Shah, son of Sultan Zainu'l-'Abidin reigned over that land. Araki had brought with him letters and a communication from Sultan Husayn Mirza. Apart from a variety of presents, he had also sent to him a fur (coat) of an animal called '*kesh*'(?). Its fringes were wrought in gold. Furriers had used their special skills to embellish it. The fur-coat carried on it the pictures of the heads of different birds and animals in exquisite shapes. Any one who saw it was amazed by the superb craftsmanship that had gone into its making. The fur coat was studded with twelve buttons of gold. Khwajeh Malik Zargar (the goldsmith) had spent six months in stitching it.[2] He was renowned throughout Khurasan for his exquisite art of gold work and the golden buttons attested to his great artistic skill. Apart from this, Sultan Husayn Mirza also sent him (Hasan Shah) set of a specially-made armour for him.

Shah Qasim directed one of his disciples, named Mir Dervish, to join the entourage of Shamsu'd-Din Araki to

[1] Dedamari tells us that Hasan Shah gave himself to a life of ease and pleasure. Twelve hundred Indian musicians adorned his court. He paid no attention to the affairs of the state so much so that people in Bahlulpora (near Sialkot) revolted against him. The uprising was quelled by Tazi Bhat, the commander of Hasan Shah. See *Waqa'at-e-Kashmir*, ed. and trans. Shamsu'd-Din Ahmad, Srinagar, 2001, p.108 seqq.

[2] This means that preparatons of dispatching Araki mission to the court of Kashmir Sultan had been going on at Herat for a long time may be for more than a year.

keep him company during his long and tiresome journey (to Kashmir). Thus, carrying with him all the presents, letters and other provisions needed by the travellers, Mir Shamsu'd-Din Araki took the Qandahar route for reaching his destination in Kashmir.[1]

In Multan

When he arrived in Multan (India), he found that famine had struck the land. The price of eatables was very high. During the few days of his halt at Multan, he arranged the distribution of food (bread and soup) among the poor, the destitute and the travellers. Poor people from adjoining areas flocked to his place and partook of meals at his *dastarkhwan*.[2] In Multan there lived a Sayyid who had actually migrated from Iraq. He had a large family to take care of. This Sayyid had a grown up daughter brought up as an pure and chaste person. One day, the Sayyid sent a word to Amir Shamsu'd-Din that in case he intended to take a wife, he (the Sayyid) would offer his daughter in marriage to him. Shamsu'd-Din accepted the offer and the girl was given in wedlock to him. At that point of time, Shamsu'd-Din was fifty-five years old and a bachelor. He had spent his years in pursuit of knowledge and for performing social service (to the people). Now at the age of fifty-five he entered into family life.[3]

---

[1] Dedamari says that Sultan Husayn Mirza deputed Shamsu'd-Din on a diplomatic mission to the court of Sultan Hasan Shah. After his return to Herat, Sultan Husayn Mirza came to know of Araki's religious mission in Kashmir.

[2] *Dastar+khwan* is a sheet of cloth spread over the utensils in which cooked food is carried. Once people sit down to eat, the sheet is spread on the floor and plates filled with food are laid on it. *Khwan o khwar* are generally used together and from *khwar* in Pahlavi, we have *khwar+nak/kwarnaq* meaning kitchen or dining room. Likewise, we have *khwan-gah* from Pahlavi meaning the place to eat and, from it we get *khwangah* and the Arabicised *khanqah*.

[3] We are not told how old the girl was.

Ghakkar route

In Multan, the mendicants and seekers of divine grace benefited from his affection and munificence. He took his newly wed wife named Bejeh (?) Agha, with him and proceeded towards the lands of Kashmir. At the border of Dana Gala[1] he entered the territory of the Ghakkars. There, he bought Maulana Bayezid for the service of his family.[2] In particular, Bejeh Agha was to accept him in her special (personal) service. From Ghakkar territories, his entourage moved towards Kashmir and in the year sixty-nine of Kashmiri calendar or AH 888 (AD 1483), he entered Kashmir from Herpora route. Sultan Hasan Shah had dispatched some of his nobles to receive him.

---

[1] "The combined names of *Darvas* and *Abhisarasi* are mentioned in various ethnographical lists, furnished by the *Mahabharata*, the *Puranas* and *Brhatsamhita*, along with those of tribes belnging to the Punjab. The position of their country was first corectly ascertained by Wilson, *Essays*, p.116sq. From the evidence available it appears that *Darvabhishara* as a geogrphical term comprised the whole tract of the lower and midle hills lying between the Vitasta and Chandrabhaga." Stein further writes that "it must be noted that the gloss of A, on our passage, *Bhimbher Danagala dese*, would restruct the application of the term to the lower hills between the limits above indicated. Bhimbhar, the first locality named by the glossator, lies at the foot of the outer hills, in the centre of the tract between the Vitasta and the Chinab, and was the country of a little hill-state; See Cunningham, *Ancient Geography*, p.134. The name Danagal appears to survive in that of an old Ghakkar fort in the lower hills near the Vitasta. I have, however, been able to obtain only oral information regarading ths place." See *Rajat*, Bk.I, verse 180 fn.

[2] Purchasing a slave for domestic or personal services was an established practice in the Islamic world. These slaves could be enrolled in the army and in many instances a slave rose to become a commander of high rank. The founder of the Slave Dynasty of Sultans of India was also a slave bought and inducted into military service. Setting a slave free was considered a virtue of much significance. Hafiz of Shiraz says:

Kilk-i mushkeen-i tu ruzi kih ze ma yad kunad
Mi barad ajr-i do sad bandeh kih azad kunad.

Hasan Shah's court

The nobles escorted him to the city (of Srinagar). The entire equipage, men and material, family, their palanquins etc. were brought to the hospice of Malik Itoo in the locality of[1] Deder (sic.)

Ministers, senior government functionaries, advisers to the government and the dignitaries, all came to pay him a courtesy visit. A grand fiesta was set afoot to which some of the leading nobles, scholars and learned men of the town were invited. Amir Shamsu'd-Din was present in the function. He carried in his hand the letters (from Sultan Husayn Mirza). The fur coat was given in the hands of Mir Dervish, and his attendants with instructions that each of them should be present by his side. Then taking the letters in his hands, Amir Shamsu'd-Din moved slowly towards the Sultan who, however, did not rise from his seat as a mark of respect to the letters (to be presented shortly). Amir Shamsu'd-Din hinted at it but there was no movement from the Sultan's side. The reason was that the rulers of Kashmir had never been at war with other rulers. They had never heard about court manners and the norms of protocol. Prior to Amir Shamsu'd-Din, no emissary had ever come to Kashmir from the Indian rulers. As such, they (the rulers of Kashmir) were ignorant about the protocol and the etiquette generally followed as mark of respect to the messages, letters and gifts from royalties. It is because of the teachings and training of Amir Shamsu'd-Din that the rulers of

[1]But, in the preceding lines the writer tells us that Kashmir royal court had dispatched a team of notables and grandees to receive Araki at Dana Gala as he proceeded towards the city of Srinagar. This repudiates the assertion that the Kashmir kings were ignorant of protocol. The last Hindu ruler of Kashmir had also formally received Shahmir somewhere in Baramulla when he entered the valley for the first time. *Baharistan* tells us that all facilities were provided to him and his large entourage. See *Baharistan-i-Shahi: A Chronicle of Mediaeval Kashmir*, (tr.) K.N. Pandit, Calcutta 1991, Chapter I et al. Envoys from foreign countries often visited Kashmir during the Hindu period. See *Rajatarangini*, tr. Stein.

Kashmir learnt the culture of extending due regard and respect to the proclamations (*farman*) and letters and presents from a ruler of another country. The fact of the matter is that the *ulema*, the *Qadis*, religious scholars, the Sayyids, Sultan's, administrators, the masses, and the high and low of this land had totally forgotten all the tenets of faith and Islam and the laws of the *sharia* of the Holy Prophet. Through the teachings, training and exhortations of Amir Shamsu'd-Din, all of them gained knowledge about doing what is permitted and what is prohibited in Islam, meaning the laws of *sharia* brought by the Holy Prophet, and the modes of behaviour and etiquette prescribed for the community of the Messenger of God. In the pages that follow, we shall describe the de-Islamisation, faithlessness, and adoption of the habits and customs of non-Muslims and heretics by the *ulema* and the (Muslim) scholars of this land. We shall also describe how the jurisconsults, theologians and men of learning did such deeds in their homes as the non-Muslims were wont to do. In particular, such aberrations were quite visible in the houses of the leading *Qadis* and the *Shaykhu'l-Islam*.[1]

Amir Shamsu'd-Din saw that while receiving the letters and presents brought by him, Sultan Hasan Shah did not stir from his seat. He became angry. "Make him a peg to be driven into the earth so that he cannot move. He does not mean to show respect to the king of Khurasan", he uttered in high emotion. The nobles made him rise and receive the letters and gifts from the auspicious hands of Shamsu'd-Din. He placed the special fur on the hands of the Sultan and lay the presents before him. Then on the behest of the *ulema* and the nobles,

---

[1] This title was given to Sufi Shykhs and learned men in the middle of the 4th century AH /11th century AD. In the beginning of the era of Memluks of Egypt and Syria the title was more a matter of courtesy than a formality. When the title was given to the Grand Mufti of Turkey for the first time, it gained special status and then was given to influential Muftis. In Iran during the Safavi period, the title was conferred upon a person who headed the judiciary. The Prime Minister appointed him. *Ency. of Islam*. Also see *Loghat Nameh*, p.152.

Sultan Hasan Shah approved the presents (sent by the ruler of Khurasan), and accepted them. He returned to his seat beckoning Shamsu'd-Din to take a special seat. First, they talked about the hardships of a long and arduous journey. Then they talked about the health of Sultan Husayn Mirza and then about the situation (in his kingdom). Amir Shamsu'd-Din conveyed the Sultan's greetings and good wishes to Hasan Shah. After exchanging these words, dinner was announced. It was a special feast to honour the guests. Dishes were laid and those present partook of soup and other dainties. After the dinner, Shamsu'd-Din was granted permission to retire to the special lodge arranged for him.

Araki's broad vision

Araki settled down at the assigned lodge. Attendants and servants were directed to bring eatables from the market. Two persons acted as interpreters and emissaries. On the next day, a package of one million (?) in cash, a thousand *trak* (one *trak* = 5 kgs approximately) of rice, flour, and a hundred heads of sheep were brought to the *Amir* from the state establishment to meet his daily requirements.

Amir Shamsu'd-Din instructed his servants and attendants to take all the sheep and cereals with them (to his residence). He found that the sheep were very lean and small in size, which did not please his eyes. He said that if the kings of these lands sent him such (degraded) meat to eat, then he was very sorry for them. Turning to the emissary of the Sultan who had been sent for conveying the message, he said," Purchase thirty heads of sheep from the butchers of this land. Each should weigh between 24 and 25 maunds (each maund equal to nearly two kilograms). In any case, no sheep should be less than twenty maunds in weight. One lakh and thirty thousand (?) were allotted for this. All these sheep were sent to the Sultan with the message (to the ambassador) that he should look at the sheep closely and send him the same kind in future. The Sultan of Kashmir found that the sheep sent to Amir

Shamsu'd-Din were really lean and unworthy of presenting to a guest. As against this, the sheep sent by Araki, were fat and strong. Sultan Hasan Shah also came to know that the sheep he had sent to Araki had been gifted away by the latter to the sweepers, beggars, destitute and those who had come to offer their obeisance to him. Not a single sheep from that flock was sent to the kitchen. This caused embarrassment to the Sultan (of Kashmir).

Thereafter the Sultan directed the functionaries that whatever was sent to him by way of presents, should be checked before it is dispatched. Since he was the emissary and the ambassador of the king of Khurasan, he (Araki) had seen persons of high class and their families. He knew of the munificence of kings and rulers. As such, in no case a sub-standard gift was ever to be sent to him so that he was not put to shame a second time.

Next day, Sultan Hasan Shah summoned the ministers, seniors and elders of the state. Men of learning and scholarship in the town were also invited. The letters sent by Sultan Husayn Mirza were opened and read out to the Sultan (of Kashmir). He came to know about their content. These revealed the purpose of procuring medicinal herbs and elixirs that could be obtained easily in those (Kashmir) parts of the land. Their procurement did not entail any special effort and labour, and these could be sent without much hassle. On knowing the contents of the letters and also on account that the King of Khurasan would remain obliged to receive these herbs everybody felt relieved and happy.

Amir Shamsu'd-Din rested at his lodging for a few days to overcome the fatigue of a long journey. After that, he occasionally came out of the house and went to the royal court. They would talk about the health of Sultan Husayn Mirza and the stories of other kings. Sometimes the elders, the nobles and men of learning would come to the presence of Amir Shamsu'd-Din at the bidding of the ruler, and sit with him for a while. Amir Shamsu'd-Din would treat them hospitably and invite them to partake of various dainties prepared in his kitchen. In particular, they would be served soup,[1] the kind of which they had never tasted before.

The fame of Amir Shamsu'd-Din's generosity and munificence spread far and wide. The number of visitors and guests began to swell day after day. He expanded the circle of his acquaintances and associates. There was a shortage of utensils in his kitchen. One day, he told the messenger of the ruler to summon some local coppersmiths and ask them to forge some plates and containers for use in the kitchen for cooking and serving food to the guests. When the ruler of Kashmir learnt about it, he ordered that some kitchenware made of copper be sent from the royal household for Amir Shamsu'd-Din. The officials executed these instructions and brought the kitchenware to Araki's place. When he desired to see the stuff he found that pots and plates sent to his place were empty. He expressed regret that there was not a single well-bred staffer in the royal household who knew that it was in bad taste to send empty vessels and kitchenware from the royal house.[2] Then he ordered his servants to cook some delicious chicken soup and varieties of excellent food and pudding and fill the platters and trays. He sent these dainties to the royal house under the supervision of Mir Dervish with the specific objective of making the royal household realize that empty plates and platters are not sent out from high place. All the people of this land, high and low, were amazed at the generosity, munificence and largehearted hospitality of Amir Shamsu'd-Din.

The general impression among the people was that this man was the emissary and ambassador of the King of Khurasan. This they thought was the reason of his lofty

[1] *shurba* (*shoor+ba*) literarlly meaning saltish water. *ba* is the reverse of *aab* meaning water. Shurba means meat soup. I don't think it is true that the household of the Kashmiri Sultans at this poin of time did not know of *shurba* or soup.

[2] This is not the first instance of Araki's contempt for the Kashsmir royalty. His treatment of common Kashmiris is totally inexcusable as we shall note in this work.

disposition. They desired to seek him and know him because he was the ambassador of Sultan Husayn Mirza of Khurasan. (But) they did not know about his spiritual attainments, and he, too, did not disclose anything about this to his circle of friends.

Trance during picnic

A couple of months later, the season for shooting ducks[1] set in. Sultan Hasan Shah told his courtiers and ministers that because the season for shooting wild ducks had started, the ambassador might want to accompany him for a cruise in the Wular[2] (lake). The nobles of the city decided that Hajji Shams and Hajji Hasan[3] accompany the royalty so that they understood what Amir Shamsu'd-Din said during the game. These were two learned persons of the town. Apart from having conventional knowledge and wisdom, they had also performed pilgrimage (*hajj*) of the twin holy shrines. They were adepts in the art of socializing when sitting in the assembly of the learned and sophisticated gentry. They had the gift of the fine art of conversation in refined circles.

At this point of time, Hajji Shams was the Shaykh and the caretaker of the (Amiriyyeh) Hamadaniyyeh.[4] Hajji Hasan also held a high position among the people of this land. Both of them had performed the *hajj* of the twin holy cities and they joined Shamsu'd-Din to keep him company and speak to him. (This means they functioned as his interpreters and in all probability spoke Arabic).

Sultan Hasan Shah took with him all of his courtiers and nobles on the game. They took boats. They also summoned

---

[1] Siberian ducks still migrate, among other places, to the Wular and Hokarsar lakes in Kashmir valley during winter.

[2] The largest lake in Kashmir valley. For the etymology of Wular see *Rajatarangini* Bk.iv.593n. and vol.II, p.423.

[3] Two Arabic/Farsi knowing courtiers at the court of the Sultan.

[4] The hospice of Amir Kabir Sayyid 'Ali Hamadani in Fateh Kadal, Srinagar. Previously it was the temple of Kali during the Hindu rule.

popular musicians of the town to accompany them. Ustad Hasan, the lute player, was the outstanding instrumentalist among the whole lot. His father, Ustad Muhammad Udi (the lute player) had come to Kashmir from Khurasan during the reign of Sultan Zainu'l-'Abidin (d. AH 880/AD 1475). He had attained perfection in (instrumental) music, and other known sciences at the feet of teachers in Khurasan and Arak. Mulla Hasan Udi, a remarkable instrumentalist indeed, walked in his fathers footsteps. He always accompanied the Sultan wherever he went and never stayed away from rendering his service.

Accompanied by a large group (of camp followers), the Sultan arrived at the bank of the lake (Wular). He and Amir Shams sat in their boats. At this time, the air was pleasant and invigorating, and water in the big lake was clean and transparent. The shore of the vast lake was immensely attractive. The mountain and its slopes were a riot of colour. The leaves of the trees had turned partly yellow, crimson and pink. This was the time when the rays of the Supreme Being illumined the hearts of the people gifted with inner light. The stunning beauty of these physical surroundings immensely attracted Amir Shamsu'd-Din. Slowly, he found himself drawn towards the hidden truths lying deep in the bosom of nature. The peal of music raised by the musicians and the lute player intensified his absorption. Losing self-control, he was overtaken by passionate sentiments. He fell into a trance and under its impulse stood up, as the Sufis do, in spiritual dance and ecstasy. Those present saw with their own eyes how he became ecstatic. For them, this was something of a wonder to behold.

Mir Dervish sat in the next boat. On beholding Shamsu'd-Din in a state of ecstasy, he drew his boat close to his. Hajji Shams and Hajji Hasan also got up. Holding one another's hands, they shifted themselves to the boat in which Shamsu'd-Din stood entranced. Thus, they formed a circle around him.

Joining the ecstatic dance is the tradition of the dervishes and the sufis.[1]

Sultan Hasan Shah was unfamiliar with the trance and ecstasy of this kind. He had not heard anything of it. Naturally, he became curious to see for himself how Shamsu'd-Din and his companions were behaving. He immediately disembarked from his boat and sat in another boat following the first one. It was a smaller boat and from there he very intently looked at how the dervishes were conducting themselves (in a spiritual dance). He also enquired from the people present about the details of how it had happened. But they were unable to answer his questions. However, both Hajji Hasan and Hajji Shams, were aware of the achievements and spiritual feats of the Shaykhs and dervishes. They made a submission to the Sultan that he had thought of Shamsu'd-Din as the emissary of Sultan Husayn Mirza. He, in fact, was among the leading Shaykhs and spiritualists of his day.[2]

After a while, the intensity of trance and ecstasy abated and Shamsu'd-Din returned to a state of normalcy. He took off his turban from his head and gifted it to Mulla Hasan Udi, thereby expressing that the trance and ecstasy had resulted because of his superb rendering of a befitting note. The practice of gifting one s turban is fully compatible with the practices of the Holy Prophet.

---

[1] Music and dancing (*wajd o sama'*) though forbidden in orthodox Islam, have been a part of Sufi tradition since long. Actually in Turkey, the cult of dancing dervishes was established by the great Sufi poet, Maulana Jalalu'd- Din Rumi. Forming a circle around a Sufi in his trance is called *halqa zadan* meaning emulating the act.

halqeh gird-e man zaned aye paykaran-e ab o gil
atashi dar sineh daram az nayakan-e shuma (Iqbal Lahori)

[2] Going into a sudden trance in such a situation, where the Sultan and his nobles and courtiers were to witness it with their own eyes, appears to be a shrewd ploy to establish his Sufi credentials and to impress them all that besides being an emissary from a powerful neighbouring ruler, he was also an outstanding religious missionary.

It has been recorded in many authentic works of the learned men of Islam (Shaykhs) and spiritualists including the notable work called *'Awarifu'l M'aarif* (and also the tradition goes) that during the period of compilation of the above mentioned work at Mecca, Shaykh Shihabu'd-Din Suhrwardy recorded that one day the Holy Prophet sat with his companions. Suddenly, Gabriel descended upon him with this divine message: "O Prophet of God! Verily the mendicants of your community shall enter the paradise half a day earlier than the prosperous ones." On hearing this message, the Holy Prophet was highly pleased. In a state of perfect happiness, he asked his companions. "*afyekum min yanashrina*" meaning, "Is there anybody among you who can recite/sing something." There were a few nomads in the assembly and one of them said he could. The Holy Prophet, now in a state of ecstasy, told him to come nearer and recite. He sang a few verses in Arabic. This recitation made a deep impact on the Holy Prophet and he fell into a trance. As the Holy Prophet remained under that influence, all of his companions followed him in this practice, which became a tradition. All of them stood up and made a circle around him and became a part of that spell of ecstasy. In that state, his shoulder-cloth slipped down. He retrieved it and cut it into four hundred small pieces, offering one piece each to his companions as an souvenir. This shows that on that particular day, no fewer than four hundred companions had joined him in his ecstatic dance. The tradition handed down to the followers and the Shaykhs of high status is that during the closing days of the Lent, all dervishes come out of their secluded cells and revel in ecstatic dancing. We shall throw more light on this tradition in the pages that follow.[1]

---

[1] For more information on *wajd o sama'*, see Qasim Ghani's *Tarikh-e Tasavvuf dar Iran* (2 vols.), loc. cit.

Mu'awiyeh's objection

Once Mua'wiyeh[1] bin Sufyan saw that the Holy Prophet and his companions were in a trance. After returning to normal state of mind, the Holy Prophet began distributing pieces of his cloak (among his companions). Mu'awiyah came to his presence and said that it (going into tance) was a remarkable thing to see. The Prophet told Sufiyan to be quiet. "Nobody should express joy or hurl sarcasm at the time of communion with God, particularly those who are not bestowed with the grace of love and affinity to God," he added.

Abu Sufyan was ignorant of the sweetness of faith and attraction to Islam. He had never had the opportunity of smelling the fragrance of the flowers in the garden of faith. To him Islam perhaps meant only outward obedience. The Prophet's ecstasy was in fact revelation of eternal truth and the guarded secrets of the cosmos, which appeared something like fun to Sufiyan's blind eye.

Abu Sufyan had actually repugnance for the ways of Islam. Instead of submitting to the tenets and principles of Islam, he only secured submission of others to Islam. Thus like a child, he considered the Holy Prophet's trance no more than fun.

The purpose of bringing in the above tradition (*hadith*) is to show that trance is the tradition inherited from the great Shaykhs. After recovering from the ecstasy, they used to distribute their clothes among the participants in the ecstatic dancing. In this way, the tradition originating with the Prophet was handed down from generation to generation.

After the ecstatic trance in the boat, Amir Shamsu'd-Din Araki bestowed his turban (*dastar*) to Mulla Hasan Udi, just to keep alive the tradition of the Prophet. This tradition is a sufficient proof in support of (Araki's) ecstatic dance (*wajd-o-sam'a*). According to the stories, utterances and traditions

---

[1] See *Loghat Nameh.*

descending down to us from the great spiritualists, some music and certain tunes are permitted for use (during the dance). Some instruments and notes are categorised as 'permitted'. Theologians and scholars, too, have issued decrees (*futwa*) endorsing the use of some musical instruments and singing of some notes. We shall have more to say on this subject in the pages of this book.

Araki and Nur Bakhshiyyeh

Sultan Hasan Shah and many great nobles (of Kashmir) put questions to Hajji Shams and Hajji Hasan about the causes and effects of the ecstatic dance. Both of these Hajjis, who had performed pilgrimage to the twin-holy cities (*harmayn* meaning Mecca and Medina), knew fully well about the trance and ecstasy of spiritualists. Sultan Hasan Shah and his nobles found that they had thought of this visitor as the emissary of Sultan Husayn Mirza. But, in fact (now they found) that he was holding an exalted position among the dervishes and spiritualists of distinction. The Sultan asked him to which order of Sufis he belonged.[1] Shamsu'd-Din Araki replied," My path is that of the exalted order of Nur Bakhshiyyeh and I have made allegiance to the great spiritualist Shah Qasim Faiz Bakhsh. He (Shah Qasim) has been staying in the capital city of Herat where he came from Arak. He had dispatched me to Kashmir on the request of Sultan Husayn Mirza. It was on his instructions that I proceeded to these lands. I have nothing to do with the service of Sultan Husayn Mirza nor am I bound to him. I have no connections with any Sultan or king."[2]

The news of his excellence in spiritual powers reached all the people, high and low in Kashmir, including those in the adjacent territories. Men of learning and parts, theologians,

[1] Seeking an answer to this pertinent questionsn contradicts the writer's earlier assertion that Sultan Hasan Shah did not know anything about Sufis, their trance, practices and *wajd o sama'*, etc.

[2] This statement is diametrically opposite to what Araki said to Hasan Shah during their first meeting.

mendicants and seekers of spiritual light, thronged to his place and benefitted from his discourses. With every passing day, larger and larger numbers that were attracted to him came to know of his virtues.

Spiritual training of Kashmiris

Before Shamu'd-Din arrived in Kashmir, Hazrat Baba(?)[1] was infused with an urge to seek a spiritual guide and mentor for himself. His intense urge compelled him to sever his filial relations with his children and other family members. He wanted to proceed on a long journey in search of a master. But, travels were not in store for him; he remained confined to his house, waiting impatiently for the great grace to descend upon him. He surrendered himself to God Almighty and waited for something unexpected to happen.

Whenever a traveller or a saintly person arrived in Kashmir, Hazrat Baba (Baba 'Ali) would present himself before him, along with his friends and companions. He would make acquaintance wih him and make detailed enquiry about him. He would ask him of his ways and methods of seeking knowledge and excellence; he would ask for details of prayers and recitations. If a sincere desire for friendship in any of the newcomers arose in him, he would maintain his friendship in all circumstances and pay him occasional visits. He would offer himself for any service to him or desired of him so that he could benefit from his company.

The story of Shamsu'd-Dins ecstatic dance reached the ears of the citizens of the town (Srinagar). Since Baba 'Ali himself happened to be in search of spiritual advancement, he took great pleasure in presenting himself along with his friends and companions before Amir Shams. More prominent among his companions were Mulla Muhammad Imam, Sufi Jamal, Mulla Yusuf and Mulla Ismail Kohi(?). Mulla Ismail happened

[1] Obviously Baba 'Ali Najjar, whose name has been mentioned earlier too.

to be associated with Hazrat Baba. This group came to the presence of Shamsu'd-Din to benefit from his association. During the couple of days they spent with him, they closely observed Shamsu'd-Din's way of life; how he dressed, ate, behaved with visitors, spoke and everything else. They also observed minutely his inner qualities and virtues, and thus, with each passing day, they felt more and more inclined to trust him and pay him obeisance. They were too happy to carry out any instructions he gave them. They strictly observed the distinction between matters permissible and not permissible as Araki described them. Each one of them established close and sincere bonds of respect with him.

Among the learned men of this (Kashmir) land was my late father Maulana Jamalu'd-Din Khaleelullah, and Qadi Muhammad Musa (known as Maulana Zeyd) who used Afsari as his pen name in his verses. Both of them became his devout disciples and paid occasional visits to him. Many students, scholars and *Khwajehgan*[1] (plural of *Khwajeh*) of the town also attended his assemblies and benefitted from his sermons and sagacious words.

People of saintly disposition and dervishes like Sufi Muhammad, Khwajeh Husayn Bandey,[2] Mulla Dedo and Mulla Nusrat and many well-known personalities of Kashmir also came to the presence of Araki and benefitted from his association. The story of his generosity, munificence, and spiritual excellence reached every nook and corner of the land (Kashmir). His personality became a catalyst as the Sun

---

[1] Followers of *Naqshbandiyyeh* Sufi order are usually called *Khwajehgan*; Hafiz says:

wafa az Khwajehgan-e shahr ba man
Kemal-e millat o din bu'l wafa kard

[2] According to some etymologists, Bandy is the corrupted Kashmiri form of Sanskrit Panday meaning priest. Most probably, after their conversion to Islam around this time, the Brahmanic priests adopted Bandy as part of their name.

of virtue and good deeds to rise over this land.[1] His breath exhaled the fragrance of belief and sincerity. The winds of Nur Bakhshiyyeh (faith) spread over the land bringing life-giving fragrance and freshness to friends and followers. In order to give direction to their material and spiritual pursuits, and to enquire into happenings and events, people began to seek from him predictions about future events through the instrumentality of his spiritual powers. The people acted upon his auguries with all the faith they had in him.[2]

Foretelling about Hasan Shah

I have heard my venerable father tell me the following story repeatedly. A couple of months after Shamsu'd-Din's arrival in Kashmir, the winter was about to end and the early spring had made its appearance felt (AH 989/AD 1484). The Sultan took ill; the efforts of curing him by the physicians did not succeed. When his illness prolonged, Shamsu'd-Din's associates and acquaintances came to him and told him that the Sultan's illness was getting prolonged with each passing day, because the physicians could not find a cure. They requested Shamsu'd-Din to address his inner self, and through his grace make a prediction (in the matter). They said they wanted to know what would appear in the cosmos-reflecting mind of Amir Shams so that they could know before hand what was going to happen to the Sultan.[3] Araki acceded to

---

[1] The metaphor light and darkness used by the historians of mediaeval Kashmir historians to state that prior to the promulgation of Islamic faith, which is figuratively light and sun, there prevailed only the darkness of sin, aberration and heresy in Kashmir.

[2] This is an old diehard habit of Kashmiris. *Rajatarangini* is replete with such stories.

[3] Curiously, Kashmir history from ancient times often alludes to this trait in the character of the Kashmiris. In Central Asia, even today, we hear people speaking about *jadu-e-Kashmir* meaning the sorcery of Kashmir. History of Zoroastrain Iran bears testimony that ancient Iranians keenly pursued the study of astrology. The practice of taking an augury and the urge to know in advance the impact of stars on one's destiny are still prevalent among some ancient Aryan groups. Included among them are the Shia and Pandit (Hindu) communities of Kashmir.

their request, turned towards the World of Essence and decided that he would apply himself to the task that night. Next day in the morning, his associates came to him and enquired about the augury.

Shamsu'd-Din said, "The hope of recovery and, therefore, of his life are lost. Whatever has been observed about his condition in the World of Essence cannot be undone by the nobles and the ministers of this land. Even the offspring of the Sultan and his close relatives, too, cannot expect to do that. As such, Sultan's recovery is not possible." The associates again asked about what the task reflected in the mirror[1] of the illuminated mind of Amir Shamsu'd-Din that could not be performed by the nobles, ministers and even the offspring of the Sultan. To this, Shamsu'd-Din answered, "The solution is that the Sultan spend all his riches and all his secured treasures. If his nobles, ministers and descendants can do it, then God Almighty would cure his disease."

It is well known that ancient kings who amassed enormous wealth and filled their coffers, had never opened these up for large-scale munificence. Had they been generous, royal treasury would have been opened for the poor. Each day twelve persons could take away skirtful of gold coins and move in lanes and market places and distribute handfuls among the poor, the dervishes, the destitute and the needy for two or three days till the treasures were emptied. Only then is there a hope that God Almighty may listen to the prayers of the destitute. This might ward off the tragedy that is about to overtake the Sultan. There is no other hope for his survival. But because it is very difficult, therefore, there is little hope of Sultan's survival. His disciples were convinced that Shamsu'd-Din's prophecy emanated from his pious dream.

[1] In the mediaeval times people known to make predictions kept a glass or a cup or a ball made of glass in their hands and pretended to see the image of coming events in it. Hafiz says:

Goftam in jam- e jahan bin be tu kai dad hakim
goft an roz kih in gonbad-e meena mi kard.

They lost all hope of the Sultan's recovery and waited for the day of his death.

Death

After a couple of days, Shamsu'd-Din Araki sent through his servants a few melons to the Sultan. The largest and the best of the melons fell from the hands of the bearer in the way. The remaining melons were delivered. When the news of the melon falling from the hands of the bearer reached Shamsu'd-Din, he remarked that the Sultan would pass away that day or the day after because the messenger from the unknown had brought the tidings in the shape of falling of the melon from the servant's hand.

Next day in the morning, he ordered the saddling of horses. Shah Qasim Faiz Bakhsh had sent him a black turban, which he wore on his head. Mir Dervish and some of his attendants were to accompany him. Riding their horses, they headed towards the royal palace. People thought he was going to enquire about the health of the Sultan but his close associates were sure that he was going only to join the funeral of the Sultan. No sooner did he enter the royal house than loud wailing and crying were heard from inside. The news of Sultan's death had reached the people. As he entered the palace, the nobles and the grandees present on the occasion offered him the highest place to sit. The Qadis, *ulema* and leading personalities of the town came to know about the sad news. People came in large groups and squatted on the spacious platform. Preparations for the royal funeral commenced. Amir Shamsu'd-Din also accompanied the funeral procession up to *Mazar-e-Salatin*.[1] After taking leave of the mourners, he returned to his residence. He paid daily visits to *Mazar-e-Salatin* to offer *fateha* (prayers for the dead person) for a few days. He would address the gathering

[1] In Zaina Kadal vicinity in downtown Srinagar near the tomb of Zainu'l-'Abidin's mother.

present there in these words: "Owing to the demise of the king, my mission is disrupted, and my return (to Khurasan) hindered. I do not know how the *mullahs* are going to interfere in my affairs." Verily all that he had said did actually happen.[1]

Muhammad Shah

Muhammad Shah was barely two years old when his father Sultan Hasan Shah passed away. The nobles, ministers and senior functionaries of the realm installed him on the throne of his late father. Since he was still a child, state power remained in the hands of the lords and administrators (of the state). As is generally the case, there arose mutual jealousy and dissension among them and the country passed into a state of instability and confusion. At times, there were clashes and fights. These rampant quarrels and dissensions among the nobles of the land led Amir Shamsu'd-Din to prolong his stay in Kashmir.[2] This apart, it was the Will of the Supreme that he stayed on for more time, and appoint Hazrat Baba and other followers to help his mission. Some of these happenings have been stated in the previous pages but something more will be said in the pages that follow.

Zadibal site

Amir Shamsu'd-Din stayed in Kashmir for about eight years during the first stint (AH 888–96/AD1483–90). In AH 896/ AD 1490, he returned to Arak. After staying away for twelve years (in Arak), he sought permission from Shah Qasim Faiz Bakhsh to return to Kashmir for the second time (in AH 908/

[1] This means that opposition to the mission of Araki continued unabatedly, and the deah of the Sultan exacerbated it.

[2] Obviously, he was keenly watching political developments that followed the death of Sultan Hasan Shah. In particular, since Muhammad Shah, the successor to Hasan Shah was an infant, it was evident that power would be monopolized by the most influential courtiers about whose support Araki was skeptical. Now he was a political observer and not just one who had gone into trance while on a cruise on the Wular.

AD 1502). Twenty years later, the site at an elevation (in Zadibal), which had attracted him so much came into possession almost without asking. In this way circumstances favoured his stay there for the construction of a hospice. He decided to build a hospice befitting men of high spiritual excellence. It was also to become his residential quarter and ultimately the shrine for the visit of pilgrims and devouts. We shall record in pages to follow the details of acquiring the site and raising a hospice and the (residential) complex on it.

Shifting to *Mazar-e-Salatin*

Amir Shamsu'd-Din stayed in the hospice of Malik Ahmad Itoo. After the death of Sultan Hasan Shah, the old servants and inmates of the hospice fomented trouble and chaos in his quarters. Since they were not friendly to him, they brought a litany of complaints to the neighbours in the locality. They approached the administrative circles in the city and raised hue and cry for justice. It caused him anguish, and he felt unhappy to continue living at that place. At last, he decided to leave the hospice. In the proximity of *Mazar-e-Salatin,* and by the bank of the river, there was an old building. It was repaired and made habitable. Then he shifted his family and his belongings to this house. Space was provided for the horses, shepherds and others associated with his mission. He stayed there for about a year along with his family. During this period, Bibi Agha, his eldest daughter was born to him. This was in AH 890/AD 1485). Hazrat Baba and other associates suggested that they arrange a wet nurse for the infant. However, he was not happy to stay (permanently) in this land and did not agree with anybody except the mother of the infant feeding her.

Shaykh Shihab Hindi

It was in this house that a debate between Shamsu'd-Din and Shaykh Shihab Hindi took place. Shaykh Shihab was an Indian *mulla* who claimed that nobody in India could stand before him in debates on rational sciences and their principles. He boasted that even in the twin holy cities nobody could be his peer in that field. In India, he would join hands with the enemies and opponents of the king and write letters and reports against him. When the ruler of India came to know about his misconduct and hypocritical nature, he sent him into exile.

Shaykh Shihab begged intercession (of his friends and acquaintances) to get permission to go to Kashmir, but the Emperor did not grant it.[1] Taking his family with him, Shaykh Shihab proceeded towards Gujarat. However, he did not feel comfortable at that place. He took a boat and proceeded to Mecca for pilgrimage. The leading personalities (in Mecca) accorded him dignified reception. He had a grown-up daughter of marriageable age. The gentry and the Sayyids in Mecca offered proposals for marrying the girl to an eligible candidate. However, he did not agree giving his daughter in marriage to somebody among the gentry and the Sayyids. After performing *hajj* obligations, many leading personalities suggested to him that they arrange the marriage of his daughter. He asked for a few days to consider the matter and submit to the Holy Prophet for right guidance. A few days later, he wrote down the following:

> "In my dream I saw the spirit of the Holy Prophet before me. I placed the matter before him and his instructions were that I should not give my daughter in marriage to anybody here (in Mecca). In the east there is a country called Kashmir whose ruler is Hasan Shah. This girl will be married to him. You should proceed (to that land) and arrange your daughter's betrothal to him. No change in this order will be entertained. Such references do exist (in history) where the Holy Prophet has said that whosoever

[1] Evidently, Kashmir was not part of the Indian Empire at this point of time. Why the Emperor refused him permission to go to Kashmir is intriguimg. At this time, India was under the rule of Lodhi dynasty.

> saw me, verily he has found the truth. How can I go against these instructions?"[1]

After performing the obligations of *hajj* pilgrimage, he proceeded towards Iraq. In Baghdad, he found that the order of Shaykh Abdu'l Qadir Gilani[2] (d. AH 561/AD 1165) was the most popular of all (Sufi) orders. He aligned himself to this order, and wrote down *Qadiriyyeh*[3] for himself and proceeded from Iraq to Jam[4] (Iran). Without stopping at any place, he arrived in India by Kirman and Siestan route, and from there, he quickly moved towards Kashmir so that the Emperor did not come to know about his movements.[5]

Mir Shamsu'd-Din had already arrived in Kashmir in AH 888/AD 1483), and Shaykh Shihab followed him. Sultan Hasan Shah dispatched nobles and lords to receive him on his arrival in Kashmir. Then he told the entire story of his dream in Mecca to the nobles who had come to receive him, who in turn, recounted the story to Sultan Hasan Shah. Sultan Hasan Shah's son, Muhammad Shah Alam was still an infant when

---

[1] Whether true or not, one cannot overlook the connection between this dream and his initial demand that the Emperor allow him to proceed to Kashmir when the order of his exile from Delhi was issued.

[2] Born in Baghdad in AH 560 or 561/AD 1164/65, Shaykh 'Abdu'l-Qadir is the Imam of Qadiriyyeh Sufi order. This order has a large number of followers in India, (Ottomon) Turkey and the Islamic lands. According to *Qamusu'l-'Elam,* his geneology is traceable to Imam Hasan. He received his early coaching in theology and Arabic from Abu Zakariya Tabrizi. His work *Futawi* is appreciated by the Shafi'i and Hambali schools. Among his works in the science of mysticism are *Bashairu'l-Khairat*, *Futuhu'l-Ghaib* and *Malfuzat-e Qadiriyyeh.* Sources: *Rawdatu'j-Jannat*, p.432 and *Rayhanatu'l-Adab*, vol.iii, p.494.

[3] A treatise dealing with the philosophy of Qadiri Sufi order.

[4] A town in Khurasan province, also called Jam-e Kharjard.

[5] The Shaykh appears to have adopted a circuitous route to Kashmir in order to avoid detection by the informers of the Indian Emperor. However, he had managed to inform the court of Sultan Hasan Shah in Kashmir of his impending travel to that land.

his father had died. As such, the reins of the government fell into the hands of Sayyid Hasan Baihaqi.[1] His grandfather had come to Kashmir from Sabzwar (in Khurasan, Iran). The nobles of this land (Kashmir) did not tolerate a government run by these Sayyids.[2] In the ensuing fighting, Sayyid Hasan Baihaqi got killed. His son, Mir Muhammad Baihaqi came to know about his father's killing. He assembled three to four hundred armed cavalrymen and marched right upon a group in the hospice. The other group, on which he had launched an attack, got scared and withdrew by another door and headed towards Idgah[3] ground. Mir Muhammad thought they were scared and had fled the field. He was enraged and gave them a hot pursuit.

Chasing the fleeing Kashmiris, Mir Muhammad crossed the bridge (on the river) and attacked the city.[4] Turning to Nowshehra,[5] he came close to the royal quarters, which he besieged. As a result big fighting erupted. Each day saw the belligerent troops shooting arrows at one another. Many

---

[1] For fuller information on Baihaqi Sayyids and their role in the mediaeval history of Kashmir, see *Baharistan-i-Shahi*, (tr.) Kashinath Pandit, Calcutta, 1991 (relevant portions). Baihaq is the name of a town in Khurasan from where the Sayyids rose and came to India. *ulhid shakl/bigu bisuz kih Mehdi-e dinpanah rasid* (Khwajeh Hafiz).

[2] The Syyids played an active role in the affairs of the state and became very powerful. Their role and domination was rented by the Kashmiris, which led to clashes and fighting. See *Baharistan*, op. cit.

[3] The large ground in the proximity of downtown Safa Kadal in Srinaagr city. The author of *Baharistan* tells us that mass conversion and circumcision of the Hindus under instructions of Shamsu'd-Din Araki took place on the Idgah ground. See *Baharistan*, loc. cit. p.

[4] Mediaeval historians have seldom mentioned the name of Srinagar. They have generally called it '*shahr*', which is commonly used by Farsi historians of Iran for a capital city. *Shahr* is the modern Farsi of Avestic *shathra*. Farsi historians have even written *shahr-e-Iran* meaning the country of Iran. Ferdowsi says: *hameh shahr-e Iran bedu shad bud.*

[5] Downtown Srinagar and the seat of mediaeval royalty.

people got killed and many more were wounded. The siege continued for nearly two months and a half with neither side winning a decisive victory.

Men of learning, jurists, Sayyids and grandees of Kashmir and the rest of the people assembled together and said that the fighting should cease because much blood of Musulmans had been shed. They said that it was incumbent upon them to tell the people to desist from further fighting. They (the troops) should assemble at a particular place and make a pledge for peace. It was possible that their opposition and enmity would lead to truce. They said that their mutual rancour should transform into mutual peace: opposition and disunity among them had to be replaced by mutual understanding and unity. (Since) the following day was Friday, they agreed that all of them would assemble in the presence of Mir Dervish (the companion of Shamsu'd-Din), to take a pledge in the presence of the elderly Sayyid[1] (?) that they would resolve their differences through peaceful means.

Shaykh Shahab opposes

On the next day, Mir Dervish, the *Qadis*, *ulema* and scholars, friends and associates assembled at the hospice. Amir Shamsu'd-Din was also invited to attend the assembly. It was said that (because) Araki was the emissary of a great king, he too should be included among the gathering. Amir Shamsu'd-Din took his seat next to Shaykh Shihab. Those attending the deliberations paid attention to the suggestions and conditions of peace offered by Amir Shamsu'd-Din. They asked him how they should carry forward the dialogue.

He said, "The first thing, which needs to be said to the sons of the soil, is that they have performed a significant task.[2] They expect intercession by the Holy Prophet (on the Day of

---

[1] It is not clear who the Sayyid is. It could be either Shamsu'd-Din Araki or Sayyid Muhammaḍ Baihaqi.

[2] The task was that of abandoning their ancestral religion and embracing Islam.

Judgement). They claim to be Muslims and observe Islamic faith but, at the same time, they have no hesitation in killing people of the Prophet's faith. None but the wretched Yezid had done such a despicable deed. For that, Yezid shall continue to be condemned and castigated until the Day of Judgement. It is incumbent upon the people to express remorse and repentance on what they have done. They should do many acts of munificence for the children and families of the Sayyids who have been innocently killed. Great consideration should be shown in serving them and extending affection towards them. They (Kashmiris) should also pray to God Almighty for forgiveness.. Then only would God accept their repentance and overlook their sins."

Then turning to the Sayyids, he said admonishingly, "The Sayyids, too, need to be advised. He said to them, "You have come to this land from a different country. After arriving in Kashmir, you banished the poor and seized their property and wealth.[1] Because of this the local people have no sympathy for you, who are strangers to them. You have brought a bad name to yourselves by indulging in such sinful and detestable deeds. It is advisable that you forgive their (of local Kashmiris) sins and leave the retribution (of the blood of your fathers) to the Day of Judgement. If you have killed a thousand people, it will not be taken as justifiable for avenging the blood of your fathers. You cannot identify persons and fix responsibilities for avenging the blood of your fathers.. The right course for you is to work for peace with them and spare taking revenge of your father's killing to the Day of Judgement. God Almighty will do that with the Yazidis."[2]

Shaykh Shahab heard Araki making damaging remarks about Yezid, the son of Hind (*t'an-e-Yezid pisar-e-Hind*).

[1] Thus here we have one of the causes of conflict between the Baihaqi Sayyids and the local people.

[2] This is a highly diplomatic statement and reveals subtly the mistakes committed by either side during their armed struggle for power.

On hearing the name of the sons of Hind he was filled with prejudice. He decided to torment and disgrace him. At this moment, his despicable son Miyan Budeh(?)[1] had taken his seat at a little distance behind Amir Shamsu'd-Din. On beholding this the ignominious Shaykh Shihab addressed his son in these words," Dear son, you are a learned man and a scholar in your own right. Why do you choose to sit behind ordinary people? Stand up and take your seat at the top". He insisted upon him to occupy another seat and made him sit by the side of Shamsu'd-Din.

This caused embarrassment to Shamus's-Din. Even the participants in the assembly found themselves exasperated by such behaviour. However, nobody said anything. Even Shamsu'd-Din did not say anything to both the jealous persons.

Reports say that the behaviour of this uncouth person in that assembly irritated Shamud-Din Araki. He said that he had tried to console his mind several times by reiterating that the utterances of that man did not cause any harm to his faith or to Islam. However, his turbulent mind could not find peace, nor could he convince himself that nothing serious was going to happen by Shaykh Shihab making his young son sit above him in that assembly. The more he tried to convince himself, the more rumbling he felt inside. He used to say that whenever somebody inflicted humiliation on him and his heart became uncontrollable and intensely restless, that person would indeed be asking for some serious trouble to his life and to person. This had convinced him that the behaviour of the person would cost him the life of his young son.

Assassination of Miyan Budehh(?)

The session of the assembly came to an end, and the participants started returning home. Amir Shamsu'd-Din called a couple of acquaintances who were present in the

---

[1] Proper identification of this name remained elusive.

assembly and said to them," You are a witness that this son of an ass (Shaykh Shahab) assumed an air of superiority. He has made way for his destruction. Because of this you should be a witness to the scene of how this youth meets his tragic death."

Maulana Zayd, the father of Qadi Muhammad, Hajji Shams, Sufi Muhammad, and a few more persons were witness to what was going to happen to the son of Shaykh Shihab. The above-mentioned assembly was held on a certain Friday. A week later, and on the third Friday, a quarrel took place between this Miyan Badeh (?) and his younger brother named Miyan Munjel (?). Both of them were usually under the effect of intoxicants and not in their proper senses. Miyan Munjal decided to put an end to his brother's life. He marked time from morning until noon but did not get an opportunity. On Friday their father (Shaykh Shahab Hindi) following the old tradition, attired in prayer clothes went to offer prayers at the Jamia Mosque.[1] His son Miyan Budeh (?) wanted to follow his father. He too wore the dress in accordance with the

[1] It should be the mosque in downtown Nowhatta area. According to Stein, it was a famous Buddhist shrine, (See *Geography of Ancient Kashmir* appended to vol.ii of his translation of *Rajatarangini* and *the Archeology of Ancient Kashmir* by R.C. Kak). Ladakhi Buddhists used to come all the way from Ladakh to pay obeisance at this Buddhist shrine. As late as 1950s and 60s, the Buddhist Lamas on a visit or business to Srinagar, used to pay obeisance by going round the mosque thereby reviving the memory of an ancient tradition. After the advent of Islam in Kashmir around AD 1339, and the replacement of the Buddhist shrines by Islamic mosques, the foundation of the ancient structures including that of Jami'a Masjid remained in place as almost of every shrine in the valley while the superstructures took different shapes and styles. The Jami'a Mosque became the seat of the biggest Friday congregations. With the beginning of a political movement under Sheikh Muhammad 'Abdullah in early 1930s for putting an end to Maharaja's rule, *Jami'a Masjid* became the main headequarter of the *Bakra* party while another ancient Buddhist shrine (converted into a mosque) at Hazratbal became the main seat of the *Sher* party. With the beginning of armed conflict in Kashmir in 1990, both of these places have also become the political venue for mobilizing public support for armed movement. Stray statues of Buddha or Bodhisattavas lying around the structure as late as 1960, are no more traceable.

tradition came out of his house and waited a while for his horse to be brought to him.

His brother Miyan Munjel was sitting in the second storey of the house and keeping an eye on him. He found the opportunity ripe to strike. Looking around, his eye caught the sight of a millstone lying in the corner. He lifted it with all his strength and dropped it down from the window straight on the head of the target. The head and neck of Miyan Budeh (?) got crushed and his dying wail reached the sky. This tragic news was brought to Shaykh Shahab. In utter desperation, he left the prayer halfway and barefooted rushed out of the mosque. On reaching his place, he found that the head and the neck of his son were crushed. A fool that he was, he sat at his side for some time looking at the dead body (of his son).

Husayn Munajjim's version

Mir Husayn Munajjim[1] reports that his father was present in that assembly. Shaykh Shihab had seated his son at an elevated place than that of Mir Shamsu'd-Din. After the assembly dispersed, he accompanied Shaykh Shihab to his residence. On the way, somebody said to the Shaykh that Mir Shamsu'd-Din Muhammad, the emissary of Sultan Husayn Mirza, had made one among those present in the assembly a witness to the (prediction of the) death of his son.

After hearing these words from the reporter, he just smiled and said, "The people in these lands are very strange; they are foolish and devoid of culture. They listen to trash and believe in nonsense. "I call them ignorant (*buduw*) and I never trust them. I just wonder why they are enamoured by imaginary stories and why they become the followers of such tricksters. They are not strong and sincere in their relations with the people of learning and erudition," he added.[2]

---

[1] I have not been able to establish the identity of Husayn Munajjim. No mention of him could be found in any relevant work of reference.

[2] This is Araki's very unsympathetic assessment of Kashmirian character.

We came to the residence of the Shaykh to offer condolences. Some of the city elders told the Shaykh that it was not good to hurt the feelings of dervishes because they were not without some spiritual powers. The Shaykh did not agree with this statement and asserted that he did not believe in the community of Sufis.

Mir Husayn Munajjim says, "My father was surprised to hear these words (from Shaykh Shihab). Since he did not believe in Sufis, he had dared to be impolite in the assembly. There was no sign of remorse and repentance in him. His son's death had not made him sorrowful or regretful. I found that Shaykh Shihab totally rejected the ways (*tariqat*) of the Shaykhs. He detested the style of *sufis* and dervishes and did not feel inclined to join their assemblies. This was the beginning of the story of wretched Shaykh's animosity towards Mir Shamsu'd-Din."

Second encounter

Another encounter between this abominable wretch and Amir Shamsu'd-Din is recounted here. Many changes took place in this land (Kashmir) through its nobles and administrators. The reins of power and authority passed into the hands of Malik Saif Dar. He called an assembly of the *ulema* at the Hamadaniyyeh hospice (*khanqah*). A large number of Sayyids, Qadis, and the *ulema*, men of learning and erudition, nobles and leading personalities and state officials of high rank participated in the meeting. Amir Shamsu'd-Din was also invited to it. Outstanding persons received special favours in this grand function.

The intransigent Shaykh Shihab took his seat by the side of Amir Shamsu'd-Din in that assembly. Soup and food was served. The custom observed in these lands (Kashmir) at that point of time was that food, pudding and dessert for the learned, the Sayyids and the Qadis would be brought on separate platters. A large platter full of dainties was placed before Amir Shams and another in front of Shaykh Shihab.

In the same manner, one platter each was placed in front of the *ulema*. Everybody uncovered the platter with covetous eyes. Driven by greed and the apprehension of incurring the displeasure of their womenfolk, the *ulema* did not muster courage to eat from the platters. They wrapped the platters in the spreadcloth and handed these over to their subordinates to carry to their residences.

Shamsu'd-Din ate a few morsels from his platter to remove his appetite. The remaining food was distributed among his servants and attendants. Part of the feast was offered to the servants and attendants in the hospice (*khanqah-e-Hamadaniyyeh*). Shaykh Shihab found that Amir Shams did not send anything to his home. Turning towards him he asked why he did not send anything to his family. Shamsu'd-Din answered that his house was full of eatables. Food was sent to those who had nothing with them so that their families and children could eat it.

This enraged Shaykh Shihab. He said that the learned men did not carry food for anybody. It was sent to their homes because God Almighty says in the *Quran* "eat and carry home". The word *tamatu'u'* meant carry home. Amir Shamsu'd-Din said that God Almighty never meant that you should order the food to be carried home for your womenfolk to eat. Thereupon Shaykh Shihab said that it meant that he (Shamsu'd-Din) did not accept the Qura'nic verse in this context. But Amir Shams said that perhaps the Qura'nic verse to which the Shaykh had referred bore a different interpretation. However, the idiotic Shaykh Shahab castigated him, and said that he was not at all a scholar and had not read a single book. He stressed that whatever he said was based on what was written in the books (meaning the *Qura'n* and its commentaries). It was not known where from he draw his interpretation.[1]

---

[1] Debates between Araki and Shaykh Shihab on contentious issues indicate wider social cleavages in the Kashmiri Muslim community. The Shia'-Sunni rift had already crept into it, while their divines were locking horn on petty issues.

Highly prejudiced clergymen, who bear enmity towards the House of the Holy Prophet, all came to support the views of Shaykh Shihab. They raised hue and cry that a person who had not acquired any knowledge and had not read any book, had no standing to enter into serious debate with the most learned scholar and *Shaykhu'l-Islam* of the lands of India. He was the one who was most venerated at the twin holy cities of Mecca and Median. Amir Shamsu'd-Din said that he may not have read anything, and may not have scrutinised any work of commentary, yet he was confident and had made research that the meaning of the Qura'nic verse in question was not what was understood by Shaykh Shihab. The altercation among the *mullas* became louder but the Amir did not accept their interpretation.

Malik Regi Dar, the brother of Malik Saif Dar, was moderately informed on theological matters. Probably, he had read some works on the science of theology. He usually supported the *mullas*. He said that the noise raised over the controversy was futile. Why not send somebody and fetch the *Kashshaf*[1] commentary so that the meaning of the verse is clarified. Malik Regi Dar thought that the commentary endorsed the views of Shaykh Shahab. He thought that when the views expressed by Shaykh Shihab received endorsement from the book (*Kashshaf*), then Shamsu'd-Din could not escape the accusations made against him.

A couple of *mullas* rose to fetch the work in question. Some of them feared that resorting to the reference book might put Amir Shamsu'd-Din in an embarrassing situation. They suggested that this debate be set at rest. They knew Shamsu'd-Din, and suggested that he should agree with the *Shaykhu'l-Islam's* interpretation. But Shamsu'd-Din could not be cowed down, and swore by God Almighty that he could never accept what the Shaykh wanted him to accept.

His friends and admirers became apprehensive lest the meaning of the verse in the *Kashshaf* ran counter to what he

[1] Famous commentary on *Qur'an* by Jarullah. See *Baharistan*, loc. cit., p.65.

himself said. In any case, when the book was brought and the verse under discussion was examined, its interpretation went as this; "*kulu va tamatu'u qaleelan inakum mujrimoon*" meaning "eat and enjoy but in small quantity. Verily you are among the culprits." This verse (*ayat*) descended (on the Prophet) to castigate despicable persons. It indicates God's wrath coming down as hell pain inflicted on evil people. However, Shaykh Shihab wanted to detach the *ayat* from its concluding part and distort the entire verse so that he could argue that it supported his interpretation. He forgot that it was the holy book and that he could be charged with distorting its text.

This wicked wretch was not ashamed of God Almighty and His Prophet. He did not realise that distortion of the *Qura'n* in any way was tantamount to blasphemy. Thereafter, Amir Shamsu'd-Din addressed the audience in these words, "Justice-loving people must open their eyes and understand that God Almighty has sent down this *ayat* (verse) for condemning the wicked people to hell. But this Shaykh wants to use it for his glory and for his examples."

Every one in that assembly was convinced that the Shaykh had taken cudgels with Amir Shams on a theological issue without sufficient evidence to prove his point, and that this was totally wrong. This exposed the Shaykh as an obstinate, prejudicial and a mean person. Amir Shamsu'd-Din's friends expressed great satisfaction and happiness for his success in the debate while his enemies met with humiliation.

Hafiz Baseer

The venerable scholar and teacher, Maulana Hafiz Baseer, said a number of times that the wretched Shaykh Shahab rejected the Shaykhs and showed bitter antagonism towards the saints (*auliya*). He was no less a rabid denouncer of the people with spiritual attainment and mystic ecstacy than the traditional non-conformists. Enmity towards those who guided people (along right path) and husbanded spiritual domain (*velayat*) ran in his blood. He had the audacity to enter into a debate with Amir Shamsu'd-Din in the *Khanqah-e Amiriyyeh* (Amiriyyeh hospice) although it was not a formal occasion. This showed that he was giving vent to his feelings of animosity and rivalry. During this debate, he deliberately overlooked some verses of the *Quran*. A number of times I recited the concluding portions of these verses so that he might hear them and thus bring to an end the meaningless debate. But because loud voices were poured from all sides, the *mullas* did not hear what I was reciting. Nobody was willing to pay heed to what I was saying repeatedly.

I found that Amir Shamsu'd-Din was not in a mood to accept anything that Shaykh Shihab said. I whispered in the ear of those who were sitting by my side that Amir Shamsu'd-Din was hotly debating the issues with Shaykh Shahab. What could be the basis of his knowledge? They replied that Shamsu'd-Din was the emissary of the Sultan of Khurasan but was not quite knowledgeable in the branch of theological learning. They said that he had not read a single book pertaining to the science. He had not read even a single text book of theology and its terminology. He has not perused the works of rational and speculative sciences. He is not versed in these branches and has nothing but a completely negative approach to the academic debate with Shaykh Shihab.

When the copy of *Kashshaf* was produced, I found that what Shamsu'd-Din had said was in complete conformity with the interpretation given in the work. It contradicted the interpretation given by Shaykh Shahab.

Making the knowledge of Amir Shamsu'd-Din the basis (of my inference), I thought that if he had not been a genius, he would never have ventured to enter into a debate with men of learning who opposed his thoughts. A person who is alleged to have read no important work and examined no source material (on the subject) cannot be expected to enter into a debate with the Shaykh.

Some students and beneficiaries of Makhdum's patronage (Maulana Hafiz Baseer) say that a large number of people were told that the *mullas* were well grounded in the branches of rational and speculative sciences. They had compiled works in each branch, such as philology and mathematics. Hazrat Makhdum (Hafiz Baseer) used to admonish his students and seekers of knowledge that such rumours about the clergy were totally baseless. He told them that they were not erudite enough to produce works on these branches of theological science. Nevertheless, he said, the *mullas* kept with them private collections, which included works by elders. All that *mullas* have done is to re-write those works of the elders and append introductions to them and dedicating the work to the rulers of the day. On the basis of this they tell people that they have authored those works.

The people of Kashmir had not benefited from these *mullas* in their pursuit of knowledge. If at all any type of learning flourished in these lands (Kashmir), it emanated from the lessons imparted by Mulla Muhammad Rumi and Mulla Ahmad Rumi. Their status as scholars is much higher than that of Shaykh Shahab; the two brothers excel him. Whosoever is a teacher or a taught in theological learning in this land, has been a student of the two scholar brothers.

In short, Shaykh Shahab was not only inimical towards Shamsu'd-Din, he was also an enemy of all God-fearing saints. From the very beginning, he was dead set against the Shaykhs and pious saints. This animus had got ingrained into his wretched nature. These detestable people, bereft of inner vision are unable to withstand the bright and glittering rays of the powers of saints and excellence of the men of purity. The bright rays of the Sun of *Velayat* (spiritual domain), which light up assemblies and gatherings, do not penetrate the dark corners of their eyes. When the light of spirit and truth casts its rays on them, they bark like mongrels.[1]

This is how the despicable wretch demonstrated his jealousy and ill-will towards Amir Shamsu'd-Din in the course

[1] It is a common belief among some Farsi poets and writers that when the moon sheds its light, the dogs bark:

Mah noor mi fishanad sag bang mizand
sag ra bego kih naz'e tu ba mahtab chist.

of his second encounter with him. During this debate, Malik Saif Dar and Malik Regi Chak became the disciples of Mir Shamsu'd-Din'. Finding that Mir Shamsu'd-Din was a person of high status the nobles and grandees (of Kashmir) became his devotees. They visited him often and thus benefited from his discourses in seeking the path of the mystics.[1]

However, a group of prejudiced *mullas* bore ill will towards *ahl-e bait* (household of the Holy Prophet). Just as the hearts of infidels and *kafirs* are replete with corruption and aberrations, their hearts, too, were full of prejudice. These *mullas* invariably demonstrated their hatred against the employees in Amir Shamsu'd-Din's establishment. They felt pride in expressing rancour towards the Amir. In this way, they tarnished their record, which God Almighty would examine on the day of reckoning. They confined their faith and Islam to the boundaries of material and the transient world. Rancour is essentially of two kinds: ingrained and circumstantial.

Decrees of infidelity (*kufr*)

During the periods of penance and spiritual training, exalted saints like Shaykh Junayd Baghdadi,[2] Abu'l Hasan

[1] Araki's ability to assume different postures such as an ambassador, an emissary, a dancing dervish, a mystic and a theologian of Nurbakhshiyyeh School is noteworthy. Above all, he has demonstrated remarkable understanding of Kashmirian psyche in general and of Kashmiri nobility in particular.

[2] Baghdad is Avestic/Sanskrit *bagha* (= Sanskrit *bagha+wana* = God the Great) + *dat* from Avestic *datan* meaning to give (Farsi *dadan*). *Bagh(a)dad* (Baghdad) means 'given by God'. Junayd's family was originally from Nehawand in western Iran, but he was born in Baghdad. A pioneer of Sufi movement, he standardized the principles of Islamic Sufism. His writings are neither mundane nor exaggerated. He asserted that the links of the Sufis with the *Qur'an* and *hadith* (Tradition) were strong and nobody could lay claim to guiding the pupil along the path of mysticism if he had not read the holy book and the *hadith*. Historians have given him various appellations like *Qutb-e 'azam*, *Sayyidu't-taifah*, *Ustadu'l-tariqat*, *Taju'l-'arifin* and etc. He studied theology from Sufyan-e Thauri, and in the branch of Gnosticism, he is a peer of Harith and Siri Saqati. Ibnu'l-'Abbas ibn Sarih learnt the subtleties of the ways of mysticism (*tariqat*) from him and his aphorisms are well known among the Sufis and spiritualists. He died in Baghdad in AH 297–98/AD 909 at the age of 91, and remains buried in the tomb at Shonezyeh. See *Nameh-e Danishwaran*, vol.v, p.15, *Rawdatu'j-Jannat*, p.163, *Tarikh*, Ibn Khallikan, vol.i, p.127 and *Rayhanatu'l-Adab*, vol.i, pp.282–83.

Noori[1] and Shaykh Shibli[2] kept the pseudo-scholarly *mullas* at arms length. They had stopped listening to the utterances of pretentious *mullas* and meeting with them. In order to escape their disquieting company and meetings, they went to sequestered and desolate places. They lived in the ruins. However, when the *mullas* of the day realised that these mystics hated them and thought it proper to avoid their company, they joined hands in a nefarious conspiracy against them and got all the three arrested. They were charged with heresy and aberration. They reported to the ruler of the day that the three persons were heretics and *zandiqs* (non-

---

[1] 'Attar records this curious incident in *Tadhikaru'l-Awliya*: When Ahmad bin Muhammad Ghulam Khaleel charged him (Noori), Junayd Baghdadi, Shibli and Abul Hamza of heresy (*zandaqah)*, they were sent to the Qadi. He referred them to the Caliph saying if they were apostates then there was no Musulman on earth. The Caliph told them to ask for something and he would grant it. They said, "Forget us because acceptance by you meant our rejction by God and vice versa." The Caliph wept and set them free. *Tadhkirah* loc. cit., fn.3 infra.

[2] In the beginning, Abu Bakr Dalaf Shibli was the Governor of Damavand (*Dumb+a+vand*) in northern Iran and then became the Usherer (*Hajib*) of Caliph Muwaffaq 'Abbasi. However, he gave up the service, became a penitent and a Sufi and came to be known for his piety and spirituality. He was originally from a village called Shibleh in Khurasan wherefrom he drew his name Shibli. He was born in AH 247, died in AH 334 and was buried in Khezran where his tomb exists. There is a difference of opinion among some of his historians about his religion. He has been dubbed as Maliki (Ibn Khallikan), Shi'a (Qadi Nurullah Shushtari) and a fanatic by others. See *Tadhkiratu'l-Awliya*, ed. Alder, vol.ii, p.127, *al 'Elam* of Zarkuli, vol.iii, p.21, *Sabk Shinasi* of Bahar, vol.ii, p.185.3 'Attar records this curious incident in *Tadhikaru'l-Awliya*: When Ahmad bin Muhammad Ghulam Khaleel branded him (Noori), Junayd Baghdadi, Shibli and Abul Hamza of heresy (*zandaqah)*, they were sent to the Qadi. He referred them to the Caliph saying if they were apostates then there was no Musulman on earth. The Caliph told them to ask for something and he would grant it. They said, "Forget us because acceptance by you means our rejction by God and vice versa." The Caliph wept and set them free. *Tadhkirah* loc. cit.

believers)[1] and that their words and deeds reveal infidelity and heresy. The ruler ordered their arrest for putting them to sword. They were sent to the *Qadi* to obtain a decree for their beheading on the verdict of the *ulema*, the learned men and the theologians. The Qadi said he would question them about Islamic law and theology to ascertain the level of their scholarship. Noori and Shibli were the first two to whom questions were put and the expectation that they would be unable to give a satisfactory reply. This would enable him (*Qadi*) to issue a decree for their execution. "In what manner is *zakat* payable in cash," asked the Qadi of Noori. The latter replied, "In your faith or in our faith?" The Qadi asked "In both". Abu'l Hasan Noori said, "In your faith, one

---

[1] *Tarikh-e-Tabari* has this sentence: *dar awail Zandiq wa Manavi be yak ma'ani bud darajeh-e chaharum az darajat-e panjganeh-e din-e Manaviyeh.*" Again, at another place, it records: *Mani zindiq be zaman-e Shapur birun amad wa zandaqah aashkar kard. Zandiq* is drawn from *Zand(a)*, the commentary on Avesta. We come across this term twice in *Zend-Avesta; Yasna* 61 *band* 3, *Vandidad* 18, *band* 53–55. Apparently, *zand (a)* means the enemy of the religion (*din*) brought by Ahura Mazda or *din-e Mazdyasna*. Early Iranian historians attributed *zandaqah* to Mani who, according to the Zoroastrains, was a sorcerer, liar, cheat and a seducer, and who, according to Ferdowsi, was a painter from China.

biyamad yaki mard-i goya ze Chin
kih chun u musawwar nadanad zamin.

Mani declared he was a prophet, and challenged *Mazdayasna*. Arab historians have arabicised the word *zandik* into *zandiq* and *zandaqah*. Islamic writers and historians gave various denigrating epithets to the followers of Mani like *mulhid, dahri, bedin* etc. (See the gloss in *Burhan-e-Qat'e* edited by Muhammad Moin.) '*Nazimu'l-Atabba* gives the meaning of *zandiq* as this: Zand is Zoroastér's book. *Zandiq* is one who has no faith in life hereafter and God, a *mulhid* and a *bedin*. Maulana says:

sa'ati kafir kunad siddiq ra
sa'ati zahid kunad zandiq ra.

Here *zandiq* is the antonym of *zahid*. By *zandiq* later Muslim writers geneally meant believers in *zend* and hence non-Muslim. Araki never fails to use this derogatory terminology when speaking about the Hindus of Kashmir. Mohsin Fani in his *Dabistanul-Mazahib* records the presence of fire-worshippers in Kashmir.

for every hundred and five for every two hundred are payable as *zakat*. However, in our faith, even if the whole world comes into the possession of dervishes, then as thanksgiving to mutual love, they place the entire world at the altar of God Almighty. However, so far we have not been able to reach that stage."

The *Qadi* was an honest and a noble man. Tears rolled down his eyes. He said, "Who among the non-believer wants the execution of these innocent people?" Then he wrote a letter to the Caliph saying that if these people are heretics and non-believers, then for certain there was not a single faithful, true and honest believer in the whole world."

Sayyid Ali and fanatical *mullas*

Mir Sayyid 'Ali Hamadani, the *Qutb* of the *Qutbs*,[1] had suffered great persecution and distraction at the hands of the faithless and detestable *mullas*. Maulana Nuru'd-Din J'afar Badakhshi quotes him in *Khulasatu'l-Manaqib* as this, "I have suffered many difficulties and conspiracies at the hands of the *ulema* and the theologians. One of their perfidies was that they tried to poison me once. But, God Almighty took me under His protection. However, the effect of the poison continues even to this day. Once in a year, I become extremely restless, and my body turns pale and the sores gradually dry up. The story goes like this. I sat in the company of some *mullas* at a certain place. I said some bitter truths to the assembly gathered there. The *ulema* were not happy with it and said to one another that if people came to know of these utterances of the Sayyid, they would withdraw their trust in them. They then hatched the conspiracy of getting rid of me alive or dead.[2]

---

[1] *Qutbu'l-Aqtab* literally means the pivot of the pivots. It is the highest spiritual status in Sufism.

[2] Throughout this narrative the author has tried to paint Mir Sayyid Ali Hamadani in Shia colour. Thus the mullas are generally painted as Sunni fanatics. See the following page.

After making consultations amongst themselves, they decided to poison me. For this purpose, they arranged a big feast to which I was invited. They pretended that my presence in the assembly would be an honour to it. On my way to the feast, I happened to meet with a saintly person who placed a few grains of *hubbu'l-muluk* (probably akin to antidote) in my mouth beseeching me to eat them. I did not object and ate it.

In the assembly, the participants showed me full respect. They brought me a cup of beverage (*sherbat*) and offered it to me with great cordiality. I drank from the cup but later on came to know that the contents had been mixed with poison. I stood up to leave though the people present insisted that I stay on. As soon as I reached my cell, I suffered vomiting and loose motions. This diluted the effect of poison but I suffered a lot before recovering. After this incident, I desisted from keeping company with the dishonest *ulema*. Behind my back, they invented many allegations against me.

Superficial and false faith

The real reason for the animosity and rancour of these detestable wretches towards Amir Shamsu'd-Din was that the wives (and womenfolk) of the *mullas* of Kashmir were mostly from the (houses of) infidels and polytheists. They had taken them in marriage.[1] The faith and solidarity which these women had developed (among their groups) overpowered them (their husbands). Habits, traditions, rituals of the people of these lands had got mixed up with those of the infidels, idol-worshippers, deviants and men of rank ignorance. It had become a normal practice in their households. Those who

---

[1] It is a curious phenomenon. If the *mullas* were originally Brahmans and had converted to Islamic faith, then naturally their women too beacame Musalman and there was no need to take them in marriage. At the best the *nikah* between the husband and wife might have been performed in an orthodox manner to legalise their previously established marital status. Alternatively, it seems that the *mullas* had taken the Hindu women as their wives against their free will.

decided in their families and homes about what is permitted and what is not in Islam, were all infidels and polytheists.[1] The *ulema*, theologians, men of scholarship and erudition of this land had accepted the customs and traditions of depraved and (innovation–liking) aberrant people instead of the traditions and the path shown by the Holy Prophet of Islam. They had discarded all Islamic laws and the basic tenets of Islamic faith. The commandments of God and the Prophet had been done away with. All of them were engrossed in material acquisitions and kept themselves busy with only transient matters. Marriages of women and girls were performed according to the instructions from the infidels and polytheists. Routine matters like hosting feasts for the bride and the groom, their schedule of daily life, including the hours of waking up and going to sleep, were fixed after seeking permission from the infidels and the polytheists.

This is why the detestable, misguided and depraved people of this land have been nursing animus and rancour against the God-fearing and religion-abiding people. One cannot fully count the detestable innovations, depravity, and levity of the *ulema* and theologians of this land. These are numerous. We recount here a story told by Amir Shamsu-Din Araki that tells us about how corrupt, depraved and heretic the local people are.

Polytheism in Kashmir

"I heard from many reliable persons and sources, in particular from Maulana Hafiz Baseer, that during the time I had been staying at *Mazar-e-Salatin*, Qadi Husayn Shirazi happened to be the Qadi of Kashmir. He had developed liaison with the ignominious Shaykh Shihab. Kashmiris called him *Shaykhu'l-*

---

[1] This is an interesting picture of the complexion of Kashmirian society as late as the beginning of the 16th century. It reveals that conversions to Islamic faith had not totally effaced the pre-Islamic traditions in Kashmir. The *mullas* were actually Brahmans converted to new faith. Surprisingly we find that the womenfolk retained strong cultural ties with their Hindu faith and held on to these tenaciously.

Islam. Later on, Qadi's daughter was married to the son of Shaykh Shihab.

On the occasion of the wedding feast, the Qadi's daughter, adorned as bride, was carried from the house of the Shaykh according to the customs and convention of the infidels prevalent in this land from the ancient times. At Shaykh Shihab's house, the bridegroom mounted a horse. About twenty to thirty beautiful but unveiled women, accompanied by some young men, mounted their horses and moved towards the river flowing through the city. In accordance with the custom and the traditions of the depraved infidels and corrupt villains, and as is the wont of the dissidents, many singing women and prostitutes walked ahead of the cavalcade, dancing, laughing and bursting into revelries. Men, women and spectators witnessed the procession in the town and moved along with it. Men and women of prominent families enjoyed the sight of this procession from housetops and walls or by sticking out their necks from the windows. A large crowd of people made up the procession. Now all this is despicable and disallowed (in Islamic faith) because it is a dirty innovation within the realm of infidelity. These practices are strictly unlawful and disallowed (in Islam). The procession finally arrived at the riverside at *Mazar-e-Salatin*.

Upon entering the premises of the burial ground of the Sultans and the governors (of Kashmir), I heard the sound of drums and flutes and the loud noise of people. I came out of my place and took seat in a house to the west of the procession scene. The clamour raised by the reveling crowds was terrible. Some of my servants and attendants gave me the details of the proceedings. Some people from the city had taken their seats by my side. They related to me what they had seen these people do in the function and what type of rituals and customs of the infidels they had observed.

The bride and the bridegroom, along with some women, dismounted their horses on the bank of the river. Two defiled, dirty and wretched *kafirs* also came to the side of the bride and the bridegroom. These polytheists raised the infidel's thread (*zunnar*)[1] from their impious and defiled bodies and wore it over their dress. One of the infidels took a tumbler in his hand and filled it with water. He recited some words of infidelity and polytheism,[2] lifted the tumbler and poured water into the river from some height. After some time, the bridegroom took a sword in his hand and sliced the water from some height. The bride followed suit. The infidels continued reciting the words of sorcery.[3] They filled the tumbler with water several times and continued the ritual, thus maintaining the customs of the infidels. They conveyed the rules and rituals of infidelity to the couple in a strange manner and made some exhortations in the language of the depraved in the hope that the couple would comply with and submit to the ways of the infidels. They performed strange acts, gestures, and rituals of infidelity for two hours. The rest of the procession, men, women and young people, all witnessed the proceedings from the *Mazar-e-Salatin*. A large crowd of men and women had come along with the dancing women to that place. These women vied with one another in gorgeous clothes, and in adornments and make up. They exchanged glances of joy and merry-making. Corrupt men, dirty youth and vagabonds of the city cast covetous glances on these women. They betrayed no sign of fear of God and His Prophet. The women also took great pleasure in exchanging pleasantries with unknown men

---

[1] The tradition of suspending three or six strand thread from the neck down under right arm is connected to the baptizing ritual among the Brahmans (Pandits) of Kashmir, called *yagnyopavita* in Vedic tradition. This tradition also prevails among the Zoroastrians, who call it *kushti*. The style of wearing *kushti* is different from the wearing of *yagnyopavita*. The fire-worshippers tie it around their waist. The name *kushti* meaning the game of wrestling is derived from *kushti* because the winner had to lay his grip on the waistband of his rival and then put him down. However, Arabs gave it the name of *zunn* and in Kashmir the complacent Pandits of post-Islamic centuries frequently mentioned the ceremony as *zunnar bandi*. The word *zunnar* seems to be borrowed by the Arabs from either Hebrew or some other language.

[2] Obviously some *mantras* or Sanskrit hymns meant for the occasion.

[3] *mantras* or *slokas*.

present on the occasion. They smiled and expressed pleasure as they looked at them. The singing women and the prostitutes danced at the gate of the complex. It was an impassioned show of music and dance and a large crowd of city's charlatans had assembled there. In the midst of all this dirty and despicable revelry, they came out from that place and headed towards the house of the Shaykh to repeat the proceedings.

No act of depravity was spared in the house of the Shaykh and the *Qadi*. Practices of infidels were performed in full. But, observance of these practices is not restricted to the house of the *Qadi* and the *Shaykhu'l-Islam*. Such atheistic and idolatrous practices continue to be observed in the houses of all scholars, theologians and leading personalities of this land (Kashmir). They observe all the festivals and feasts of infidels and polytheists. The family members of the elders and leading persons of this land, especially their womenfolk, do not do anything without the permission of the infidels and permission of astrologers.[1] In fact, in all activities of daily life like eating, drinking, sleeping, rising from sleep, travel and rest, astronomers and polytheists have a role to play. This is why all scholars and men of learning in this land, high or low, nurse deep enmity and opposition to the people who believe in prayers and penance, purity and cleanliness.[2] They have always indulged in inciting animosity and fanning opposition towards the people of heart and spirit. It is in their nature to be the sworn enemies of God-loving spiritualists. They have done all they could to perpetrate oppression against the spiritually-

[1] An allusion has already been made to *jadu-e Kashmir,* meaning sorcery of Kashmir in the pages of this work. The Shias of Kashmir usually evince interest in the science of astrology. Even al-Biruni also speaks of it in *Indica* (*Tahqiq-e Mali'l-Hind*). So far no scholar has taken up the subject for research and study. In Tajikistan everybody wanted me to reflect on *jadu-e-Kashmir*. Unfortunately, I had no information on the subject.

[2] By these qualities, the author means true Musulmans. In these paragraphs, he has made a distinction between pseudo-converts and true Musalmans. The two were locked in mutual confrontation at this period of Kashmir's history. Araki was writing more than two hundred and fifty years after the advent of Islam in Kashmir.

inclined Shaykhs and feel proud of their jealousies and prejudice against them. They have not spared efforts to poison them or get them killed. Shaykh Shihab, the wretch, sparked many disputes and confrontations with Amir Shamsu'd-Din. All this is because of expressed or unexpressed animus.

Third encounter

This transient world undergoes changes and revolutions. The reins of power of this land (Kashmir) went out of the hands of Malik Jahangir Magray,[1] the son-in-law of Shaykh Shihab. It will be recalled that Shaykh Shahab had turned down a proposal of his daughter's marriage to some nobleman of Sayyid descent in the holy city of Medina. He intended to give her in marriage to Sultan Hasan Shah of Kashmir. But her destiny did not favour the girl, and after the death of Hasan Shah, she was married to Malik Jahangir Magray.

During the administration of Jahangir Magray, Malik Saif Dar, along with his brothers and friends had been defeated in Kashmir and had fled to the Indian mountains (Pir Panchal). Many soldiers of Kashmir also fled the land and joined Malik Saif Dar. Following this development, Malik Magray arrested the guides and the guards watching the roads. Some of them were put to sword for which decrees were obtained from Shaykh Shihab.

In one of his decrees, Shaykh Shihab said that Jahangir Magray was the *Imam* of his times and the *khalifa* (Caliph) of his days. According to the people of Sunni faith, it is important to have achievements to ones credit in order to reach the status of *Imam* and *Khalifa*. Anybody who acquires the high status and dominates others becomes the *khalifa* of the day. This is what the people of Sunni faith say.

Today in this land (Kashmir), the *Imam* of the times and the *Khalifatu'l-lilah* (God's vicegerent) is Jehangir Magray.

---

[1] Magray is the corrupted form of Margresha, the name of a powerful clan of mediaeval Kashmir. See, Jonaraja's *Rajatarangini*, tr. J.C. Dutt.

There is no doubt that one who opposes him is in fact a rebel. One, who rises in rebellion against him, is to be beheaded. Therefore, in accordance with this decree, the followers of Malik Saif Dar who were captured were to be beheaded. In this way, the Shaykh was responsible for the killing and destruction of many innocent people.

When the reins of power once again passed into the hands of Malik Saif Dar, he did not forget the destruction of innocent people caused by the deep-seated enmity of Shaykh Shihab and his false decrees. He was keen to avenge the bloodshed caused by Shaykh Shihab. A big assembly was organised to which the theologians of the town were invited. They were asked to give their opinion on the decrees issued by the detestable Shaykh.

A sumptuous feast was arranged in the Hamadaniyyeh *khanqah* in Srinagar. A large number of *ulema*, scholars, grandees, noblemen, Sayyids and *Qadis* were invited to it. Amir Shamsu'd-Din was also invited to the feast. He took a boat from his residence. At the time of his departure, Mir Dervish, one of the devotees of Shamsu'd-Din, politely submitted to him that they were strangers in the land (Kashmir). There were no supporters and defenders for them. As such, he (Amir Shamsu'd-Din) should take utmost care not to take part in argument with the Kashmiri people. He suggested that in the case of a debate on any issue, Araki should desist from using impolite words. All of Mir's devotees and associates agreed with Mir Dervish's suggestion. Amir Shamsu'd-Din also accepted it. Mir Dervish took with him a few of his associates and came to the assembly. His main anxiety was to see how deliberations were conducted and that the atmosphere was not vitiated by any indiscretion.

When Amir Shamsu'd-Din joined the assembly, he found Shaykh Shihab sitting by his side. After the dinner was served, a debate was initiated. But before the proceedings started, Amir Shamsu'd-Din turned towards Shaykh Shihab and said," You speak indecent words and make indiscreet utterances in the course of a debate. I do not mind whatever you speak about my person because I have the capacity to swallow it all and forgive you. But, you should not speak anything about my attendants, associates and servants. You are prone to using hateful and indecent language. You will take care that no disrespect is shown to my associates. I cannot tolerate any misbehaviour of that kind. As such, you must keep in mind this warning."

At the outset, Malik Saif Dar asked the *ulema* to tell him what the Islamic injunction has to say about a person who issues a decree of infidelity against *kelima*-reciting Musalmans and sheds their blood? Shaykh Shihab realised that the debate would certainly go against him. He now understood the ultimate purpose of the debate. In order to refute the allegation, he began a speech by taking recourse to pretexts. Some of the *mullas* who supported Malik Saif Dar took part in the debate. It was the habit of Amir Shamsu'd-Din that whatever he had to say, he would quote it from Hazrat Shah Qasim. He would say that he had heard so and so from Shah Qasim. In the course of this debate, too, he quoted Shah Qasim a number of times.

Forgetting the warning that had been given to him by Shamsu'd-Din right in the beginning, Shaykh Shihab said that he (Shamsu'd-Din) had referred to Shah Qasim several times in his speech only to project him (Shah Qasim) as a scholar more than what he actually was. "I know him not. He was an alchemist and spent his entire life in seeking unattainable things. He only spoilt his life, and there is no point in feeling proud of him," the Shaykh said. Amir Shamsu'd-Din could not tolerate these words spoken against Shah Qasim. He gave a strong slap on the face of the Shaykh with the back of his hand that broke his two teeth. He fell flat where he was sitting. Mir Dervish witnessed this happening from a little distance. He rose and came quickly to the side of Amir Shamsu'd-Din and kicked the Shaykh several times on his back.

All those participating in the assembly rose from their places. The meeting was disrupted. The *mullas* raised uproar.

People inside the hospice raised a loud noise so much so that people who heard it outside thought that the nobles and grandees were perhaps attacking one another. They caught hold of the horses and the carriages standing outside the hospice and joined in the great scuffle in which the strongly built persons overpowered the weak ones and looted and vandalised them.

When this row was taking place, some of the associates and followers of Amir Shamsu'd-din stood within the walls of the hospice. They entered the hospice and took him away to the secluded cell of Sayyid Muhammad Hamadani in the hospice so that he could be secured against sudden assault. The windows and doors of the cell were very strong and had to be broken to take him out. A boat kept ready at the riverbank ferried him to his residence.

The supporters of the people who were at the helm of administrative authority (of Kashmir) stood at the gate of the hospice and announced that the pandemonium was created by the *mullas* and that there was no friction between the ruler and the nobles. They warned miscreants not to do anything untoward, not to indulge in loot and arson; otherwise they would face the wrath of the authorities.

When the turmoil and disturbance subsided, the rulers and nobles left for their places. The *ulema* and the *mullas* also headed towards their homes. As soon as Amir Shamsu'd-Din came to his residence, his followers and associates, who had heard of the incident in the hospice, came to him and desired to know what had happened. Amir Shamsu'd-Din called Mir Dervish to his presence and asked him, "At the time of our departure, you had advised me that I should not lose my cool and should avoid everything that would disrupt the proceedings. But when I struck a blow at the face of the Shaykh, why did you rush to the spot and deliver several kicks to him?" Mir Dervish defended his action in these words." I had tried to advise you with the purpose that a debate does not turn into a scuffle. But, when I saw that you had raised the hand in bravery and had come out to challenge him, I realised that the matter had gone far beyond persuasion and advice. I acted courageously, and unmindful of consequence, decided to strike him."

Message to Saif Dar

The clergy of the city decided to support Malik Reg (Regi) Dar. A message was sent to Malik Saif Dar through one of them. It is said that ever since the world came into existence, the *ulema* have always indulged in debates and discussions but they never behaved in such a way with the elders, scholars, grandees and the learned community. They have never been humiliated or treated with disrespect. In no city and in no town are humiliations hurled when an assembly of learned men is in progress. This is unheard of. If this situation continues, then it will be humiliating for them to continue staying in this land. They said, "Your Lordship, the principles of justice and equity determine every action of human beings. Please implement these principles out of your concern for the people. Your officials ought to examine this episode with justice and equanimity and try to understand the vicious things that have cropped up. If the Great Malik chooses to ignore the event, it will be a big mistake on our part to continue to live in this land."

Kashmiri *mullas* in revolt

The message was brought to Malik Saif Dar. Initially he cared very little to do justice because of his long time malice and ill will (towards his detractors). But then the clerics made it an issue of the entire community. They came out of their homes and residences and proceeded to the outskkirts of the town (of Srinagar) for a sit down strike.[1] They demanded that Mir

[1] This kind of a show of resentment to the policy of the ruling authority by the clerics was not the first of its kind in Kashmir history. During the Hindu rule, the Brahmanic priests would lodge protests like that. They would also resort to hunger strike. See, *Rajatarangini*, tr. Stein, 2 volumes, Lahore, 1889, chapter dealing with the reign of Harsha.

Shamsu'd-Din be banished from Kashmir as he was their enemy. They said that they would not return to their homes unless their demand was met. They even took an oath to that effect. (Thereupon) Malik Saif Dar sent them a message that he could not break Shamsu'd-Din's heart, because he happened to be the emissary of the King of Khurasan. He asserted that nobody had ever heard of a host causing embarrassment to an envoy from another country or region. He declared that he would not allow anybody to put the emissary of the ruler of Khurasni to inconvenience just because the *mullas* wanted to derive pleasure out of it.[1]

He declared that Amir Shamsu'd-Din was not at fault in this disorder. Before the debate ensued, he had clearly told Shaykh Shihab in the presence of the entire audience that no contemptuous words should be said about his followers or his Shaykhs. Shaykh Shihab had made some indecent remarks. The *mullas* were offended by the remarks of Mir Shamsu'd-Din. The king told his courtiers that the purpose of the assembly was to take revenge against Shaykh Shihab, make him uncomfortable through the spoken word. Amir Shamsu'd-Din had only fulfilled his mission. How could such a dear person be subjected to any kind punishment?

Mullas threaten exodus

The (Sunni) clergy now came to know of Malik Saif Dar's reaction to the issue. He had given them a bit of his mind. Thereupon all of them left their homes, and came to a place that was one or two stations outside the outskirts of the town. A day or two later, Malik Regi Dar came to Malik Saif Dar for

[1] It is intriguing that while Saif Dar is conscious of the norms of protocol in treating the "emissary" of a foreign country, he meticulously avoids even the slightest mention of the interference of the "emissary" in internal matters of the host country, an act disallowed by the same set of norms of protocol. Obviously, Saif Dar's policy is not based on any principle, but is politically motivated. This is a significant event in the history of Shia-Sunni relationship in Kashmir at that point of time.

consultations. He told him that they (the clan of Saif Dar) lacked the competence to administer the state. The *ulema* and scholarly persons[1] were migrating from their land (Kashmir) to the lands of Hind, and this would certainly earn them a bad name. He said that the matter needed careful consideration. If these people migrated to Hind, then the people in those lands would have a very poor opinion about them (the rulers). Malik Saif Dar said that he was not going to win the goodwill of the clergy at the expense of Amir Shamsu'd-Din. He added that he knew the *mullas* were miserly, greedy and wretched. Then he asked Regi Dar to request them to return and that Shaykh Shihab would be given additional (12?) estates (*jagirs*). Regi Dar went to the *mullas* and brought them back from Khan Marg(?)[2]

Shahab and Hamadaniyyeh hospice

A few days later, instead of punishing Shaykh Shihab, he was entrusted with the trusteeship of the Hamadaniyyeh hospice, a position previously held by Hajji Shams.[3] With this assignment in hand, Shaykh Shihab became greedy person. He began indulging in reprehensible deeds. He interfered with the procedure of giving stipends provided by the hospice that had been there from the days of Amir Sayyid 'Ali Hamadani. The practice had continued among the followers of that

[1] This shows that opposition to Araki was not limited to the clergy only but to the men of learning as well. In other words it was a broad-based movement against the political structure of the day which was behaving in a prejudicial manner.

[2] We have today a small town called Khan Sahib in Budgam districtg. It lies along the Tos Maidan pass over the Pir Panchal. It.is possible the adversaries of the (Sunni) clergy would have lebelled those who left their homes "*mufroor*" (absconders) as the Pandits were labelled following their mass exodus in January 1990 because of the rise of militancy in Kashmir Valley. Even the revenue officers are reported to have entered "*mufroor*" in the residence column for the Pandits in state revenue records.

[3] It appears that Regi Dar negotiated a deal by which the Sunnis were given some concessions including the important concession of making Shaykh Shihab the trustee of the Hamadaniyyeh hospice (*khanqah*). However, the dmand for banishing Araki from Kashmir was not conceded.

line (*silsilah-e Hamadaniyyeh*).[1] He abolished the established rules and practices of offering prayers and recitations introduced in this hospice from the time of the arrival of Amir Sayyid 'Ali Hamadani. He also stopped the stipends and daily allowance that had been provided since long time. He was emboldened in dispensing with the established norms to the extent that recitation of the psalms called *awarad-e-fathiyyeh* was also stopped. Recitation of these psalms was the choice practice of the devotees of this land by which they used to show their allegiance and special regard for Amir-i Kabir Sayyid 'Ali Hamadani. Succeeding generations of people of this land (Kashmir) observed the practice of reciting some special hymns. He forbade the recitation of *awarad-fathiyyeh,* and, in its place, he introduced the recitation of *award-i-Qadiryyeh*[2] at the time of offering morning prayer *(namaz)*. The followers of the line of Shaykh Abdu'l-Qadir Geelani (Jeelani)[3] had compiled these psalms and he (Shaykh Shihab) brought these with himself (when he came to Kashmir). Thus the practice of reciting *awaraad-e-fathiyyeh* ceased to be observed in the hospice. He told the inmates and casual residents of the *khanqah* that he would not permit anybody to recite them because the Hamadaniyyeh era had ended and was now replaced by Qadiryyeh era. He said that anybody desirous of reciting the *awraad* should recite *Awraad-e-Qadiryyeh.* He also declared that Hamadaniyyeh line had to be uprooted from the town and added that whatever practices of

---

[1] Obviously, these stipends generally went to the students of Shi'a faith.

[2] The inference is that the *award-i fathiyyeh* were attributed to Nurbakhshiyyeh order of Sufis while the *award-i-Qadiriyyeh* to the Sufi order of Abdul Qadir Jeelani (Geelani)

[3] Born in Baghdad in *cir.* AH 470–90/AD 1077–97, Mohiu'd-Din 'Abdu'l-Qadir Gilani is called the Imam of Qadiryyeh order of Suifs, which has a large number of followers in India and the erstwhile Ottoman Empire and the Islamic lands. According to *Qamusu'l-Elam*, he traces his origin to Imam Hasan. He received early tutoring from Abu Zakariya. His work *Futawi* is appreciated by the followers of Shafi'i and Hanbali schools. He died in *circa* AH 560–61/AD 1164–65 in Baghdad. See *Rawdat'u-Jannat*, p.432 and *Rayhanatu'l-Adab*, vol.iii, p.494.

recitation, prayers and related matters were prevalent in Kashmir (according to Hamadaniyyeh order) would be effaced lock, stock and barrel. He warned that nobody would be permitted to bring the name of Hamadaniyyeh on his tongue. In short, Shaykh Shihab wanted to efface from the lands of Kashmir all traces, systems and the line of the Hamadaniyyeh order.[1]

God Almighty ordained that the *tariqat* (system/way) of Hamadaniyyeh order and of Nurbakhshiyyeh line would flourish in all regions of this land and this state. The dark hearts of the heretics and the doubt-ridden minds[2] of the ignorant people of this land were to be illumined by the light of the instructions given by the followers of the path of truth. Thus came to be lit the candle of Nurbakhshiyyeh beliefs and the venerable man of parts, Mir Araki, carried this task ahead.

Araki's firm resolve

These unbecoming and undignified acts of the Shaykh were brought to the notice of Amir Shamsu'd-Din. The report of banning the recitation of *awraad-e-fathiyyeh* in the Hamadaniyyeh hospice in particular, pained and depressed him. He recollected that the auspicious steps of Sayyid 'Ali Hamadani had bestowed light upon the people of this land. This made his line and his order very popular. But now the situation had been reversed to such an extent that even the recitation of *Hamadaniyyeh* psalms was forbidden; stipends and alms were terminated. They (those against Hamadaniyyeh

---

[1] This could be called the first mass-scale propagation of discarding Hamadaniyyeh Sufi order and replacing it with Qadri Sufi order. This is symptomatic of Shia-Sunni strife in the Kashmirian society in the 15th century AD. It may be inferred that the *Awraad-e-Fathiyyeh* originally introducd by Amir Kabir had a pro-Shia tilt. That is why Shaykh Shihab replaced it by *Awraad-e Qadiryyeh*. This matter should invite the attention of researchers. Is the current *Awaraad-e Fathiyyeh* an amalgam of the two?

[2] It shows that people who had converted to Islam two enturies ago still had doubts on various aspects of the new faith.

order) wanted to eradicate fully the system brought by Amir Sayyid 'Ali.

He considered it incumbent upon him to revive the practices and (Sufi) order of Amir Sayyid 'Ali. The followers of Amir-e-Kabir needed to be introduced to the ways and systems of penance and other formalities. His traditions and recitations had to be revived and promulgated. People seeking his path had to be taught how to undertake the Lent (*chillah*) and they needed to learn the specific rules of etiquette laid down for the followers of that order. He held consultations with his associates and supporters to find out the ways of achieving this objective. These consultations further strengthened his resolve of reviving the Hamadaniyyeh traditions. Thus through his courage and persistence, the *khanqah* of Hamadaniyyeh was restored to its past glory. Circumstances leading to this development will be recorded here as faithfully as possible.[1]

Amir Shamsu'd-Din Araki mad a firm resolve to give a crushing defeat to the enemies of the people and the opponents of the religion of Islam in this land of mischief-mongers, and a hotbed of corrupt people. He determined to raise high the banner of Islam, demolish the customs and traditions of idol-worshippers, and eradicate all symptoms of infidelity and ignorance (about Islamic religion) from the misguided people of this land.[2]

---

[1] This paragraph reveals that the Islamic traditions and the Sufi order brought by Mr Sayyid Ali Hamadani, the well known 14th century Iranian missionary to Kashmir, were replaced by the traditions of the Sunni sect and the Qadiryyeh order of Suifs. Arak undertook the mission of restoring the original traditions and system, which, as we shall see, were reversed again after Araki's decline.

[2] This statement categorically indicates that Araki had a religious and not a political mission. Propagation of Nurbakhshiyyeh order and not the failing health of Sultan Husayn Mirza of Herat was his priority. It is ironic that in order to bring "true knowledge of the right faith" (Shi'ism) to the converted people of Kashmir, he thought it necessary to undertake the destruction of the Hindus who had stuck to their old faith.

Sufi Jamaal

To begin this difficult task, Amir Shamsu'd-Din looked for an augury[1] and sought divine support to his mission. Among his devotees and associates, there was one named Sufi Jamaal. Whenever Amir Shamsu'd-Din began doing something new and sensitive, he would seek an augury from Sufi Jamaal.[2] He told Sufi Jamaal that he was planning a difficult mission. He wanted to know how the mission would go. However, Araki did not tell him the exact nature of the contemplated mission and did not explain to Sufi Jamaal the precise objective he was aiming at. Sufi Jamaal sat down in the night to take an augury. In the morning he came to the presence of the Amir and recounted his dream as this:

"A person carrying something on a covered platter came to me and placed it in front of me. I took off the cover and found that there were fresh pomegranates. I counted them and found they were forty. I broke open each pomegranate and found there were forty granules in each." Having heard the story from Sufi Jamaal, Amir Shamsu'd-Din was certain that if that (?) dervish went into lent, he would receive God's special favours.

Taking an omen

He did not rest content with the omen taking practice of Sufi Jamaal. One day he prepared himself for inner purification to receive the omen in his mind's mirror. He wanted to examine how sincere his intention was and also the ultimate result of the task underway. Once, Mir Dervish too, had desired to take an omen in order to ascertain the divine dispensation. Mir Dervish's cell was located next to that of Shamsu'd-Din. Around midnight, Mir Shamsu'd-Din called Mir Dervish and

[1] Taking augury in order to find propitious moment for beginning a new task has been an old practice with the Iranians. See Introduction.

[2] In all probability, he seems to be an indigenous Hindu who had converted to Islam.

knocked at the wooden partition between the two cells. He wanted to know whether Mir Dervish was awake or sleeping. He told Mir Dervish that he had found a strange omen on his own. He had found that in fact Suleyman[1] was a hypocrite. People with clean heart know that Dervish Suleyman was considered one of the most faithful disciples and followers of Imam Nurbakhsh.

For a long time, he tended camels, as did Oveys Qarni.[2] Wherever Sayyid Muhammad Nurbakhsh went, Dervish Suleyman would load the camels with his master's belongings. But he was given the negative title of a hypocrite (*makkar*). Indeed, he had rendered a great deal of service to the venerable Imam. Owing to his (Dervish Suleyman's) selfless service, intense penance and strict observance of ascetical practices, he was admitted to the circle of his lieutenants. He was given (religious/Sufistic) authority and the freedom of exercising it as he wished. In the matter of interpreting dreams, the venerable Imam had bestowed upon him the status of Yusuf. "But in the course of my seeking an omen, I found Suleyman a hypocrite. He rode a camel as big as an elephant with a big bell suspended from its neck. It rang so loud that its sound reached the ears of the people of this world. Coming

---

[1] I have not been able to identify this person.

[2] Oveys ibn 'Amir was from Bani Murad tribe whose ancestors had come from Yemen. He had not seen the Prophet personally but came to 'Umar ibn Khattab and, along with 'Ali, took part in the battle of Siffin. Some historians believe that he attained martyrdom in that battle in AH 37/AD 657. Ibn Batuteh, who had visited his grave in Damascus, tells us that he had read in *al-Mu'alim fi Sharh Sahibu'l-Muslim* of Qurtabi that Oveys joined a group of Prophet's Companions in Medina and left for Syria with them. However, before arriving at his destination, death overtook him at a place where there was neither a drop of water nor a blade of grass. His fellow travelers were disappointed and did not understand what to do. Then, suddenly they found that a shroud, some water and a little scent for sprinkling over the dead body appeared from nowhere. Then they resumed their journey. However, after going only a short distance, one from among the group turned back saying that he would put something on the grave by way of a signboard. But, to his surprise, he could not find any trace of the grave. See *Loghat Nameh* (under Oveys Qarni), p.510.

close to me, he dismounted, and brought down a big water container from the seat to place it in front of me. On opening the container, I found it full of almonds and currants (*kishmish*), which I distributed among the people around me. I too, tasted some of these. Beneath the dry fruit, I found a heap of gold coins and gold and silver. The more almonds and currants I distributed among the people present, the more gold and silver appeared from underneath. After a couple of hours, I found that Dervish Suleyman was doing sorcery (?). At my place, I could discern the hazy visage of Hazrat Imam Nurbakhsh. Thereafter Imam Nurbakhsh appeared at my place as well as that of Dervish Suleyman. It was bewildering, and I woke up. Mir Dervish wanted to know from Shamsu'd-Din how could the dream be interpreted. They deferred its interpretation to next day when all devotees and servants would be present in his assembly.

Interpretation

Next day, the devotees, friends, associates and sympathizers all gathered together in his august presence. Then Shamsu'd-Din addressed them, "The camel and its seat represent intense penance and spiritual exercise; the ringing of the bell means that the fame of penance and meditation of my followers and dervishes would resound in the four corners of the world. This was an indication that the religion of the Prophet would spread in the world and that Islam would gain strength from step to step. Word about my effort, in the service of religion will reach many ears. The imparting of religious and spiritual instructions will reach lands far and near. The distribution of almonds and currants indicates promulgation of recitations and prayers besides conveying the meaning of spiritual inspirations, which are destined to flow to my followers and devotees. Blessed will they be with the fruit of their spiritual exercise. Regular refurbishing of gold coins, as seen in the dream, means that many spiritualists of eminence and fame make a name under my guidance and training."

In short, many ascetics and dervishes retold the story of Mir Shamsu'd-Din Arak is well-known interpretation of a dream. These truths had dawned upon him just because of his great service to leading spiritualists who had given him their blessings.

Mir Shamsu'd-Din desired that a secluded place be found so that independent cells for the seekers of the path of spiritualism could be provided. His followers said that there were many hospices (*khanqah*) in the town. Whichever hospice Hazrat Mir Shams selected, they would obtain permission from the ruler (to occupy them). He said that hospices in the city (Srinagar) were useless and not worth the name; at best these were like a caravanserai or the traveller's inn. No hospice in the town was fit for lent for the seekers of the path to divinity, even the Amiriyyeh hospice, too, was not a fit place for the purpose. (That hospice was built under the instructions of Amir Sayyid 'Ali Hamadani). Actually, the father had raised the platform and the son[1] had built the hospice on it.

Sayyid Muhammad Hamadani

He was hardly three or four years of age when his father passed away. After reaching adolescence, he did not accept the tutoring of Khwaja Ishaq for spiritual guidance. Wicked and satanic persons misled him into opposition to and animosity with that spiritualist. Owing to these differences and quarrels, he went into self-imposed exile. From his birthplace Khatlan (in today's Tajikistan), he came to the lands of Kashmir.[2] He could not go to any of the followers of his father. As such, he remained somewhat ignorant of the ways and procedures of the seekers of divine path and the systems of

---

[1] Sayyid Muhammad Hamadani's differences with the followers and disciples of his father (Amir Kabir Sayyid 'Ali have been told in this work at its proper place).

[2] Full details of these differences are not available. However, we may infer that Sayyid Muhammad Hamadani was inclined towards the Sunni and not the Shi'a faith, though it is a moot point.

penance. However, he ordered the construction of the Hamadaniyyeh hospice, which was not according to the principles and procedure of the people of the path and system (of mystics).[1] He might have ordered the builders to build a hospice. But the masons and carpenters built a structure according to their own wishes. As such, that hospice was not built keeping in mind the custom of the dervishes going into Lent.[2] The spiritual guides and the Shaykhs of divinity, too, built hospices for their pupils. The doors of private cells opened in the compound of the hospice. The frame of the door was hardly an inch or two above the level of the compound.[3]

He directed his friends and devotees to look for a site with the provision of a private cell that would be away from the crowds, a place purified by the steps of some seer. He said that Shaykh Bahau'd-Din had built a hospice somewhere, which he would like to use for lent and secluded penance.

Shaykh Bahau'd-din Kashmiri

Araki's devotees and followers said in one voice that Shaykh Bahau'd-Din[4] had not attained a level of fame in this land that he would arrange secluded penance for his followers and pupils. They said that they had yet to see a hospice or a lent house that the Shaykh had built for himself.

---

[1] This sentence, besides the one in the preceding paragraph, indicates that the type of hospice Araki recommended for the Nurbakhshiyyeh dervishes must have been modelled differently from the ones used by the Sufis of other orders like the Naqshbandiyyeh or Qadiriyyeh or Suhrawardiyyeh. Since the Hamadaniyyeh hospice built by Sayyid Muhammad did not fulfil the requirements of Nurbakhshiyeh models, it further clarifies that Sayyid Muhammad was inclined towards Suuni sect. The subject merits investigation by serious scholars.

[2] Ibid.

[3] A look at the *khanqahs* of mediaeval times in Tajikistan, particularly the one in Hissar, answers the specification given here. No such *khanqah*, standing or in ruins, is comparable in style to the Central Asian hospices.

[4] His tomb is preserved in the Nowhatta locality of downtown Srinagar and is known to the locals by the name Bahau'd-Din Sahib.

Shaykh Bahau'd-Dins residence was situated close to the Amiriyyeh Khanqah (*Khanqah* of Amir Sayyid 'Ali Hamadani) to its south. It was a small and dark house in which his family lived. He lived on a handful of cooked food that he carried from the kitchen of the hospice to feed his family. Every month, he used to go in for lent on selected days in one of the cells of the hospice. He observed lent in strict conformity with the tradition of the dervishes. At last, some people came to know about it. They marked the details of his schedule and came to know that he was a perfect dervish. He spoke a few words and did not maintain links with any of his relatives or associates but remained engrossed in his own world of spiritual introspection. He had no source of income and depended on whatever little he found to eat from the hospice kitchen. He had never gone in pursuit of any regular income. Men of substance took pity on his condition as they came to know the details of his life. Thus, they sympathized with him. Some of the grandees of the town brought information about this saintly person to the notice of Sultan Zainu'l-'Abidin (d. AH 880/AD 1475). They said that since the God-fearing man had neither any source of income nor demanded anything from anybody, the Sultan might be pleased to grant a stipend to him from the alms received at Hamadaniyyeh hospice establishment and meant for mendicants and dervishes. They recommended both a stipend and daily allowance because his family members deserved this succour. They pleaded that this virtuous deed would earn good merit to the Sultan.

But that king followed the ways and customs of the infidels, the corrupt and the *zandiqs*[1] (apostates). He said that he would put Shaykh Bahau'd-Din to test before fixing a stipend for him.

---

[1] Supra, p.112fn.1.

The test

Elders and grandees waited to see how the matter would proceed. One day, the king took a boat and came to the Amiriyyeh hospice. After learning about the place of residence of Bahau'd-Din, he disembarked and ordered a couple of his servants to set the house of Bahau'd-Din on fire. Then he ordered a few men to go close to the window of the secluded cell in which the Shaykh had gone into lent and speak loudly that his house had caught fire. The Shaykh heard the loud noise, opened the window and saw the flames engulfing his house. Some people say that the Shaykh was in deep introspection. He came out of the door of the hospice and, leaning against the wall of the hospice, kept looking at his house as the leaping flames consumed it. He did not know that the house had been set on fire by king s order. When the house turned into ashes, he returned to his cell and resumed his penance. He did not utter a word.

But the king did not approve of the Shaykh for coming out of the cell on hearing that his house was on fire. "A true dervish and an absorbed *sufi* would not have left his cell. Had he not come out, I would have ordered that a new house be built for him. But I have lost faith in his asceticism," said the Sultan.

A foolish king puts his subjects to a test in these perfidious (*jehudaneh*)[1] ways and loses faith and confidence in saints and ascetics: he is not ashamed of treating seers and divines in that way: he does not know that the learned, the theologians, the Shaykhs and the divines, all need to respond to the call of nature when in lent. It is perfectly right and permitted.

The servants of the hospice learnt about the indifference of the king. They stopped the Shaykhs daily supply of food and even had the audacity to make him feel uncomfortable.

[1] The Muslims call the habit of hard bargaining attributed to the Jewish people as *juhudbazi*. It is always used in a derogatory sense.

This brought the Shaykh to the brink of disaster. A generous woman, descending from the line of Baihaqi Sayyids,[1] learnt that the king had put the Shaykh to a test. She cursed the king, calling him unjust for putting dervishes and mendicants to test and ordering the burning of the Shaykh's house.

Bibeh (Bibi) Khatun

This woman, a member of the royal *harem*, was Bibeh (Bibi) Khatun. She sent one of her confidants to the Shaykh for enquiring about him and his family. Then she fixed a quantity of ration of rice and other eatables and cash dole for the Shaykh, from the budget of royal household. With the succour provided by this noble woman, the Shaykh managed to make both ends meet.

When Bibeh Khatun learnt about Shaykh's demise, she told her officials that expenditure for the burial of the dead should be debited to her private account, and his body be buried in her private graveyard. The officials did as directed, and the dead body was laid to rest in the graveyard of the Baihaqi Sayyids. The *mullas* in charge of the graveyard had dug a grave for the Shaykh at a place that lay below all graves in that graveyard. The dead body of the Shaykh remains buried there.[2]

Burial place rebuilt

Amir Shamsu'd-Din Araki came to know from his friends and admirers about the story of Shaykh Bahau'd-Din. He regretted the misfortune and wretchedness of the people of this land. He said it was sad that none among the grandees, elders, and seniors of this land was gifted with insight into the truth because they were unable to recognize an outstanding saint

[1] For details about the history and role of Baihaqi Sayyids in Kashmir, see *Baharistan-i-Shahi (A Chronicle of Mediaeval Kashmir)*, Cal.1991, chapter iii, et seq.

[2] Curiously, no historian of Kashmir has mentioned any controversy over Shaykh Bahau'd-Din and the story of putting him to a test.

among them. He then proceeded to the grave of the Shaykh to offer prayers. It was a modest grave of a poor man with a couple of unchiselled slabs and a handful of soil spread over it.[1]

After offering prayers for the dead person (*fateha*), he told his followers and *sufis* to bring a square stone for reconstructing the grave with a befitting structure over it.[2] At that time, there was a platform on the grave, which was dismantled under Shamsu'd-Dins instructions; a new superstructure was raised in its place.

Araki visited the grave of the Shaykh very often to pray for the soul of the dead. This increased (peoples) respect for the burial place of the Shaykh, and, thereafter, it began to be called *Mazar-e-Sayyidan* instead of *Mazar-e Sadat*.[3] Indeed *Mazar-e-Shaykh Bahau'd-Din* attained much fame. The size of offerings made at the burial place increased manifold and it became a place which people high and low visited.. Having done that, he asked his associates if there was any hospice in the city in the name of Shaykh Sultan Kashmiri.

---

[1] Araki was a staunch Shi'a of Nurbakhshiyyeh order. This work profiles him as an uncompromising fanatic. Why should he have developed a sympathetic attitude towards Shaykh Bahau'-Din, and subtly accuse Sultan Zainu'l-'Abidin of his atrocious treatment of the Shaykh? If we presume that Araki considered the Shaykh of Shi'a proclivity, then we shall have to look for Araki's sources of information. It remains to be investigated whether reconstruction of the tombs was Araki's ploy to attract the attention of the local people who believed in shrine-worship.

[2] This means that Nurbakhshiyyeh did not oppose the raising of tombs over the graves of the dead, a practice strictly forbidden by the Wahhabis.

[3] The difference between the two is that *Sadat* (plural of *Sayyid*) is Arabic while *Sayyidan* (plural of *Sayyid*) is commonly used in Farsi. The real reason for Araki to re-name the place could have been to detach it from the history of the Baihaqi Sayyids who were not Shi'a but Sunni and Araki was not comfortable The difference between the two is that *Sadat* (plural of *Sayyid*) is Arabic while *Sayyidan* (plural of *Sayyid*) is commonly used in Farsi. The real reason for Araki to re-name the place could have been to detach it from the history of the Baihaqi Sayyids who were not Shi'a but Sunni and Araki was not comfortable with that.

Khanqah-e Sultan

Knowledgeable persons told him that there was a hospice of Shaykh Sultan; the people of the land called it Khanqah-e-Shaykh Sultan Kubra. The Shaykh had gone into lent several times in that hospice. They told Araki that the said hospice stood at the foot of Koh-e-Suleyman and the place was called Drugjeh (*sic.* Drugjan).[1] On learning the name of the place, he immediately proceeded to the site to have a look at the hospice and its environs. He found it a small place, but was happy with its interior and secluded cells.

He sent blessings to the soul of Shaykh Sultan and said that the model of the hospice met the conditions set forth by Shaykhs and penitents. He conveyed to all those who had accompanied him that he was willingness to stay in that particular hospice along with his family. His intention was to impart training to the seekers of divine path while staying in that hospice. He wanted to find how God Almighty bestowed His grace upon his servants and dervishes.

Bahau'd-Din meets Sultan Kubra

People gifted with inner purity and truthfulness are aware that Shaykh Bahau'd-Din and Shaykh Sultan both hailed from Kashmir. Shaykh Bahau'd-Din came from Phak[2] (?) and Shaykh Sultan came from Geyur[3]. This is the reason why Hazrat Imam (Nurbakhsh) called both of them Kashmiri in his work *Silsilatu'z-Zahab*. At the time of compiling this work, both of them were alive. Both were the followers of the teachings of Khwaja Ishaq[4] from whom they learnt various

---

[1] This locality is at the foothill of Shankaracharya hill to the south of Srinagar city. It is now renamed as Sulaiman Koh.

[2] Phak is the old name of a pargana lying to the northof Srinagar

[3] Name of a village in Anantnag district. Kashyapa Bandhu, the popular leader and one time close associaate of Sheikh Abdullah, too, hailed from Geyur.

[4] He was the spiritual guide of Sayyid 'Ali Hamadani also in Khatlan. See p.69fn.3 supra.

things such as mysticism, penance, Lent meditation, innovation, and the manners and etiquette and expression of regard for others. Under his spiritual guidance, both of them attained high position and reached a prominent stage in their mystic journey. Hazrat Khwaja permitted them to accept allegiance from the pupils of mystic pursuits, repentance, and guidance and instructions for the seekers of spiritual excellence. Both of them have received encomiums from the Imam in the above-mentioned work.

When the Imam wrote *Sahifatu'l-Awlia*,[1] Shaykh Sultan Kubra had left this mortal world. That is why his name has not been included in the *Sahifa*. Shaykh Bahau'd-Din was still living. The Imam had included the names of only the living saints and godly men in his work. In fact, the said work begins with praise for Shaykh Bahau'd-Din.

After obtaining permission from Khwaja Ishaq Khatlani (martyred AH 826/AD 1422) to guide the mystics under training, to accept repentance and allegiance from devotees, both of them returned to the lands of Kashmir. At that time, infidelity, apostasy, polytheism, corruption and dualism were at their peak (in Kashmir). These conditions had come into being because of the support and encouragement from Sultan Zainu'l-'Abidin (d. AH 880/AH 1475). Nobody cared two hoots for religion. The development of religion and its expansion had been brought to a halt, rather stonewalled. This is why nobody showed any regard for or respect to Bahau'd-Din. He advised people but they did not accept it.[2] Although he had in his possession the letter of authority from Khwaja Ishaq that he could guide the seekers of knowledge, the people behaved like strangers and declined to pay heed to his words of wisdom, let alone making allegiance at his hands.

---

[1] It is the work of Imam Nur Baksh.

[2] This phenomenon needs to be studied in depth. I suspect he was inclined towards the Nurbakhshiyyeh.

Under these circumstances, he decided to retire to a place of seclusion and spend his days away from the din of material life.[1]

Uthman Makhdum

Mir Hasan Munajjim has recounted the following story a number of times: "Maulana Uthman Makhdoom's hospice stood in the neighbourhood of Shaykh Bahau'd-Din's hospice. The Maulana often enquired about the welfare of the Shaykh. He would watch him making penance or observing fasts for purification. His attendants would bring information to him about the ascetic. In due course of time, he developed association with him. He occasionally invited the Shaykh to his place and spent some time in his company. He heard from him the story of the Hamadaniyyeh dervishes too, meaning dervishes related to or associated with Mir Sayyid 'Ali Hamadani. Sometimes he asked him questions about the life of Khwaja Ishaq. After a while, Maulana Uthman passed into a state of ecstasy and absorption. For this reason, the people of this land used to call him Makhdum Uthman *majzoob* (the absorbed one).

I heard from my illustrious father, who, in turn, had heard it from others that Maulana Uthman had accepted the Shaykh as his spiritual guide and had made allegiance to him. Whatever Maulana Uthman had attained (in the realm of spirituality) was because of the company and association of the Shaykh. The people of this land recount many interesting stories about the status, miracles and extraordinary feats of Maulana Uthman. People of Kashmir, commoners as well as distinguished ones, talked a lot about his miracles. Many people, high as well as low, reposed trust in Maulana Uthman.

---

[1] This statement explains the reason why Sultan Zainu'l-'Abidin put him to a test and ordered the burning of his house. See p.143 supra.

We shall record the stories of his supernatural feats at a proper place in this work.

Shaykh Sultan and Araki

Shaykh Sultan usually kept with him a group of people from his native place Geyur (in Anantnag district). The Sultans and nobles of Kashmir saw that a large number of people owed allegiance to him. They ordered the construction of a modest hospice for him and allotted twelve endowments (*waqf* lands) for his maintenance.

For some time he remained in seclusion doing penance. He used to recite *Hamadaniyyeh* prayers (*awrad*). Though he prompted dervishes to go into Lent, but for himself he chose to undergo specific training meant for a mystic. None of his followers could become his deputy because they were not of outstanding ability.

Some times later he went back to Geyur, where he breathed his last. Without Shamsu'd-Din's help he could not have achieved much fame in Kashmir. Finally, the name of Shaykh Sultan became very popular with the people of this land.

To Sultan Kubra's hospice

After a couple of days, Shamsu'd-Din sought permission from the Sultan to shift from *Mazar-e-Salatin* to Sultan Kubra's hospice. The family took a boat for carrying them and their belongings to the new place of residence. In that locality lived the community of Lankhors (*sic*. Lanjikhors).[1] Family members as well as household goods of Mir Shams were brought to the house of one Khazir Mir Lanjihkhor (*sic*) where they rested for a couple of days. Mir Shams directed his followers and associates to take in hand the repair work of the hospice, and arrange all facilities for those taking to Lent. The

---

[1] A sub-cast common to both Muslims and Hindus of Kashmir is inow known as Lankar/Langar.

devotees began the work of repair and renovation with great enthusiasm and speed. In a very short time all necessaries were provided (to make the family comfortable.)

Chilleh

The summer went by and the autumn was about to set in. Shamsu'd-Din told his associates and followers that he would be going into lent with the onset of the autumn. Dervishes were asked to go in for *'etekaf* meaning penance in seclusion, and he himself would impart lessons in the science of mystical practices. All of his followers waited eagerly for the day when this would happen. At last, one night, Mir Shams asked his disciples to be ready, as he would go into seclusion on a specific Friday night. Dervishes would follow suit. On hearing this news, they became happy as if they had been liberated from some deep distress.

From early morning of the appointed Friday, Amir Shams kept himself busy with arrangements for the event. He called all devotees, associates, and seekers of the path of mysticism to his presence. Those who were found capable of undergoing lent and seclusion were instructed to be ready. Others were found useful for rendering service to the dervishes. Mulla Abdu'r-Rahman was the first to perform the duty of distributing food among the dervishes. Araki called him to his presence and taught him how a prayer was sent for a dead person's soul. He was also educated on the principles of equal treatment to the mendicants. We shall take up this subject at the end of this tract. He ordered that one of the dervishes should take charge of the kitchen. A couple of sheep would be slaughtered and meals served before the time for prayers so that those coming to say goodbye could partake of it.

Mir Dervish was assigned the job of lighting the candles in secluded cells of dervishes. He received training in making candles. He took with him two dervishes to help him as candle holders. In this way, one or two persons at the most would be given a particular assignment, the rules and regulations for which were explained to them. Even the meanest of chores like sweeping the floors, lighting candles and baking bread were also taught to the servants in the hospice.

Call for the prayer

Araki allowed the old caller for prayer (*mu'ezzin*) to continues assignment. He advised him to be regular in giving call for prayers. Mir Shams directed one of the dervishes to give a call for prayer for the penitents. Instructions were that he should give the call from inside the hospice but only after the call given by the *mu'ezzin* from outside the mosque was over.

Mulla Muhammad Sabahi received instruction to lead the prayers and *namaz* for dervishes gone into seclusion. He was also to transmit all the rules and procedures of offering *namaz* and other rituals to those who went into seclusion until mid-day.

In short, Amir Shamsu'd-Din stayed in the hospice of Shaykh Sultan for six years. Each autumn, he directed his followers to go into lent. He imparted training to the seekers of divine path. People drew benefit from his teachings and many of his followers rose to distinction in their godly mission. He offered them green robes and a black turban. Among the more prominent divines who benefited from his special favours were Sufi Jamaal, Mulla Saeed, Hazrat Baba, Mulla Muhammad Imam, Mulla Yusuf, Mulla Ismail and many others.

His second daughter Thania Bibi was born during his stay in the hospice of Sultan Kubra. His close associates proposed engaging a wet nurse for the baby. He excused himself by saying that he was moving frequently and Hazrat Bejeh Agha (wife) herself breast-fed the baby.

Interpreting dreams

Malik Saif Dar was the Governor of the country (Kashmir). Once he came to the presence of Shamsu'd-Din and recounted his dream:

He had entered the treasury of the ruler where he found many precious objects. Diamonds lay scattered in open, and gold and silver coins filled the boxes. Among this treasure was a trouser, which he wore and came out without coveting the precious jewellery.

On hearing the dream, Shams beckoned Saif to come closer to him. Then he whispered into his ear that there had been a scandal in the *harem* (ladies establishment) of the Sultan and that someone among the womenfolk had cheated. He advised Saif Dar that he should keep away from evil deeds. On hearing these words from Shamsu'd-din, he thought he had done something wrong. Somebody must be privy to his movements; otherwise the secret could not have leaked out. However, he was convinced that Shamsu'd-Din had known it intuitively and this increased Malik Saif Dar's faith in his supernatural powers.[1]

Saif Dar invited

Once, Malik Saif Dar accompanied by about fifty horsemen in attendance paid him a courtesy visit. Others came on foot. On enquiry, Mulla Abdu'r-Rahman informed Araki that there was nothing ready to serve the visitors. He said that pudding and rice mixed with millet had been cooked for the dervishes. Besides, some quantity of ghee (margarine) and honey was also available. He told the cook to look into the containers, for God Almighty might grace them with plenty of eatables so that the visitors are served a meal. The cook found that he could have twenty-five platters filled with eatables which were enough to feed all the persons in the entourage of Malik Saif Dar.

The author and Araki

Maulana Khaleel, the father of this writer, was one of the disciples of Shamsu'd-Din. Among others were Maulana

[1] This is yet another example of the gullibility of ordinary Kashmiris. Araki fully exploited this weakness in their character.

Dervish Bandey, Maulana Suleyman, and Maulana Nusrat. I have heard from my father many stories of dervishes and sufis who were the followers of Mir Araki.

My maternal uncle, Maulana Muhammad, too, was among the followers of Araki. He had declared his allegiance to the sufi-saint and learnt from him the ways and methods of the Sufis and sufistic pursuits. He would occasionally take me to the presence of Araki and we benefitted from meetings with him. Shamsu'd-Din asked my maternal uncle who I was. He said that I, his nephew, was interested in visiting the spiritualist and learning the ways of dervishes. Amir Shams showed great affection for me whenever my maternal uncle took me to his presence. One day, after offering mid-day prayers, he ascended the platform where he generally sat. A large number of dervishes, Sufis, and disciples sat around him. I was also present on that occasion. Shams told my maternal uncle that he wanted me to show allegiance to him. My maternal uncle stood up, took my hand and brought me to the presence of Amir Shams. Then he told him to keep his hand also under my hand so that Shamsu'd-Din would put his hand on mine. My maternal uncle recited the prayer along with Shamsu'd-Din. I repeated the words, which my maternal uncle uttered. Thereafter the *kelima* (words of faith) was recited and a *fateha* (thanks) was recited on this success. People present on the occasion also joined Amir Shams in reciting the *fateha*. After performing the ritual of prostration, Shamsu'd-Din planted an affectionate kiss on my forehead. During this exercise, I kept perspiring. Then he advised me to offer prayers regularly and know its procedures. I was twelve years old at that time. Two years after this incident, Amir Shams left for Arak, as he wanted to be in the service of his spiritual mentor Shah Qasim. I shall record the details of this journey at a proper place.

He had raised a structure for the devotees to offer *namaz*. During the rainy season, people would offer prayers inside the hospice. However, during summer, it was inconvenient to sit inside. He desired that a sufficiently spacious place with twelve doors and windows be constructed for the dervishes to offer prayers. An imposing structure came up. During rainy days, people could offer five-time prayers with comfort. In winter, people would spend the entire day in this hall. However, with the passage of time, termite ate up the wood of the pillars and windows and the foundation gave way. Nine years after its construction, a storm blew off its roof and the structure collapsed. In AH 909/AD 1503, Sultan Husayn Shah built a new mosque at the behest of Shamsu'd-Din at that site.

Preparations for journey

Amir Shamsu'd-Din Araki was satisfied that a prosperous Hamadaniyyeh School[1] (of Sufis) had been established in the land of Kashmir. The Nurbakhshiyyeh way of life had attained popularity and all dervishes and disciples were in complete agreement (with one another) individually as well as collectively that it was the right Sufi order for them. All this brought him immense satisfaction.

His separation from the service and company of his preceptor had been a long one. He wanted to re-unite with Shah Qasim Faiz Bakhsh, the son of Sayyid Muhammad Nurbakhsh. Indeed, he felt an inner urge to return to his presence. Therefore, he sought the permission of the Sultan of Kashmir, his ministers, and men in authority. At that time Sultan Fath Shah[2] was the ruler of Kashmir and the reins of administration rested in the hands of Malik Saif Dar.[3] The noblest and the leading personalities of this land

---

[1] Obviously he means the School of Nurbakhshiyeh order of Sufis. There are many allusions tha confirm that by Hamadaniyyeh School, Araki means Nur Bakshiyyeh School of Sufis.

[2] AH 925/AD 1519.

[3] This period of Araki's six year long stay seems to have led to the rise and expansion of Nurbakhshiyeh order in Kashmir. One of the reasons for its rise could be the political rivalry between Fath Shah and Hasan Shah and the resultant polarisation of Kashmir nobility.

who always wanted Araki to be among them were loath to allow him to return to his native place. But he insisted on his return journey and the nobles and grandees of the kingdom could not stop him. He collected nick-nacks needed for the journey. Government officials issued instructions to local physicians and perfume dealers to collect elixirs that were required for the ailing Sultan Husayn Mirza. All of them got busy with collecting presents for the ruler of Khurasan. One Maulana Husayn Shangi, a courtier adorned with the ornaments of knowledge and acumen, was to accompany him as the emissary of the Sultan of Kashmir to the court of Sultan Husayn Mirza.

Chapter III
Araki's Return to Iran

Araki's return and the events thereafter are divided into three parts.

Part I

Acrimony of the People of Khurasan Towards Shah Qasim

This part deals with the acrimony of the people of Khurasan towards Shah Qasim during the period when Araki was away in Kashmir.

Devotees and followers came to know that Shah Qasim had come to Khurasan and was engaged in giving treatment to Sultan Husayn Mirza. The cure had been successful and the ailment was controlled. Now he could occasionally walk up to Jami'a Masjid to offer Friday prayers. From the beginning of his reign, Sultan Husayn Mirza had given administrative power in the hands of Mirza Kichak Khan who had already paid allegiance to Shah Qasim and found entry to a special group of his followers and devotees. As long as Kichak Khan was alive, nobody dared to express overt hostility towards the house of 'Ali. The death of Mirza Kichak Khan caused deep anguish to Shah Qasim. The reins of the administration then passed into the hands of Mir 'Alisher (Navai),[1] a follower of

[1] Born in AH 844/AD 1440, 'Alisher Navai was a classmate of Sultan Husayn Mirza, a descendant from Chingiz Khan's Chaghatai line. The two classmates had made promises of lasting friendship. While Sultan Husayn inherited the kingdom of later Timurids and ruled over Transoxiana, Kashghar, Balkh and Badakhshan, 'Ali Sher dedicated himself to the pursuit of learning and attained great heights of scholarship. He could write and compose verses both in Turkish and in Farsi, using *Navai* as his pen name... (*takhallus*) in Turkish and *Fani* in Farsi. Sultan Husayn summoned him from Samarqand and offered him the post of the Lord of the ...

Khwaja Naqshband and a student of Mulla 'Abdallah Hajji. He took pride in being the follower of Khwaja 'Abdallah (Naqshbandi)[1] and a student of Mulla 'Abdu'r-Rahman Jami.

Jami and the Sayyids

Mulla 'Abdu'r-Rahman Jami nursed no less rancour against the holy Imams, grudge towards the House of the Holy

---

... Royal Seal (*mohardar*). Owing to his qualities of head and heart, he achieved great eminence and rose to become the Prime Minister (Vizier) of Sultan Husayn in Herat. Himself a renowned scholar, Navai set up a famous library in Herat to which renowned scholars of the day, including the historian Khwandamir (the author of *Habibu's-Siyar*) used to visit. He built nearly 370 tombs and shrines over the graves of great saints, savants, religious and literary personalities of Central Asia, including the shrines of Imam Reza (in Meshhad), Faridu'd-Din 'Attar, (in Nishapur) and Qasimu'l-Anwar in Langar. At last, he resigned from his high office, became a recluse and then a dervish interacting extensively with Mulla Nuru'd-Din Abdu'r-Rahman Jami. Probably owing to the influence of Jami, he became an ardent follower of Naqshbandiyyeh Sufi order. He has left behind a *diwan* of his verses, one each in Turkish and Farsi besides at least nineteen other works. Sources: *Majm'a'l-Fusaha*, vol.i, p.3195, *Tadhkira Nasrabadi*, p.470, *Fihrist-e Kitabkhaneh-e Sipah Salar, Habibu's-Siyar*, (Khayyam Pub.), vol.iv, pp.137, 159 et al. *Tohfeh-e Sami*, p.179, *Mir'atu'l-Khayal*, p.172 and *Fihrist*-e Kitabkhanneh-e Majlis, Tehran, vol.iii, p.367.

[1] Born in Kharjard Jam in AH 817/AD 1414, Nuru'd-Din Abdu'r-Rahman Jami was a studious student who picked up almost all branches of learning of his times. He became an outstanding prose writer and a poet who wrote in traditional style. He was attached to Naqshbandiyyeh order of Sufis, a disciple of Sa'adu'd-Din Muhammad Kashghari the successor to Khwajeh Bahau'd-Din Naqshbandi, the founder of Naqshbandiyyeh orderl. Jami had met with eminent personalities of his times like Khwajeh Muhammad Parsa and Fakhru'd-Din Luristani. He has showered great praise on Naqshbandi Sufi Khwajeh Ahrar (Ahrar-e Wali), the contemporary of Mirza Shahrukh, and the ruler of later Timurid House in Herat. Some of the contemporary or later historians and biographers (*Tadhkira* writers) portrayed him as a controversial figure and accused him of anti-Shi'a proclivities. (See 'Allama Muhammad Qazvini's *Epilogue* incorporated by 'Ali Asghar Hekmat in his work *Jami*). Curiously, some near contemporary staunch Nurbakhshiyyeh writers produced two works whose titles they borrowed from Jami's works. These are *Baharistan-i-Shahi*, a history of Kashmir (translated into English with annotations by this writer and published in Calcutta in 1991), and *Tohfatu'l-Ahba*b, the wok now in hand. Jami has *Baharistan-i-Jami* (which in turn appears to have been inspired by *Golistan* of Sa'adi), and *Tohfatu'l-Ahrar*. See, *Rayhanatu'l-Adab*, *Jami* by 'Ali Asghar Hekmat, *Rawdatu'-Jannat*, *Ateshkadeh* of Azerbegdili, *Majalisu'n-Nafais*, *Habibu's-Siyar* and *Riyadhu'-'Arifin*.

Prophet, and malice towards the family of 'Ali than ibn Muljim[1] did. One can get an idea of the extent of his prejudice and hostility (towards 'Ali) from what we state in the lines that follow.

From the Ummayids and the rulers of the House of Marwan[2] down to Mulla Abdu'r-Rahman Jami, people nursing rancour against the House of the Prophet have existed in all ages. They are there even today and they will be there in the future as well. They support Abu Sufiyan and Marwan rulers. We have sufficient proof of their animosity towards the House of the Prophet and malice towards 'Ali. We know of their hand in the murder of the descendants of the Holy Prophet. Obviously, despite proof of their crimes, showing goodwill towards these tyrants and wretches is tantamount to misleading oneself as well as others. They consider it advisable to maintain friendship with people of depraved thinking.

Mulla Jami found that *Amiru'l-Momineen* 'Ali is the chief of the Sayyids. Yet he had the audacity to say: "I can take the sword of prejudice and malice and strike it on the head of the Prophet in order to satisfy my rancour".

---

[1] Abdu'r-Rahman ibn Muljim had taken an oath in Ka'aba to assassinate 'Ali, Mu'awiya ibn Abu Sufyan and Omr ibnu'l-'Aas so that differences among the Muslims were put an end to. He succeeded in assassinating 'Ali on 9th of Ramadan AH 40/AD 660. For this felony he earned the bad name of *ashqiu'l-ashaqqiya*

[2] Born in the second year of *hijrat*, Abu 'Abda'l- Malik Marwan became a secretary of the third Caliph. Ater the assassination of that Caliph, Marwan accompanied Talha, Zubayr and Ayesha to Basra. After getting defeated in *Jang-e Jumal*, he went into hiding. However, 'Ali pardoned him for fighting on the side of Mu'awiyeh in the battle of Sifin. Declaring his allegiance to 'Ali, he came to Medina in AH 42/AD 662, but 'Abdullah ibn Zubayr turned him out of the city and he went to Syria. When Mu'awiyah bin Yezid became the Caliph, Marwan, though of advanced age, declared himself the Caliph in Northern Horan. In AH 64/AD 683 the people of Jordan declared their allegiance to him. He went to Syria and then to Egypt, entrusting the governorship of Syria to his son 'Abda'l-Malik. Some historians believe his wife Umm Khalid strangulated him to death. He was the first to strike the Shami *dinar* (coin) with the Qur'anic words *qol hu allah* inscribed on one side. See, *al-'Elam* by Zarkubi, vol.viii, p.94, and *Muntahau'l-'Arab*, Also see *Loghat Nameh Dehkhda*, p.227.

Undoubtedly Mulla Jami descended either from the line of Abu Sufyan or from the Kharijites of Nehrawan.[1] That is why he wanted to unburden his heart of enmity against 'Ali. He decided to avenge the killing of his distant ancestors. He incorporated many baseless and senseless things in his works. He filled journals with this trash. He filled his writings with derogatory remarks and observations against the house of the progeny of the Prophet and 'Alavi Sayyids. This audacity is in no way less than of Ibn Muljim.[2] It is surprising that ignorant, prejudiced, revengeful and idiotic persons try to find justification for all nonsense that has been written by writers like Jami.

Enmity towards 'Ali

Mirza Haider Gorkani[3] (Haider Baig Duglat d. AH 958/ AD 1551) lodged with Khwaja Hajji. It was the month of *Ramadan* (fasting). Mulla Barkhordar had arrived from *Ma'wara-an-Nehr* (Trans-Oxiana). Mirza Haider showed him extraordinary regard and brought him to Khwaja Hajji's lodging. When dinner was served, Mirza Haider spoke about Kashmir and its people. He started bragging about himself and indulged in backbiting. He said that infidelity and anti-religious (Islamic) trends had become rampant in Kashmir. People had acknowledged the Caliphs and had ignored the

---

[1] Khaariji means one who secedes. Khariji was the name given to a sect that rose in opposition both to 'Ali and Mu'awiyah on the question of arbitration, following the battle of Siffin in AH 37/AD 657. They were part of 'Ali's army but when the succession for the Caliphate was left to arbitration, they left him raising the cry that arbitration is only with God. Their starting point was puritanism and many of them were *qarra'* meaning public reciters of Qur'an. 'Ali attacked them in the battle of Nahrawan (AH 38/AH 658).

[2] P.122 supra, fn.1.

[3] Gorkan means son-in-law in Uighuri language. Timur is also recorded as Timur Gorkani in some Farsi historical works. The descndents of Timur's line were called *Timuryan-i-Gorkani*. The Mughals of India are also called *Maghulani Gorkani-e Hind*. Haider Beg also descended from the House of Timur and was related to Babur.

Companions of the Prophet of God. "I (Mirza Haider) changed their thinking and the traces of infidelity were removed from Kashmir. I cleansed people small and big of this aberration."[1] Mulla Muhammad Barkhordar wanted to know if learned Islamic scholars and members of the clergy were found in Kashmir. Why did not the clerics dissuade local people from indulging in aberrations? The Mirza said that the *mullas* and the *ulema* themselves were *Rafizi* (Shi a). They themselves practised *rafz*. Why should they disallow the practices observed by the people? One of the *mullas* named Qadi Muhammad was known to people for his fanatic adherence to *rafz*. He had composed a satire on Mulla 'Abdur-Rahman Jami. Mulla Muhammad asked about the nature of the satire. Mirza Haider said that in the satire, the composer alleged that Mulla Jami had adopted double standards in his work titled *Silsilatu'z-Zahhab*. It was a combination of praise and satire.

Bold step

During the days of Mir Shams, one Mulla Farhi arrived from Khurasan. He was shown due respect in Kashmir. In his library was a volume of Jami's *Silsilatu'z-Zahhab*. It had beautiful binding but its contents were repugnant. "Once Qadi Muhammad and I (this writer's father) were going through his books and the above mentioned volume (*Silsilatu'z-Zahab*) was among them. We examined it in part, and came to know that Mulla Jami had been arrogant towards *Amiru'l-Momineen*, Hazrat 'Ali. We read through the derogatory remarks; our sense of faith was aroused and our Islamic identity sensitized. The book was brought to Kashmir for the first time: it was not found in any part of Kashmir before the arrival of Mulla Farhi (*sic*) although its contents were talked about in these lands. After studying all the derogatory remarks, Mulla Farhi was told that Jami had composed a satire on 'Ali and had been very

[1] Obviously he was hinting at the ascendancy of Shi'sm of Nurbakhshiyyeh order.

arrogant towards him. But he said that they (Qadi Muhammad and my father) were accusing Jami of prejudice against 'Ali whereas he (Jami) had actually composed an encomium to 'Ali. There was no proof of condemnation or satire. He said that they had not understood the text because of their inadequate knowledge and lack of analytical ability.

Thereupon Qadi Muhammd read out a few verses from the above-named book and asked him (Mulla Farhi) to explain and bring out the meaning of a few verses. Mulla Ahmad was head and shoulders above in sectarian prejudice and said that they were not able to comprehend the meaning of Mulla Jami's verses. He said that even men of learning and eminence were unable to understand what Jami had said. How then could people of lesser intellectual faculty be able to comprehend him? He snatched the book from the hands of the Qadi and asked he had nothing to do with it? The Qadi showed great patience and restraint but the writer's father could not stomach the remark. He stood up and overpowered the foreigner placing his feet on the latter's chest. He snatched the book from his hands and gave it to Araki. Qadi Muhammad also followed the writer's father (Maulana Jamalu'd-Din Khaleelullah) to the presence of Mir Shams. They just wanted to know what Araki had to say about the work. Mulla Ahmad Khwajeh, too, accompanied the Qadi. They recounted the whole story to Shamsu'd-din Araki. He said that that was not the volume which contained Jami's canard. The Qazi, however, said that it was the same book. Thereupon, Shamsu'd-Din said, "Oh *Mulla*!! Take this book to the kitchen and burn each of its leaves." With these instructions given to us, we stood up and departed to our cells. However, I came to the kitchen where Qadi Muhammad and Mulla Ahmad Farhi (*sic*) also joined me. He made supplication and wanted a few leaves of the book to be given to him. He said we might retain the rest and do with it whatever we pleased to do. He said if a portion of the book did not remain in his possession, he would feel broken down because he had taken great pains to procure it.

I was unmoved by what he said, and put each leaf to the leaping flames in his presence. With the tearing away of each leaf of the book, it appeared as if his heart was being rent into pieces. I tore up many leaves and then cast the scraps into the burning flames. On beholding the torn pieces, that filthy man tore his clothes and beat his breast. With each leaf flying into flames, he would tear away a small sheaf of his beard and throw it into the flames along with the burning leaf. It appeared as if he was going to consign himself to the flames. Although a pupil of Jami, nevertheless, he was not as bold and courageous as his teacher, to consign himself really to flames.

When the entire book was consigned to the flames, he fell at my feet and begged that the cover of the book be returned to him so that he could preserve it as a souvenir. We did not spare the cover and left no trace of the work for its wretched owner. When the burning of the book was over, he besmeared his head with ashes and cried loudly. Back in his home, he sat mourning the loss of the book. Qadi Muhammad also proceeded to his home while I kept myself busy with the chores of the hospice and of Mir Shamsu'd-Din's (household). Next morning I came to the presence of the Qadi. He said that we would go to the house of Mulla Ahmad that day and spend some time in his company. I asked him how we could sit in his company in view of the things that had happened the previous night. The Qadi said that the previous night they had burnt his heart and today they would rub salt into his wounds.

On finding us at his residence, Mulla Ahmad flew into rage. He said we had almost killed him the previous night and now we had come to be with him. He asked whether we had any new mission to accomplish. The Qadi told him that he had come to recite to him some of the panygerics composed by Jami so that he would do justice by realising what type of encomium were composed. The *mulla* was not prepared to listen. He said that he nursed deep hatred for them and was not prepared to sit in their company. But, the Qadi was determined to sit with him and I, too, sat by the side of the Qadi. He took out the paper from his pocket and began reading the *mathnavi*. He read it out as Jami had penned it down in *Silsilatu'z-Zahhab*. He read each verse of Jami twice while this wretched *Khariji* sat like a coiled snake. The Qadi asked whether they considered those verses as encomiums in praise of Hazrat 'Ali and or a satire and condemnation for Jami. What answer would they give to the Holy Prophet on the Doomsday? It is better that I put the verses of the *mathnavi* (with the Qadi) on paper here so that friends and well-wishers would enjoy reading them and send blessings to the soul of the Qadi.

(verses)

Enmity towards Faiz Bakhsh caretaker

Mirza Kichak expired, and Sultan Husayn Mirza was sick. The (advisory) role in the affairs of the state shifted from Shah Qasim to the depraved Mulla Jami—the incarnate Ibn-i Muljim.[1] He was the teacher and guide of Mir 'Ali Sher (Navai), a powerful person at the royal court. Mir 'Ali Sher had developed acquaintance with the associates and attendants of Shah Qasim. He showed his friendship towards them. However, after the death of Kichak Khan, Mir 'Ali Sher no longer supported or co-operated with them, rather took recourse to animosity that had prevailed between the Hashimites[2] and the Umayyids.[3]

[1] loc. cit. The author means to say that so far the Nurbakhshiyyeh were in ascendancy at the royal court in Herat but because of these two events—the death of Kichak Khan and illness of Sultan Husayn—the Sunni Naqshbandi group became strong and influential.

[2] The Arab tribe to which the Prophet belonged.

[3] The Umayyids was the first ruling dynasty of the Muslims that began with the reign of Mu'awiyeh in AH 41/AD 661, and ended with that of Marwan in AH 132/AD 750. Mu'awiyeh ibn Sufiyan established the capital of the Caliphate in Damascus when he was the Governor of Syria under Uthman the third Caliph. The family name is derived from a clan Umayyah, descendants of the Quraysh. 'Abdu'r-Rahman was the only survivor of the Ummayid house after their defeat at the hands of Abu'l-'Abbas in the battle of Zab river in AH 132/AD 750. The fugitive 'Abdu'r-Rahman founded the Ummayid kingdom of Cordova in Spain in AH 138/AD 756, which lasted till AH 422/AD 1031. See *Encyclopedia of Islam*, pp.408–09.

One Friday, he sought a meeting with Shah Qasim in the Jamia' mosque. They met for some time and talked about various matters. Following this meeting, he (Jami) disclosed his hidden malice towards his friends and associates. He made slight of Shah Qasim in front of his known circle. He betrayed hatred and contempt for Shah Qasim. He said that it had been ascertained that Mir Sayyid Muhammad Nurbakhsh was a munificent person. He illuminated the minds of the people of the world and a host of followers and associates. However, it appeared that he had left no fleck of light for his son (Shah Qasim).

Indeed, Mulla Jami was devoid of divine light; black-hearted man and a *Kharijite*[1] (dissident). He did not know that Mir Sayyid Muhammad Nurbakhsh—a reservoir of divine light—had declared his son a rare person who had come into existence with the movement of time and stars. He called him a compendium of virtues and high values. The fact is that he (Jami) was incapable of perceiving the truth (about the status of Shah Qasim)

This Mulla Jami had crossed all limits of enmity against Shah Qasim, so much so that he would not have hesitated to compass his assassination and plunder through his associates and colleagues. The wicked people of *Mawara an-Nahi*[2] (Transoxiana) and the devilish men of the time, the poisonous snakes that they are, all joined hands (against him). Jami told them that Shah Qasim Nurbakhshi had become very arrogant. He (Jami) wished that the Shah did something that gave him a pretext to bring him harm. Shah Qasim had called a physician from India and kept him by his side. The physician attired himself like *jogis* (Indian mendicants). Through him, Shah Qasim learnt about the properties of medicines and the manner

---

[1] Supra, p.122fn.3.

[2] Arab historians invariably use this term, which literally mens 'beyond the river'. Farsi and Tajik historians genrally use the term *vara rud,* which has the same meaning. However, Turanian historians call the lands beyond the Oxus *vilayat-e-bala.* Oxus is the name given by Herodotus, while the Arabs call it Jayhun and Tajiks/Iranians call it Amu Darya.

in which these were administered.[1] Sometimes he would also indulge in explaining the colour, effect, and chemistry of medicines and such other things. Shah Qasim took interest in learning the basics of medical science. Actually, behind the profession of a physician, he concealed his divine powers and status.

Propaganda campaign

The first thing that Jami did in the process of launching a propaganda campaign against Shah Qasim was to spread the rumour that Shah Qasim had become a riddle for Sultan Husayn Mirza, because of which the latter's disease increased day after day. This allegation was unacceptable to people gifted with common sense and practical wisdom. The second allegation brought against him was that he had equated the *Kashshaaf*[2] commentary with the Holy *Qura'n*. The third allegation was that according to Shah Qasim, the commentaries on the *Qura'n* were not in conformity with the tenets of the Prophet or that they ran counter to it.

---

[1] The Persians and Arabs knew of Indian medical science as early as the days of Sassanian rulers. In particular, the names of Sushrud, Waghbhatta and Charak were well-known in that part of the world. See the scholarly work *Tarikh-e ulum-e 'aqli dar tamaddun-e Islami ta qarn-e panjum*, by Zabihullah Safa, Teheran, 1948.

[2] It is the title of the famous commentary on the *Qur'an* by Jarullah 'Allama Zamakhshari. Born in Zamakhshar (*zam* = cold in Avestic, *akh-akht* = bound and *shar* =*shathra*=*shahr*, meaning a cold town/place) in AH 467/AD 1074, his one foot was amputated because of frostbite. He traveled to Baghdad several times and became a *mujawer* (retainer) in Ka'aba. That is why he is called Jarullah. He died in AH 538/AD 1132 in Jurjan. In the beginning, he, as a follower of Abu Nasr Isfahani, took to *'etezal* (professing *Mu'tazila* faith) and towards the last days of his life embraced Shi'ism, (See notes of Dehkhuda recorded by Muhammad Moin in *Loghat Nameh*, p.437). He is one among the great Islamic scholars of commentary (*tafsir*), linguistics (*ilmu'l -lughat*), tradition (*hadith*), grammar, (*sarf o nahv*) and epistology (*bayan*) of Hanafi school. The exact title of his commentary is *al-Kashshaf ana Haqaiqu'l-Tanzil*. See *Elam-e Zarkuli*, vol.iii, p.1017, *Safarnamah* Ibn Batutah, *Wufayatu'l-'Ayan*, *Khandan-e Nav Bakhti*, *Tarikh-i Guzideh*, *'Ayunul-Akhbar*, *Rawdat'u-Jannat*, *Lubbu'l-Albab*, *Habibu's-Siyar* and *Tatamatu's-Sawanu'l-Hikmat*.

One day he talked to Mulla Jami about exaggerating the facts. He told him that such things could not do any harm to the body of Faiz Bakhsh. A few days later, miscreants and cronies of Transoxiana and Samarqand floated the rumour that a group of students had gathered at the place of Shah Qasim and he told them that the holy Prophet was illiterate while his father Muhammad Nurbakhsh was a scholar and a treasure-house of all rational and revealed sciences. As such he had placed his father higher than the holy Prophet.

This prejudiced group made such (nonsensical) heresy a basis for their enmity and rancour against that saint. They spread rumours like these in all the four corners of the land and among the people of all ranks. In this way "the banner of animosity was planted in the ground of prejudice." Ultimately, these rumours reached the ears of the disciples of Shah Qasim who conducted enquiries into them. He was convinced that the opponents from Transoxiana and inimical persons from Khurasan had demonstrated their intention to bring harm to his person. They had even asked for the remuneration of putting Shah Qasim to death. However, Shah Qasim wrote all these things and brought them before Sultan Husayn Mirza. The latter summoned Mir 'Ali Sher (Navai) and apprised him of all the intrigues that were being hatched against him. He instructed him not to give quarter to those satanic persons. He was enjoined not to remain complacent, for ensuring that no harm was done to or oppression allowed against Shah Qasim Nurbakhshi and that the attendants of Shah Qasim did not suffer at their hands in any way.

Though Mir 'Ali Sher attended to these matters, things did not improve. Finally, he called to his presence all the *ulema* of Herat who were hostile to and prejudiced against him. He used threats, intimidation and other antics to contain them.

Pilgrimage

Aware of deep-seated animus of his adversaries towards him, Shah Qasim felt ill at ease in Khurasan. Through the instrumentality of Khadija Begum, he sought the permission of and assistance from Sultan Husayn Mirza to proceed to the lands of Arak. When permission was granted, he began preparations for the journey. Before bidding him farewell, Sultan Mirza consulted Khadija Begum and his nobles; he ordered providing him with twenty-two horses for the proposed journey. This was to enable him to proceed to the holy shrine of Imam Musa at Meshad. Shah Qasim bade farewell to his benefactors and the devotees of Khurasan and took the path to Meshad. Among his closest disciples and pupils were Maulana Hatifi, Maulana Husayn Waiz Kashifi,[1] and several others. All of these luminaries had established cordial relations with him. The party arrived at the shrine of the eighth Imam, circumambulated it and observed all rituals prescribed for such visits. Having done that, he bade to all of them farewell. Mirza Kichak and his soldiers also returned home.

From there, he proceeded to Arak, along with his friends and attendants. As soon as the news of his arrival in Simnan reached people, all the young and old flocked to his presence. His relatives, elders and all known persons in Solgan came out to welcome and felicitate him. He came to his home. The people of Arak and Azerbaijan were very glad about his safe return. People—known and unknown—relatives, friends, acquaintances and the public showed him great love and respect. They felt overjoyed by his presence among them. In this way, he got rid of his enemies through his wisdom and

[1] A profound scholar of Islamic studies and mysticism and a contemporary of Sultan Husayn Mirza in Herat, Kashifi was gifted with a melodious voice that attracted large gatherings to his sermons. He has composed a *qasida* (panygeric) in praise of 'Ali. However, there is some confusion among historians about his faith in one or the other sect. In Herat, the majority of people during his days were Sunnis and he was accused of being of Shi'a faith. But in Sabzwar, the cradle of Shi'a faith, he was branded a Sunni. Among his works are *Anwar-e Suhayli*, a rendition of *Kalileh wa Dimneh*, *Rawdatu'sh-Shuhada*, *Rashahat 'aynu'l-hayat*, the last one being about the Naqshbandis. He died in AH 910/AD 1504. See, *Kashfu'z-Zunun*, *Rawdatu'j-Jannat*, p.256 and *Hidayatu'l-'Arifin*, vol.1, p.416.

sagacity. His enemies and opponents were no less hostile than the enemies of Imam Husayn were in Kufa and Syria. He returned to his peaceful home along with his servants and devotees in complete security. He stayed in this abode of peace without any worry and distraction

Part II

In Service of Shah Qasim

Araki had spent seven or eight years in the lands of Kashmir. For five or six years, he continued to impart spiritual training to his pupils. He bestowed benefactions on the seekers of truth. People wanted him to stay on for more time and the Sultans and the high officials all wished him to delay his departure. They offered many excuses to hold him back, but these did not work. His inner urge did not permit him to continue staying in Kashmir. When all persuasions to make him change his decision had failed, the Sultan of the day and the high-ups in the government relented. He then kept himself engaged in collecting the necessary paraphernalia for the long journey. Medicines and elixirs were collected for Sultan Husayn Mirza. Physicians and chemists in the country were ordered to procure these medicines, herbs and elixirs. They got these collected from the peaks of mountains, deep forests and grasslands. Maulana Husayn Shamnagi was to accompany him as the emissary (of the Sultan of Kashmir). He was a learned man and had many accomplishments to his credit. He was an excellent orator and conversationalist. He, too, was ordered to prepare the wherewithal of his journey. Many wonderful gifts such as crowned birds, wild cows, and expensive artifacts were procured for presentation to Sultan Husayn Mirza.

Malik Saif Dar

At this time, Sultan Fath Shah was the Sultan of Kashmir and Malik Saif Dar was the vizier. The Sultan ordered that all gifts meant for Sultan Husayn Mirza be stored in the house of Malik Saif Dar. He requested Shamsu'd-Din Araki to proceed to that house to select gifts befitting the rulers of the lands of Khurasan. Whatever he thought was not worth presenting, was to be replaced with befitting ones. In the house of Malik Saif Dar, Shams 'Araki examined the items one by one. He did not approve of even a single item. This was the reason why Malik Saif Dar showed his resentment. He was somewhat blunt in saying that whatever they could procure according to their power and resources was stored there. But, whatever was beyond their power, he (Araki) should not expect them to produce for his perusal.

When people heard about strained relations between Malik Saif Dar and Shams Araki, they thought that the Malik disliked him and wanted to send him away from this land. However, this was not the truth. Malik Saif Dar was devoted to him. When Araki visited this land for the second time, he would pray for the dervishes and the Shaykhs of the land in the course of recitation of didactic verses. At that time, prayers were offered for Malik Saif Dar and Malik Regi Dar also. But, somehow, the rumour spread that Shah Qasim had told Shamsu'd-Din Araki that Malik Saif Dar was his enemy in Kashmir and since he was dead, therefore Araki should proceed to Kashmir This was an unfounded story. Actually, Shah Qasim had told Araki that it was Shaykh Shihab who had died in Kashmir. People mistook him for Saif Dar. The truth is that Saif Dar never nursed any ill will towards him. Shamsu'd-Din Araki' in turn, showed much affection for him. For many years during lent, Malik Saif Dar would be asked to sit behind the dervishes at the time of reciting thanksgiving in which prayers for Malik Saif Dar would also be recited. This practice continued from the times of Malik Saif Dar to the days of Mirza Haider (d. AH 958/AD 1551).

In short, many delicate and befitting gifts were collected for presentation to Sultan Husayn Mirza. Shamsu'd-Din Araki completed preparations for the ensuing journey. His pupils and devotees, very close to him in the endeavour of attaining training and excellence, wanted to accompany him. However, their entreaties were not accepted. He desired that the Hamadaniyyeh line and the Nurbakhshiyya system should prosper in these lands and the devotees left behind were to continue that mission. He exhorted them not to make any more entreaties, and that they should remain steadfast on their chosen path. He assembled them and advised them to remain united, offer five-times-a-day prayers regularly, and continue the recitations as had become the custom of the day. He advised them never to show slackness in reciting *awarad-e fathiyyeh amiriyyih* (special prayers prescribed by Amir Sayyid 'Ali Hamadani or Shah Hamadan as he is known to Kashmiris). He bade them to do all they could in reviving the traditions and system of *Nurbakhshiyyeh* order.

Sufi Jamaal

The person who was assigned the duties of leading the group of disciples to offer prayers and recite the *awrad* was Sufi Jamaal. He was known for his good qualities and strict morals. He was the first whom Araki interviewed and asked several questions in order to assess his ability of leading that group.

He put this question to Sufi Jamaal: "If you were designated as the chief of the hospice and the leader of the group, how would you meet the material requirements and other necessities of life?" Sufi Jamaal began thinking of resigning to the will of God. He said that he would order the widening of the pond of water situated at the height. The stones lying around would be removed to make space for the cultivation of crops. The pond would help them in irrigating the fields. This would provide subsistence to the dervishes. This proposal of Sufi Jamaal was not approved.

Mulla Isma'il

The same question was put to Mulla Isma'il. He was a man of lofty ideas in comparison to Sufi Jamaal. He said that God

Almighty provides sustenance to his creatures out of his munificence. If we are steadfast in His path, God will certainly provide us with means of subsistence. He said it was important that we ignore the question of the means of subsistence, and concentrate on praying to the Creator. God Almighty would take care of them. All this depended on resigning to God Almighty's will. Araki liked it and accepted it. Thus, Mulla Isma'il became the pointman of the Sufis, with these instructions (a) he will show no laxity in taking care of the dervishes and the group of devotees placed in his charge, (b) no laxity is allowed in winning their goodwill and their security so that they are not forced to disperse in different directions, (c) five-time prayers are offered regularly, (d) recitation of *awarad-e-fathiyyeh Amiriyyeh Hamadiniyye*[1] is made a regular and permanent feature, (e) as the leader of the group, he should recite *navad wa noh nameh* (Book of 99 verses[2] (?) while rendering *awradh*, (f) in winter, they should take to lent (*chilleh*), exercise penance in accordance with the training imparted to them. The purpose was to perpetuate the Hamadaniyyeh and Nurbakhshiyyeh system in these (Kashmirian) lands. As the leader of the group, he should not lose his head and become haughty, for it may be lead him astray from the right path.

Shamsu'd-Din Araki did not speak to Hazrat Baba at this point of time. He did not send him to the presence of the group of Sufis so that Satan did not seduce him. Perhaps he might also nurse the ambition of becoming the leader of the group and its Shaykh. He had not as yet developed a strong claim for that assignment.

Mulla Isma'il had shut himself up in the hospice of Shaykh Sultan Kubra.[3] The building was neither new nor did it have

---

[1] It is curious that the writer mentions it severally as *Awraddh*, *Awradh-i-Fathiyyeh*, *Awradh-i-Amiriyyeh*, *Awradh-i Hamadaniyyeh* and *Awradh-i Fathiyyeh Amiriyeh Hamadaniyyeh*. This suggests that Mir Sayyid 'Ali might have subsequently made interpolations in the text of the *Awradh*.

[2] I have not been able to find a copy of this work nor could I understand what it was?

[3] See *Baharistan-Shahi*, loc. cit., p.189, fn.18.

new cells for those who wanted to sit in Lent. Thus anybody not occupied with the constructional and other administrative matters of the hospice, would not allow him time to perfect his spiritual excellence.

Fath Shah's letter

Maulana Zayd was the father of Qadi Muhammad Qudsi. He was the Secretary of Sultan Fath Shah. He was directed to draft two separate letters one for Sultan Husayn Mirza and the other for Shah Qasim. He prepared the draft in two days and sent it to Sultan Fath Shah. The *ulema,* the learned men, the ministers and the scribes of the land appreciated and approved the draft. The text of the letter written to Shah Qasim ran thus: "Sultan Zainu'l-'Abidin, the ancestor of Sultan Fath Shah received correspondence from the exalted Hazrat Nurbakhsh. These carried instructions for the mendicants and the dervishes. Shaykh Shamsu'd-Din, the guide and teacher of many parts arrived in this land. My brother Sultan Hasan Shah died suddenly. Then there were dissensions among the nobles of the state. Mir Shamsu'd-Din Araki had to stay here because he was helpless and in discomfort. With God's grace he propagated the right system (theological) for the common people of this land. Through his undaunted courage and efforts, the people (of Kashmir) who did not observe the forbidden in religion, were liberated from that malaise. They turned away from the forbidden and joined the fold of the faithful. Now he has decided to return, and we have great pleasure in permitting him to undertake the journey for which we have provided him all the facilities he needs."[1]

---

[1] It is a subtle reference to the liberal policy of Sultan Zainu'l-'Abidin, as a result of which orthodoxy had become weak in Kashmir. The writer has, in earlier portions of this work accused Zainu'l-'Abidin of allowing revival of Hindu traditions in Kashmir following the destruction caused to it by Sultan Sikandar, the Iconoclast. Kashmiri historians have not mentioned anything about Zainu'l-'Abidin's interaction with contemporary Timurid rulers of Herat. Furthermore, the contents of the letter from the Sultan of Kashmir to Sultan Husayn of Herat are an official recognition of stupendous proselytising effort made by Araki in Kashmir.

Departure

Mulla Husayn Shamnagi[1] was in his entourage. Kashmiri scholars, nobles and dignitaries, all bade him farewell. He chose the Pakhli[2] and Shamnagi[3] route for his exit from Kashmir. A large number of his followers and disciples accompanied him up to Baramulla. The parting was emotional. People raised a peal of din. Nearly a hundred thousand followers gave vent to their pulsation and disappointment on his departure. By getting separated from him the pain was as severe as of the day of reckoning. At Baramulla, he bade farewell to his followers and devotees and adopted the Pakhli (Hazareh) road to Nilab[4] (Nilabhata) and to Kabul.

Ulugh Beg

At that time, Ulugh Beg Mirza Khord was the ruler of Kabul. Earlier Amir Sayyid J'afar, the son of Imam Sayyid Nurbakhsh had passed through Kabul on his way to India. Because of his interaction with Amir Sayyid J'afar, Mirza Ulugh Beg had become a devotee of Imam Muhammad Nurbakhsh. He evinced interest in the ideology of his sect. When Shamsu'd-Din Araki came to meet with Mirza Ulugh Beg, he was briefed on the background of the ruler's relations. Thus, Ulugh Beg confirmed his adhering to the teachings and convictions of Araki and through him sent exquisite gifts and a letter to Shah Qasim. He requested that a copy of the Imam's theological work, namely *Ahwat,* be sent to him and expressed his desire

---

[1] Shengi or Shamnagi is not clear. Shamnag is a place name in Kashmir. Shengi could be the corruption of Shanki, which is the abbreviation of Hindu name Shankar.

[2] A part of Taluqan region on ancient Central Asian route to Kashmir.

[3] In NWFP.

[4] Nilab is the name used by Farsi/Tajiki/Dari historians and biographers for the Indus River. Generally, the crossing point for travellers from Kashmir along Pakhli route was Attock. For more details, see *Akbar Nameh* of Abu'l-Fazl.

to follow the theological principles laid down in the work. He also said that he would adopt his faith and sect.

To Arak via Samarqand

In Kabul, Araki came to know that Shah Qasim had proceeded from Khurasan to Arak. He, therefore, delayed his departure to Khurasan and told Mulla Husayn Shamnagi that since Shah Qasim had proceeded to Arak, he did not find any important mission calling him to Khurasan. However, Mulla Husayn insisted that since he (Araki) had lived in Kashmir for a long time, and many precious gifts besides many useful medicines and elixirs not found in Khurasan had been brought for Sultan Husayn Mirza, he should, therefore, proceed to Khurasan. He also said that the Sultan would be pleased to receive these gifts and he would bestow munificence on him (Araki). Araki said that he had not decided to return to Khurasan because of any greed for the favours of the Sultan. He had come only in deference to the wishes of Shah Qasim. He said he now wanted to travel to Samarqand and meet with Khwaja 'Abdallah Naqshbandi. "I want to see with my own eyes how Khwaja 'Abdallah Naqshband impresses the world with his spiritual excellence and leadership through Sufi music (*sama'a*)? I want to see how he raises the banner of his spiritual guidance and how he handles the delicate matters of spirituality? I want to gather information about his special spiritual powers." Saying this, he bade farewell to Mulla Husayn Shamnagi and crossing the Hindu Kush, came to Badakhshan.[1]

With a large number of gifts, medicines, elixirs, letters and books brought from Kashmir for Sultan Husayn Mirza, Maulana Husayn Shamnagi proceeded towards Herat and came to the court of Sultan Husayn Mirza. He was bestowed

[1] It is curious that notwithstanding his profuse show of respect and reagard for Sultan Husayn Mirza when he was at the court of the Sultan of Kashmir, Araki turned to Samarqand and did not accept the plea of Shamnagi to proceed straight to Herat. This needs to be investigated.

favours and was introduced to the *ulema*, the nobles and the poets of Herat. When he came to the presence of Mulla Jamai, he asked him whether anybody knew about his verses in the lands of Kashmir. Mulla Husayn told him that people knew them and some of his verses were very popular. Jami asked which of the verses were popular. Mulla Husayn said:

> *Jami chih laf mizani az pak damani*
> *bar khirqa-e tu in hameh dag-e sharab chist.*
> (O Jami! You boast of your puritanism/ why all these stains of wine on thy gown?)

People present on the spot were immensely delighted. Word reached the ears of Sultan Husayn Mirza that the emissary from Kashmir was taking liberties with Jami. However, Mulla Husayn Shamnagi received many rewards and favours from Sultan Husayn and then returned to his native land.

Araki crossed the Hindu Kush Mountain, and arrived first at Khatlan (now in Tajikistan). Here exists the burial place of Amir Sayyid 'Ali Hamadani. Then he proceeded to Badakhshan to visit the shrine of Khwaja Ishaq, the Martyr. His next stage was Balkh, the place where Khwaja Ishaq had been martyred. The body of this martyr remains buried by the side of the mosque in Balkh. He kissed the grave dutifully and rubbed his forehead on the earth, which brought him to the end of his pilgrimage to the shrines. Thereafter he left for Samarqand.

In Samarqand

Araki said, "In about two months, we arrived in Samarqand. We spent another term of two months just to take rest. On the first Friday (in Samarqand), I prepared to offer the Friday prayers. I tied round my head the black turban, presented to me by the iconoclast, Shah Qasim Nurbakhshi himself. I proceeded to the Jamia' Masjid. After offering *namaz*, a large crowd of people came to me and then my dialogue with them proceeded along these lines:

> Samarqandis: To which *silsila* (Sufi order) are you linked?
> Araki: The exalted *silsila* (order) of *Hamadaniyyeh* meaning of Sayyid 'Ali Hamadani.
> Samarqandis: Whose followers are you?
> Araki: Hazrat Shah Qasim Nurbakhshi.
> Samarqandis: Wherefore have you come and where are you going?
> Araki: I have come from Kashmir and am on my way to Arak.

They asked me the reason of my going to Kashmir and I apprised them about it. They asked me about the conditions in Kashmir and about the people of that land. They asked for the position of the people about their faith in Islam and their observance of the principles of religion etc. I said that the tenets of the path of the Prophet and the rules and principles of the community of the Apostle of God were not flourishing in that land. They said that Amir Sayyid 'Ali Hamadani had visited Kashmir and they were told that his presence in Kashmir had popularized Islamic tenets and the religious covenants in Kashmir. Why had the religion of the Prophet declined there? I said Amir Sayyid 'Ali Hamadani had visited those lands but he did not stay there for more than forty days. During that short period, some groups of people came to his presence and he blessed them with forgiveness. They decided to enter his circle of followers.

Khanqah-e Shah Hamadan

Amir Kabir (Sayyid 'Ali Hamadani) had raised a platform at the place where he stayed in Srinagar. He called it the mosque. He used to offer *namaz* five times a day on that platform together with his followers. After his return, his disciples continued offering five-time prayers from that platform and punctually recited *awarad-e-fathiyyeh* and *awrad-e 'asriyyeh,* meaning the recitations meant for the morning and for the evening. After the death of Amir-e Kabir, his son Mir Muhammad Hamadani stayed at that place (Srinagar) for a few years. On that same platform, he built a hospice.

During the visit of Amir Sayyid Hamadani, Sultan Sikandar was the ruler of Kashmir. This ruler expressed his allegiance to Amir-e Kabir and became his disciple and sincere follower. In accordance with the guidance and instructions of Amir-e Kabir, this religion-abiding ruler became the instrument of strengthening the religion of Muhammad and the community of Mustafa.[1] He brought prosperity and embellishment to the faith of the Prophet. He razed to ground all the idol-houses in his country. The idols of the infidels and their idol- houses were destroyed. He cleared his country of the customs of the community of infidels (*kafirs*) and of vices, aberrations and oppressions of the heretics (*zandiq*).[2] He ordered the infidels and the polytheists to leave the country. For breaking and destroying the idol houses, temples and idols, he is known by the title of Sultan Sikandar, the Iconoclast (*but shiken).*[3]

---

[1] The inference is that it was on the instance of Mir Sayyid 'Ali Hamadani that Sultan Sikandar undertook his grand mission of iconoclasm. Lines that follow this sentence substantiate the inference.

[2] *Zandiq* has been explained in an earlier footnote, p. supra. However, some more minformation may be added.The word *zanda* occurs twice in *Zand-Avesta* (*Yasna* 63, *band* 3, *Vandidad* 18, *band* 53–55. Apparantly, *zanda* means the enemy of Mazdayasna religion. *Zanda* or *zandaqa* was attributed to Mani who, according to Zoroastrians, was a sorcerer, liar and a cheat calling himself a prophet and challenging Mazdyasna. The Arabs arabicised and wrote *zandik* as *zandiq*. Bal'ami (the translator of Tabari's history) writes: "*Mani-e zandiq be zaman-i Shapur birun amad wa zandaqa ashkar kard*". Thus, the followers of Mani were called *zandiq* (pl. *zandaqa*) and other words used synonymously are *mulhid*, *dahri* and *bedin*. Also see gloss in *Burhan-e Qat'e'* edited by Muhammad Mo'in.

[3] Details of Sikandar's inconoclasm are found in chapter III. *Baharistan-i-Shahi*, pp.28–58.

Sultan Zainu'l-'Abidin

When the virtuous Sultan Sikandar, the Iconoclast, left this house of toil for the house of comfort, his son Sultan Zainu'l-'Abidin succeeded him. This Sultan reversed the policy of his father and adopted the path of prevarication (*fisq*) and heresy (*zandaqa*). He brought some of the infidels close to himself and on some others he conferred ministries. He revived all customs and rituals of infidels and polytheists. He rebuilt all the idol-houses and temples that had been razed and destroyed. By rebuilding the temples of the infidels and the people of darkness and prevarication, this ruler—who was not God-fearing—popularised their religion. In this way, the fallacious beliefs and oppressive vices of the heretics and dualists gained strength to such an extent that in every household, most of its members returned to infidelity, heresy and despicable innovation.[1] Only a small number of people expressed adherence to Islam. Islamic tenets and the customs of idolaters had got mixed up in a way that the nobles, officials, and the Sultan, all considered the heretics, the infidels, the wretched and the innovators as their close associates to drink and dine with. In his *mathanavi,* of which we bring a few verses here, Qadi Muhammad Qudsi, has properly depicted the condition of those days:

kufri ki qadeem bud nav shud
waz mehr-e munir-e shar'a zau shud
Shud bar-e digar berasm mo'tad
atashkadeh o kinisht bonyad
Islam be kufr gasht makhlut
arkan hameh mand ghair marbut

[1] This belies the view that conversion had taken place out of free will of the people. Had it been so they would not have opted to return to their original faith and its traditions.

Gasht tawaif-munafiq
Ba kufr mua'awin-o muwafiq
Har jahili(?)waziri bud
dar shirk shareek-e mushiri bud
butkhaneh-o khanqah baham
yak masjid-o yak kalisa baham
gar mardi guzardi namazi
mi goft zanash be dev razi
war zankih padar shudi be masjid
mi kard pisar be kafiri jadd

> Infidelity, rampant during olden days, was revived. The sun of *shariat* (Islamic law) illuminated it. In line with old tradition, the fireplace and the temple flourished side by side. Islam got mixed up with infidelity and its elements disintegrated. The ambivalent groups joined and compromised with heresy. The stupid became the minister and he was party to infidelity. The idol house and the hospice stood side by side, the mosque and the church (perhaps meaning Buddhist temple) were seen in close proximity. If a man offered Muslim prayer (*namaz*), his wife would interact with (pray to) the devil. If the father went to the mosque, his son attempted to fraternise with the infidels (*kafirs*)

The people of Samarqand asked him, "Did not the *ulema*, the learned men and the intellectuals of those lands forbid the infidels and the lost people from diluting (the principles of) Islam?" Araki answered, "The *ulema*, and the learned men of those lands showed no interest in the propagation of the Islamic religion, *sharia*' and the tenets (of faith). The *Qadis* and theologians of that land had become indifferent towards the traditions and the ways of Islam. They had mixed up with the infidels, the heretics and the misguided people. The acts and ways of the *ulema* and the theologians could not be differentiated from those of the ignorant and the wretched. Their customs and habits had got mixed up. (verses)

> Despite the fact that learned and distinguished men of the times are always amidst them each one experienced in his own right and each one having examined the books a thousand times, none of them is really aware of the basics of faith. Nobody is able to show the path of true religion. Nobody cares for the religion (Islam). Everybody is on the path of falsehood and ignorant about religion and the ways of faith. They care for riches that are expendable but unmindful of that which lasts long, he said.

The people of Samarqand were shocked and surprised on knowing that the learned men of Islam in those lands had adopted the ways and customs of the infidels. I told them that I had seen the *ulema* and the *Qadis* of those lands with my own eyes and witnessed their (mis)deeds.

Customs of heretics

"I shall recount a story about the relations between the Qadi and the Shaykhu'l-Islam. I shall inform you of the perfidy and un-Islamic deeds of these people. This will give you a glimpse of the ways, deeds and conditions of the people of those lands. My house was situated on the bank of a stream in the city of Kashmir (Srinagar). Two learned men lived nearby. One was the *Qadi* of the city and the other was Shaykhu'l-Islam. They entered into matrimonial alliance between their children. The daughter of the one was given in marriage to the son of the other. The nuptial ceremony and the reception function were performed according to the customs of the innovators (*bid' at*),[1] the infidels and the heretics. Forty to fifty pretty women, clad in gorgeous costume and adorned with ornaments, came riding to that place. They were without a veil, and dismounted

[1] Arabic root *bid'a* means innovation. It means bringing something new into the social structure that obviously repudiates the known customs and traditions of orthodoxy. Pehaps in social interaction among the people during this period of Kashmir history there might have been an element of accommodation seen by the author and by the orthodoxy as *bid'at*.

by the bank of the canal close to my residence. Imagine their shamelessness, notoriety, and disgrace, the like of which one does not find anywhere else in the world. Forty to fifty beautiful young damsels rode their horses along with males without displaying an iota of reservation. Female drummers, singers, prostitutes and flirts, all dancing and reveling, led the party with music flowing from long flutes. Menfolk of the town stood on both sides of the pathway besides onlookers who had taken vantage points on windows and balconies. Wicked people, charlatans and vagabonds among the young males also accompanied them to the bank of the canal. Two or three infidels and polytheists also came along with the bride and the bridegroom. They carried a glass filled with water. The bride and the bridegroom carried a sword in their hands and indulged in strange movements. They uttered the words (meaning *mantras*) of infidelity and polytheism and observed the rituals and customs of the infidels. The bride and the bridegroom also performed the rites and rituals of the infidels. In the feast, all customs of infidels and misguided people were fully observed.

A few days later, the *Qadi* and the Shaykhu'l Islam both hosted a feast at their respective residences. A large gathering of musicians and dancing girls came together on the occasion. Onlookers came from here and there and made a big crowd. These types of aberrations and detestable things of infidelity and heresy were freely observed in the house of the Shaykhu'l Islam and the *Qadi*. I have been a witness to all this. It shows the extent to which infidelity, aberration, corruption, anti-Islamic customs and irreligiosity were rampant in this land."

After listening to these details, the *ulema*, the learned and the elderly people of Samarqand expressed their regret and surprise. They bit their fingers in utter disappointment saying that owing to the irreligiosity of the *ulema* and the learned men as well as owing to the faithlessness of the nobles and men of authority, the place of Islam (*daru'l-Islam*), has been converted into a place of battle (*daru'l-harb*). The city of Islam becomes the city of *kafirs* (heretics).[1]

In the service of Fayz Bakhsh

Araki stayed in Samarqand for two months and then prepared to go to Arak. He went to Astarabad via Taif and Merv. Then he came to Rustamdar and Mazandaran. He entered Gilan. At Shaft Koreh, he visited and circumambulated the Nurabad shrine. Thereafter he proceeded to Solghan where Shah Qasim stayed in all peace and security. Solghan was the place of Hazrat Imam. Angels descended from heaven to bless this spot and all spiritualist desire to set their foot on this soil. Shah Qasim was extremely happy to know that Araki had returned along with his family. He said that when Shamsu'd-Din left the place, he was alone and had now returned with a large family. We bring to mind the incident of Hazrat 'Ali. When he conquered Khyber, J'afar Taiyyar returned from Ethiopia. The Holy Prophet had said at that time that he did not know whether he should celebrate the victory of Khyber or the return of J'afar. In the same way, Shah Qasim said whether he should celebrate the return of Araki or the appearance of his family.

In Solghan

Shah Qasim laid the foundation for another house close to his own. This had been brought to completion. Gardens were added to it. He gave it to Araki with a choice to raise more

---

[1] It may be presumed that the reason for Araki to go to Samarqand and float the stories of "innovation and apostacy" in Kashmir was to mobilize the opinion of Sunni *ulema* of *Mawara-an-Nahr* in support of his mission of Nurbakhshiyyeh order and also to reduce the anti-Nurbakhshiyya trend at the court in Herat, leaving him supreme in his Kashmir adventure. He had had disclosed that he was going to meet with Naqshbandiyyeh in Samarqand. The purpose was obvious. The Muslims have the religious duty to fight against *daru'l-harb* till it is converted into *daru'l-Islam*.

constructions on that piece of land if he so desired. Araki laid the foundation of a spacious garden, which was divided into two parts. One part was developed into an orchard with a variety of fruit trees. In the second part, flowers of different colours and hues were planted. It was made into a very attractive flower garden. Shah Qasim gave it the name of *Bagh-e-Kashmir.* Sometimes he would ask his attendant to fetch him fruits from *Bagh-e-Kashmir.* Sometimes he would come out into that garden and orchard for a stroll. This made him very happy.

Shamsu'd-Din Araki spent eight years in the company of Shah Qasim. During this period three daughters were born to him. Two daughters had already been born and now he had five daughters and no son. His wife Bibi Agha had a lurking desire that God blessed her with a son. Somehow, Araki came to know about this desire of his wife. He told his young daughters to go to Solghan and stay with his relatives. He advised them to make daily attendance at the shrine of Sayyid Muhammad Nurbakhsh and submit a request to his pure soul (to bless him with a son). Undoubtedly, with the blessings of that exalted soul, they would get a brother. From among his daughters, Sania Bibi, Fatima Bibi and Rabi'a Bibi went to the shrine at Solghan and stayed with their relatives. Every morning they visited the shrine and prayed that their parents be blessed with a male child. On the third day, while they bowed their head in prayer, a voice reached their ears saying, "God Almighty has given you a brother." As they raised their head, they did not find anybody around. This caused them some consternation and they came out of the shrine and went to their home recounting to their relatives all that had happened. They became happy and in the company of a female relative sent the girls back to Daresht. The whole story was repeated to Shamsu'd-Din Araki. He said that surely God Almighty would bless them with a brother.

Daniyal's birth

A couple of months later, Bejeh Agha's pregnancy was announced. The news of the birth of a son was conveyed to Shah Qasim, requesting him to propose a name for the male child. He suggested Daniyal, and that was accepted. The child was born on the day of *Navroz* or New Year's Day according to Iranian calendar. It will be remembered that the Holy Prophet had installed 'Ali on the same day (*Navroz*)[1] as his successor. Shah Qasim drew in his hand the horoscope of the infant. A year after the birth of the child, Shamsu'd-Din Araki proceeded to Kashmir for the second time. We shall speak about it at a proper place.

Part III

To Kashmir

After obtaining formal letter of permission from Faiz Bakhsh, Araki left Iranian territory in the month of Muharram of AH 902/AD 1496. Shaykh Daniyal had come of two years of age at that point of time. Araki lost no time in proceeding to Kashmir. In the course of this long journey, he had many strange experiences.

Converses with Khwajah Khizr[2]

Araki has recounted the following story, "After leaving the peripheries of Rey and Arak, and placing his foot on the soil of Khurasan, we went a stage or two further and then rested. Tents were pitched and the members of the entourage and

---

[1] Novroz (Avestic *Naok roch*) falls on 21 March, the day of vernal equinox and is the first day of new Iranian year. The tradition of celebrating Navroz, a pre-Islamic festival, continued with unabated zest after Iran beacame Islamic. By stating that the Prophet installed 'Ali as his successor on Novoz, is a subtle way of providing space to an important tradition of Zoroastrian origin in the Shi'a and Nurbakhshiyyah culture.

[2] An imaginary figure that is believed to have attained immortality.

his family were asked to halt for rest. There lay a wide and spacious ground around and I strolled over it. After reaching a short distance from my camp, I beheld a man sporting grey beard with a very attractive visage. He came close to me. I wished him and he asked me where from I had come and where I was headed to. I said I had come from Arak and was heading to Kashmir. He asked the purpose of my mission of going to Kashmir. I said that my master Shah Qasim Fayz Bakhsh, the son of Imam Nurbakhsh, had directed me to go to Kashmir and provide guidance to the people there. He said "God Almighty will bless you with success in the lands of Kashmir. The infidels and polytheists will be bestowed the fortune of accepting Islam when you place your auspicious foot on that soil. The Islamic way will flourish there. Your enlightenment, your urge of strengthening Islam and the faith will stand in the way of the unbelievers, non-Muslims and wicked people. However, I would still like to give you some advice. I told him that I would accept these with pleasure."

"God will support and bless your efforts in Kashmir. You should remain steadfast in your mission so that ignorant people who are following a false religion and whose hearts are darkened by prejudice will be shown the religious path of the Innocent Imams. They will be guided along the righteous path of the followers of Imams. Trust me if God Almighty gives you a life of thousand years like that of Hazrat Noah, He will give you the strength to convert a thousand *kafirs* and polytheists to Islamic faith each day. They will be brought into the fold of Islamic faith. The conversion of heretics to the faith of the elevated Imams carries more reward in the other world than strict penance, prayers and other virtues. I said that I would follow this advice with all my heart and soul."

This celestial person then withdrew into the direction wherefrom he had come. I returned to my tents. I was convinced that this could be nobody other than Hazrat Khizr.

Conversion of Hanafis[1]

It has already been stated that groups of infidels, heretics, polytheists and lost people were found everywhere in Kashmir. The customs and traditions of infidelity and heresy had got mixed up with the life style of the *'ulema* and the *Qadis*. Then some of the local people, partly through the guidance of the noble guide (Araki) and partly through the power of the strokes of Haideri (Islamic Shi'a) sword had been brought into the fold of Islam. Many Muslim *Qadis*, *'ulema* and learned men of Kashmir, who professed *Hanafi* and *Shafi'i*[2] faith, left their respective sects, under the guidance and admonishing of Araki, rejected their (previous) beliefs and entered the fold of the righteous and true faith of 'Ali Murtaza. They changed their community and faith.[3] Imam Nurbakhsh has clearly explained in his theological work *Ahwat* that he had recorded without distortion or alteration all the procedures of religious law that were prevalent during the lifetime of the Holy Prophet. *Risaleh-e 'Aqaid* (A Treatise on Beliefs) and *Fiqh-e Ahwat* (*Ahwat* theology) both have been authored by him. Both of these books contain the beliefs and procedures of the Muhammadan community and the theological principles of the faith brought by the Prophet that were in vogue during his days and on which rested people's conviction. He has stated this in his work.

He has said that some superfluities and discrepancies crept into the Sunni and Shi'a faiths in the course of history. At times, the foundations of these two faiths were built on weak and inconsistent arguments. Some unsubstantiated stories and interpretations were interpolated into the texts. Both are contrary to the faith of Imam Nurbakhsh. We know that the faith brought by Imam Nurbakhsh is free from all these

---

[1] Rey is almost the present Tehran region.

[2] One of the four theological schools of Islam. See also *Sufism in Kashmir*, p.83.

[3] From Suui Hanafi sect to Shi'a Nurbakhshiyya order or sect.

superfluities: it is pure and unadulterated. Among the most outstanding persons following Nurbakhshiyyeh thought were Maulana Kamalu'd-Din Baseer, Jamalu'd-Din Muhammad Qudsi, this writers father Maulana Jamalu'd-Din Khaleelullah and Maulana Zia Muhammad bin Salman. There were many others among the learned men of the time, who had spent their lives as Hanafis and Shafi'is supporting controversial ideas and beliefs. All of them came to the presence of Shamsu'd-Din Araki.

Imam Reza shrine

After his interface with Hazrat Khizr, Shamsu'd-Din returned to his tent. He intended to proceed to the holy shrine of "Shah-e Khurasan", meaning Imam Reza.[1] After kissing the dust of the shrine at Meshad he circumambulated it and thus received the grace (of the Imam). His servants and attendants too had the good luck of making a pilgrimage to the holy shrine. After completing formalities (of pilgrimage), he left Meshad. He arrived in Kandahar and had planned to return to Kashmir via Kabul. But he carried with him a copy of Shi'a theological work *Ahwat* authored by Sayyid Muhammad Nurbakhsh. It was a gift for Mirza Baig (Ulugh Baig), and he wanted to hand it over to him in person. At this time came the news of the demise of this righteous ruler. The people of the town confirmed the veracity of the news. Therefore, he changed his mind and came to Hindustan by Multan route. Covering one stage after another, he arrived in Ghakkar.[2] It was winter, and owing to severe cold, he stayed there for some time. The news of his arrival in Ghakkar was brought to Kashmir. At that time his disciples and followers (in Kashmir) had gone into lent. They sent two *sufis* to his presence carrying some clothing and letters. The messengers arrived shortly. They asked him about his journey and also told him how eager

[1] Ali Reza, the 8th Imam.

[2] Western Pir Panchal range.

his followers and disciples were to receive him (in Kashmir). At the end of winter, he took the Poonch route.[1] At this point of time, apart from the high ranking Cheni Renu [*sic*], the people of Rachapal[2] (?) had declared allegiance to Mulla Ismail. All of them sought the permission of their ruler and came to receive Shamsu'd-Din. They had decided to conduct the horses and the entourage from Poonch to the pass (Hajji Pir) and onwards with full care and security. The Malik of Chunu accompanied by the people of Kalor and the pargana of Chunu came to Poonch. They lifted his luggage and his children on their backs and proceeded towards the pass. Snow-clad mountain pass was crossed with ease and the whole entourage arrived in Baramulla safely. It was the Shivratri[3] of the people of Kashmir.

In Baramulla

By this time, Mulla Ismail and all his disciples had completed the lent and were out of it. They received the news of Araki's arrival in Baramulla. All the disciples as well as ordinary people came out to join his reception. Malik Chuni Renu came to Bachehbal: he was [*sic*] accompanied by his family members and associates. A grand feast was hosted. He and all his family members made their allegiance to Araki. From that day down to present times all his progeny have declared allegiance to Araki's faith (converted to Nurbakhshiyyeh faith).

---

[1] It is difficult to ascertain the precise route he chose for entering Kashmir. In all probability, he might have taken the Poonch—Hajipir—Baramulla route. Hajipir pass lies on this route. 'Ghakkar' is the name of an ethnic group living in the highlands of western Pir Panchal that divides cold Kashmir from the wam plains. I presume that Ghakkar stands for eastern part of the Punjab, the present Mirpur area. Poonch is Parnotsa of *Rajatarangini*.

[2] Cheni or Chunu Raina could have been a highland chieftain holding sway over some part of the territory through which he travelled. Rachpal should be a site along Poonch—Hajji Pir route.

[3] It is the most important and popular religious festival of the Pandits of Kashmir valley commemorating the marriage of Shiv and Parvati. The Pandits were mostly Shaivites.

Then Araki was brought to the city in a procession. Soon after receiving the news of Arakis arrival in Ghakkar, Mulla Ismail arranged the construction of a new house for him and his family. He did not like that Araki's family be put up in the shabby and worn out houses of the Kashmiris. He arranged all necessary household equipment and kitchenware. Eatables such as rice, flour and fat lambs were provided. The stuff was handed over to his servants and housekeepers.

By the time of Araki's return, Mulla Ismail had become fairly rich and prosperous. He demonstrated his large heartedness and placed all his wealth and belongings at the disposal of Araki. He told Araki," We first came out of the skin of our grandfather (meaning I converted from the faith of my grandfather) and now I have to come out of my skin as well (meaning he had to adopt Nurbakhshiyyeh faith). Therefore I want to withdraw my hand from all my wealth and belongings and give it in the control of Araki." Shamsu'd-Din praised his love for lofty courage and established his control over all his wealth.

Differences

But regrettably his mind had been vitiated by poisonous thoughts. Like a venomous snake, the poison rested deep in his mind and was not visible outwardly. Apparently, he had gone into seclusion and forsaken wordily pursuits, demonstrating that he had liberated himself from the prison house of this material life. But alas he was unmindful of the disabling ego and inherent avarice in a human being. He did not realise that mind and soul could be vitiated by wicked thoughts. He did not know that these things could mislead even a wise seeker of truth. This is how Satan works to seduce human beings. He had not given up these negative traits in his character.

Satan overpowered him. He submitted to the evil force of ego, which began to drag him towards decline and darkness.

People came in large groups to pay obeisance to Shamsu'd-Din Araki and made allegiance at his hand. He admonished Mulla Ismail and forbade him to accept allegiance from anybody without his permission. This restriction created in him a sense of rejection, and thus was laid the foundation of corrupt dealings. He took a wrong direction. He made wrongful objections and took to defiance. Thus he with a large group of his people plunged into hell.

Musa Raina

The first among the nobles and rulers of the lands of Kashmir to win Araki's special favour was Malik Musa Raina. The Zadibal[1] site, where Nurbakhshiyyeh hospice has been erected and where the tomb and the grave of Araki are located, was actually given in endowment (*waqf*) by Musa Raina.[2] Owing to continued efforts of this noble and courageous man the banner of Islam, the religion of Mustafa, and the system of 'Ali Murtaza reached the pinnacle of glory. Shamsu'd-Din first visited this place (Zadibal) in AH 888/AD 1482. His perceptive eye had chosen this place and had liked it immensely. We have already described it in these pages. He desired that a beautiful and spacious hospice or mosque be raised at this attractive site. During his first visit to the place he had not made up his mind to choose it for his stay. But during the current visit, he showed much liking for it. At that time, the site was neither anybody's property nor in anybody's possession. It was state land.

After the murder of Malik Saif Dar, Chadura[3] nobles seized the reins of power. Fath Shah, the Sultan of Kashmir,

---

[1] It became the headquarter of Araki in downtown Srinagar.

[2] Originally from Chrar, this powerful commander rose to become Governor of Kashmir AD 1501–10.

[3] Chadura village is located in present day Budgam district. It is known in Kashmiri's mediaeval history for giving rise to a famous house of nobles called the Maliks, who, after their conversion to Islam, continued to wield immense influence in the affairs of Kashmir. In particular, Haider Malik Chadura rose to become a commander in the army of Emperor Jehangir. He is also the author of Tarikh-e Haider Malik, now available in English version.

ordered that the people of Chadura could take up their residence in Nowshehra and settle down around the place. He allotted land to them and the Zadibal estate passed on to Malik Musa Raina who built some houses there and took up his abode in one of them.

Feast in Araki's honour

After announcing his allegiance to Shamsu'd-Din Araki, Malik Musa Raina made arrangements in summer for a grand feast in his honour. He wanted all disciples and followers of Shamsu'd-Din Araki to join the feast and thus grace his house with their auspicious steps. Araki acceded to his request and permitted him to arrange the feast. On the night of the proposed feast, Araki summoned all his followers and disciples. Heading a crowd of people, he came to the house of Malik Musa Raina. The fortunate Malik hosted a lavish feast and people high and low all partook of many dainty dishes. The dinner having been served, Malik Musa Raina requested Araki to move to his private apartment. The family members of the Malik including womenfolk, children and close relatives were assembled in his residential quarter. He wished them to make allegiance to Araki and receive his blessings. Araqi granted him his request and consequently the family of the Malik received initiation and blessings of Shamsu'd-Din Araki.

Musa donates property

Thereafter Malik Musa Raina offered to donate all his land in Zadibal and the old houses that stood on it to Shamsu'd-Din. It was a voluntary gift and he renounced his claim to the entire estate. Then he told his family members, one and all, his servants, and the peasants who worked there that they should offer all their possessions to Araki as a gift. Among the gifted articles were gold and silver ornaments, necklaces, bangles, ear rings, cash, costly costumes, precious silver ware, and woollen clothes. He said that those who did not have possessions to offer should bring whatever small articles they had. He promised to compensate them by paying double the cost of the articles gifted. Thus women and men, children and servants raised a mountain of gifts, such as clothing, corn, cash, gold, silver, emeralds, pendants, rings, wrappers, turbans, and many other things. On beholding the generosity of Musa Raina, Araki showered lavish praise on him and accepted the gifts. He offered a prayer for him.

The Malik offered his personal belongings, such as horses, saddles, weapons, and other war material to him. He retained only one pair of clothing for each member of his family. In this way all the immovable property of Malik Musa Raina, such as houses, land, orchards etc. passed into the hands of Araki.

Araki in Zadibal

With the onset of spring, Araki began the construction of the building at Zadibal. He also ordered cultivation of land (now available there). Melons and other crops were sown. Although Araki had desired to raise the construction a year before but because the land did not belong to him, he could not fulfil that wish. Twenty years later, in AH 922/AD 1516, a mysterious combination of stars made it possible for him to bring his lurking desire to fruition, and the Nurbakhshiyych hospice came into being on which angels descend from heaven and became the centre for training of spiritualists seeking the right path.

When Mulla Isma'il saw that Araki had settled down at Zadibal and people were going in large numbers to announce their allegiance to him, and that they brought enormous presents to him, he felt jealous of him. This was the reason for his enmity towards Araki.[1] Mulla Ismail turned away, and renounced the faith to which he had been (previously) admitted.

---

[1] Perhaps political rivalry and lust for power and influence at the royal court were the underlying cause of their mutual rift.

Ismail afflicted

(In course of time) Mulla Ismail was afflicted with leprosy. When he told about his ailment to Hazrat Baba, he took him to Araki. On examining him and after hearing his story, Araki said that the possibility of curing the patient lay in his hands. He said that Mulla Ismail should lock himself up in a room and not allow anybody to see him, nor should he come out to see anybody. Then Araki would prepare food for him with his own hands and serve him. But evidently this was not acceptable to Mulla Ismail.

After his meeting with Araki, Mulla Isma'il held consultations with his advisers and counsellors. One of them was his nephew (sister's son) who had returned from *hajj* pilgrimage. People nicknamed him *Hokeh Hajji.*[1] He was the key adviser (to Araki) and could mislead other counsellors. He said that Araki's advice to Mulla Ismail to lock him in a secluded place meant that nobody could interact with him. It would distance him from people, high and low. Prescribing a special diet would lead to the deterioration of his physical health. This was how the disease would spread and prove fatal. He told Ismail that these steps would end his life. Even poison could be administered slowly. He suggested that they shun the company and association of Araki. He added that the faith that he had preached and taught, he had not found anywhere: in Mecca, Medina, Syria, Turkey, Egypt or Yemen. He had not found traces of this faith anywhere. He pleaded strongly to move away from him for the same reason.

These arguments of *Hokeh Hajji* made an impression on Mulla Ismail's mind. The Mulla owned a house in the city (of Srinagar), and a mosque stood by its side. His father began

[1] *Hokh* in Kashmiri means dry. In slang it means absurd, pretentious, fake etc. *Hokheh* means dried up. It is a favourite pastime of Kashmiris to invent sadistic and satirical sobriquets of this kind. However, another interpretation of the term is that *huqqeh* in Farsi means fraud/deception. Thus *huqqeh* Hajji means a fraudulent Hajji.

calling *azaan* (Muslim call for prayer) from this mosque. Mulla Ismail left the company of Araki and shifted to his own residence. He did not join him for offering five-time Muslim prayer. He would stay in his mosque the whole day and retire to his residence late in the night. He would not meet with anybody, nor would permit anyone from among his group to be with him.

A few days later , Hazrat Baba and Mulla Muhammad Imam learnt about his (Mulla Ismail) recantation of faith. They admonished him excessively and warned him of having been led astray by Satan. But destiny had abandoned him to recantation. The rock-hard man refused to accept advice and guidance. Their efforts were of no avail. With each passing day, he reinforced his apostasy, surrendering his faith and his conscience to the temptations of material world.

The cause of enmity

In the beginning of spring, Araki cultivated melons and melons in the garden of Mulla Ismail. Melons began to ripe. A stray cow entered the farm and began eating and destroying the crop. In anger Araki asked whose beast it was. Somebody said that it belonged to Mulla Ismail. In rage he said that Mulla Ismail had given up all his land and possessions. He had accepted in the presence of a large gathering that I was the new owner of the property. It was not in his possession. Then wherefrom did this beast appear? Does he (Mulla Ismail) still possess this property?

He was informed that when Mulla Ismail had taken to seclusion, this cow had been left in the village, and now he had brought it here. In order to admonish Mulla Ismail, Araki said that the cow be passed on to the kitchen to be butchered and the beef be served to the *sufis*.

The slaughter of the cow further prompted Mulla Ismail to reject Araki's faith. He took liberty in raising objections against Araki. Backbiting escalated. In order to influence common people, he claimed that it was a calf and not a cow.

He further objected how Araki could serve beef to his followers and disciples when the cow was not his property? A suckling calf could do no damage to the melon field. He said that Araki did not regret what he had done.

Ismail's allegations

Mulla Ismail said, "We remember very well in what guise Amir Shamsu'd-Din Araki came to us when we stayed for the first time in the hospice of Shaykh Sultan Kubra. One day when we came out from our residence for a stroll and proceeded towards the ground at the foot of Suleyman Mountain, three or four persons accompanied Araki. It was summer. I plucked some grapes in a vineyard, and ate the delicious fruit. Suddenly turning to me, he (Araki) asked if the vineyard belonged to me as I was eating the fruit so freely. I told him that did not belong to me or to any of my relatives. I added that I did not know who the owner of the orchard was. Having said that, he was furious and said to me that I pretended to go along the path of the *sufis* and that I was making a great effort to tread along that line. Which religion and which community permitted plucking of fruit from the property of other people without their permission? How were you to seek permission from the owner, he inquired.

You can see that this was one face of Shamsu'd-Din Araki; and now he had ordered butchering of a cow that belonged to others and eaten beef. "He does not care for anything, nor is he deterred by a misdeed. How can such type of people be eligible to guide and lead others" Ismail asked.

Alas, the unwitty and arrogant Mulla Ismail did not understand that Araki had become the owner of the cow the same day on which he had called Araki *maula* meaning the holder and possessor. His claim on the animal was wrong and illegal. All the grass and cattle-feed provided to the cow by Ismail was illegal (*haram*). Mulla Ismail used to watch the cow so that Araki did not order its butchering. But being a dark-minded and wicked person Mulla Ismail proved a poisonous snake. He did not understand that blessings of godly saints worked as panacea for removing ailments. Blowing out of proportion the incident of butchering a cow that Mulla Ismail claimed was only a calf, he began misleading people from the path of righteousness. He virtually dragged them and as well as himself to the abyss of darkness.

Mulla Ismail aroused filial sentiments among his kinsmen and friends on the trivial issue of the slaughtering of a calf. Along with them he hatched conspiracies to force the displacement of Araki from his present location. All of them wanted to shift to Mulla Ismail's old mosque. After performing morning *namaz* (prayer), Mulla Ismai'l took a couple of his associates with him and came to that old mosque. They stayed there for the whole day and after performing the evening *namaz* returned to their houses. They did not join the congregational prayers with Araki. They did not participate in reciting *awradh* (psalms).

Hazrat Baba and others repeatedly cautioned him (Ismail) about this situation. But he was not willing to listen to them. He was not prepared to change his attitude. God Almighty aggravated his disease (leprosy). Both his hands dried up and became stiff so much so that he could not lift a morsel to eat. He had to be fed by others with spoons. Despite this state of broken health, he was not prepared to listen to anybody's advice. Entreaties of his friends, followers and well-wishers made no impact on him.

Shifting to Zadibal

Araki's inner voice confirmed that Mulla Ismail would never return to the path of righteousness. It confirmed his recantation. One day, after offering afternoon prayers and reciting the psalms (*awradh*), Araki showed up in his hospice. Araki's disciples and devotees were present there. He beckoned one particular person, who was very close to Mulla Ismail. As already said Mulla Ismail had donated his belongings to Araki on the day he declared he had renounced the world. Araki had distributed some of those possessions among the *Sufis*. Whatever had remained, he returned to the associates of Mulla Ismail. These were mostly utensils and kitchenware like pots and pans. Some books, which he had gifted to Araki, were also returned. He said that the purpose of Ismail in gifting these articles to him was to win his heart. But when Ismail had changed and wanted to move away from his company, those commodities had no utility for him. "What value do these material things have for me?" he asked.

Then addressing his dervishes (disciples), he said, "This man has adopted the path of apostasy and recantation. He has given up my company. He is out of my heart, and I consider him a renegade. All those from among you who have some love for me and who are resolved in following me should accompany me. Those who are inclined towards him (Ismail) may stay on." Saying so, he stood up and came out of his hospice. He carried a staff in his hand and proceeded towards Zadibal. A crowd of dervishes followed him. Those who were destined to face disaster and adversity stayed on. Apart from Mulla Salman, Hajji 'Ali and Mulla Bayezid, there were some more people who had access to the family of Araki. They stayed on so that they would accompany the womenfolk after dusk. He arrived at Zadibal along with his followers.

His family members joined him in the evening. They brought all their belongings with them. He took his abode in the old house of the virtuous Malik (Musa Raina). Those who arrived with him were Hazrat Baba, Maulana Muhammad Imam, Maulana Nusrat, Maulana Saeed, Maulana Khalleullah (this writer's father), and several others. Dervishes requested him to grant permission to their families for joining them. He allotted a garden to them from the estates of Malik Musa Raina so that in summer they could cultivate the land. The dervishes quickly built small rooms and huts and brought their families to live in them. He engaged himself in the rehabilitation of the *sufis*.

So far we have recorded the biographical events of Araki's life, in their chronological order. In pages to follow, we shall give details of his major achievements. It is better to distribute these details (into sub-chapters). We shall begin with the construction of the Shamsiyyeh hospice and the account will begin with the story of repair and reconstruction of Nurbakhshiyyeh hospice.

Chapter IV
Mission in Kashmir

Part I

Stewardship of Hamadaniyyeh Hospice

Sultan Muhammad Shah was the ruler when Araki arrived in Kashmir. With the consent of his advisers, government functionaries and the nobles of the land, he (Muhammad Shah) offered the stewardship of the Hamadaniyyeh hospice to him for his stay in Srinagar and to meet his expenses. The powers invested in him included recruitment of attendants, their dismissal, their stipends or replacement etc. The documents in this regard were formally signed.

The royal farman

> "By the order of the chief of the nobles, Sayyid Muhammad Husayni, and in the presence of Malik Ibrahim Magray, Malik Shams Chak, Malik Edi Raina and all the top functionaries of the state and the nobles, it is stated in writing that the stewardship of Hamadaniyyeh hospice is entrusted to Shamsu'd-Din Araki. Only he and no other person in the state will deal with all matters pertaining to the maintenance and continuation of the hospice. No person of a higher or lower rank or one from the governing group shall go against his wishes or interfere in his work. He will exercise authority over all that he finds necessary. He will issue directions to the inmates of the hospice of Amir 'Ali Hamadani. It has to be mentioned that in the endowment document bearing the signature of Sayyid 'Ali Hamadani it is stated that the inmates of the hospice shall revive the tradition of reciting

prayers, hymns and psalms laid down by Sayyid ‘Ali Hamadani.”

Sayyid Muhammad Baihaqi

At this time, Mir Sayyid Muhammad Baihaqi[1] occupied the seat of vizier in the state. He desired to marry the daughter of Araki. Bibi Agha was his eldest daughter and the Sayyid proposed marriage to her which Araki did not accept. He said he did not like to be in the company of the Sultans, high-ranking nobles and men of substance. Mian Muhammad was furious to hear about the rejection of the proposal. Araki told Hazrat Baba and my father (Maulana Jamalu’d-Din Khaleelullah) to look for a traveller from the lands of Khurasan, Iraq, Rum or some other land.[2] He directed them to bring that person to his presence and he would give his daughter in marriage to him. He instructed them to ensure that the man was honest, faithful and lived a humble life.

At that time, a man named Mulla Fazil had arrived from Rum (Turkey). Hazrat Baba knew him. My father had seen this traveller from close quarters. He said he had no intention of staying permanently in this land. But that a gentleman had accompanied him from the lands of Rum and he wanted to stay here permanently. If Shamsu’d-Din desired, he might consider the alliance of his daughter with that gentleman. This man was called Shaykh Abdus Salam. He was brought to the presence of Araki, and asked him about his community and tribe. His answer convinced Araki that the gentleman was descendant of a house of learned men of Rum.

Bibi Agha married

He told my father to be the *vakil* (spokesperson/guardian) from the side of Bibi Agha. The alimony was settled at nineteen and a half *misqal*s (grams) of gold, and a camel load

---

[1] See *Baharistan-i-Shahi,* p.87.

[2] It may be inferred that the more important reason for Araki to reject the proposal was that the Baihaqi Sayyids were of Sunni Hanafi faith.

of silk and brocade called *diba-e shastari*. My father performed the marriage rites of Bibi Agha with Shaykh Abdus Salam. He was also told to arrange a room for the Shaykh. He got it modestly furnished and handed it over to the servants of the Shaykh. Shamsu'd-Din also sent him some money through the treasurer to meet the household expenses. He also instructed that whatever had been cultivated in the village, called Potwav,[1] be given to Bibi Agha.[2]

When Mian Muhammad came to know of Bibi Agha's marriage, he began to nurse animosity against Araki. His opponents and enemies fuelled the flames of jealousy. They taunted Mian Muhammad saying that that person (Araki) had considered it a humiliation to give his daughter in marriage to him. They said that he (Araki) had not considered his power and status equal even to that of an ignominious person.

Mantji case

One day, Araki went for an excursion to the Koh-e-Maran[3] to have a look at the melon farm. Suddenly there appeared a horse rider. He drew closer but did not offer obeisance to Araki, and did not show him any respect. Araki asked him the reason for not wishing him. A few *sufis* were present on the scene. They said that the horse rider was not a Muslim but an infidel wearing *zunnar* (ceremonial thread). Araki asked if he was a *kafir* (infidel), why did he ride like Muslims. Why is there no distinction between the dress he wore and those of Muslims[4]. A *sufi* said that the rider was the secretary

[1] This village is situated somewhere between Pattan and Baramulla towns in the valley.

[2] It shows that Araki had already got this village allotted to his daughter. After her marriage she had the right to own its produce in cash or in kind.

[3] Hari Parbat.

[4] Islamic history tells us that Jews of a land freshly conquered by the Muslims became second rate citizens—*dhimmis*—in their own land, the nascent Islamic state. They were required to wear a mark—usually a patch of yellow cloth—below the neck across the shoulders so that their identification was quick and easy. Araki and Nurbakhsiyyeh did not consider the *kafirs* (Hindus) men of the book (*ahl-e kitab*) and as such they had no right to be trated at par with the Muslims.

of Mian Muhammad, the Governor. He was arrogant because of the support of his master. Araki ordered that the man be pulled down from his horse and taken into custody. The *sufis* obeyed and Araki threw him down on the ground and thrashed him mercilessly, so much so that he lost the hope of survival. Thereafter he was let go.

The infidel presented himself before Mian Muhammad in that very miserable condition. This incident further ignited the flames of jealousy, enmity and prejudice. He (Mian Muhammad) became mad with rage. He ordered his musclemen to enter the house of Mir Shamsu'd-Din Araki apprehend all males and bring them to his presence. Children and women were to be spared. The ruffians entered the residence of Araki. Many elderly persons were busy with their work in the orchard. Among these were Sufi Dawood, Sufi Junayd, Nunu Sufi and others. Even the gardeners, cooks, hewers of wood and drawers of water all were rounded up. They were beaten with batons and lashes.

When the news of this incident reached Araki, he came out of the melon farm and went straight to the residence of Mian Muhammad. Standing in the premises, he sent him a message asking what the fault of his *sufis* was. Why were they subjected to oppression and why their hands were chained? Mian Muhammad replied harshly asking what the fault of his official who he had beaten mercilessly was? Araki said, "The secretary was punished according to the *sharia* (religious law) of *Mustafa* (the Prophet). Why did he not wear the clothes of the infidels? The clothes he wore (of Muslims) were not permissible according to the religious law of the Messenger of God. I have, therefore, disciplined him and taught him a lesson.[1] But what was the fault of our *sufi*?" Mian Muhammad thundered that he was the Governor of the land and caretaker of the city and he (Araki) had not been

[1] This incident, also recorded in some more histories of Kashmir, gives us an idea of the religious persecution of the Hindus of Kashmir by Araki and his local supporters among the nobles and plebians.

appointed as a superintendent to take care of peoples' morals. Likewise, nobody had been appointed to oversee his (Araki's) code of morals. He asked him why he had taken upon himself the task of calling the people to book without formal permission from the authorities of the land. Araki answered that Shah Qasim had assigned him the duty of directing and guiding the people of this land. If he (Mian Muhammad) were determined to obstruct the guiding of people on the right path, he would not stay in his country as long as he (Mian Muhammad) was its Governor. He demanded that he be given formal permission to leave for Baltistan so that he stay there till the last day of Mian Muhammad's administration.

Mian Muhammad had little knowledge of worldly affairs. He was arrogant and conceited. He did not mind if he broke the heart of dervishes or inflicted pain on them. He did not even take into consideration the words and wishes of his ancestors. In a spate of anger, he ordered his scribes to give Araki the formal order for permission to leave. The permit for travelling to Baltistan via Tibet was given. Many close associates of Mian Muhammad requested Araki to come to the upper story (of the house of Mian Muhammad). Their purpose in making this request was that he should not become a victim of Mian Muhammad's fury. But despite much effort to induce him to come up, he refused to oblige them. He boastfully said that as long as he was alive, he would not step into that house. When the permission of travelling via Tibet was handed over to him, Araki said that he had come to the lands of Kashmir in deference to the instructions of his spiritual masters. The purpose was to guide the people of these lands along the right path. But Mian Muhammad had created obstructions in his mission. He was answerable to his God and ancestors. Mian Muhammad as well as his ancestors knew about the mission for which Araki was in Kashmir. Saying these words, he and his followers came out of the house of the Mian. The *sufis* who had been rounded up were set free.

Malik Musa Raina was in Chadura at that time. On learning about the happening, he moved out of Chadura and came to Mian Muhammad and admonished him. He told him to stop Araki from his travel to Tibetan region and suggested that both of them go together to meet Araki. Musa Raina came to the presence of Shamsu'd-Din and entreated him to cancel his visit to Tibet. He told him that Mian Muhammad would be coming the day after to clear misunderstanding and unpleasantness. But Shamsu'd-Din was too determined to accept the entreaties of Malik Musa.

A couple of days were spent in collecting nick-knacks for the travel. Leaving the construction work at Zadibal halfway, Araki prepared for the long journey. About fifty *sufis* comprised his entourage. He left behind Hazrat Baba and other dervishes to look after the construction work of the hospice. Doors and windows had to be fixed. They were to ensure that five time prayers were offered with regularity and the *awrad* (recitations) were made at the stipulated time.

Reception at Skardu

Bukha of the ruling line of Maqpun dynasty was the ruler in Skardu when Shamsu'd-Din arrived in those lands. He came out at the head of a large crowd to receive Shamsu'd-Din Araki. At that time, there were no traces of a religion and community (of Muslims) in Tibet.[1] Nobody knew anything about the religion and doctrines of Islam. The ruling class and the subjects in those lands were all infidels and heretics. There were big idol houses in all the forts. People used idols as objects of worship.[2] With his auspicious steps on this soil, all

[1] Farsi historians have always spoken of two Tibets, *kalan* (large) and *khord* (small). Baltitan formed part of *Tibet-e Khord*, while Ladakh was part of *Tibet-e Kalan*.

[2] It needs to be ascertained whether these were the statues of Buddha or of other Hindu deities. It is beyond the scope of this work to go into the details of expansion of Hinduism and Buddhism in the regions of Baltistan.

rajas, nobles, elite, peasants and common people were admitted to the religion of Islam. High and low, declared his allegiance to Shamsu'd-Din Araki. Men, women, children and old people all embraced Islam and were admitted to its fold. They recited *kelima* in his presence and renounced the customs, traditions and practices of infidels. He ordered his *sufis* and dervishes to destroy the idol houses and prayer houses[1] (temples) of the infidels wherever they found them. These had to be demolished and razed to the ground leaving no trace behind.[2] The *sufis* carried out his instructions faithfully and raised mosques and hospices on the ruins of temples and idol houses. With the blessings and guidance of Shamsu'd-Din Araki, ruins of torched idol houses and idols yielded their place to the praying houses of the people of Islamic faith. The arch and the pulpit took the place of idols for the worshippers. Through the instrumentality of this virtuous saint, and guide on the path to the other world, doctrines of the religion of the Prophet and the law of Islamic religion flourished in each and every nook of that land. The hearts of the inhabitants of those lands were enlightened and illuminated by the love and allegiance they showed to the House of the Prophet and the descendents of Haider (meaning 'Ali). Under the spiritual guidance of this saint of many parts, some people of those mountainous regions emerged as the bearers of high morals. The names of Dervish Zirak and Dervish Kemal could be mentioned in this context. We shall speak of their spiritual powers and excellence at a proper place.

Presents and gifts

Araki travelled in those regions for two months. The owners of big fortresses and the learned men of those areas brought

[1] Idol houses and prayer houses are usually clubbed together in the text. It means the idol houses of the Hindus and the *mathas* or *viharas* of the Buddhists.

[2] No research worth the name has been conducted by archaeologists in the region of Baltistan and Balawaristan that would reveal the existence of the temple structures of Hindu period. Nevertheless, any effort made in this direction in future is likely to be amply rewarded with exciting results.

him silver plates, each filled with a hundred *tolas* (one *tola* = 10 grams) of gold. The viziers and the nobles each brought about forty to fifty *tolas* of gold as a gift. Women, officials and nobles all offered him their ornaments. Ordinary people also brought him gifts according to their ability. The father of this writer narrated several times that the gifts of white and brown colour (meaning silver and gold) were made in heaps. Expenses for the entire team right from the beginning of the travel in Kashmir up to Tibet were entrusted to the care of my father. Total weight of gold and silver offerings was in the neighbourhood of thirty kilograms. Half of it was gold and the other half silver. Woollen clothes gifted to Shamsu'd-Din also piled up and some of these were given away by him to the accompanying dervishes.

Baihaqi's high-handedness

While Mir Shamsu'd-Din was touring Baltistan, Sayyid Muhammad did not permit me (this writer's father) to come to his place out of deep-seated animosity and malice. He stopped the staff and elders in Shamsu'd-Din's team from performing their assigned duties or stewardship of Hamadaniyyeh hospice, and usurped the sources of income and possessions.

Malik Musa Raina demonstrated deep attachment and sincerity towards Araki. He hated and disliked the attitude of Mian Muhammad. Driven by his Islamic fervour, he (Musa) openly demonstrated his his opposition and enmity towards Mian Muhammad. At that time, Sultan Fath Shah and some of his nobles were stationed on Indian mountains (Pir Panchal).[1]

[1] "The Sanskrit chronicle of Shrivara, iii, 433, relating the return of Kashmir refugees by the route of Shurpura (Herpur) in the time of Hassan Shah (*circ.* AD 1472–84), tells us of a fatal chill he caught on the top of the Panchaladeva. It is clear that the name here used corresponds exactly to the modern Pir Pantsal, Pir being the nearest Muhammadan equivalent for Deva. Dr. Berner's account has already shown us that popular superstition had not failed to transfer also the supernatural powers of the Deva to the Pir who acted as his represenative on the Pass", *Rajatarangini*, vol.ii, pp.397–98. For full detail on Pir Panchal (*Pantsal*) see Stein's excellent note *Rajatarangini*, vol.ii, p.392 *et seq.*

Malik Musa Raina sent him a secret message offering to align with him. He told the Sultan to return to Kashmir and he would give him his support. Fath Shah's entourage took the Hirpora[1] route and Malik Musa Raina moved away from Chadura and joined them.

On the other side, Mian Muhammad took Sultan Muhammad Shah with him and prepared for a battle. They encamped in village Duru. After halting at that place for a couple of days, Mian Muhammad proceeded to face the adversary. In a battle that took place somewhere near Hirpora, Mian Muhammad was killed. Sultan Muhammad Shah was defeated and fled towards Hindostan.[2] Sultan Fath Shah assumed the reins of the kingdom of Kashmir and the administrative power passed into the hands of Musa Raina.

The lucky Musa Raina entered the city the same day. At that time Daniyal was of twelve years of age (AH 912/ AD 1506). Heading a group of *sufis*, Hazrat Baba went to offer felicitations to Musa Raina. He bestowed on him gorgeous costumes and other gifts. In return, Musa Raina endorsed the stewardship of Hamadaniyyeh hospice for Baba, a right bestowed by Shamsud-Din Araki in his will. All possessions and sources of income of the hospice were restored to the functionaries of the hospice.

A foretelling

Two years after Araki's departure for Tibet, Bejih Agha, the mother of Shaykh Daniyal saw a dream that all dark trees

---

[1] The ancient Shurapura (Hurpur) was founded by Shura, the minister of Avantivarman, in the ninth century, evidently with the intention of establishing a convenient emporium on this important trade route. See, *Rajatarangini*, vol.ii, p.394, section 42.

[2] In mediaeval times, Kashmir always remained a separte kingdom, outside the territorial jurisdiction of Hindostan. The mountain range (Pir Panchal) that divided them has usually been called Indian Mountains (*kohistan-e-Hind*) by Farsi historians. During the Hindu period, the territories of the sovereign Kingdom of Kashmir extended as far as Gandhara (Kandahar) to south- west and Stadru (River Satluj) to the south.

of the Poneh Renu[1] idol house bowed to Shaykh Daniyal in front of the hospice. The trees lay prostrate on the ground. Araki interpreted the dream like this: The said temple will be razed to the ground but that credit will not go to me. God Almighty has destined Shaykh Daniyal to achieve that act of faith. At his hands the idol house will be destroyed and trees will all be cut down.

When Malik Musa Raina became (Hasan Shahs) prime minister, Hazrat Baba sought his permission to pull down the idol house. On the following day, Hazrat Baba took Shaykh Daniyal and a team of *sufis* with him, and came to the bank of the canal where the temple stood. It was razed to the ground in front of Shaykh Daniyal. Following the instructions of the Shaykh, all trees were cut down. Araki's interpretation of the dream of Bejih Agha came true.

Return from Tibet

Prime Minister Malik Musa told Hazrat Baba to send a couple of *sufis* post-haste to Tibet (Baltistan) to persuade Araki to return to Kashmir. He issued strict orders that there should be no delay in dispatching the emissaries. After providing them with travel expenses and other necessary requirements, two to three *Sufis,* under the leadership of Mulla Jowhar proceeded towards Tibet. But before they could convey to Amir Shamsu'd-Din the news of Malik Musa Raina's victory, the Amir had already learnt of it through intuition, and resolved to return to Kashmir. But the ruler of Tibet and the Khans of that land told him that it was the peak of winter season and the time of snowfall. They said they hardly knew anybody undertaking the difficult journey to Kashmir at that time of the year. Not even birds ventured a flight in that harsh winter and over the difficult and dangerous route. But Araki did not heed their advice and made preparations for journey to Kashmir.

---

[1] I have not been able to identify this temple and the place where it stood. Probably the temple was situated somewhere close to Zadibal, where Araki had built his hospice.

Raja of Khaplu

Raja Bahram was the ruler of Khaplu at this point of time. He told Shamsu'd-Din that the work of construction of a lofty mosque over the ruins of a temple destroyed by Amir Kabir (Sayyid 'Ali Hamadani) was still incomplete. He requested Araki to leave behind one of his successors (*khalifa*) who would impart them the *kelima* and teach how to offer *namaz*. Araki acceded to their request and left behind Malik Haider whom he used to call by the name of Haideri but he submitted that he would proceed to Kashmir as part of his entourage and would return to Tibet in summer along with his son Mulla Ismail. Thereupon Araki advised Bahram Khan to wait till summer when his dervish would return along with his family. Araki bade them farewell and proceeded towards Kashmir. He expressed his displeasure with those who brought him the bad news of the death of Mian Muhammad. He ordered that they be lashed because they deserved punishment for bringing him the bad news of the killing of Sayyid Muhammad.

The ruler, high ranking officials, nobles, ministers one and all came to receive him in Kashmir and brought him to Zadibal hospice.

Zadibal hospice

Within a few days of his arrival, he engaged himself in completing the construction work of the hospice. After the western projection, the raising of its four walls was undertaken. The wall was ten yards high. The ground within and outside the wall was levelled and an attractive house and platforms were raised all around it.

Towards the east, south and west of this hospice, there were ponds of clean water, which met the requirements of the hospice. Expansive gardens and orchards sprawled on all sides at the site. In the beginning he ordered *sufis* to lay out a garden towards the north of the hospice. Flowers and roses of various hues were planted in it. Private houses were constructed on one side of the garden where people began to live. Another garden was laid out close to the first gate. These gardens were also purchased or bought on lease or were donated by the owners and houses were built on these, too.

The first door was named of *Babu'sh-Shariat*. There was an open space just outside the gate, which was set aside to serve as a stable. It was enclosed with a wall so that nobody encroached on it. An enclosure was also raised around *Babu'sh-shariat* so that horses and mules of infidels and non-Muslims did not trespass and the *sufis* had all facility of access. That land was uneven at that time and was strewn with rubble. The rubble was removed and dumped in the pond close to *Babu'sh-shariat*. It was desiccated of water and then turned into a garden where fruit bearing trees of many varieties were planted. The floor of the hospice was made pucca.

When devotees and mendicants came to meet with Araki, they dismounted from their horses at the *Babu'sh-shariat* and walked the distance down to the wall of the hospice. But officers, nobles and high-ups would pass through the gate and come to *Babut-tariqat*. The guards and doormen entered through the second door.

Araki had named the second door *babut-tariqat* and its boundary was also demarcated. Some of the rulers and top nobles would alight from their horses at this gate, tie the horses there and then go inside. During the days of Araki, no ruler or noble passed mounted through *babu't-tariqat*. The horses would be left outside the walls. Inside *babut-tariqat*, there was a wide stretch of land without any structure on it. Araki used to come to this gate and distribute gold, silver and clothing among the people. A crowd of *sufis* and other people usually assembled here. Shaykh Daniyal would be seated on the rostrum at this door.

Pilgrims and visitors to this holy shrine enter through *Bab-e-Shariat*. Then they turn to northwest towards *Bab-e-Tariqat*. The distance between the two points of entry is about a hundred steps. After going through the second door, they proceed towards *Bab-e-Haqiqat*. The distance again is about a hundred steps. The devotees enter through this door and walk about twenty-five steps towards the west. Then turning south, they take about forty paces, and this brings them to the walls of the hospice. The grave of Shamsu'd-Din is situated on the right side while that of Bibi Agha is on the left. The actual shrine has these dimensions: towards east facing the platform twenty-four yards, from south to north fifty yards.

Circumambulation

Circumambulation pathway is like this: 10 yards towards the south, 10 yards towards the west, and width of the western side of the platform 5 yards, distance between northern flank and the graveyard of Araki 12 yards, distance up to eastern porch 6 yards.

I have heard from my father that Araki used to say that every devoted believer will go round his grave seven times thinking that he virtually circumambulated the holy Ka'aba. He would receive grace equal to circumambulating the Ka'aba.

It is said that one of his followers (*sufis*) desired to make a pilgrimage to Mecca. He collected a good amount of gold for meeting the expenses and came to the presence of Araki to seek his permission and blessings for the pilgrimage. He asked him to place the gold before him. The devoted follower immediately brought to him all the gold he had collected. Then he asked him to deposit the gold with him and circumambulate the hospice seven times a day regularly. God Almighty would bless him with all the virtues of circumambulating the Ka'aba. These words are like the words of Bayazid Bistami,[1] as we learn from biographies.

During his lifetime, this hospice commanded as much respect as the mosque in holy Ka'aba. One could enter the premises only for offering five-time prayers. A few *sufis* kept an eye on those who entered into Lent in its cells. These (supervising) *Sufis* would come to the hospice at mid-night and not allow anybody to come in.

---

[1] p.204, supra.

Outside the *Bab-e-Haqiqat*, there is an enclosure on the left. Many platforms have been raised on its fringes. Their southern side remains hidden behind tall wooden planks. Araki used to spend most of his time on these platforms. People high and low, state functionaries and spiritualists, learned men and nobles all would meet him at that very place.

Reminiscences

I was five years old. Once I was taken to pay my regards to Araki. We reached a spot and then sat under a mulberry tree, waiting for my father to join us. He came and took us with him. Araki bade me come closer to him. But giving due regard to his personality, we sat down at some distance. But he bade us come closer to him. He put his hand on my knees and pulled me so close that my knees almost touched his. He was murmuring something and gently wiped his slightly perspiring face. Then he ran his hand on my face. He repeated it seven or eight times. He was chewing a sugar cube in his mouth, which he took out from his mouth and placed on my hand. I put it in my mouth. He talked to my father who felt happy, and Araki, too, smiled. Then he asked for more sugar cubes and, a *sufi* brought a handful of grey sugar. Araki said that the sugar be tied to my waist. He pulled out a leather bag (with his own hands) and something square in shape, which he placed on my hand. My father tied it around my waist. Thereafter Araki asked for something to eat. A *sufi* went out and brought back a plateful of yellow rice, some bread and soup, and placed it in front of me. He lifted a morsel in his hand and put it in my mouth. Then he ordered that a plateful of minced meat and thin bread be sent to my house along with me so that I partook of it along with my brothers. A *sufi* brought the eatables and accompanied me to my residence. This was when I saw him closely. I looked at his face intently and found spiritual rays emanating from it and illuminating me. I have an indelible impression of his face, personality and thoughts. Thereafter, I got several occasions of meeting him.

Destruction of Pandrethan temple

Qazi Muhammad Qudsi had declared his allegiance to Shamsu'd-Din Araki. He often came and sat in his presence. He also used to accompany Araki in his visits and short travels. Once he expressed his intention of destroying the idol house in the village of Pandrethan.[1]

---

[1] *Rajatarangini* Bk.v, verse 267 runs as this: "The sons of the minister Meruvardhana, the one who built at Puranadhishthana the illustrious (shrine of) Vishnu called Meruvardhanasvamin ..." In his note to this verse (*Rajat*, Bk.v, 267) Stein writes, "Regarding the identity of Puranadhishthana with the modern Pandrethan, see note 99 of Bk.iii. In the well-preserved little temple still standing in the village of Pandrethan, we may safely recognise with Cunningham the Meruvardhanasvamin of our passage..." Stein visited the site in 1895 and wrote, "The building stands at present in the water of a shallow tank, which has occupied the place of the original courtyard. The temple has been noticed already by the earlier European travellers; *cf.* MOORCROFT, *Travels*, ii, p.240, HUGEL, *Kaschmir*, i, p.260; VIGNE, *Travels*, ii, p.38. For a full description see *JASB* 1848, pp.283 *sqq* and COLE, *Ancient Buildings in Kashmir*, p.29, Bk.iii, verse 99 of *Rajatarangini* runs: "Afer having consecrated the first shrine of Pravareshvara together with 'circle of the Mothers' (*matrichakra*), he consecrated various holy shrines at Puranadhishthana". The construction of the shrine(s) is alluded to King Shreshthasena, whom the people called Pravarsena and Tunjina. The identity of Puranadhishthana (the ancient capital) with the present village of Pandrethan, about three miles above the present Srinagar on the right bank of Vitasta, has been first shown by General Cunningham (See *JASB* 1848, pp.283 et seqq). Stein thinks that the name of *Puranadhishthana* must have already been in use in the first half of the seventh century, as Hiuen-tsiang evidently refers to it when speaking of the "old city" situated about 10 *Li* or *circ* two miles to the S.E of the new city (See *Si-yu-ki*, i, p.158) *Rajat*, Bk.iii, 99 fn. Kalhana mentions Puranadhishthana once more in the reign of Partha (*Rajat*, Bk.v, verse 267) when gloss A2 explains the name by *Pamydrthan iti prasiddhegrame* meaning *Pamydrthan* (present Pandrethan) is a well-known village. The temple of *Meruvardhanasvamn* whose erection is related in that passage, has been recognised by General Cunningham. Kalhana records the erection of various buildings by the minister Rilhana 'in the towns of the two Pravarsenas'.

In a note to verse 99 of Bk.iii, Stein records: "The slopes rising immediately to the N of Pandrethan show considerable remains of ancient buildings in the form of carved stones and architectural fragments, which can be traced along the foot of the hillside for about a mile and a half. Among them several broken *Lingas* of colossal dimensions attract attention. The *Lingas* or shrine of Pravaresha, which seems to have been the most prominent among them, is distinguished by the designtion '*purvam*' from the great temple of the same name, which Pravarasena II built in his new capital of Pravarapura.

He took a boat to reach this place. The Qadi accompanied him. He told the Qadi that he wanted the names of famous and outstanding Shaykhs and saints to be arranged in a verse form and inscribed on the walls of the hospice.

After reaching the above-named village (*Pandrethan*), he, along with a large group of *sufis* got engaged in destroying the idol house. Scraps of paper, pen and inkpot were brought for the Qadi. He sat under a tree and began compiling the line of leading Shaykhs in verse form. Thus he produced a *mathnawi* (long poem) by the afternoon prayer. After offering prayers, Araki started to return. The Qadi also sat by his side and said he would like to recite a few couplets he had just then composed. He was permitted to recite them and when he read a few verses, he began to cry out of deep sentiment and bowed his head in praise of God. The *Qadi's* intense feeling for spiritualism moved Araki. He sent for Mulla Rabi Ganai and Mulla Hajji Ganai both known for their excellent calligraphic skill. The *mathnawi* composed by Qudsi was divided into two parts one each for the calligraphers who inscribed it on the walls of the hospice, and these can be seen there.

Destruction of Zadibal hospice

The hospice and the complex around it and in its proximity came up as a result of great effort made by Shamsu'd-Din Araki. It remained in tact for a long time. But forty-two years after the domination by the Turks,[1] this complex suffered severe damage during the reign of Mirza Haider Gorkan in AH 929/AD 1522. Mirza Haider demonstrated his stone heartedness, deep animosity and prejudice in destroying the hospice and razing it to the ground. The entire hospice, all of its cells, and structures of the complex were razed to the ground. The inscribed timber and its arches were taken to *Band Kol* (?). Walls of his tomb were smashed and razed to the

[1] Allusion is to Mirza Haider Dughlat, a warrior from Eastern Turkestan and an Uighur by extraction who invaded Kashmir and succeeded in removing the Shahmiri house of rulers. He was an ethnic Turk.

ground. We shall describe the details of this perfidy of Mirza Haider Gorkani at its proper place.

Part II

Araki's Mission of Destroying Idols and Temples of Infidels

The foremost of the saints (Araki) wanted to strengthen Islam in this land (Kashmir) for which he made a great effort. On the ruins of destroyed idol houses and the temples of the infidels, mosques and hospices (*khanqah*) were raised. The groups of polytheists, infidels and heretics of Kashmir were converted to the Islamic religion, some by force and others through strong persuasions. The banner of the law of Mustafa and of Islam as well as the religion of the community of the Prophet was raised high in the skies. In the chapter that follows, we shall describe this story.

Friends with clear conscience and lofty souls are aware that Shamsu'd-Din arrived in Kashmir during the last days of winter. The first thing he did after arriving in the city was to occupy the house of Baba Isma'il that stood at the foot of *Koh-e-Maran.* Here he offered prayers and recitations, and his family rested there. At this time, all parts of the region had been converted to *daru'l-Islam* (the place/land of peace) by the untiring and auspicious efforts of Sultan Sikandar Butshikan. But with the passage of time and because of being misled by the Satan(s) and Lucifer(s), the region had reverted to *daru'l-harb* (plac/land of fighting). People who had been admitted to Islamic faith as a result of efforts of the late Sultan (Sikandar), one and all turned away from allegiance and submission to the laws of Islam and set their foot once again in the valley of infidelity, darkness and aberration.

Through the support of the Sultans (reference to Zainul 'Abidin) and co-operation of mischievous officials, polytheists, infidels and *zandiqs* were encouraged to such an extent that every part of Kashmir region flourished with idol houses. The foundations of Islamic tenets and the laws of Islam were fully smashed. Proselytizing, defiance and repudiation (of Islamic ways) had become widespread. At every step a stone was given the name of a deity. Idol houses were raised in every village and habitat. Along the passages and at every conspicuous place, idol temples were built. Something of this has already been said in an earlier chapter. Thus Mir Shamsu'd-Din had made a great effort in demolishing these idol houses. He exhibited courage in spreading Islam and Islamic law in Kashmir.

Temple at Koh-i-Maran[1]

Shamsu'd-Din Araki began his enterprise (of destroying temples) with the temple at *Koh-i-Maran* (*Hari Parbat* hillock). According to the Hindu astronomers of Kashmir, when the Sun enters the Pisces, it is called the day of spring. However, according to Islamic astronomers, this is the day of coming together of two stars (conjuction of Sun and Moon in Pisces).

There existed a big idol temple on top of *Koh-i-Maran*.[2] In Kashmiri, it was called *Hareh Blari* (Hareh Brari).[3] Groups and clans of Hindu infidels, heretics and unbelievers circumambulated it. The tradition descended from ancient infidels[4] of the land was that on the day of spring (*roz-e-*

---

[1] Muslims gave this name to Hari Parbat (*Sharika Parvata*) hill situated in downtown Srinagar. Akbar is said to have built a rampart wall around this hill. For the legend of Sharika, see *Sharikamahatmaya* and *Rajat*, Bk.iii, verses 339–49 fn.

[2] Stein notes, "The goddess Sharika which has given to the hill its name, has been worshipped since ancient times on the north-west side of the hill. Certain natural markings on a large perpendicular rock are taken by the pious as representing that kind of mystical diagram which in the *Tantrashastra* is known as *Shrichakra* See note K 192 in *Rajat*, vol.ii regarding the worshiip of such diagrams.

[3] Sharika > Harika > Hareh and Bhattara > Brari as Bhattaranadvala > Brarinambal. See *Rajat*, vol.iii, Bk.vii, verse 1038.

[4] See *Jonaraja*, Bodlein ed. pp.472, 767.

bahar)[1] they would assemble here to pray at the idol temples. These people would go up the hillock and offer prayer. They observed the practices and rites of infidelity and polytheism. The people of this land resorted to idolatry and were joined by the Sultan, the officials, the nobles, the heretics, the miscreants and the wretched lot.

A festival was observed during the spring at this place. Musicians, drumbeaters, singers, dancers etc. made a big crowd on that day. Many loose women and dancing girls joined them and thus enlivened the assemblies of dance and music. People from all walks of life in the town, merchants and shopkeepers, artisans, labourers and professionals all came to witness the festivities of dance and music. People from the suburbs, villagers and peasants all subscribing to infidelity and heresy came along to get pleasure from the pageant. Hindus and the corrupt people came to see the prostitutes and singing women.

No means of enjoyment were spared; bouts of drinking wine and indulging in other corrupt practices. These activities disallowed by Islamic law and falling within corrupted morals were conducted openly. The *'ulema*, *Qadis* and *Sayyids* of this land did not perform their duty of judging and enforcing what

---

[1] Kashmiri Pandits observe two festivals in connection with the beginning of spring. The first is called *sont* in local idiom, which appears to be a corrupted form of Sanskrit *vasanta* and Punjabi *basant.* The second and more popular spring festival is *Novreh* or the New Year according to Laukika calendar. It almost sychronizes with the ancient Zoroastrian *navroz,* or the New Year's day. A tradition is curiously common between the pre-Islamic Iranians and the Kashmiri Pandits. It is called *haft seen* in Farsi and *thaal barun* in Kashmiri. Iranians gather together seven things beginning with S sound as a symbol of the advent of the new year. Pandits fill a platter with several things like grains of paddy, rice, a cup of milk, sugar, the new year calendar, image of a Hindu pantheon, a pen and and an inkpot. Early on the morning of the New Year (*Navreh*) family members are required to have a look at the filled platter and take a spoonful of milk. In all probabiloity the author referes to *Novreh* or the new year of Kashmiri Pandit calendar which almost synchronizes with the vernal equinox (21 March). That is why the author says that on this day the Sun enters the Pisces. He does not say *Novroz* but *rbz-e-bahar* (the day of spring) because he abhors traditions of pre-Islamic Iran. An excellent write up under the title 'Navreh—The New Year of Kashmiri Hindus' by Upender Ambardar appeared on page 11 of *Kashmir Sentinel*, vol.13, nos.4–5, May 2008.

is allowed and what is not allowed in Islamic law just because they did not want to displease the Sultan and his administrative officers.

Amir Shamsu'd-Din Araki stayed in the house of Mulla Isma'il during the spring season. He heard a loud peal raised by the beating of drums and other musical instruments, in addition to the deafening noise made by the cheering and yelling crowds. He inquired of his followers what the noise was about. They explained the situation. He said that the purpose of his visiting Kashmir region was to pull down the idol houses of infidels and polytheists. His first task was to put an end to the customs, traditions and habits of the *kafirs* (infidels) and also stamp out corruption and aberration (that had seeped into their life). "Now it is my duty to eradicate these innovations and the customs of the infidels", he exclaimed.

Thereupon he ordered a band of *sufis* and devotees to come to his presence. Taking this group along with him, he came to the *Koh-i-Maran*. He entertained no apprehension from the loud noise of the people and the crowds. Oblivious of the displeasure of the ruler and unmindful of the reaction of law-makers and the law enforcing apparatus, he made all the polytheists, corrupt and dissipated people run away from that place. He ordered baton charging of dancing and singing women, musicians and drumbeaters until they disappeared. Wine and liquor assemblies that had been set up all around were closed down. Pitchers of wine were broken and in this way dark customs of infidels were put to an end.

A prayer house of the infidels existed at that place.[1] Its foundation was dismantled, and the idol house was set on

[1] Verse 460 of Bk.iii *Rajat* records: "The royal couple (Ranaditya) built the temple of *Ranarambhasvamin* and *Ranarambhadeva* and a *matha* for Pashupata (mendicants) on the hill of Pradyumana" Explaining the alternative name of the hill (*Sharikaparvata* = *Harparvat*), Stein, in a footnote to verse 460 above writes, "By *Pradyumnamurdhan* is meant the *Sharikaparvata* or *Harparvat* in Srinagar (See note Bk.iii, 339–49). The E slope and foot of the hill is now covered by extensive buildings, including *sarais* connected with the famous Muhammedan shrines of *Muqaddam Sahib* and Akhund Mulla Shah. These probably occupy the sites of earlier Hindu structures such as the *mathas* referred to in the verse."

fire till it was fully consumed in flames. The bright candle of religion and Islam brought by the Prophet, and the law of his religion and the path of Mustafa and Murtaza ('Ali) was lighted. He initiated the task of breaking the idols and idol houses. From this place began the guidance for the people of the world and the progeny of Adam.

With this event began his differences and disagreement with Sultan Fath Shah. The infidels, polytheists and irreligious aberrants came to Fath Shah with their plea. They told him that the Sultan had been kind and affectionate to the ancient people of the land. They said that they had the tradition of coming to *Koh-i-Maran* at the beginning of spring and enjoying themselves a while after leaving behind cold and frosty days of winter. They added that in ancient times, the rulers and officials joined the commoners in enjoying themselves at this place. This really helped the common people, traders and professionals to snatch moments of joy and happiness. The tired and exhausted peasants and ordinary people would get rejuvenated by participating in the festivities. Everybody prayed for the Sultan's health. But they did not know wherefrom this Mir Shams had appeared. He had disrupted all these festivities and caused pain to the onlookers. He had forced the people to disperse and run away and thus to close the spring festival. Now he, along with a band of his disciples, was busy destroying temples.

Fath Shah annoyed

Owing to his satanic impulse and susceptibility to flattery as well as his haughty demeanor, Fath Shah thought of sending his musclemen to punish Araki as well as his band of *sufis*. He even ordered that the *sufis* be executed, which, however, was not liked by his courtiers. Maulana Muhammad Ganai was a pupil and a trainee of Araki. He exhorted the Sultan not to cause obstruction in the mission of Araki because the customs (of the infidels) were extraordinarily abominable. When he was informed of Fath Shah's anger and wrath, Araki just laughed it away. On the following day, after having finished recitation of *awrad-e-fathiyyeh* and before taking breakfast, he took along with him a group of his associates and *Sufis* and went up the heights of *Koh-i-Maran* (Hari Parbat). Together they destroyed even the smallest remnant of the idol house and scattered pieces of the idols (previously broken by them).

Baitu'llah

He directed that the ground where the temple stood be levelled so that the foundation for a 'God's House' (*bait-ullah*) could be laid on it. Construction material needed for the project was collected at the place. In a few days, a mosque for praying and obeying the Creator came up on the site where a temple of the infidels and the Hindus previously stood. He appointed a person for calling people to prayers (*mu'ezzin*). He instructed a few *sufis* to take up their abode there. This was done to ensure that people were summoned to prayers five times a day and congregated in that mosque. He also instructed that *awrard-e-fathiyyeh* and *'asriyyeh* (morning and afternoon recitations) be regularly chanted.

A garden at the foot of the *Koh-i-Maran* (Hari Parbat) was the endownment property of the destroyed temple. After raising the mosque on the site of that demolished temple, he engaged himself in reclaiming the garden and in raising structures on it. Saplings of trees bearing a variety of fruit were planted in it. These were almond, walnut, pistachio and grapevines of *husaini*, and *fakhri* variety.[1]

---

[1] Herat and eastern regions of Khurasan are famous for growing the finest varieties of grapes. In all probability, he might have asked travellers and visitors from those regions to bring vineyards of different varieties to Kashmir for plantation. Names of some varieties are found in *Chehar Maqala* of Nidhami 'Aruzi Samarqandi', ed. Muhammad Moin, Teheran.

From the hospice of Mulla Isma'il and his locality, Araki shifted to Zadibal. But even then he did not give up nurturing the saplings he had planted in the above-mentioned garden. Its regular repair and reconstruction lasted till the end of his life. A few *sufis* were stationed there for performing the duty of making the call for prayers and offering prayers (*namaz*). Another purpose of rehabilitating them at that place was to look to the protection of the structures. Vegetables of different variety and fruit like melons, watermelons, beans, beet root, green vegetables and spinach etc. were cultivated in every season. Fruit and vegetables of excellent quality were produced under his supervision. The like of these were not to be found at any other place in Kashmir. Melons produced in this farm were the sweetest one could find in the land.

Araki was enamoured of this farm and delighted in taking care of it. He always engaged the *sufis* to do one or the other job on the farm. He would usually cite the words of the Holy Prophet, viz. "we like Ohod and Ohod Mountain likes us" (*nahubbul ohod wal ohod yhubbana*).

Tombs on Koh-i-Maran

He arranged tombs, graves and graveyards for the dervishes and *sufis* in this garden[1] so that his associates and devotees and

[1] In all probability the graveyard complex in close proximity to the tomb of Bahau'd-Din Sahib in Nowhatta, Srinagar has replaced the spacious ground that was attached as *Agrahara* to the temple on Sharikaraparvata by King Pravarasena. Some tombstones over the graves bear bilingual inscriptions viz. Sharada and Farsi. About the temple of Pravarasena, Stein records: "A short distance to the SE of *Bhimasvamin* rock and outside Akbar's fortress has the *Ziart* of Bahau'd-Din Sahib, built, undoubtedly with the materials of an ancient temple. The cemetery which surrounds it maintains also many ancient remains in its tombs and walls. To the SW corner of this cemetery rises a ruined gateway built of stone blocks of remrkable size and stil of considerable height. This structureis traditionally believed by the Srinagar Pandits to have belonged to the temple of *Shiva Praveshvara* which Kalhana mentions as the first shrine created by Pravarasena in his new capital. See *Rajat*, Bk.ii, p.447 paragraph 96.

sufis regularly visited the place. Maulana Muhammad was the Imam of dervishes. He wore black turban. When he died (in this world of annihilation), his was the first dead body to be shifted (buried) to this garden. A tree stood to the north of the mosque and Araki desired that the deceased Maulana's tomb was erected under that tree. He was buried at that place. After a short while, Maulana Saeed also departed from this transient world. He, too, had been bestowed a black turban, and his remains are buried at this spot. A little later, Sayyid Sharif, who hailed from a noble family, died near the residence of Araki in Zadibal. When asked about his burial place, Araki said that leaving some space to the west of the grave of Mulla Muhammad, the Sayyid be buried at that place so that the dervishes remain buried at the back of the Sayyids.

Thereafter dervish Zeerak Tibeti passed away. In reply to the question as to where the body of the Tibetan dervish is to be buried, Araki said that his place would be at the feet of Sayyid Sharif. He desired to be buried towards the foot of Zeeraks grave. This will be recorded at its proper place. Most of his distinguished *sufis* remain buried at the site under reference. Some of them died during his lifetime and were buried there. Others got the resting-place at the spot after the death of Araki.

Enlightened friends and associates are aware that the light of the dawn of Islam and the illuminating Sun of the path of the Imam enlightens the dark minds of idolators and those abandoned to darkness. The Sun of Islam first shed its bright rays on the *Koh-i-Maran* (Hari Parbat). Shamsu'd-Din Araki had selected this place for the tombs, graves and resting place of distinguished *sufis* and dervishes so that it would be easier for him to visit the site after reciting *awrad-e fathiyyeh* and *'asriyyeh.* He used to walk the distance from Zadibal to *Koh-i-Maran* to attend to the farm.

Two idol houses destroyed

Between *Koh-i-Maran* and Zadibal, there stood two temples. These were quite strong. He destroyed both.[1] Many stones of the destroyed temples were brought to Nurbakhshiyyeh hospice. The stones were square in shape and brittle. These were used in the boundary wall of the hospice (at Zadibal). One of these temples stood close to the locality of the Baihaqi Sayyids. Local people objected to its destruction and this denied him a good opportunity of laying the foundation of a mosque at this place.

Chamkundi temple

The temple known as Chamkundi was destroyed.[2] Its walls, five to six yards high, were made of stone. The wall was left as it was but stones and earth that had formed the foundation of the temple inside were taken out. A beautiful mosque was raised inside the compound where the temple stood previously. Some adjoining orchards and gardens were endowed to this temple. He planted melons there and a few *sufis* were also stationed in the mosque to give call for prayer and to offer congregational prayers. They were also asked to take care of the farm.

---

[1] Stein tells us: "Not far from Bahau'd-Din Sahib's *ziarat*, to the SW, stands the Jami'a Masjid, the greatest Mosque of Srinagar. Around it numerous ancient remains attest the former existence of Hindu temples. Proceeding still further to the SW, in the midst of a thickly-built city quarter, we reach an ancient shrine which has remained in a comparatively fair state of preservation probably owing to its conversion into *Ziarat*. It is now supposed to mark the resting place of the saint styled Pir Haji Muhammad. It consists of an octagonal cela of which the high basement and the side walls are stil well-preserved. The quadrangular court in which it stands is enclosed by ancient walls and approached by ornamented gateways.

[2] Chamundi is a form of goddess Durga, *Rajat*, Bk.iii, verse 46. Kalhana refers to the legend of Chamunda killing Daitrya *Rura*. See *Padma Purana* v.xxxvi, 59 – 95. Chamkundi (Chamnundi) temple was consecrated to Durga and its location has been described in the text.

Mahasen temple[1]

In order to procure timber for the construction of the hospice (at Zadibal), Araki proceeded to Kamaraj. A temple existed there. Groups of infidels and Hindus used to visit this temple for pilgrimage. They would circumambulate it. It was called Mahasen. Within the precincts of the temple, there stood an idol made of stone. It was the object of veneration of the Jews[2] and the infidels.

Felling of tall fir and deodar trees that surrounded it was prohibited out of respect for the temple. On his arrival at this spot, the first thing for Araki to do was to raze this famous temple to ground. Every trace of the idol and the idol house was effaced. After breaking idols and setting the temple on flames, he engaged himself in felling trees. Some strange things happened in the course of that exercise; it has already been recorded at its proper place. At the site of the temple that was destroyed, he built a Jami'a mosque. The Imam and the *mu'ezzin* were asked to take care of the mosque and hold Friday congregational prayers. He managed to obtain from the officers and nobles of the time one *kharwar* and nine maunds[3]

---

[1] It could be the temple of *Mammasvamin* built by Mamma. Kalhana writes, "The clever, wise and rich Mamma built (the temple of Vishnu) *Mammasvamin*, and gave, when (on the occasion) for the consecration of a multitude of sacrificial cups *(kumbha)* eighty-five thousand cows (to Brahmans) and provided for each cow five thousand *dinnaras* as an outfit." See *Rajat*, Bk.iv, verses 698–90. Mamma has been mentioned as the uncle of King Chippatajayapida (*Rajat*, Bk.iv, verse 679). Kalhana syas that Mamma took for the endowment of his temple (Mammasvamin) the villages granted to the temple of *Matrguptasvamin* (Bk.iv, verses 698–90 fn.). Stein could not trace the site of Mamma's foundaion. However, it is clear that the temple was located in Kamaraj *pargana*.

[2] This is a very curious sentence. *Dabistanul-Mazahib* of Mohsin Fani does mention that Jews were to be found in Kashmir but that they had veneration for a Hindu temple is not understandable.

[3] 1 *kharwa*r = 80 kilograms and one maund = little more than one kilogram. One *kharwar* and nine maunds of land mean the measurement of land that would need 89 kilograms of seed to be sown. According to a rough estimate, 20 kilograms of seed mean 25 kanals of land. This is the old Kashmiri agricultural measuring terminology still in use in rural Kashmir.

of land, which was endowed to the mosque and was used for the maintenance of its caretakers.

Warblaru[1] (?) temple

A big temple existed in Baramulla area in Kamaraj pargana. It was called Warbalaru in Kashmiri language. Araki destroyed it and erected a mosque over its ruins. An Imam and caller of prayer (*mu'ezzin*) were appointed for the mosque. They were to arrange Friday congregational prayers and exhort people to offer group prayers five times a day. Since there were fewer chances of Araki visiting this area, he permitted Hazrat Baba to obtain allegiance of the people and appointed him his vicegerent. The purpose was to induce Baba to go on excursion to the suburban areas of Kashmir. He was to reach each village and hamlet so that people volunteered to show him their allegiance. In deference to the wishes of Araki, Hazrat Baba paid visit to the adjoining areas once a year. As a result of his auspicious steps, many people in the adjoining

[1] It could be Varabal Agrahara called Barvul by the locals. The Agrahara was established by King Jaluka. (*Rajat*, Bk.i, verse 121). Stein gives this information: "Varabala can be safely identified in view of the close agreement of the names with the modern hamlet of Barvul situated on the right bank of *Kanknai* (*Kanakavahini*) River, about a mile above its confluence with the Sind. When passing through the hamlet on my way to Bhuteshvara in August 1891, I found close to the path a sculptured linga-base or *bhadrapitht* of considerable dimensions, and was shown on further inquiries, another large carved slab lying in the fields below the houses. According to the statement of the aged Muqaddam, Barvul had formed for a long time the *jagir* or Agrahara of a Pirzada family of Srinagar, until it was resumed by Maharja Gulab Singh. The temple and *Agrahara* stood on the route to the shrine of Bhuteshvara (Bothser)" See *Rajat*, Bk.i, verse 121 fn. In a note on verse 107 of Book i, vol.i of *Rajatarangini*, Stein (writing in 1891) adds, "In the narrow gorge of the Kankanai River (*Kanakavahini*) which flows past the south foot of this spur (Harmukh), and some two miles above the hamlet of Vangath (*Vasishthasrama*), are found ruins of some seventeen temples of various age and dimension. These ruins, which are now almost hidden by the luxuriant vegetation of the forest, have been described by Bishop COWIE, *JASB* 1866, pp.101 sqq., and Major COLE, *Ancient Buildings in Kashmir*, pp.11 seqq., under the name of 'Temples near Wangath'. *Rajat*, vol.i, Bk.i, verse 107 fn.

villages and areas became his disciples. Many people in the villages of Baramulla, small traders and businessmen, expressed their reverence for the Baba. Even up to this day, most of the people of this area continue to be in the circle of Baba's disciples.

Nandraja temple[1]

A village named Shivaz (*sic*. Shiv?) in the pargana of Kamaraj is well known. An imposing temple existed there. It was called Nandraza in Kashmiri. At this temple the infidels and the misguided people used to celebrate a festival. Araki destroyed the temple. A *jami'a* mosque was raised on the ruins of the destroyed temple. Mulla Muhammad, the uncle of Mulla Nasir, was made the *mu'ezzin* of the mosque. They were charged with the duty of assembling people for Friday congregational prayers. Two or three *kharwars* of land was allocated to the mosque for the subsistence of the staff. The call for prayers five times a day and offering of Friday congregational prayers at this mosque continue till this day.

Bomar temple

A village called Chogul in pargana Kamaraj was well known to local people. There existed a massive temple.[2] In Kashmiri it was called Bomar. It used to attract big crowds of people. A dervish among the disciples of Araki was known as Shri

---

[1] Though Shiv, the name of a village does exist in Baramulla district, yet not much could be known about the Nandraza temple. However, Kalhana tells us that Nanda, the queen of King Gopalavarman, who descended from an unblemished family, founded, though yet a child, the *Nandamatha* and (the temple of *Nandkeshava*). See *Rajat*, vol.i, Bk.v, p.245. A few miles downstream of the town of Sopor, there is a shrine on the left bank of Vitasta called Nandkeshwar. But the name of a village where the shrine is situated is Seer usually called Seer Jagir, which does not become Shiw as indicated by the author.

[2] Chogul villlage lies to the north on Sopor-Kupwara road just after descendng Vataven heights (*vudar*). Village Bomar is situated at a little distance from Chogul. I have not been able to trace the ancient history and geography of the temple in this village. Stein does not make any mention.

Bhat[1] who was a leading personality among the infidels of Shahabu'd-Din Pora.[2] God Almighty blessed him by guiding him for conversion to Islam. He accepted the true faith in Araki's presence. Thus he was admitted to the circle of his dervishes and devotees.

Shamsu'd-Din Araki dispatched him along with many dervishes and disciples for the task of destroying the Bomar temple. As the contingent of disciples (of Araki) passed through Sopor town, the people in Chogul got wind of it. Villagers of Bomar were mostly soldiers by profession. A powerful person among the people and tribes of this village was called Ahaldwar (Haldar?). He enjoyed the confidence and trust of high government functionaries and nobles. Prompted by him, the people in this area prepared to give the followers of Araki a fight. They maintained nullah Pohru[3] as the dividing line and stood to defend the temple and the villages on their side of the stream. The dervishes and *sufis* encamped on the other side of the stream. The contesting groups fought for two days. The villagers withdrew and the group of the *sufis* overpowered them. A victory was recorded.

---

[1] His Muslim name has not been found though Bhat remained the suffix of main names even after conversions to Islam. Many Hindu names continued in their original form for a long time. For example Shanki Raina of Muslim chroniclers is Shankar Raina of Hindu chroniclers. Likewise, this name could be Sher Bhat after he embracd Islam.

[2] Locality raised by Sultan Shihabu'd-Din, now in downtown Srinagar between Nowhatta and Haval For more information, see *Baharistan-i-Shahi*.

[3] About four miles below Sopor, the Vitasta receives its last considerable tributary within Kashmir. It is the Pohur, which, before its junction, has collected the various streams draining the extreme north-west of the Valley. This portion of Kashmir Valley figures but little in *Rajatarangini* and we find no reference to the Pohur or any of its affluents. Stein writes: "The old name of this river is uncertain. Jonaraja in a passage which is found only in the Bombay edition, calls this river *Pahara*; the *Mahatmays* vary between *Prahara* and *Prahaara*. (See *Jonaraja*, Bombay, ed.1150, 1152; *Vitastamahatmya*, xxvii). Of the side-stream the Mavar flowing through Machhipur Pargana is named in *Nilamata Purana* as Mahuri (*Nilamata*, 1322 sqq.). The stream gives name to the area (Mavar in Langayt Jagir). Some Farsi versifier has praised the water of Mavar stream in these words: *ab-e Mavar, gar kuni bavar, khushtar az ab-e kausar*. (Should you trust me, the water of Mavar is sweeter than the water of the spring of Paradise).

They crossed the river and pulled down the temple house. The place was densely forested. The trees were felled and the site was made plain for laying the foundation of a mosque. The idol pulled down from the temple was placed under the threshold of the mosque so that visitors to the mosque would trample it under their feet. The practice of calling people for five time prayers and offering congregational prayers on Fridays was put in place.

When Araki was told about fighting and also of the bravery and courage of Shri Bhatt, he assigned to him the task of enforcing permissible and non-permissible in Islam in the rural area of Kamaraj. This dervish proved to be a person of firm faith and true dedication. He destroyed the famous temples and idol houses of Kamaraj, which for example, included those of Uttarasher (*sic*), Badakot, Kubisher (*sic*), and Gushi temple in the localities of Kandi, Shaki Shiraz (*sic*), Kupwarah and Drang.[1]

---

[1] All these places are situated in the *pargana* of Uttar, and lie to the north of Sopor town. Badkot could, in all proability, be the Kashmiri form of Sanskrit Bhatta Kota in which Kota means a fort.This village is situated at a distance of about a mile and half from Handwara (Skt. *Hanandwara*) on the road to Bhadrakali shrine in present Kuprara district. Gushi or Gush is a village in *pargana* Uttar and appears several times in *Rajatarangini* especially in connection with pilgrimage to Sharada made by the Hindus of ancient Kashmir. According to Stein it was at Gushi that *Mahadevi* (*Sharada Mata*) appeared to Muni Shandilya—the son of Matonga—who had been practising great austerities in order to obtain the sight of the goddess *Sharada* who is a *Shakti* embodying three separate manifestations. Mahadvi appears to him and promises to show herself in her true form as *Shakti* in the *Sharada* forest. The goddess vanished from his sight at *Hayashirashrma* (Kashmiri Haeyhom) situated about 4 miles to the NNE of Gushi.

Stein, depending on oral history recounted to him by Chandra Pandit of Goteung, a learned Brahman whom he met during his travel, has made a curious piece of research. He says that owing to insecurity and hazards of pilgrimage to *Sharadatirtha*, the Brahmans created a few prototypes of original Sharada Tirtha in the valley. One of these was close to Gushi. He writes, "Finally I may note as a characteristic fact that even in the comparative neighbourhood of the ancient *Shardatirtha*, and on the very route to it, a substitute shrine has ben created to suite the circumstances already indicated. Immediately adjoining the groove at Gushi' known as *Rangavor* (Skt. *Rangavatika*) and mentioned above (*Rajat*, vol.ii, p.281) is small walled enclosures in which a few fragments of ancient relieve images are kept. This place is locally considred a shrine of *Sharada*, and is visited in stead ...

These temples were pulled down and destroyed. In the remote areas of the towns of Sopor and Baramulla, and in inner rural areas of Kamaraj, he pulled down all temples and built mosques in their place. From those times down to present day, Islamic system and way of life prevail in full force in those vast areas. The religion of the Prophet and the customs of the community of Mustafa are prosperous everywhere. The temples of Jatti Renu, Kandi Renu, Bachhi Renu[1] in Kamaraj and Satwal[2] (?) temple in Sopor were all razed and destroyed.

Araki had built the Nurbakhshiyyeh hospice (*khanqah*) in the locality of Zadibal. To the right side of this hospice, there existed a big temple well known (to Kashmiri Hindus). In local language it was called Paneh Renu. There existed a spring by

... of *Sharada* temple on occasion of the *Sharadayatra* by Brahmans of neighbourhood" (*Rajat*, vol.ii, p.288).

Drang designated in Kashmir any frontier watch station closing a route through the mountains. *Drang* is also the name of a small village situated on the direct route from the Uttar *pargana* to Sharada Tirtha on the Krishnaganga. *Drang* lies half a mile to the NW of *Haeyhom*. It is known to local Brahmans as *Sona Drang* (Skt. *Suvarnadrangaka*) Commenting on *Sunadrang*, Stein writes, "The prefix *Sun* may have been originally intended to distinguish this *Drang* from other *Drangas* (See Note D, iii 227). I am tempted to connect it with the notices quoted below note 16, about gold found in Kishanganga River. Classical notices already show that gold-washing was carried on in old times by the *Dards* of Kishenganga Valley and the Upper Indus. Cf. Herodot. iii, 105, Magasthenes in Strabo, xv, p.706 with BUNBURY *History of Ancient Geogaphy*, 1883f., p.229." See also Bk.viii, verse 2507n.

[1] *Renu* the Kashmirian form of Skt. *Rajana/Rajanaka* was used for a State dignitary of high rank. See *Rajat*, vol.ii, Bk.viii, verse 756 fn. According to the author of *Baharistan-i-Shahi, Raina* or *Renu* is the title given to distinguished warriors. (See *Baharistan*, Index R). Three temples mentioned here with *Renu* as suffix were situated in the interior of Hamal (Skt. Shamala) *pargana* lying between Baramula and Uttar *pargana*. In all probability these temples were built by local chieftains of *Damara* warriors and consecrated to gods or deities popularly worshipped by the local people. Deformation of Rajana into *Renu* can be easily found in *Rajanakavatika* deforming into *Re'n+vor* of present day. See Stein's tr. of *Rajat*, vol.i, Bk.viii, verse 756 fn. The exact location of these three temples and the fourth one near Sopor could not be found nevertheless these were situated in Kamaraj *pargana*.

[2] Location of this temple could not be established.

its side, which was skirted by tall fir and other kinds of trees. Araki wanted the temple to be destroyed and the trees felled. A person named Khwaja Gharami lived close to the temple. He and his men obstructed the destruction of the temple. Satan's prompting had entrapped them. They were enslaved by infidelity and aberrations, had accepted falsehood and believed in what the corrupt people said. This had made them stone-hearted. Khwaja Gharami was highly influential with the people in that locality. Men, women, wives and husbands all came out to obstruct the destruction of the temple. Thus Araki was denied the opportunity of destroying that temple.

Foretelling

Araki nursed the secret desire of destroying the aforementioned temple. One night, Bejeh Agha, the mother of Shaykh Danial saw a dream. She saw that lofty trees around the temple in question bowed their tops before Shaykh Daniyal while he was still a child. She recounted the dream to Araki who interpreted it to say that while he himself could not fulfil the task of demolishing the temple and felling the trees, his son Shaykh Daniyal would accomplish it. The fortune of accomplishing that task actually fell to the lot of Shaykh Daniyal. Although he was yet to reach adolescence, he performed the act of pulling down the temple.

To Tibet (Baltistan)

Following this event, relations between Araki and Sayyid Muhammad Baihaqi came to a head-on collision. We have already alluded to it. This was the reason why Araki undertook a journey to Tibet. He raised the banner of Islam in Tibet (Baltistan). He engaged himself in strengthening the teachings and laws of Islam and Sharia in those regions.

The situation led to the exacerbation of differences between Amir Sayyid Muhammad Baihaqi and Malik Musa Raina. This drove them to the brink of actual fighting in which Amir Sayyid Muhammad Baihaqi was killed. Victorious Musa

Raina entered the city (Srinagar). The *ulema*, the Qadis, the Sayyids, the nobles, and leading personalities came to extend felicitations to him. Hazrat Baba took care of the family and children of Araki. He took Shaykh Daniyal with him and proceeded to offer their felicitations to Malik Musa Raina. The Malik expressed his happiness to see Hazrat Baba and Shaykh Daniyal. He made them sit at a special place in the court, and they were presented with robes of honour. The government (of Musa Raina) gave the trusteeship of Hamadaniyyeh hospice in the hands of Shaykh Daniyal. It had been taken away from the hands of Araki by late Amir Sayyid Muhammad Baihaqi owing to his enmity with Araki and had forbidden him from coming to that place.

Paneh Renu temple

It was in this meeting with Malik Musa Raina that Hazrat Baba sought the permission of destroying the temple of Paneh Renu. On the next day, after reciting *awarad-e-fathiyyeh*, Hazrat Baba took along with him Shaykh Daniyal and a group of dervishes and proceeded towards the pond.[1] He seated Shaykh Daniyal by the bank of the canal and directed his followers to begin the felling of trees. They hewed down trees that did not bear any fruit. Since Shaykh Daniyal was seated facing *qibla* (the Mecca, generally the West for the people in the East) the falling trees fell towards the west as if bowing to Shaykh

[1] Location of this temple could not be traced. However, as it is reported to have stood by the side of a pond or pool of water, I have tumbled on this footnote of Stein to *Rajat*, verses 125–26, Bk.i: "On visiting Sudrabal in June 1895, I was shown on the very shore of the *Sudrakhun* and close to the village Masjid two small pools which were then covered by the water of the lake but according to the uniform statement of the villgers, are fed by two perennial springs. A tradition which I gathered from the old men of the village, relates that many hundred years ago, Brahmans were in the habit of making pilgrimages to these springs. The name Buttpora which survives to this day as the name of a now deserted part of the village area, was pointed out to me as evidence of the former habitation of Battas i.e. Puruhits. No ancient remains can now be traced near the springs but huge carved slabs are said to have been carried away (*Rajat*, Bk.i.125–26 fn.).

Daniyal. Thus the dream of his mother Bejeh Agha came true. When Araki returned from his travels in Baltistan, he built a mosque on the ruins of the temple and appointed staff to look after it.

Bhimasvamin temple

A few days later, he said that a big temple existed close to the graveyards of the Sayyids and Shaykh Bahau'd-Din.[1] Many infidels, polytheists and corrupt persons invariably assembled there and performed the blasphemous rites of infidelity and heresy. In Kashmiri it was called Bomeh Swami.[2] He said that pulling down the temple and destroying it was incumbent upon the Muslims. He came in person to supervise the demolition of the temple. Stones and earth at the site were heaped into a small mound on which a platform was raised equal to a man's height. A mosque was constructed on it and a *mu'ezzin* was appointed. Shaykh Daniyal gave this place to Malik Regi Chak for burying the dead of his family and close

---

[1] The locality between present Nowhatta and the southern slope of Hari Parbt hillock is called Bahadu'd-Din Sahib.

[2] Verse 352, Bk.ii of *Rajat.* runs as this: "Owing to his (Pravarasena's) devoted worship to the image of *Vinayaka* called *Bhimasvamin*, of its own accord turned its face from west to east in order to show that he was not averse to his city." In a footnote to this verse, Stein writes, "*Ganesha* (*Vinayaka*) is worshipped to this day under the name of *Bhimasvaminganesha* in a rock lying at the foot of the southern extremity of *Harparvat* (*Sharikaparvata*)." Describing the ancient sites of Srinagar, Stein records, " Close to the foot of the southern extremity of the hill (Hari Parbat) is a rock which has from ancient times received worhip as an embodiment of *Ganesha* and the name of *Bhimasvamin*. A legend related by Kalhana connects this *suyambhu* image with Pravarsena foundation of Pravarapura (See *Rajat*, vol.i, Bk.iii, verse 352n.). From regard for this pious king the god is then said to have turned his face from west to east so as to behold the new city. The rock is covered by the worshippers with so thick a layer of real paint that it is not possible to trace now any resemblance to the head of the elephanat-faced god, still less to see whether it is turned west or east. In fact, if we are to believe Jonaraja, the rock image has changed its position yet a second time. The chronicler relates that *Bhimasvamin* from disgust at the inconoclasm of Sultan Sikandar *butshikan* has finally turned his back on the city. See *Jonaraja*, Bod. ed. p.766 and *Rajat*. tr. Stein, vol.ii, section iv, p.446.

relatives and friends. The dead of his (Regi Chak's)[1] clan remain buried here. The infidels and polytheists considered both of those temples sacred.

Makhdum's foretelling

Here lived a learned and austere man known for his miracles. People, high and low, showed him great reverence. He was Makhdum Maulana Usman Majzoob. His house and seat were situated near the Hamadaniyyeh *khanqah* (hospice) in Srinagar. Occasionally, he would come to Nowshehra to meet with the Sultan. In doing so he had to pass by *Koh-i-Maran*. Whenever he passed by the Bimeh Swami (Bhimasvamin) temple, he would get down from his horse, and bow his head while facing the temple. It was to show regard to the idol house. He used to walk some distance, and only when the temple was out of his sight would he mount his horse. While visiting Zadibal, this man, absorbed in the divine, always dismounted, showed reverence to the temple and then started walking on foot. When both the temples were out of his sight, he would mount the horse. Shams Ganai, a close associate of Araki, asked him why he did that unbecoming act. He asked, "It is so strange. You are a learned man and one who does miracles. But you dismount your horse while passing by the temple. Common people will try to follow your bad example." Maulana Uthman answered, "This temple is an abode of all satanic and devilish spirits of this land. We did not have enough strength to fight with them. So we adopted a conciliatory attitude so that they did not disturb and obstruct our prayers and submission to God. We did not want that they should create distraction in our minds. If we had not adopted a conciliatory attitude, they would have unleashed untold oppression on us because we did not have the power to resist them.

---

[1] He was one of the four chieftains of Kashmir who divided Kashmir kingdom among themselves and installed Muhammad Shah on the throne. See *Baharistan*, p.124.

"God willing, very soon a godly man will arrive in these lands who will be the friend of all blessed people. God Almighty will give him the strength to win a decisive victory over the satanic and devilish groups of this land. He will drive away from this land all forces and groups of satanic infidels and wretched hypocrites so that the lands (of Kashmir) are cleansed of stains and stigma of polytheists, dirty infidels, idols and idol houses. He will relieve us from having anything to do with the temples, idol house and idols."

This writer heard the above story several times from his teacher Mir Husayn Munajjim. Since Maulana Uthman had spiritual links with Shaykh Bahau'd-Din Kashmiri it could be the reason why he sometimes did strange things.[1]

Whatever he foretold had already happened. After planting his steps on this land, Amir Shamsu'd-Din embarked on demolishing of the temples and idols of the community of darkness. He purged the whole land of traditions, laws, beliefs and rituals of infidels. He lifted to sky the banner of Islam and Islamic community. He banished from this land Satans and devils that misled the people along the path of aberration. The fiends who entrapped the people were extirpated from the land.

Dervishes gifted with powers of foretelling found that some large groups of infidels of satanic and devilish disposition (from Kashmir) crossed the Indian mountains and proceeded towards the lands of Hind in large numbers. These armies comprised men, women and children. People who saw them proceeding to Hind asked them who they were and what was the reason of their exodus? They expressed deep anguish. Giving out loud cries and moans they said, "We are the *devas*[2] (angels) and *pari*[3](s) (fairies) of this land (Kashmir). Our ancestors lived there from times immemorial. Nobody ever interfered with or obstructed our affairs. But Mir Shamsu'd-

---

[1] I have not been able to explain the "spiritual links".

[2] *Deva* or *devta* in Skt. means angel. But in Farsi it means evil spirit.

[3] Pahlavi *paerika* meaning a celestial body usually of feminine gender.

Din arrived in this land from Arak at a time when we were living there. He has forced us to leave our homes. He has destroyed our houses and temples, and razed them to ground. Some groups from our community adopted his faith of Islam and its tenets and laws. As such, they have been allowed to continue staying in Kashmir. But those who did not conform to his faith and its *sharia*, were not at all allowed to stay there." The fact of the matter is that what happened was precisely what they had reported. Those who stayed back surrendered to Araki and his followers.[1]

Hazrat Baba

Dependable and knowledgeable persons recount that Hazrat Baba got up in the early hours of morning for ablution. He came out from his cell and moved towards the sanctum. Somebody in pain appealed to him to listen to his supplication. Hazrat Baba uttered a few words, which the supplicant must have understood. He went away. Hazrat Baba went to the sanctum after some time. The aforementioned visitor returned along with two or three more persons. They talked among themselves. Hazrat Baba uttered a few words, finished ablution and joined them. He was angry with one of the persons standing and kicked him on his back and shin. The person began crying but his cry was not like that of a human being. It was a shrill sound like that of a monkey. He quickly got up and took to his heels.

After a while Hazrat Baba went to the hospice of Amir Shamsu'd-Din. One of his wives had seen all that had happened. On the next day, Zi Maji, the mother of Hazrat Baba's children recounted the previous night's incident. She said that she got frightened on seeing all that had happened and she could not come out at night to perform household chores. Family members enquired of Hazrat Baba the details

---

[1] This confession totally rubbishes the assertion that conversion of the Hindus to Islam was voluntary.

of the incident. He told the story like this: "There is no need to fear anything. The person in fact was a gini having taken up abode in this town. He appealed to me that there was a vacant house in Alau'd-Din Pora, which was his abode. But some other gini had forcibly turned him out of that house and occupied it and turned him out of that house. His wife and children were also thrown out. He had caught hold of one of the intruding gini and brought him to me. I caught hold of that gini and told him to vacate the house. But he excused himself saying he had no other place to go. Then I kicked him a few times and he began to cry. I gave him something to vacate the house and return it to the owner. Don't get disturbed; he is not going to harm you."

In short, the groups of *jinns* were subordinated to the authority of the spiritual descendents and Shaykhs of Shamsu'd-Din Araki. They would come to him with their disputes and stories of oppression by one against the other for seeking justice, because they expected justice and favour from them. These spiritual descendents (Sufis in the service of Araki) are the Suleymans and Sultans of the invisible world; therefore nobody can disregard their orders. The question of disobeying the commands and instructions of Arakis disciples and associates did not arise at all. The question of harming any servant or *sufi* connected with the order did not arise nor could anybody even think of taking revenge or creating any hurdle in their way.[1]

I swear by God that in these times (after the tradition had been laid down by Araki), many men of parts and spiritual excellence were born who pulled down huge temples and destroyed them completely. Innumerable idols and statues were struck down and thrown into dust. None of his disciples or attendants was harmed in any way. He demolished

[1] The jinnis seem to be persons of extraordinary physical strengh. After admitting them in the order of sufis, they were foremost in demolishing and destroying strongly built temples all over Kashmir. Araki calls them dervishes because they lived in hospices with their families and ate from general kitchen.

numerous imposing and stately idol-houses, yet nobody ever had the courage and strength to bring even the slightest harm to the family members of these noble men (*sufis* and *dervishes*). The possibility of bringing harm to Hazrat Baba did not arise.

Shah Qasim's blessings

Shah Qasim came to know the story of destruction of temples and idols at the hands of Shamsu'd-Din Araki. In great surprise he asked Dervish Salman, Dervish Walid and the group of other dervishes who had proceeded to Arak as emissaries, as to how it was possible for Araki to raze to the ground such lofty temples and the idols as these places are the habitat of the ginii. He asked whether his *sufis* had encountered any mishaps. The dervishes (from Kashmir) answered, "Your Holiness! We have pulled down and destroyed so many temples and idol houses; we have razed to ground so many imposing and lofty structures (of infidels). Never did any one from among our *sufis* ever come to grief or suffer a mishap or contract a disease. On the contrary, as a result of the blessings thereof, we all remained in good health and we feel glad and satisfied." Having heard this happy news, he raised his hands for thanksgiving; dervishes (from Kashmir) also raised their hands and prayed to God Almighty that He blessed Araki with profound courage and victory in his mission. They offered *fateha* (thanksgiving) and prayers. God Almighty bestows munificence on His beloved and obedient followers. He helps them with success.

From among the Shaykhs of high order and stalwarts among the spiritualists, none had the honour of breaking so many idols and destroying so many temples as Shamsu'd-Din Araki had for the sake of propagating, and strengthening prosperity of Islam. Only he was blessed to eradicate lock, stock and barrel the dark and depraved customs of the community of darkness, their rituals, laws and beliefs. No

Sultan, Padishah, Governor or noble could claim credit for an achievement like that. We shall take up this matter again in this work.

Musa Raina's allegiance

The reins of power and authority had passed into hands of Malik Musa Raina. He had become a devotee of Shamsu'd-Din Araki, and had made it a point to do everything for his mentor's satisfaction and pleasure. He carried out his orders and instructions with great earnestness. In fact, Araki had doled out lengthy lessons and pieces of advice to him in matters of faith, and had succeeded in roping him into following his line. He had emphasized that such noble deeds would ensure his entry into paradise (in hereafter). Thus he had prepared Musa Rainas mind for raising high the banner of Islam, the *sharia* of Mustafa and the community of the Prophet. Musa Raina devoutly worked to translate this mission into practice. He wrecked the very roots of idolatry, infidelity and heresy. He raised to the heights of the sky the heads of those who followed Islamic faith. It was a matter of great pride and honour for them.[1]

Sultan Sikandar (AH 796–820/1393–1417)

As a result of the very special grace of God Almighty, all the infidels and polytheists of this land were converted to Islamic faith during the reign of late Sultan Sikandar, the Iconoclast. Large groups of infidels (*kafirs*) and idol worshippers joined the Islamic fold. Small and big people of this land converted to Islam happily or unhappily.. They surrendered to the commands of Islamic faith.[2]

---

[1] For more details on Musa Raina's zeal for destruction of temples and conversion of the Hindus to Islamic faith and Nurbakhshiyyeh order, see *Baharistan-i-Shahi*, p.106.

[2] It means the conversion took place as a matter of compulsion. It did not matter whether the people converted to Islam were willing or not. Araki's orders had to be carried out.

Zainu'l-'Abidin (AH 826–79/AD 1422–74)

After some time during the reign of Sultan Zainu'l-'Abidin, clans and groups of people rejoined the infidels and idol worshippers and thus revived traditions and practices of infidels and polytheists. At the time of the death of Sultan Sikandar, Sultan Zainu'l-'Abidin was still a minor. As such, he could not benefit from the upbringing of Sultan Sikandar. He mixed up with the children of the infidels. The company of despicable progeny of heretics led him astray from the path of guidance, devotion and belief (in Islam).[1] Indeed, he had gone astray even when Sultan Sikandar was still reigning.[2] Abducted by satanic people and fraternizing with atheists had made him a *zindiq*[3] and a *mulhid*[4] (apostate and proselyte).[5] He permitted the community of polytheists and groups of infidels to practice idolatry and infidelity: he allowed reconstruction of old idol houses and temples that had been demolished; he allowed that smashed idols be replaced: he ordered that these (worshipping places) be rehabilitated. All heretics, proselytes and deviators, who had feigned allegiance to the Islamic community and the people of faith but secretly nursed false beliefs and heretical customs, were given the freedom to return to their original faith.[6]

---

[1] It means the indigenous Hindus were still influential. They might have been lying low during Sikandar's anti-Hindu rule but re-emerged once he was gone and then influenced the entire power structure beause Zainu'l-'Abidin was still a young boy.

[2] Some histrians have said that in his young age he was as much fanatical and prejudiced against Hindus as his father. He changed after he ascended the throne. But this sentence contradicts assertions like that.

[3] Loc. cit., p.112, fn.1 supra.

[4] Ibid.

[5] Use of such strong derogatory words against this Sultan is unknown to Kashmiri historians notwithstanding their disapproval of his pro-Hindu policy.

[6] *Baharistan* tells us that the proselytes used to place the copies of scripture under their haunches while making idolatorous prayers. *See Baharistan-i-Shahi*, loc. cit., p.117.

With the permission of this blasphemous ruler, many groups of people withdrew from the circle of Islam and the community and religion of the Holy Prophet. They adopted the path of darkness, apostasy and acrimony. High and low of this land, all turned apostates and returned to infidelity and idol worshipping. Practices of heresy and infidelity were revived. Reconstruction of temples was carried out with full force. In Kashmir there was hardly a village or a locality that did not have two or three temples. There was hardly a day when a festival of the infidels would not be observed in a locality or village or when an idol would not be installed in a temple. Lowly as well as distinguished people, senior and the learned, everybody was not only opting for idol worshipping but was also pursuing it with all seriousness. Housekeepers in urban and rural localities, traders, shopkeepers, artisans and commoners, all decorated their houses with five or six idols of various shapes and size. They worshipped these idols at dawn and dusk as is the practice of idolaters and infidels. People took to the practices of heretics, and those wearing the thread (*zunnar*). No respectable person (*khwajah*), trader, or artisan was circumcised. Every one among the nobles and the commoners, low or high followed the ways of idolatry, did not go for circumcision. Apart from indulging in these prohibited practices, many people considered it a matter of pride to take to drinking and merry making. Everybody considered that whatever was not permitted (in Islam) was permitted (for them) and thus proper for adoption. Outwardly the festival of *Eid* and Fridays were observed in towns and villages and although some of the *Qadis* maintained the laws and tenets of religion, yet the Islamic laws and the essence of Islamic religion did not enjoy full flowering and effect. No theologian, *Sayyid* or *Qadi* prohibited flouting of religious law and adoption of what was not permitted in Islam.

How could the *ulema* and *Qadis* prohibit these vices when all these customs and traditions sprang from within their own houses. Their womenfolk practised infidelity, and engaged themselves in corrupt deeds. It was not possible for them to stop others from indulging in awful practices. The learned men of this land had become so demoralized and imbecile to such an extent that they did not object to the indulgence of their womenfolk in irreligious, heretical and polytheistic practices. On the contrary, it made them happy. We have said about this in detail in the context of Shaykh Shihab Hindi's account.

Verdict (*Futwa*)

Shamsu'd-Din Araki fully understood the phenomenon of infidelity, heresy, apostasy and *zandaqa* (proselytizing) of the people of this (Kashmir) land. He found that none from the lowest to the highest in this land was free from defilement and irreligiosity. Thus some of the *'ulema* and theologians of those times, who were above fault in their faith, piety and austerity, like Maulana Baseer, Qadi Muhammad Qudsi and others, enquired of Araki for a decree regarding the treatment to be meted out to the proselytes who had defied the principles of Islam. Many learned men, including the above- mentioned theologians, said with one voice that an injunction (*futwa*) be issued saying that the proselytes and renegades were directed by the Mohammedan law (*sharia*) to return to the Islamic fold. They should abide by the tenets of Islam; by doing so they will succeed in attaining the aim of their life. And if they do not do so, then the only other way is to put them to sword. No excuse will be entertained thereto nor will the poll tax (*jizya*) be accepted from them (for continuing as non-Muslims. They have only two options: either to accept Islam or death).

With the help and support of Malik Musa Raina, Shamsu'd-Din Araki issued a decree that groups of infidels, worshippers of idols and the rest of people of other communities return to the fold of Islam, abandon proselytizing and heresy, give up all innovations and aberrations of the customary dark and ignorant ways and recite the *kelima* once again for the renewal of their faith in Islam. They should strengthen and rejuvenate their faith, and make their intentions clean. This order was promulgated throughout Kashmir whose lands extended from the borders of Maraj to those of the extremes of Kamaraj. People should give up customs of polytheists for good. They should be bold and strong and uphold Islamic faith and community and the law of the Prophet and ensure its full growth so that with their individual efforts the banner of Islamic faith is raised to the sky.

The benefits

Shamsu'd-Din Araki issued this order on the basis of the support of Malik Musa Raina. Consequently, every day groups of infidels numbering five hundred to two thousand or even more came to the residence of Shamsu'd-Din bringing with them their ceremonial thread (*zunnar*) for re-conversion to Islam. Dervishes and *Sufis* of Araki spread out in different parts of Kashmir.[1] None among the nobles or the men of authority in the land had the courage to cause them obstruction in their mission.

When infidels began to pour in at the seat of Shamsu'd-Din Araki in such large numbers, his subordinates and dervishes, particularly the father of this writer (Maulana Jamal u'd-Din Khalilullah) would take off the ceremonial threads from the necks of the infidels and polytheists, administer *kelima* to them, make them eat beef and get them circumcised. A large number of barbers was kept at hand to undertake the task of circumcision of all fresh converts to Islamic faith.[2]

In each village, locality and habitat, a "master-*mulla*" was appointed to educate the converts on the *Qura'n*, principles of Islam, system of offering prayers (*namaz*), fasting, Islamic laws and tenets of faith etc.

Thus all infidels, apostates and polytheists once again became Musulman. No person was left without circumcision or reciting the *kelima*. Infidels in villages and rural areas were

---

[1] To mange wholesale conversion to Islamic faith and Nurbakhshiyyeh order.

[2] This is corroborated by the author of *Baharistan*, loc. cit., p.117.

also converted in the same manner. Only a very small group did not convert. Their fathers and forefathers had fled to Nagarkot[1] during the reign of Sultan Sikandar, the Iconoclast. Some of them had settled in Kishtwar and others had fled to Jammu. As they had not converted to Islam, their descendants were spared the compulsion of conversion and were left in whatever condition they were.[2]

Subsequent achievements

Having accomplished the mission of converting infidels and heretics to the Islamic faith, Shamsu'd-Din Araki now addressed the task of reviving Islam. He paid special attention to the reformation and rehabilitation of the re-converts. The situation at this point of time was as follows.

Inhabitants of the city (of Srinagar), traders, vendors who apparently called themselves puritans (*momin*) and Musalman, were, in fact, obstinately perpetuating the customs of the infidels and polytheists in their homes. Their women continued idol-worshipping. Womenfolk in the town were infidels to the core, and observed the festivals of their (original) faith with regularity. These apostates (*zandiq*) were Musalmans only in name; secretly they worshipped the idols, which kept them happy and satisfied. In most of the homes, together men and women worshipped idols. First of all aristocrats (*khwajah*), the elite, businessmen and small traders were called in. Araki enquired of them about their acquaintance with the tenets of Islamic faith, its elements, duties it enjoins upon the Musalman, ablution, *namaz*, fasting etc. Nobody could give a proper answer because these people were not conscious of it at all. When it was confirmed that elders and leading personalities of the town were ignorant

---

[1] In Kangra, in present Himachal Pradesh. The strong fort of Nagarkot is said to have been attacked by Mahmud Ghaznavi in one of his attacks on India.

[2] Does it mean that the present Kashmir Pandits are descendants from that particular group?

about the basic tenets of Islam, they were immediately ordered to recite once again the Islamic *kelima*. They were taught the basics of faith and apprised of the elements and rules of Islam. All of them had to go through circumcision.

Some of the prominent personalities of this land, who wielded power and authority, had reservations about getting circumcised together with common people. They requested that barbers and circumcision operators be brought to their homes to get them circumcisioned. They would stay in their homes for some days (to recover). Their request was not granted (by Araki). It was feared that barbers and operators could be bribed and that they would avoid circumcision on one pretext or the other. Thus aristocrats were also subjected to circumcision along with commoners and none of their arguments was accepted. The intention was that religion, community and Islamic law (*shariat*) should prosper, leaving no scope for any kind of corruption.[1]

A unique experience

I heard the following story from my father. "There was an aristocrat, much respected (in his community). He enjoyed great credibility with the people. He was a middle class trader but people gave him great respect. His name was Ladar Mantji (Rudraman Ji?). He was summoned for circumcision, but he made humble supplication and feigned poverty. He requested that his head be tonsured in public, and a dependable witness be sent along with him to his house to verify that he had undergone circumcision. I did not accept his statement that he was a destitute. I opened his belt with my own hands and down came on the floor five golden coins concealed in his loincloth. I picked up the coins and asked him how these had come into his possession? He said he had brought these as a gift to be presented to me so that I allowed him to get circumcised in his own home. I tied the coins in one corner of his belt and made

---

[1] Also see *Baharistan*, loc. cit., p.116 et. seq.

him sit with others in a special room to be called on his turn for circumcision."

In the early days of the rise of Islam, such activities were undertaken with full ceremony. The purpose was that Islamic religion, Muslim community and the Islamic law had to be fully promulgated and made to pervade in the land of infidelity (*kufristan*). It is hoped that with God Almighty's grace, the prosperity and prevalence of Islamic faith will not meet with adversity and demoralization till the Doomsday. People of all walks of life, aristocrats, elites, nobles, artisans, professionals and commoners came in large groups and they were circumcised and made to recite *kelima*.

Planned conversions

It is said that one day the barbers and circumcision operators kept an account of their performance. They found that the total number of tonsuring and circumcision operations made by them numbered five hundred. Sometimes it would be in the neighbourhood of one thousand. These people were busy from dawn to dusk in these operations. This is how the people were converted and admitted to the Islamic faith.

When Araki accomplished the mission of converting people and training and guiding them in the new faith, he addressed the task of converting and guiding the womenfolk. Pious, puritanical, honest and trustworthy dervishes and *sufis* were selected and the task assigned to them. They were sent to all villages, localities and towns. In fact they reached each and every house. When they came to a homestead, they would get hold of the cow belonging to the housekeeper, kill it and sit down to eat beef in the company of womenfolk and family members. Along with this they administered the recitation of *kelima* to the womenfolk of the household, and taught them the basics of religion, the pillars of faith and the teachings of Islam. Distinguished vicegerents and sincere dervishes would enter the houses of aristocrats and the elite in order to administer *kelima* to them and make them eat beef. They would honour them by accepting their expression of repentance and make them promise that they would regularly offer prayers (*namaz*), observe fasts and other obligations. They also undertook to abstain from what was not permitted (in Islam). These special vicegerents and dervishes spread out in the suburbs of the towns and cities such as Pampur, Kani Pore (?) Shihabu'd-Din Pora etc. Men and women in these areas were apprised of what was permissible and what was not permissible in Islam.[1]

Araki organized a brigade of dervishes with instructions to move about in towns, villages, habitats, and localities. Wherever they found an idol house or an idol or a trace of idolatry, they would swoop on it, pull down the temple and eradicate the customs and practices of idolatry. He personally supervised the destruction of the idol houses that were found in the peripheries of the city (of Srinagar). At a few places, he had to fight battles against the heretics. In such cases, he would consider the opportunity a boon and declare the resisting folks as the 'people of war' (meaning enemy). He would turn to God for thanksgiving and say that the duties and obligations to which they had been called were accomplished. This would bring them success in the clashes (with the infidels).

Bakhi Renu temple[2]

A temple existed at the low-lying part of the city (of Srinagar). In local dialect it was called Bakhi Renu. It was a site for the grouping of infidels, apostates and corrupt people. Festivities would be held here several times in a year in which singing, dancing and music playing women would participate. People from around that locality—men, women, young and old—all used to flock to the temple to enjoy the festivity. Many un-Islamic and corrupt practices would be observed here. In one

---

[1] *Amr wa nahi munkir.*

[2] See footnote i p.200 infra.

part of its premises, people grouped and enjoyed drinking alcohol and wine. On hearing the details of these corrupt practices observed in that temple, Shamsu'd-Din Araki took with him a handful of *sufis* and proceeded to raze the temple to ground. People who came as spectators in the festivity were baton charged and dispersed.

Udran temple[1]

In the neighbourhood of the above-mentioned temple, there stood another idol house called Udran by the infidels of Hindostan and Jammu. It was pulled down and destroyed. When the infidels came to know about the destruction of the temple, they took bows and arrows and other arms and came out to fight with the group of the *sufis* of Amir Shamsu'd-Din. The *sufis* and dervishes were locked in a battle with the infidels for several days. In this great *jihad*, the infidels and polytheists received reinforcement, which forced the group of the dervishes and *sufis* to assemble on the open fields towards Zaldagar so that Araki was protected from enemy's attack. The infidels saw that the Muslims withdrew towards Zaldagar plains. This infused courage in them and they launched an attack on the Musalmans. Many *sufis* received wounds. The infidels overpowered them and the *sufis* were defeated. They had to run away towards the city.

Araki was brought under security to the house of Abdal Magray.[2] He remained unscathed in that fighting. At that time, Abdal Magray was not at his residence. His wife was the daughter of Malik Musa Raina. Another house stood in close proximity to the house of Abdal Magray. From the windows, doors and ventilators, womenfolk and servants hurled garbage at the *sufis* because they had demolished their temples and broken the idols.

[1] Ibid.

[2] *Margaresh* is the name of a Damra group which corrupted into Magray.

This news was brought to Malik Musa Raina. He dispatched his son Malik 'Ali Raina at the head of a contingent to disperse the *kafirs*. Araki did not stay in the house of Musa Raina. He demanded that permission of demolishing the temple be issued forthwith. He said that either he (Musa Raina) punish the culprits and show them the path of religion or banish him along with his family from the land so that he would return to Arak.

Musa Raina was deeply moved by the sight of Araki's impatience and chagrin, and the wounded *sufis* and dervishes. He accompanied Araki on the mission of demolishing the temple. Malik Musa Raina sent his son Malik 'Ali Raina to arrest the leading personalities of the infidels. Many of them were sent to prisons and many were banished to the regions of Hindostan and Jammu. Araki then engaged himself in the demolition of the temple. Even the smallest trace of the temple was effaced. The stone-idols were broken into pieces and crushed. Wooden idols were set on fire and the temple complex was inundated. After destroying the temple completely traces of not even a single stone were left behind; stones and earth were removed from the site of the temple and the ground was levelled. After completing the construction of a mosque on the site, Araki appointed an *Imam* to lead prayer assemblies and also a caller for prayers (*mu'ezzin*). He gave it the name Islampor.

Sayyid Badla

Sayyid Badla reports, "One day, I came to the presence of Amir Shamsu'd-Din Araki. He was preparing to leave his place of residence along with a group of *sufis*. They were about to proceed on the mission of demolishing a temple called Bakhi Renu (?). I also joined the band of his followers. When we reached the site, I found a big crowd of people busy enjoying themselves and indulging in merry-making. *Sufis* baton-charged and dispersed them. After some time, many people came from the regions of Udaran[1] (?), and *Sipahiyan-e-Hind*[2] (?), all equipped with war material. They were ready for a battle. We came close to them. I found that Araki stood in front of the infidels like a hungry tiger ready to pounce on the flock of goats. Every *kafir*, with a sword in his hand, was moving towards Araki and beating the earth with sticks. A contingent of the *sufis* followed Araki. They made a charge on the enemy and overpowered them. This was followed by the demolition of the temple. From among the infidels of Udran, three or four tried to obstruct Araki. Amir Sayyid Badla turned to this writer and said that my father had become a shield for Araki in the manner of a moth making rounds of a burning candle. The infidels dealt repeated blows on Araki but my father warded off each stroke and did not allow him to go a single step forward. The contingent of the *sufis* engaged the infidels. We saw that the infidels were receiving reinforcement intermittently and their fighting strength was increasing

---

[1] The location of Udaran could not be ascertained. If we read the text as Udar instead of Udaran, a far-fetched explanation could be possible. *Udar* in Kashmiri is *Uddara* in Sanskrit meaning alluvial plateau (See *Rajat*, vol.viii, verse 1427n).Who were the people referred to as *sipahiyan-e Hind* meaning Indian troops? Assuming that the two contiguous temples of Bakhi Renu and Udaran were situated in the low-lying area of Srinagar, it could be somewhere between present Idgah and Zaldagar. The nearest Udar is that of Hanjik Udar, the one where the HMT Watch factory stands today. Hanjik Udar has been a strategic site in mediaeval times and some decisive battles were fought around the ridges between the troops defending Srinagar city and the incursionists coming from Tosmaidan or Tangmarg routes. But the intriguing point here is that at this point of time there were no exclusive Hindu troops in Kashmir. Thus the "Indian troops with war material" mentioned in the text would be interpreted as some incursionists from the plains of Punjab trying to loot and interfere in the affairs in Kashmir. They might have decided to lend support to the indigenous people whom they found engaged in a fighting with the Muslim missionaries assisted by the state forces. Even ousted Muslim commanders and rulers enroled Hindu soldiers in Poonch, Rajouri and adjoining areas to reinforce their troops when launching an incursion into the valley to regain their positions.

[2] It should be *sipahiyan-e Hindu* meaning Hindu soldiers. May be contingent or a platoon of Hindu soldiers cut off from the rest might have tried to put up resistance. But then the text would carry "Hiduvan" in stead of "*Hind*".

numerically. Some of us received wounds and some others showed signs of exhaustion. Thus all the *sufis* headed towards Zaldagar.[1] A large crowd of infidels gathered on the battleground. The *sufis* wanted to come back from Zaldagar and fight against the infidels. However, this writer's father stopped them from making that move. One of his hands was wounded but despite that he held Araki with both hands and did not let him move forward.

Meanwhile, numerical strength of the infidels increased. The contingent of the *sufis* that had proceeded towards the city came to the house of Malik Musa Raina. They hoped to carry Musa Raina with them to demolish the temple. Meanwhile, Araki told my father," Oh Sayyid! I have demolished so many idol houses in this land but nowhere did I have to face resistance. Here at this place I seized an opportunity of fighting a *jihad* against the infidels and the polytheists. Therefore I shall name this place Islampor". This writer's father got up and congratulated Araki and said that God willing, with the blessings of this *jihad*, with the guidance and training imparted by him (Araki), the tenets of Islam and its laws would prosper. Since he (Araki) had waged a *jihad* against the infidels (*kuffar*) at this place it came to be named Islampor.

He (Araki) took great care of this place. Melons and vegetables like beetroot, spinach, beans, cereals, etc. were cultivated there. Its fencing was as high as the height of a man. A two-storey structure was also raised here.

Maulana Khaleelullah

A couple of years after this event, Araki told this writer's father, "Mulla, I permit you to obtain allegiance (*bai'at*) from disciples. I also empower you to accept repentance (*tauba*) from the seekers of the path of spirituality. I want that a

---

[1] The area of Zaldagar is situated on the left bank of Vitasts across the present Fateh Kadal.

hospice is built in Islampur. I nominate you as my successor and also the Shaykh of the proposed hospice. You will look after the spiritual training of disciples, *sufis* and dervishes. You will take care of and enforce the practice of retreat (*chilleh*) and the etiquette of spiritual behaviour. You will teach seekers and devotees the methods and procedures of pursuing knowledge." This writer's father declined the offer of becoming the Shaykh of the hospice or becoming its keeper. He told Araki that his heart was not in that kind of work because that would alienate him from his (Araki's) association and service. He added that he would not like to be away even for a moment from his auspicious presence.

Amir Shamsu'd-Din was very happy to hear this answer from my father. He sent him blessings. However, Araki remained busy for a couple of years in connection with the raising of some structures.

Qadi Muhammad Qudsi

Having brought the structures to completion, Araki told Qadi Muhammad Qudsi that since he belonged to that area and there existed a house for him, he should change his residence and build himself a house in Islampur. The aforementioned site and the hospice were placed under his supervision. The site (land) was leased out in his name. He was also given permission to accept allegiance and repentance from people. But the Qadi did not give up his old house and did not shift to Islampur. For this reason, the orchards (attached to the hospice) remained neglected.

But after some time, the Qadi moved to Islampur and began imparting training to his disciples. Qadi Muhammad Qudsi composed an excellent *mathnawi* (ballad) in praise of Shamsu'd-Din Araki in which he has given the details of demolition of the temple, turning it into a mosque, and the efforts of the spiritual leader (Araki) in demolishing the temples. He has also recorded all that Araki had permitted him to do. The *mathnavi* is recorded here so that readers might enjoy it and send prayers for the soul of the Qadi. God Almighty bless his soul!

Pre-Islamic Kashmir

(Free translation)

Kashmir in earlier times
Had no tradition except that of infidelity
For idol- houses and lots of idols
It was famous among lands and climes.
*On all sides along the road stood a temple (**kalisa**) with a strong encirclement*

Of idol houses, along the road side existed Fire–temples
By every temple there were wicked persons
Except them, there existed no other group of people
But idols, idol worshipper and idol maker
Each side (corner) was made of solid stone
A large variety of colourful stone idols therein
Every community was of thread–bearers
Crowds of them everywhere by the road
Would flock to the temple
For merry-making and for pilgrimage

After Shah-i-Hamadan

Then owing to dissensions among communities
Islam met with weakness day after day
. . . .
Nobody cared to promulgate religious law
Commandments of religion met with decay
Infidelity of olden days was revived
The bright sun of religious law illuminated it
Once again, according to the prevalent custom
Foundations of fire-temples and temples laid
Islam got mixed up with infidelity
Fundamentals of religion got disjointed.
Monks and heretics with their wooden gong

Sent flattering words high in the sky
The groups of dissemblers
Supported and agreed with heresy

Wherever was found a shrewd and wise man
He shared the heresy of a polytheist
Together stood the idol house and hospice
And a mosque and a temple

If a husband offered **namaz** *(prayer)*
His wife deliberated with the devil
If a father proceeded to some mosque
The son made full efforts to stick to heresy
Despite the learned of the times
Were always there amidst the people
Each dignified and experienced
Having read each manuscript repeatedly
Yet not aware of the basics of faith
Nobody was on the path of essence of faith
. . . . ?

No body ever cared for religion
They all had adopted the path of falsehood
They remained unmindful of real task
In the pursuit of perishable riches
They were oblivious of perennial torture

Araki's arrival and achievements

He raised the banner of faith high in the sky
He effaced all idol houses and idols
Within the confines of Kashmir territory
Temples that had been erected
He demolished them wholly with God's grace
He brought a new dispensation in the country
He uprooted traces of temples wherever they were
And laid the plan for a mosque instead

Wherever he demolished a prayer house
In short in this ancient valley
With the efforts of this spiritual guide
Every idol house that was laid waste
Became the site for a hospice
Today instead of each fire-temple
There is either a garden or a paradise

Demolition of Islampur idol house

A temple in that land of infidels
Was the object of their circumambulation
From ancient times, nay from antiquity.
This was the place where people
Of opposite faith lay prostrate in front of idols
At this place three times in a year
Came together men and women of Kashmir
Be they young or old in years
Staunchly bound to the tradition of idolatry
Some groups for fun and merry-making
Used to come there regularly
Nobody initiated discarding this custom.
From the calendar brought by the revealed Prophet
Passed nine hundred and thirteen years
With Hindu community and crowds of ***kafirs***
There ensued a fighting for that place
That supporter of faith and of truthful community
Against the forces of rank heretics
A great ***jihad*** for the sake of Truth
At which warriors would give three cheers
For the propagation of the law of Islam
He fought battles against the people of idols
That with the grace of God the Great Cause
The religious preceptor was so victorious
Even the intellect failed to comprehend
As it proved that small numbers shall prevail
He uprooted the foundations of idol-worshippers

He laid waste the whole structure of atheism
He ordered construction of a building at that site
Elegant, adorned and attractive
But since this land from the very beginning
Was defiled enormously by infidelity
It asked definitely for purification
By the decree of the Powerful Creator
There came a flood and washed the earth
And purified it absolutely of heretical impurity
Thus it got a good washing and cleaning
That no trace of infidelity was left in it

Mankeh Renu (?) temple

There were other idol houses (in Kashmir). He went personally to supervise their demolition. A temple stood on the island of Kol Blareh[1] (?). In local language it was called Mankeh Renu. It enjoyed great respect and credibility in the eyes of local infidels and idol-worshippers. Araki came to this temple in person and got it demolished. He built a mosque on its foundation. Having done it, he left behind one of his dervishes for conducting five-time Muslim prayers and for giving call for prayers (*azaan*). One *kharwar* of land and ten *kharwars* of paddy per annum were allotted to him for his maintenance.

Every year melons and melons were cultivated on its land. *Sufis* were assigned the duty of taking care of fruits grown there, such as melons and grapes. Grapes were carried to the

[1] *Kol* in Kasmiri is *kulya* of Sanskrit meaning a stream, and *blareh* < *bror* in Kashmiri is *bhattaraka* of Sanskrit. See *Rajat*, vol.ii, p.372. It is difficult to locate *Kol blareh* (sic) in absence of fuller detail. One of the possibilities is what is known today as *brarihnambal* which is the distortion of Sanskrit *bhattaranadvala.* See *Rajat*, vol.ii, verse 1038. In the footnote to this verse, Stein writes, "The name *bhatttaranadvala* survives in that of the *brarinambal*, a lagoon fed by the *Mar* (*Mahasarit*) and situated between south-eastern quarters of Srinagar in front of Bagh-i-Dilawar Khan. (*Brari/blari* is an obl. case of *bror*, the Kashmiri derivative of *bhattaraka.* Kashmiri *nambal* < Skr. *nadvala* is a term commonly applied to lagoons and marshes. *Rajat*, vol.i, verse 1038 fn.

locality of Zadibal for distribution among the dervishes and *sufis*. Nobles and peers of the city who visited him enjoyed eating delicious fruits. He took great care for the maintenance of this orchard.

Janak Renu temple

A big idol house stood towards the north close to Idgah. Kashmiris called it Janak Renu. Today this place is known as "Kalanveth" (*sic*). Araki demolished the idol-house. A beautiful mosque was raised on the site. Orchards endowed to the temple were turned into melon and melons growing farms. Many saplings were planted here. A *mulla* with a couple of sentries was appointed to look after it. Araki supported them partially from his own funds. Occasionally he would take the *sufis* with him and pay a visit to the place.

Vetalun temple[1]

Situatead near Rainawari,[2] it was a well-known temple. Infidels and idol worshippers attached much importance to it. *Jogis* (mendicants) from Hindostan and other parts came in large groups on pilgrimage to this temple and indulged in idol worshipping.

Araki came to this place and got it demolished. An imposing mosque was built on its ruins/site. The ground lying all around the temple was cleared of dirt, and cells were erected on it. A couple of *kharwars* of land was earmarked for

---

[1] Verse 191 in Bk.vi of *Rajat.* says, "The (fire) reaching as far as Bhikshukipraka (present Butspora, tr.) near the (shrine of Vishnu) *Vardhamanswamin*, destroyed the great buildings within the (limits of the) Vetala's measuring line (*Vetalasutrapata*)." In the footnore to the above verse, Stein records, "The term *Vetalasutrapata* contains clearly a reference to the legend told in iii, 348 sq. of the demon which indicated to Pravarasena the site for his new city. The territory which was supposed to have been originaly marked off by the demon's measuring line, might have borne the same *Vetalasutrapata*. Regarding the position of the oldest parts of Pravarapura, see note iii.339–49."

[2] Rajanakavatika of *Rajat.*

the Imam (who conducts prayers) and the *mu'ezzin*. Thereafter, congregational prayers were offered at this place. Adjoining lands were converted into orchards. The sons of Maulana (?) were in possession of these lands for some time. Later on, supported and assisted by Sayyid Ibrahim Khan, Shams Bhatt wrested the lands from the possession of Maulana's sons. Many buildings were raised on it. No noble or official of authority could obstruct Shams Bhatt (from maintaining his hold on that property).

Tashwan temple

The temple called Tashwan[1] was destroyed. Most of its big stones were used for building the Zadibal hospice. Some of the stones retrieved from the destroyed temple were carried to Islampur for use in the hospice at that place. Some stones were used in the construction of a canal at the same place. Foundation of a mosque had hardly been laid when Kaji Chak[2] showed himself up. He met with Araki. Till that day, Kaji Chak did not have a plot of land or a house in the city to live in. He requested Araki that the land in question be handed over to him. Araki congratulated him and distributed the land among his sons and grandsons. It was here on this spot that Kaji Chak ascended the throne of Kashmir.[3] It was all owing to the

[1] Tashwan is the name of a locality in down town Srinagar on the left bank of the river between Fateh Kadal and Zaina Kadal. Local folklore says that it was originally called Sadashiv temple of Hindu period. *Tasha*, a Turkish word means a consort. In all probability the *dasni* or the dancing temple girls after conversion to Islam became prostitutes locally called *hafizeh*, and the place got the name Tashwan (*Tash* in Turkish means a consort + *wan* in Kashmiri means randezvous). This is just a surmise and needs to be verified.

[2] A powerful descendant from the Chakk house of Drav, Kaji Chak(k) played a significant role in the history of mediaeval Kashmir.The house was converted to Islam. His Hindu name was Kanchan Chakra. His sister named Saleh was married to Sultan Muhammad Shah. Kaji Chak and Ghazi Chak both had accepted the fatih preached by Shams Araki.

[3] There seems some error. Not Kaji Chak but Ghazi Chak was the first among the Chaks to ascend the Kashmir throne in AH 961/AD 1553. See *Waqa'at-e Kasshmir* (Urdu tr. Shamsu'd-Din Ahmad), Srinagar, 2001, p.143.

blessings and prayers of Araki that he reached the highest position of kingship.

Another temple

There was another big temple called (*missing*). Araki personally went to demolish it. A Hindu lived in its outhouse. He had full command over the tradition of idol-worshipping and was a well known sorcerer of his times. On learning that the temple was being demolished, he returned to his cell and indulged in sorcery expecting some physical calamity to befall Araki.

Araki had chosen a place to sit down and watch the demolition of the temple. Suddenly, a splinter flying away from a stone struck his face leaving a small wound on his forehead and face. The Hindu priest came to know of what had happened. He called his sons and associates and directed them to make preparations to see him dead.

He told them that he had ascertained that this man (Araki) would be struck by a calamity but he could ward off death through his inner strength. Now this sorcery would boomerang on him. Therefore they should make preparations for his death rites.

It was mid night when the sorcerer became a victim of his own sorcery, which carried him to hell. Next morning, Araki returned to the scene where the demolition of the temple was underway. He and the *sufis* saw that the dead body of this Hindu was being carried for cremation.[1]

The temple was completely demolished. A mosque was raised on its ruins. Few *kharwars* of land were allotted to dervish Taju'd-Din for its maintenance and for calling the people to prayers. This Taju'd-Din had accompanied Araki on latter's visit to Arak and had spent six years in the service of Shah Qasim. He had also spent many years in Araki's kitchen. His duty was to distribute food and soup among the dervishes.

[1] He might have committed suicide.

When Araki returned to Kashmir for the second time from Arak, Taju'd-Din was among the first to receive him. During the lent, he called people to prayers. The aforementioned place is now in the possession of Taju'd-Dins heirs.

Udernat (sic) Temple

A temple stood on the island of Dal. Kashmiris called it Udernatau. Araki demolished it and on its ruins built a small mosque. He put this mosque and the trees around it in my fathers (Maulana Khaleelullah) possession. Delicious grapes and fruits were produced from this island garden. For many years peasants used to bring fruits and grapes to our house. After many years, tyrants and oppressors snatched the orchard and the trees from us and became its (new) possessors.

Sadasmolo temple

A temple stood close to the *Bazar-e Misgaran.*[1] Kashmiris called it *Sadas Molo*. Araki ordered its demolition. The site was levelled and Khwaja Taju'd-Din, the most respectable and dependable person in the city happened to be a devoted follower of Araki. Once Araki told him that he desired to offer that site to him (Tajud-Din). He was to construct a house and live there.[2]

The Khwaja was one among the top-ranking nobles of the town. He considered it below his dignity to grab the endowment property. He had second thoughts but Araki insisted and bestowed it upon him along with the mosque. His progeny continues to possess the estate.

---

[1] In downtown Srinagar.

[2] It could be either present Khwajeh Bazaar locality or the Misgar mohalla locality in downtown Srinagar.One possible reading could be Sadeh Mol temple. Sadeh Mol is a common Kashmiri form of address for a venerable ascetic raised patriarchal icon. A temple consecrated to him could be called Sadeh Mol temple. But this is only a conjucture and nothing conclusive can be said on the site of the temple.

Modrenu (?) temple

A temple existed in the village of Sudrabal[1] near Nowshehra.

[1] Stein has given us this information: "Proceeding to the east of *Andbhavan* for about a mile we come to the large village of Sudrbal situated on a deep inlet of the Dal known as *Sudrakhun*. The name of the village and the neighbouring ortion of the lake make it very probable that we have to place here the sacred spring of Sodara (see note *Rajat.*, Bk.i.125–26). An ancient legend related by Kalhana represented this spring as an *Avatara* of the Sodara Naga worshipped Close to the mosque of Sudrabal and by the lake shore are two pools fed by perennial springs originally near the sacred site of *Bhuteshvara* below Mound Haramukata (For this Sudara the present Naran Nag see notes I, 123; v.55–59)." Stein further says "Close to the mosque of Sudrabal and by the lake shore are two pools by by perennial springs. These, according to a local tradition were in old times visited by numerous pilgrims. Now all recollection of this *Tirtha* has been lost among the Brahmans of Srinagar. But the name of a portion of the village area Battapur points to a former settlement of Battaas or Purohitas. It is curious, too, that we find only half a mile from the village the *Ziarat* of Hazrat Bal, perhaps the most popular of all Muhammadan shrines in the Valley. It is supposed to be built over the remains of the miracle-working Pir Dastgir Sahib. Is it possible that the presence of the rather ubiquitous saint at this particular spot had something to do with the earlier Hindu *Tirtha*?" *Rajat*, vol.ii, p.457. Commenting on verses 125–26 of Bk. i of *Rajat.* Stein states in the footnote as this: " In order to give full sactitity to *Jyeshtharudra*, which Jalauka had eastablished near Srinagar, the presence of the Sodara spring was also needed. The Tirtha which the legend represens an Avatara of the latter, must after what has been said regarding the position of Jalauka's Jyeshtharudra (Note C), be loked for in the vicinity of the present Srinagar. I have, therefore, no hesitation in connecting the name Sudar, which appears in the designation of a portion of Dal, called Sudarkhun and in the name of neighbouring village Sudarbal, with this legend. The Sudrakhun (*khun* from Sanskrit *kona*) is a narrow inlet on the west side of the Dal stretteching between the suburban villages of Arampor and Sudarbal on visiting Sudarbal in June 1895, I was shown on the very shore of the *Sudarkhun*, and close to the village Masjid , two small pools which were then covered by the water of the lake, but according to the uniform statement of the villagers, are fed by two perennial springs. A tradition, whfrom the old men of the village, relates that "many hundred years ago" Brahmans were in the habit of making pilgrimage to these springs. The name Battpor, whch survives to this day as the name of a now deserted part of the village area was pointed out to me as evidence of the former habitation of *Battas*, i.e. Purohitas (Skt. *bhatta)*. No ancient remains can now be tracd near the springs, but large carved slabs are said to have been carried away from that site to serve as building material for the new temple erected by Maharaja Ranbir Singh at Ranvor in Srinagar. I cannot find any reference to the Sodara spring of Srinagar in the texts accessible to me nor can I trace any tradition relating to it among the Brahmans of the capital. The marginal gloss of G (Sodarabal Gagaribal), however, indictes that the same identification as proposed already has been made by some modern reader of the *Rajat.*" *See Rajat*, Bk.i, 125–26fn.

It was called Modrenu (?). A canal had been dug on the heights of Lar mountain. It always remained full of water and Kashmiris called it Gangabal. After every eight or ten years, they used to say that the waters of Ganga would flow down. Men and women of this land visited it for consigning the bones of their dead into its waters. The Hindus used to take a dip in it. They observed the customs of dualists and infidels, which they called supreme meditation. They thought that pilgrimage to this place meant pilgrimage to all the holy places of (the Hindu mythology). The people of Hindostan considered it as holy as the water of the Ganges. Anybody visiting this country definitely paid a visit to the Sudarabal temple and had a dip in the waters of its spring. Anybody who did not take a dip was considered dirty and impure. After bathing in the spring, people returned to their places.

Araki demolished this temple and built a mosque on its ruins. The temple lands were seized as endowment, and a *mulla* was appointed to conduct five-time congregational prayers according to Islamic tradition; its vineyard was given to be the property of the mosque. During the lifetime of Araki, infidels didn't have the courage to go on pilgrimage to Gangabal shrine not to speak of going around the place.

Story of Hamadaniyyeh hospice

A more enviable achievement than that of demolishing idol houses and laying them waste was purifying the pious hospice of Hazrat Amir from the contamination of polluted people, atheistic mendicants and detestable foreigners. It is necessary to recount this story.

People with enlightened souls are aware that there is no place more sacred and venerable than Mecca. Before the creation of Adam, this place had the honour to be the prayer house of the whole world and also of the angels. After God Almighty accepted Adams repentance, that place (Mecca) was earmarked as his native land where he had to take up his abode. After a short time, there came the divine command that an auspicious house be built at that site, and prayers be offered to God the Creator, so that his (Adams) progeny would see how God is to be worshipped.

This holy house underwent changes at the time of Noah's (Great) Deluge. Hazrat Ibrahim Khalilullah was ordered for the second time to rebuild *Ka'aba* so that it became the place of circumambulation for exalted angels and a prayer house and mosque for the prophets.

After a long time, this sacred House of God became a place of circumambulation, a place of obeisance for the devotees, an object of visitation for the angels, a source of *zam zam* water, a place for the idols and a house for the statues. Some Quraysh chieftains, known for their defiance and stern disposition, turned this House of God into the abode of devilish and satanic people. For innumerable years, this house of divine light and bliss became the worshipping place for sorcerers and depraved people and the centre for worshippers of idols (made of stones). When the last of the prophets (Muhammad) saw this situation, he lifted Imam 'Ali Murtaza on his shoulders so that defiled and impure idols and images were struck down in the House of God. In this way the *baitu'l-haram* (the House of Sanctity) was cleansed of idols and images.

In the same manner, Kashmir was a den of wicked people, the source of infidelity and a mine of corruption and aberration. The auspicious steps of Amir Sayyid 'Ali Hamadani, the peer of 'Ali, turned it (Kashmir) into a place where the law of the religion of Mustafa and the fundamentals of the faith brought by the Prophet flourished fully. Under the guidance and preaching of Amir-e Kabir (Sayyid 'Ali Hamadani), the banner of Islamic religion achieved supreme heights. The result of the preaching of His Holiness was that the place of war (*daru'l-harb*) turned into a place of peace/ security (*daru's-salam*). His precepts and preachings were as follows.

Hamadani in Kashmir

Credible reporters say that when Amir Sayyid 'Ali Hamadani arrived in this land, the administrators of the time and the ruler allotted him an inn at 'Alau'd-Din Pora[1] for his lodging. Sultan Qutbu'd-Din was the ruler then and he used to pay him occasional visits. Then the Sultan ordered the construction of a hospice for him.

Debate with a yogi

A mendicant (*yogi/jogi*) lived nearby. He was known for his trickery and many ignorant persons had become his disciples. They considered his sorcery and tricks as miracles, and his performances as extraordinary feats. Many people brought amusing stories about the mendicant to Sayyid 'Ali Hamadani. At last the Amir himself went to see the *jogi*. When he came to his presence, the Amir spoke a few words by way of an advice. But the miserable and wretched *jogi* rejected Amir's words. He boasted and said that he would show him whatever he knew while he would also like him (the Amir) to prove to him what he knew. Because of satanic pride he considered himself above the Sayyid. As the *jogi's* do, he raised himself above the ground till he came up in the air up to the height of a man. People present in the audience were surprised thinking that it was a miracle. Amir Sayyid 'Ali realised that this jugglery of the *jogi* was only to mislead the people. He, therefore, decided to demonstrate his religious sense of honour and his Islamic bravado. He pointed towards his shoes, which rose up in the air and came down on the head of the mendicant. Because of repeated shoe beats he came down to his original position. This exercise could be compared to a falcon swooping on its

[1] The locality of 'Ala'u'-d-Din Pora lying between present locality of Khanqah-e-Mu'alla and Malik Angan in downtown Srinagar was raised by Sultan 'Ala'u'd-Din who ascended the throne in AD 1347, and ruled for 12 years. See *Tarikh-I Hasan*, vol.ii, p.169).

prey. Humiliated and debased, the *jogi* was made to sit on the ground.

Then Amir Sayyid Ali provided advice and guidance to him and made him aware of the torture of hell. But the black-hearted *jogi* was not prepared to concede. Amir Kabir felt greatly dismayed at his aberration and returned to his abode. Repenting at what had befallen him and tormented by his inherent wickedness, the *jogi* gathered his belongings and left for Hindostan.

Amir Kabir ordered that the place of residence of the mendicant be levelled. An Estrada rose at the spot. A mosque and praying space were provided for God-fearing men. Here he conducted five-time congregational prayers. In compliance with his directions, his disciples and devotees would recite *awrad-e fathiyyeh* and *awrad-e 'asriyyeh* at this place. This practice continued for a long time. Sultan Qutbu'd-Din (AH 788–99/AD 1386–96) had seen his followers making these recitations.

Amir Kabir gave valuable bits of advice to the ruler and his courtiers. Only a small number of people of this country became his followers and disciples. The Sultan was one who had been admitted to the Sayyid's circle and recited the *awrad-e fathiyyeh* and *'asriyyeh*. Maulana Nuru'd-Din Ja'afar Badakhshi (d. AH 787/AD 1385) has recorded its details in his work *Khulasatu'l- Manaqib.*

Sultan Qutbu'd-Din (AH 788–99/AD 1393–1417) did not strictly follow the exhortations of Arki owing to administrative constraints. He did not promulgate the tenets of Islam and *sharia*. Thus the path of religion did not flourish under his rule. Nonetheless, he did abide by the advice of Sayyid 'Ali Hamadani that marriage with two uterine sisters was prohibited in Islam. On his biding Qutbu'd-Din separated from one of the two sisters but kept the other one as his wife after entering into a fresh *nikah* (betrothel). He did not do much to promulgate Islam and the faith. Thus Amir Kabir spoke to Sultan Qutbu'd-Din:

> "Evil forces of self aggrandisement and greed have not allowed authority to rest in your hands so that you could be a source for the propagation and flourishing of true faith and the traditions of the Holy Prophet. But I hope God who is to be will bring forth some one from your offspring who will have the blessings of attaining this supreme authority. There is no doubt that God Almighty will bestow on you an auspicious son from the woman with whom you have re-entered into a bond of matrimony. The child will be named Sikandar. My son, Sayyid Muhammad, is in Khatlan and when this Sultan Sikandar ascends the throne, he (my son) will arrive in and prosper this land. With the able management of Sayyid Muhammad and thorough laudable efforts of Sultan Sikandar the tenets of pure religion and the rules and regulations of the religion of the Prophet will receive full flourishing and prosperity. Through his guidance Islamic traditions and doctrines will reach the pinnacle of glory. Traces of infidelity, heresy, corruption and aberration will be stamped out from this land. That dear and auspicious son of yours (Sikandar) will break the idols and destroy idol-houses and uproot the customs of infidelity and heresy to such an extent that he will be called Sikandar-i *Butshikan*/Sikandar the Iconoclast.

Return from Kashmir

After doling out pieces of advice to the King of Kashmir, and after making the above prophecy Amir-i Kabir prepared to depart from Kashmir. He took the Baramulla route. On entering the territories of Pakhli,[1] local officials requested him

[1] Pakhli is in Hazara region of Pakistan. Low lands along the right bank of Kishen Ganga River were included in Pakhli. Pakhli was included in the kingdom of the Sultans of Kashmir.

to break his journey for some time and provide religious guidance to the people. It was here that he breathed his last. Full details of this story are to be found in *Khulasatu'l-Manaqib* of Maulana Nuru'd-Din Ja'afar Badakhshi (d. AH 787/AD 13).[1]

Sikandar Butshikan (AH 796–820/1393–1417)

Sultan Sikandar succeeded Sultan Qutbu'd-Din as the *Padishah* of this county. He proved to be the iconoclast for the Muslims of this land. Amir Sayyid Muhammad Hamadani placed his august steps on this land during his reign. With the support of this Islamophile *Padishah* and the efforts of the choicest of saintly persons of this land, the banner of Islamic faith and law was hoisted atop the pinnacle of honour. The customs of infidelity and idol worship and the foundations of polytheism and heresy were uprooted. After demolishing the prayer houses of idolaters and breaking idols, hospices and mosques were built on their ruins.

Shah Hamadan hospice

On the site where Amir Sayyid Muhammad Hamadani's father had raised an estrade for offering prayers in Alau'd-Din Pora, he built an imposing hospice. When it was completed, two villages of Batlal and Vachi were given in endowment to the hospice. He purchased these two villages from the Sultan out of his private funds and then gave them to the hospice by way of endowment so that its attendants would provide soup and food to those who spent mornings and afternoons in the hospice reciting the stipulated prayers. The endowment documents in respect of two villages mentioned above were signed by him and have been preserved. Many conditions and restrictions have been laid down in this document. These, for example, are:

---

[1] *Pata+khsha+yati+ya* of Avestic works. *Khsha* in *Khashayarshah* (Xerxes), of Achaeminian dynasty.

"Nobody other than a clean and abstaining person is allowed to enter this sanctorum. People given to immorality and debauchery should not be allowed to settle down or take up residence in the vicinity of the hospice. In fact recluses who confine themselves to the cells of the sanctum sanctorum should be free from all attachments except that of God. Mendicants at the hospice should be free from caring for their children and family so that they can attend themselves fully to the recitation of specific prayers stipulated by my father."

Later on, with the passage of time, rulers and administrators changed their attitude. From among the Islamic community, some turned heretics and atheists and others were given to levity and debauchery. Arrogant people settled down in the neighbourhood of the hospice. They turned the noble *khanqah* into a den of debauchery and adulterous acts. What is more, they ate two meals from the kitchen of the hospice but surrendered themselves to base instincts. When Sayyid Muhammad Hamadani departed from this transient world, the wretched employees and neighbours of the hospice claimed to be its keepers. They allowed debauchery and vice to be committed there. At one time the same hospice was the lighthouse for the people of saintly disposition.

The cells meant for seclusion and retirement were used for drinking wine. Liquor was stored and served in them. Women came to the place to sell fish, curds and vegetables. These eatables would be brought inside the cells and then followed a thousand corrupt practices. High or low, nobody was denied access (to the cells). Thus an angelic place of spiritual bliss was turned into a house of satisfying carnal desires, debauchery and devilish acts. No official or administrator or nobleman stopped them or intimidated them.

Hospice in Araki's trusteeship

When Shamsu'd-Din Araki arrived in this land and demolished the temples of infidels and polytheists, the rulers of the time and the nobles entrusted him with the trusteeship of the Hamadaniyyeh hospice. The first thing he did was to expel the corrupt and faithless heretics from the complex. This hospice (*khanqah*) had attained the position of the second *Ka'aba* in this country. Owing to carelessness of the officials and the oppression of vicious and iniquitous people, it had become the idol house of the debauch. It was cleansed of contamination of liquor and the muck of repugnant impurities of atheists. All of them were thrown out of the hospice. It was restored as the visiting place of angels, a place of pilgrimage for the devout and prayer house for the benevolent.

Extensions were made to its structure and it became quite imposing and attractive. Three additional structures were raised close to it. The biggest one served as a storehouse for storing rice, corn, cereals and other commodities. It was the storehouse for all that was needed in the kitchen. Close to it stood the kitchen. The entire structure was renovated so as to look more elegant. Now it befitted the status of its builders.

During his (Araki's) life time, nearly 400 kilograms of rice was cooked in the kitchen for morning and afternoon meals. It was served to scholars, pious people, the needy and the poor. Five times-a-day, group prayers were offered and the *awradh* were recited regularly twice a day. It was among the major achievements of Shamsu'd-Din Araki to cleanse the holy hospice of the dirt and defilement of atheists and innovators. People in the neighbourhood, high or low, all consider this achievement of Araki no less than iconoclasm. Many senior and venerable scholars of Islam have considered the cleansing of the hospice a better and more meaningful service than the demolition of the idols.

Maulana Hafiz Baseer

Maulana Hafiz Baseer was the teacher and guide of all high and low among the Kashmiris. He has said it a number of times that Amir Shamsu'd-Din Araki has made many achievements of iconoclasm in this land. He brought luster to Islam and its law and propagated Islamic religion among the local people. In this field, he rendered yeoman's service. But his greatest and the best achievement is that he cleansed the holy *khanqah* of Amir Sayyid 'Ali Hamadani of the dirt and filth of wicked and corrupt attendants. Sometimes he would say that he had once occupied a cell in the hospice of Amir Kabir keeping himself engrossed in studies. But many people, who had occupied other secluded cells, indulged in many vices. He had himself witnessed them doing irreligious deeds. His eyes had seen them indulging in a thousand vices. There was nobody to stop them. "If at any time, I ventured to admonish them, they hurled abuses on me and expressed their hatred towards me." He would sometimes tell his pupils that there was hardly any sin and vice that was not committed by these wretched people at a place which was meant for praying and meditation. Indeed cleansing the hospice of these vices and impurities required more courage than the demolition of temples and destruction of idols.

Demolitions at Jogi Lankar

A *langar* (?) is included in the idol-breaking spree of Araki. This *langar khaneh* (alms house) was located in the locality of Raenwor close to the waters of Dal Lake. Former rulers had built it and officials and administrators carried out its repair and maintenance work during their days. Mendicants (*jogis*) were provided facilities of halting and staying at this place. Sultans and rulers of Kashmir, who were alien to Islam, *shari'a* and its commandments, had endowed Panzgam[1] in

[1] Skt. *Panchiigrama* is probably the present Panzgom, a large village in Uttar, situated close to the left bank of Kahmil River. The village lies on the route which leads up the valley of the Kahmil River and over the 'Nattishannar' Pass (Bates; map 'Naschan Galli) into Karnav. See Rajat, vol.i, verse 3124 fn. In the direction of the sacred Mount Haramukuta points also the other name *Ishtikapatha*, by which is probably meant the locality referre to in the *Nilamata*, 1081, as *Patheshvara ishtah*. The latter place is identified by a gloss to another passage, 1208 with the modern hamlet of Ramaradan, in the Lar Pargana, from which the ascent on the *Haramukuta* pilgrimage begins. *Rajat*, vol.i, verse 467 fn.

pargana Kamaraj, Nadihal[1] and other villages to this 'alms house (*langar khaneh*) for the maintenance of its inmates. Hindu mendicants (*jogis*) from India and the countryside and other pilgrims used to stay in the almshouse and pray to the idols. The almshouse was their base camp wherefrom they would proceed on pilgrimage to all temples in Kashmir. At the time of returning to their respective places, they re-assembled here. Some of the pilgrims and *jogis* would return to India but some would stay on at this place for the whole year and derive consolation from worshipping idols.

The community of the *jogis* and the group of heretics did not adhere to any faith and community. There was nothing by the name of religion and religious law for them. In fact, these people had forsaken Islam and faith. They were people with no faith at all. The *zandiqs* and atheists were aliens to any faith not bound by the rules and principles of religion. They considered all forbidden, illegal and disallowed things genuine and permissible. Such type of people resided in the aforesaid almshouse at Jogi Langar.

These people drank (liquor) and took intoxicants openly in the almshouse. They would do irreligious deeds. They indulged in debauchery and other vices openly and with no reservations. None among Islamic scholars, Qadis and police supervisors taught them what was allowed and what was forbidden in Islamic religion. Despite all these lecherous

---

[1] Commenting on *Rajat*. I, verse 467, Stein writes: *Nandishila* is probably a site connected with the legend of *Nandin*, located on Mount Haramukuta; comp. note on *Nandikshetra*, i, 36. According to the *Nilamata*, vv.1061 sqq., Nandin was produced by Shilada from pulverised rocks (shila) and perormed his austerities in the lake named after him while holding a large rock *(shila)* on his head. On the other hand it may be noted that *Nandishila* is the name given to the modern village of Nadhel in Hamal Pargana by the *Vitastamahatmya*, xxiv, 32; but no sanctity attaches to this place.

In the direction of the sacred Mount Haramukuta points also the other name *Ishtikapatha*, by which is probably meant the locality referre to in the *Nilamata*, 1081, as *Patheshvara ishtah*. The latter place is identified by a gloss to another passage, 1208 with the modern hamlet of Ramaradan, in the Lar Pargana, from which the ascent on the Haramukuta pilgrimage begins. *Rajat*, vol.i, verse 467 fn.

deeds, some foolish kings, nobles and Sultans provided support for drinks, clothing and other expenses of the community of darkness. They considered these facilities gifts or alms.

Demolition of *Langar Khaneh*

Shamsu'd-Din Araki came to know about the ways and practices of the lost people; he was also informed about their actions. Therefore, he mustered courage and began thought of destroying the temple (of Jogi Langar at Rainawari). He dispatched this writer's father to the presence of Sultan Fath Shah to obtain his permission for the demolition of the almshouse. The aforesaid ruler was of bad conviction, inimical and not without prejudice (towards the Nurbakhshiyyeh). He made many pretexts for not giving permission to do so. He said that the almshouse had been built by Sultan Zainu'l-'Abidin and he would not permit the demolition of a structure that had been raised by that great king as it perpetuated blessings for that departed soul. My father used to do good deeds apart from working for Shamsu'd-Din. He spoke plain to everybody. He told the Sultan that Sultan Zainu'l-'Abidin was neither Shaykh Junaid Baghdadi[1] nor any other local Shaykh so that the structure raised by him could not be dismantled. As that corrupted prevaricator of a king had built many other buildings, it was better that the ones in question were demolished. He said there were many old structures that deserved to be demolished and destroyed. The king was upset on hearing these words. He became enraged and furious and

[1] Ibn Muhamad bin Junayd was born and died in Baghdad. He originated from Nehavand and is considered the foremost of the *Sufi* order. He was a staunch supporter of trandition and the revealed bok. In theology he was a pupil of Sufyan Sauri and in mysticism he followed Ibn Harith and Siri Saqti. Abul Abbas was his student in the science of mysticism. His death is reported in the year AH 297 or 298/ AD 910 at the age of 91. He remains buried in the graveyard of Shunezeyeh in Baghdad. Sources *Nameh-e-Danishwaran*, vol.5, p.15, Ibn Khallikan, vol.1, p.27 and *Loghat Nameh.*

wanted to punish my father. But his senior ministers and courtiers interceded and my father was saved from the kings wrath. He recounted the story before Araki.

Magray permits

Shamsu'd-Din Araki then sent my father to Ibrahim Magray who headed the justice department of this land at that time. The purpose was to seek permission from him for the demolition of *Jogi Langar*. Ibrahim Magray was too glad and ready to give permission. The letter authorising demolition was given to him (this writer's father).

On the following day, Araki took *sufis* along with him and engaged them in demolishing the structure. The site was levelled for the construction of a mosque and a prayer ground. A big mosque came up on the estrade. Its walls were raised high. It took them one full day to raise the foundation. As a result of the efforts of Araki, the mosque was built in a short time. On its completion, he said that the mosque was so imposing, spacious and grand that it could be equal to *masjidu'l-haram* (the mosque in Mecca). He said that anybody desiring to imagine the height and grandeur of the mosque in Mecca may visit this mosque and look at it intently to get the idea of what that mosque is like.

Infidels resist

There existed several groups of infidels and idol worshippers in the locality of Raenwari.[1] The chief of the community was a powerful and staunch idolater. He had established relations with some of the nobles and senior government functionaries. The infidels got his support and joined hands to confront the *sufis*. Apart from being inimical towards the dervishes and *sufis*, they were even prepared to fight against them. Thus fighting took place between the two sides. Araki called this fight a *jihad*.

---

[1] Ranavatika of *Rajat*.

Araki brought the construction of the mosque to its completion. A number of single-storey cells were also built in it. During the time of retreat, three to four *sufis* occupied one cell. Some *sufis* (of lesser status) were assigned the duty of rendering service to those who had gone into seclusion. All necessary requirements including food and eatables were provided to them. Araki would attend to their training and reformation.

Pandrethen[1] idol house

Araki also demolished the idol-temple at Pandrethan with his own hands. Its structure was lofty and massive. Sultan Sikandar, the Iconoclast, had brought stones from this very idol temple for use in *Jami'a Mosque*[2] and the tombs of the Sultan(s). Stones in the exterior of the temple were pulled down and put in the walls of *Jami'a Mosque*. The boundary wall of *Mazar-i-Salatin*[3] was also built with these stones. No resistance had been faced (by the demolishers) either during the demolition of the temple or while taking away its stones. The temple (ruined by Sikandar the Iconoclast) was rebuilt and restored to its previous glory by Sultan Zainul-'Abidin. He had allowed the revival of the customs and practices of the wicked and corrupt infidels in this temple. Every year, festivals in the name of goddess were celebrated in it. Singing and dancing assemblies were also organized on the occasion as in other idol temples.

Amir Shamsu'd-Din arrived at the spot with the intention of demolishing the idol temple. He found the structure lofty and massive. An idol stood planted in the ground besides the building. Sultan Sikandar, the Iconoclast, had not succeeded in breaking it. It had been put to flames several times but

---

[1] See *Rajat*. Bk.III, p.99, Bk.i, 104n.

[2] See *Waqa 'at-i Kashmir*, (tr.) Shamsu'd-Din, Srinagar 2001, p.73.

[3] See *Baharistan-i-Shahi*, loc. cit., p.56fn.55.

in vain. It was pounded with iron rods and other strong metals but it did not break. Not a single limb of the statue could be broken.

When Shamu'd-Din came close to the statute that was placed in the lower storey, he ordered that it be broken, and removed from its place. The site thus obtained was prepared for the construction of prayer houses and cells for the dervishes going into retreat (*chilleh*). He put in great labour for destroying and breaking the idols of the infidels. However, the statue in question did not break and Araki felt rather dismayed. It was then decided that earth and stones underneath the idol be removed to make a deep crater. This and other statues were buried in the ditch and covered with earth and stones.

Other groups (of dervishes) raised four cells on each of the four corners of the complex. The stones were cut with care and the surface was made smooth so that these looked attractive. The (new) structure that was raised (on the ruins of the demolished temple) comprised two floors. The first floor was prepared for the devotees to offer five-time prayers and Friday congregational prayers. During the days of retreat, Araki would make a few *sufis* sit in the mosque and the hospice. He guided and trained them out of his inner grace. He showed his affection and goodwill for the dervishes and the seekers of spiritual excellence.

Idol temple of Metna (?) spring

In the same way, he demolished the building at Metna[1] (?) spring. It was converted into a mosque. The site was developed. Not a trace of the demolished temple was left behind. A mosque built close to the spring still exists.

[1] The site could be identified either with Mattan or with Methun, the latter being situated on the outskirts of Srinagar on road to Chadura ahead of present day *Bagh-i-Mehtab* locality. But the presence of a spring by the side of which the temple stood excludes the second possibility. There is a well-known spring in Mattan by the side of which now there stands a mosque.

Kharboshtaz (?) Temple

He also demolished the temple of Kharboshtaz (?). This one was more popular than many other idol temples of Kashmir.

Ten temples demolished

There existed ten temples in a certain village. They were given different names, such as Jwalamukhi, Khodrenu, Lankeh Renu, Bakhi Renu, Luti Renu, Soneh Renu, Parzdan, Tsarenmal, Kupwur and Zachaldor.[1]

Shamsu'd-Din demolished these temples and built mosques at their site. A few *kharwars* of land was endowed to these mosques for the maintenance of the Imam and the *mu'ezzin* so that they were able to discharge their religious duties without distraction. Apart from the call for the prayer, five-time prayers, Friday congregational prayers were also offered here. The Imam used to deliver sermons to the villagers on religious (Islamic) duties and obligations. They would acquaint them with the tenets of Islam and Islamic faith and exhort them to be Musalmans.

Sonwar[2] temple

A temple stood in the village called Sonwar. On the ruins of the (demolished) temple, a mosque was raised so that five-time a-day *namaz* (prayer) could be offered.

---

[1] Last two place names are well known. In all probability the author intends to say that the forementioned temples were located in the regions of Handwara and Kupwara. We find that generally "renu" is suffixed to the main name of the temple. It is not clear why this practice has been followed. Two possibilities are suggested. One is that 'reun' is the deformation of '*renu/raina*' obtained from *Rajanaka* of Sanskrit, a qualifying adjective for a man/official of higher dignity. The other is that in Kashmiri 'reun' mens belonging to or of the. Bakhihreun could be Bakhi+reun meaning of Bakhi/Bachhi. But this is just a flight of imagination. It needs further research.

[2] Originally *Swarnavatika* of Sanskrit, it is known by the same name today. The entire area forms the cantonment of Badami Bagh. Sonwar is located on the National Highway leading to capital Srinagar.

Advin[1] *Pargana*(?) temple

A temple stood in Advan *pargana*. It was demolished and a mosque was built at the site. *Mullas* were appointed to bring Islam to the place. They were taught the obligations of faith and Islam, *namaz* and ablution, etc.

Kalehbod temple

In the locality known Kalehbod,[2] there existed a big temple, which was demolished and on its ruins a *Jami'a* mosque was built. Around it stood a willow plantation. The trees, thick and tall, were felled and timber was brought to the city. Logs obtained from this timber were used as cross bars for the roof in the compound of Nurbakhshiyeh hospice. These long and big logs were used from inside the hospice stretching from one wall to another that stood outside in order that these could bear load.

Since Shamsu'd-Din Araki had left the hospice without a pillar, it was felt necessary that strong logs of good length were used so that it bore the weight of the roof. Despite the heavy load that these logs bore, they did not show any sign of damage.

Narvora temple

A temple stood close to the spring in the village of Narvor Narwol *(sic)*.[3] Shamsu'd-Din Araki demolished it and built a

---

[1] Jonaraja's *Ardhavana* is the name of a *pargana* of Maraz (*Madavarajya*). See Rajat. vo.lii, p.494.

[2] The site could not be identified.

[3] "Yukadevi, (another) wife of the king, who was eager to compete with her rivals, built at *Nadavana* a *Vihara* of wonderful appearance" *Rajat*. iii, verse 11. Adding a footnote to this verse, Stein writes, "By *Nadavana* may, perhaps, be meant the present quarter of *Narvo*r situated in the north-western part of Srinagar, between Sangin-darwaza, and the Idgah. The modern name goes clearly back to a form *Nadavata*. In this form—*vata* (or *vataka*) 'garden' might correspond to—*vana* of Kalhana's name—*vor* or its feminine form—*va'r* (Sanskrit *vatika*) is frequently found at the end of Kashmiri local names; comp. ...

mosque on its ruins. A *mulla* was appointed to take care of it and arrangement for calling for the prayer and offering five-times-a-day prayers was also made. Three to four *kharwar* land was given to the mosque by way of endowment. The land has been in the possession of the descendants of the *mulla* till this day.

Vejnath Temple[1]

There was a temple in the town of Vejehbrara *(sic)* (present

... notes on *Bhuksiravatika*, I, 342; *Rajanavatika*, viii, 756; *Rangavatika*, vii, 1653. *Narvor* shows like most parts of Srinagar in its cemeteries and *Ziarats* ample remains of ancient buildings. It is, however, impossible to identify any of these from the remains found overground." *Rajat.*, vol. iii, verse 11fn.

[1] Describing the Tirtha of *Vijayeshvara*, Stein gives this detail: The ancient town which once stood in the position indicated, was evidently succeeded by Vijayeshwara, the present *Vijbror.* The latter place situated less than two miles above *Chakradhara*, received its name from the ancient shrine of Shiva Vijayeshwara (*Vijyesha*, *Vijayeshana*), the present *Vijbror*. This deity is worshipped to the present day at *Vijbror*. The site has evidently from early times been one of the most famous *Tirthas* of Kashmir. It is mentioned as such in the *Rajaratangini* and many old Kashmrian texts (*Haracar*-x). The tradition regarding Ashoka's connection with it supplies historical proof for its antiquity. According to Kalhana's account which may well have been based on genuine local tradition or even insriptinal evidence. Ashoka had replaced the old stuccoed enclosure of the temple by one of stone. The great king was also credited with having eected within this enclosure two temples called *Ashokeshvara*.

The old shrine, which is often mentioned by Kalhana, and which has been the scene of many a historical incident has now completely disappeared. According to the tradition of the local Puruhitas it stood at the site close to the river-bank and nearly opposite to the bridge over the Vitasta. When I first visited *Vijbror* in 1889 I still found some ancient slabs and fragments at this spot. It was then some fifteen feet below the level of the surrounding ground,(General Cunningham, who saw these remains in 1847, rightly attributes them to the temple of *Vijayesha*, but calls the place 'Vijayapura'. He justly points to the difference of level as an indication of the antiquity of the structure; see *Ancient Geography*, ii. p.98) and has since been partly built over. Stone materials are said to have been removed from here for the new temple of *Vijayeshvara* which was built by Maharaja Ranbir Singh some thirty years ago higher up on the river-bank.

It is probable that a temple so much frequented had undergone more than one restoration in the course of the fifteen centuries, which passed between the time of Ashoka and the end of Hindu reign in Kashmir. Some time before AD 1081, while King Ananta was residing at the *Tirtha* of Vijayeshvara, the temple was burned down in a general conflagration, caused by his son Kalasha. The latter, however, subsequently restored the shrine. The old *Linga* of Shiva Vijyeshwara seems to have been destroyed by Sikandar *Butshikan*. (See *Jonar*, Bod. Ed, 762 and 127.)" *Rajatarangni*, vol.ii, p.463.

day Bijbehara). Kashmiris called it *Vejnath.* It had no parallel in its beauty and artistic splendour. The top was capped with four rising pinnacles. When Sultan Sikandar the Iconoclast arrived at the said temple to undertake its demolition, he got the pinnacles removed without causing them any damage. These were placed on four well-known structures in the city. One was put atop the *Jami'a Masjid*, the second atop the hospice of Amir Sayyid 'Ali Hamadani, the third on top of the cupola of Sultan Sikandar's (?) tomb, and the fourth atop the palace of Sultan Sikandar in Hairan Bazar (?).

The aforesaid temple was rebuilt during the reign of Sultan Zainu'l-'Abidin. It was bestowed with the splendour of earlier days. Idolatry was revived and festivals of the infidels and their feasts were also revived as before.

Shamsu'd-Din Araki came to that place in person and saw to the demolition of the temple. The foundations of the prayer house of the infidels were demolished, and its stones were brought to the city, where these were used to build the boundary wall of the Hamadaniyyeh hospice. A splendid mosque was raised in place of the temple. The task of raising the mosque had been entrusted to the father of this writer. Seven *kharwars* of land was allotted to the mosque and this was also given in the trusteeship of my father. He (my father) assigned the land among his brothers along with the duties of conducting prayers and religious discourses. These lands continue to be in the possession of the descendants of my uncles.

Inn of Jogis

There was one more temple in the town of Vejeh Belarah (*Vijbror*) called *Prezyar* in Kashmiri language. This too was razed to the ground and the customs and shrines of idolaters and polytheists were effaced from the surface of the earth for all times to come.

Perzehyar Temple

Another temple stood in the same locality (Vejehblareh/ *Vejebror*). In Kashmiri language it was called Perzehyara (?). It was also demolished and with that all traces of idol worshipping and polytheism and also the customs and shrines of the infidels were uprooted once for all.

Kuther Temple[1]

A temple stood in Kuther by the side of the spring. Araki dispatched a group of *sufis* to demolish it. Arrangements were made for five-times congregational prayers in that mosque. A *mulla* was appointed to look after these duties.

---

[1] Stein notes: "At the sacred spring of *Papasudana*, Shiva is worshipped under the name of *Kapateshvara,* having shown himself there according to the legend under the disguise (*kapata*) of pieces of wood floating on the water. The *Tirtha* is situated close to the village *Kother* (derived from Skr. *Kapateshvar* in the pargana of Kuthar. It consists of a large circular tank fed by springs and enclosed by a massive stone wall, which the tradition, refered to by Kalhana in vii.190 sqq. and still locally remembered, ascribes to King Bhoja of Malava. For a detailed account of the extant remains at *Kapatesvara*, see note vi.190.

The legend of the *Tirtha* is related in *Nilamata*, vv.1150–68, and at considerable length in *Haracar*, xiv, from which the extant *Kapateshwaramahatmya* is taken; comp. also *Shrikanthac*, iii.14.

Albiruni had heard of the *Kapatesvar Tirtha* and its legend. He records, *India*, ii, p.181, the story told by people from Kashmir that pieces of wood sent by *Mahadeva* appear annually in "a pond called *Kudaishahr* to the left of the source of the *Vitasta*, in the middle of the month of *Vaisakha*."

Kudaishahr is easily accounted for as a clerical error for *Kavadeshwar*, a prakritized form of the name. The date given for the miracle coincides with that indicated for the pilgrimage, *Haracar* xiv, 122. The indication as to the position of the *Tirtha* is also approximately correct. Abul Fazl, *Ain-i-Akbari*, ii. p.358, mentions, " in the village of Kotihar, a deep spring surrounded by stone temples. When its water decreases, an image of *Mahadeva* in sandal-wood appears." The story related by Kalhana in vii.190 sqq. together with the legend heard by me on the spot in September 1891, as to the miraculous cure of King Mujukund (see note l.c.) seems to indicate that healing powers were once ascribed to the water of the Tirha." See *Rajatarangini* vol.I, 32 fn.

Achhabal Temple

An idol temple stood in the village of Achhabal[1] by the side of the source of water.[2] It was annihilated, and a mosque was raised at the site. One of the Sufis named Mulla Shankar was appointed Imam to lead congregational prayers and to be its *mu'ezzin.*

Temples at Sagam and Lokeh (Bhavan?)[3]

Many temples stood in the villages of Sagam and Lokeh (Bhavan?) by the side of the springs and away from these. These were annihilated and mosques in their place built. *Mullas* were appointed to conduct prayers.

Ver (Verinag)[4] village temple

Close to the spring in the village of Ver, there existed a big

---

[1] Verse 338 in Bk.1 of *Rajatarangini* says," His (King Vasunanda) son Nara II was king for sixty years, and for the same period the latter's son Aksha, who founded the village *Akshaval*." Stein's footnote to this verse says that *Akshavala* is undoubtedly the modern *Achabal* in Kuthar Pargana famous for the beautiful springs described by Bernier, *Travels*, p.413; Vigne, I, p.347, etc. The fountain is named in the *Nilamata*, 917, *Akshipalanaga*. See *Rajat*. I, 338 fn.

[2] Obviously meaning the spring of *Akshaval/Achabal*.

[3] "After constructing at *Lokapunya* a town, which was provided with the requisite accessories, the victorious king (Lalitadittya) made it, together with villages, an offering to Vishu." *Rajat*, i, 193. "At the western end of the *pargana* of Bhringa (Bring) and about five miles to the south-west of *Achabal*, is the village of Lokabavan, which an old gloss identified with Lokapunya of the *Rajatarangini*. The numerous passages which mention the place agree with this location. The name *Lokabavan* applies also to the fine *naga* adjoining the village, and this explains the second part of the present name, – *bavan* (Skr. – *bhavana*). Kng Lalitadittya is said to have built a town here. A small garden-palace erected in Mughal times near the spring is partly constructed of old materials." See *Rajat*, vol.II, p.468.

[4] The description of the *Tirthas* of Kashmir begins with the *Nilanaga*, who is placed by ancient tradition, surviving to this day, at the head of all the Nagas or Spring-deities of the land (see *Nilamata*, vv, 69, 901). He is considered a son of Kashyapa (ibid.95). His residence is the famous fountain near the village of ...

temple. This was also demolished and a mosque was raised in its place. Again, a *mulla* was appointed to conduct prayers, give call for the prayer and deliver sermons. After the demolition of this temple, bands of dervishes and *sufis* came to every place in the village and along the road where there were temples. They destroyed not only the temples of the infidels but also uprooted their customs and traditions. They wiped out all signs of idols and their remains so that the banner of Islamic religion and the *shari'a* (law) began fluttering all over that region.[1] The lands of this region were purified once for all from the traces of the polytheists and the infidels and their corrupt and debased customs.

God Almighty be the witness. God blessed that venerable person (Shamsu'd-Din Araki) with strength and divine approval. That is why he succeeded in breaking the idols of the polytheists of this land and the prayer houses of the infidels. No Sultan, monarch or ruler in the world ever had such great success to his credit. This special felicity and bliss were not to be theirs. After a long time, of epochs and century,

---

Vernag, situated in the Shahabad *Pargana* at the foot of the *Banahal* Pass. For a description of the magnificent spring, enclosed by the Emperor Jehangir in a fine stone basin, see Abu'l-Fazl's *Ain-i-Akbari*, ii, p.361; Forester, *Journey*, ii, p.4; Moorcroft, *Travels*, ii, p.250, Vigne, *Travels*, I, p.332, Ince, *Handbook*, p.184.

Near the Nilanaga, Vishnu is said to have first placed the ploughshare with which the *Satisaras* was drained (*Nilamata*, 331); and there Parvati was brought to light in the form of the river *Vitasta* by a stroke of Shiva's trident. Comp. ib.248 sqq., and the full account of the legends regarding the origin of *Vitasta* given in *Haracar*, xii. Hence the *Tirtha* bears the threefold name of *Nilakunda*, *Vitasta* and *Shulaghata* (*Nilamata*, 1290, and *Haracar*, xii, 17). The Nilanaga is now commonly known by the name of *Vernag*, which is evidently derived from the old designation *Ver* of the present Shahabad *pargana* (See *Ain-i-Akbari*).

The pond, which is now of an octagonal shape, must, as the use of the term *Nilakunda* shows, also in ancient times, have approached a circular form. It is, therefore, compared by Kalhana to a 'royal parasol'. The stream which issued from it, and which is conventionally taken as the origin of he *Vitasta*, is described by the poet as the stick supporting the parasol." See *Rajat*. I, 28 fn.

[1] Meaning Maraz (Maraj).

an outstanding personality appears to devote himself to the laws of the Prophet.

Hazrat Amir Shamsu'd-Din took great pains in breaking idols and smashing statues. He succeeded in his mission. Islamic faith and the laws of religion were strengthened (in Kashmir). The number of idol houses (temples) of the infidels in this land was so large that one could not give a full account of them. My pen is helpless in counting each of these. I, therefore, pull up the reins of my pen at this point and leave the count and account of the demolition of temples by Araki at this point although one is unable to make the count. We now turn to the munificence and large-heartedness of Araki.

Chapter V
Araki's Munificence

Araki's Munificence

Everybody said that people from all walks of life, low and high, locals and aliens all derived benefit from Araki's munificence and generosity. Nearly 700 dervishes and *sufis* in his camp were engaged in chores like lifting stones, mowing earth, looking after orchards, planting trees and cultivating melons. Winter or summer, they had no time to sit under shade and relax. They would not find time to warm up their hands in winter. Araki usually joined them in their manual work on the farms. He worked so assiduously along with his band of dervishes and *sufis* that he would perspire profusely. By working too hard at lifting stones and overturning earth, his hands had become hard and rough. He showered praise in profusion upon his team engaged in farming.

The Pantry

A large number of helpers and servants worked in his kitchen. They included chefs, drawers of water, hewers of wood, butchers, collectors of hides etc. all numbering about one hundred.

Every day nearly 3000 seers (600 *trak*) of rice were cooked and served to the *sufis* and dervishes. Beef and cereals were cooked on alternate days. Each day, one ram would be slaughtered for preparing soup. Dishes of yellow pilau, black pilau, shola pilau and soup were prepared for the guests. Sixty kilograms of flour was consumed every day for baking bread and distributing them among the *sufis* and dervishes. Besides bread, pudding, soup, meat cooked in yogurt, soup, curds and yogurt were also available. Every morning about one hundred kilograms of flour were used for making bread. During one particular year, the wheat crop failed and fine flour became expensive. The matter was reported to Araki with the suggestion that consumption of fine flour be reduced. He said, "I think that all my *sufis* can eat food at other places. Since wheat and flour have become a bit expensive in the town, henceforth the consumption of fine flour would be restricted to sixty kilograms so that nobody remains hungry and we do not have the kind of situation that prevails at other places."

It is reported that once the workers at the hospice were fed up with slaughtering cows for meat. They told him that the price of cows had increased. The animal was procured with great difficulty. If he agreed then a cow would be slaughtered on alternate days. Araki said, "Why did you people not inform me earlier. I had thought that my *sufis* are provided beef from the kitchen on one day. On the next day, they would eat at their respective places. If the cost of beef has increased in the town, how are we to procure it for the dervishes? From today onwards, a cow will be slaughtered in my kitchen every day so that my humble folks get beef to eat every day." For quite some time, a cow was slaughtered every day for his kitchen. Gradually this became a routine. Although the staff made a submission for reducing culinary expenses, yet he did not pay heed to what they said. He rather increased the expenses.

About one hundred men were engaged in different chores at his establishment. They worked on the farm, looked after the farming and took care of orchards. All of them were fed at his kitchen. The number of family members of these *sufis* was three hundred. In addition, he also took care of one hundred orphans. The *sufis* and the children all lived collectively. There were wooden platters, which they carried one by one to the kitchen and came back after filling these with cooked food and meat. They would eat out of platters outside the door of the kitchen. Lunch and supper were served. All children ate two meals a day. The children of the *sufis* were asked to perform service. After taking mid-day meals, they took small leather bags and went to the foothill of *Koh-i Maran* (Hari Parbat). There they collected pebbles and cobblestone, filled their bags and returned to the hospice where it was strewn over the pathways. This was done so that the path was not muddied in rain and snow. The children were asked to bring cobblestones only once in a day. After performing the errand, they were let off to go for playing and enjoying themselves. Special food was cooked particularly for the children.

The number of *sufis* ranged between five hundred and one thousand, though at times it would rise above a thousand. All of them were engaged in his service. Some of them brought their wives and children with them. Their children were young as well as grown up. The numbers of children were seven, eight or even ten. According to an estimate, nearly ten thousand persons were connected with his establishment. All of them expressed their reverence to him and benefited from his kitchen.

This large humanity was associated with his kitchen. God the provider of food had immensely increased the scope of his establishment in providing victuals to people. Apart from this, Araki used to give away 15 to 20 maunds of paddy to his *sufis* every year in order to strengthen their material capability and to help them feed their families without distraction and worry. For Hazrat Baba and the father of this writer, he allotted twenty-five maunds each, adding that actually only twenty-three maunds of paddy were gifted and two additional maunds were by way of *zakat* or surcharge. We accept *zakat* for the spiritualists. But the *zakat* that you are to pay is remitted. These grants would be offered twice or thrice a year besides occasional cash grants.

It is reported that there was a footman at the complex of Araki. Once he brought him a few boiled eggs and requested him to pray to God to give him a son. He prayed for the supplicant and ordered the storekeeper to help the man in meeting the expenses of his wife's delivery. He was provided with a hundred kilograms of rice, hundred kilograms of firewood, three kilograms of ghee, and two kilograms of salt. He would give away alms of this kind several times in a year. His *sufis* also received such gifts. Nobody ever grumbled.

A clever gardener

It is said that a *sufi* among Araki's staff was a gardener by profession. He behaved like a mad man when quarreling with people. But he was an adept in his work. Araki used to call him the mad gardener (*diwaneh baghban*). Once Araki said that the mad gardener had given him a headache and he should be sent back to his house. He was given forty kilograms of paddy. The gardener reached his home and a *sufi* followed him. The gardener prepared for him a meal of one kilogram of meat and two kilograms of rice. He told the *sufi* that after depositing the food for his dependents, he (the gardener) would tell him about his conditions. The gardener had ten children. He took along with him his own children and a couple of children of his neighbours and came to the presence of Shamsu'd-Din. He made a supplication saying that the children ate up the entire paddy given to him. Therefore, he had brought all of them to his presence. Either the paddy be recovered from these children or they be taken under his patronage. On inquiring whether all of those children were his siblings, the gardener said that he had many children. Araki ordered that forty more kilograms of paddy be given to him so that he could feed the kids. Other *sufis* would also be his beneficiaries in the same way.

This work titled *Tohfatu'l-Ahbab* was brought to completion on thirteenth of *Jamada-ath-thani* in the year of Hijra one thousand and fifty two/AD 1642.

The End

Index

C

D

E

F

G

H

I